Pastel

3

TOSHIHIKO KOBAYASHI

Translated and adapted by David Ury

Lettered by Foltz Design

BALLANTINE BOOKS • NEW YORK

A Del Rey Trade Paperback Original

Pastel copyright © 2002 by Toshihiko Kobayashi

English translation copyright © 2006 by Toshihiko Kobayashi

Published in the United States by Del Rey Books, an imprint of The Random House Publishing Group, a division of Random House, Inc., New York.

DEL REY is a registered trademark and the Del Rey colophon is a trademark of Random House, Inc.

Publication rights arranged through Kodansha Ltd.

First published in Japan in 2003 by Kodansha Ltd., Tokyo

Library of Congress Control Number: 2005932019

ISBN 0-345-48689-7

Printed in the United States of America

www.delreymanga.com

1 2 3 4 5 6 7 8 9

Translator and Adapter—David Ury
Lettering—Foltz Design

Pastel

CONTENTS

A Note from the Author

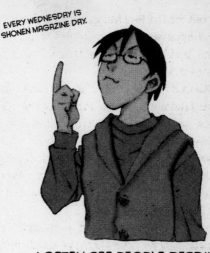

EVERY WEDNESDAY IS
SHONEN MAGAZINE DAY.

I OFTEN SEE PEOPLE READING
SHONEN MAGAZINE ON THE
TRAIN. I USED TO SEE THEM
AND JUST THINK, "OH YEAH, THE
NEW ISSUE CAME OUT TODAY."
RECENTLY, I SUDDENLY REAL-
IZED THAT THEY WERE ACTUALLY
SITTING THERE READING MY
MANGA. NOW WHENEVER I SEE
THEM, I GET THE SUDDEN URGE
TO RUN AS FAR AWAY AS I CAN.
I'M SUCH A COWARD....

Honorifics Explained

Throughout the Del Rey Manga books, you will find Japanese honorifics left intact in the translations. For those not familiar with how the Japanese use honorifics, and, more important, how they differ from American honorifics, we present this brief overview.

Politeness has always been a critical facet of Japanese culture. Ever since the feudal era, when Japan was a highly stratified society, use of honorifics–which can be defined as polite speech that indicates relationship or status–has played an essential role in the Japanese language. When addressing someone in Japanese, an honorific usually takes the form of a suffix attached to one's name (example: "Asuna-san"), as a title at the end of one's name, or in place of the name itself (example: "Negi-sensei" or simply "Sensei!").

Honorifics can be expressions of respect or endearment. In the context of manga and anime, honorifics give insight into the nature of the relationship between characters. Many translations into English leave out these important honorifics, and therefore distort the feel of the original Japanese. Because Japanese honorifics contain nuances that English honorifics lack, it is our policy at Del Rey not to translate them. Here, instead, is a guide to some of the honorifics you may encounter in Del Rey Manga.

-san: This is the most common honorific and is equivalent to Mr., Miss, Ms., Mrs., etc. It is the all-purpose honorific and can be used in any situation where politeness is required.

-sama: This is one level higher than "-san." It is used to confer great respect.

-dono: This comes from the word "tono," which means "lord." It is an even higher level than "-sama" and confers utmost respect.

-kun: This suffix is used at the end of boys' names to express familiarity or endearment. It is also sometimes used by men among friends, or when addressing someone younger or of a lower station.

-chan: This is used to express endearment, mostly toward girls. It is also used for little boys, pets, and between lovers. It gives a sense of childish cuteness.

Bozu: This is an informal way to refer to a boy, similar to the English terms "kid" or "squirt."

Sempai/

Senpai: This title suggests that the addressee is one's senior in a group or organization. It is most often used in a school setting, where underclassmen refer to their upperclassmen as "sempai." It can also be used in the workplace, such as when a newer employee addresses an employee who has seniority in the company.

Kohai: This is the opposite of "-sempai," and is used toward underclassmen in school or newcomers in the workplace. It connotes that the addressee is of a lower station.

Sensei: Literally meaning "one who has come before," this title is used for teachers, doctors, or masters of any profession or art.

-[blank]: This is usually forgotten in these lists, but is perhaps the most significant difference between Japanese and English. The lack of honorific means that the speaker has permission to address the person in a very intimate way. Usually, only family, spouses, or very close friends have this kind of license. Known as *yobisute*, it can be gratifying when someone who has earned the intimacy starts to call one by one's name without an honorific. But when that intimacy hasn't been earned, it can also be insulting.

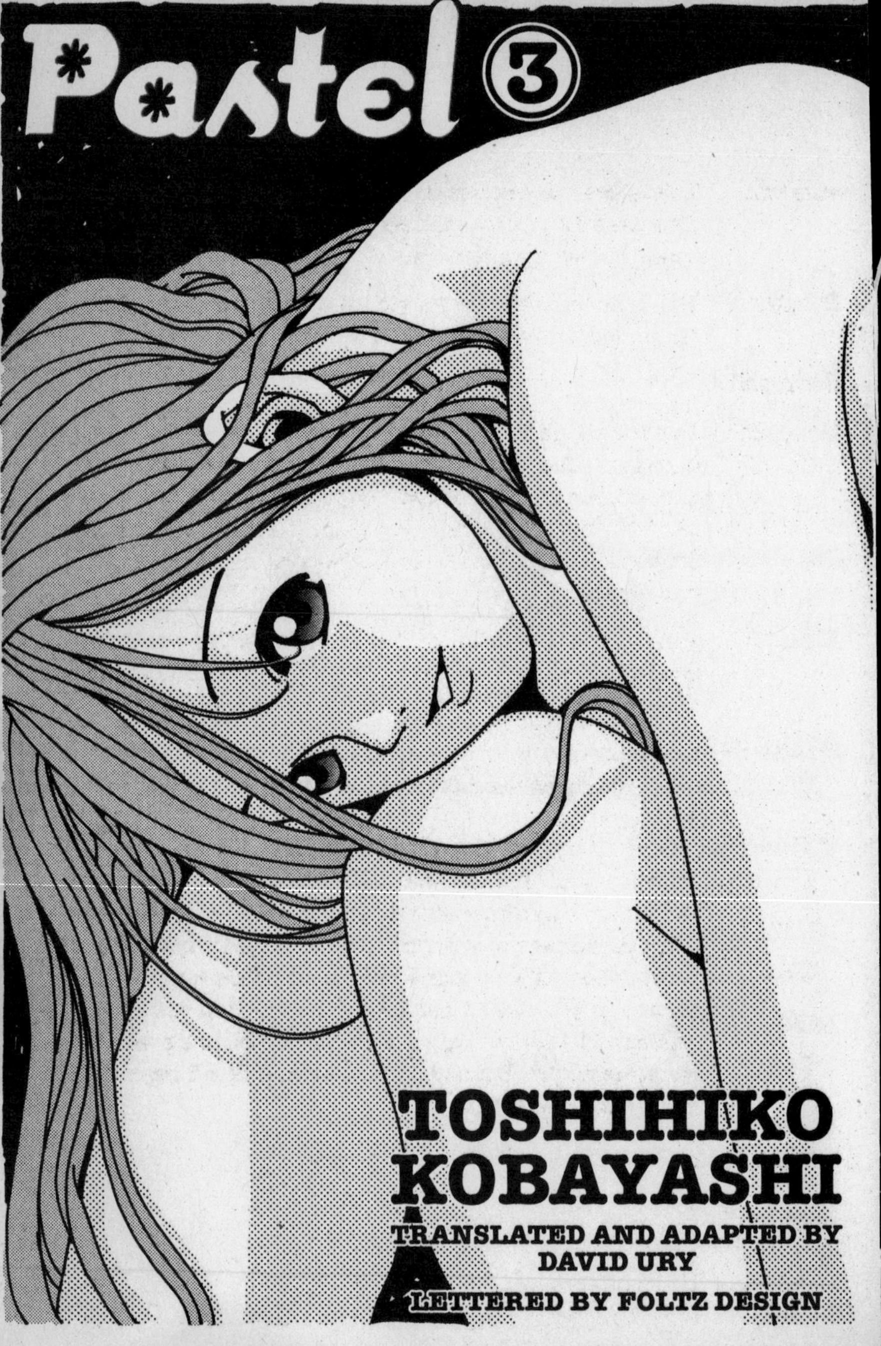

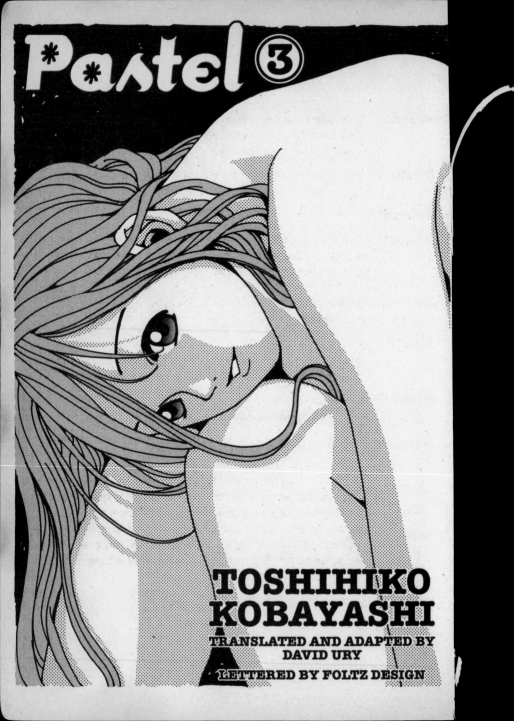

Pastel 3

TOSHIHIKO KOBAYASHI

TRANSLATED AND ADAPTED BY DAVID URY

LETTERED BY FOLTZ DESIGN

Pastel

CONTENTS

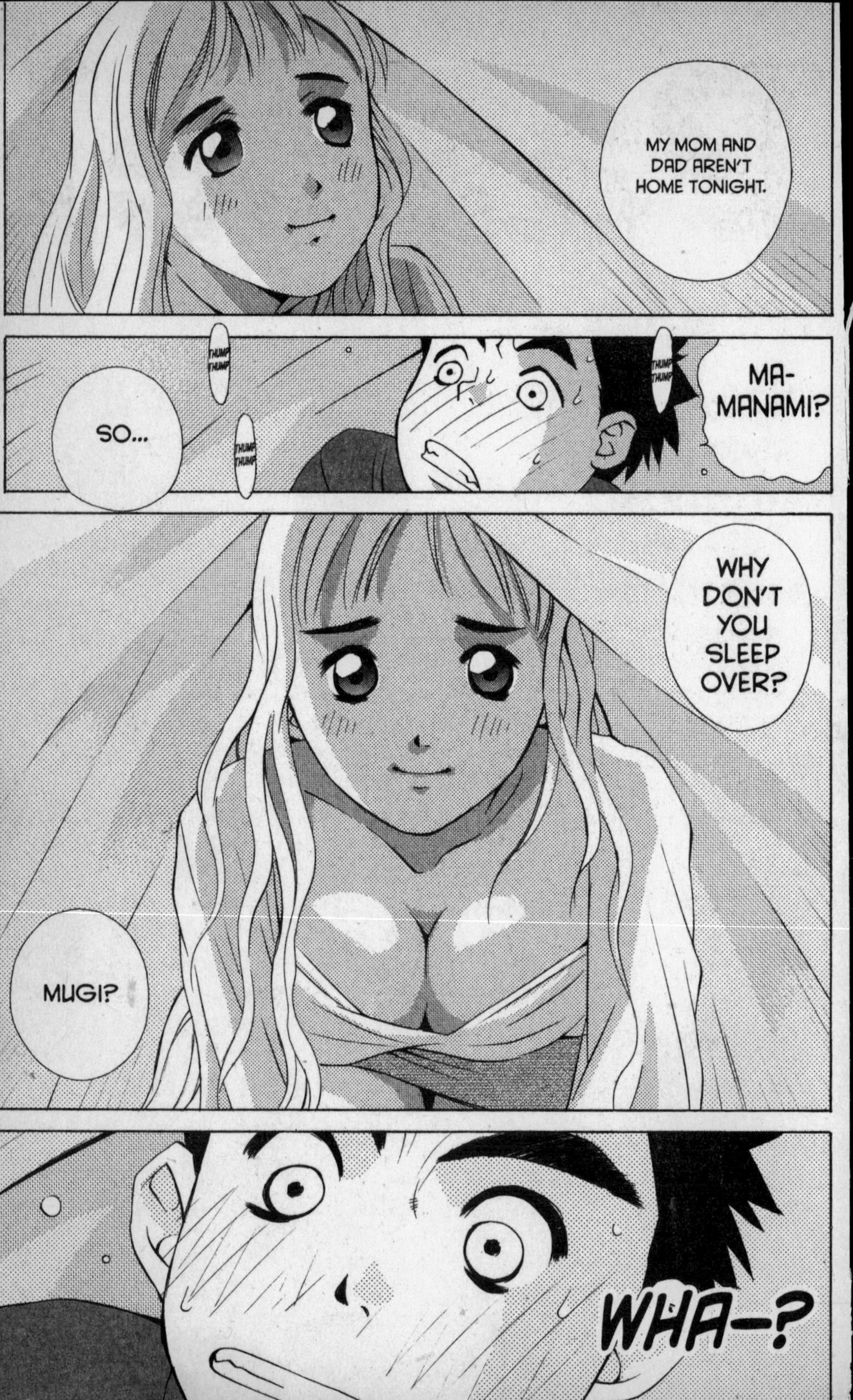
MY MOM AND DAD AREN'T HOME TONIGHT.
MA-MANAMI?
THUMP THUMP
THUMP THUMP
SO...
THUMP THUMP
WHY DON'T YOU SLEEP OVER?
MUGI?
WHA-?

*Pastel

8-23— Today, I went to the river with Mugi. We didn't catch any fish, but Mugi did manage to fall in.

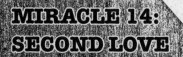

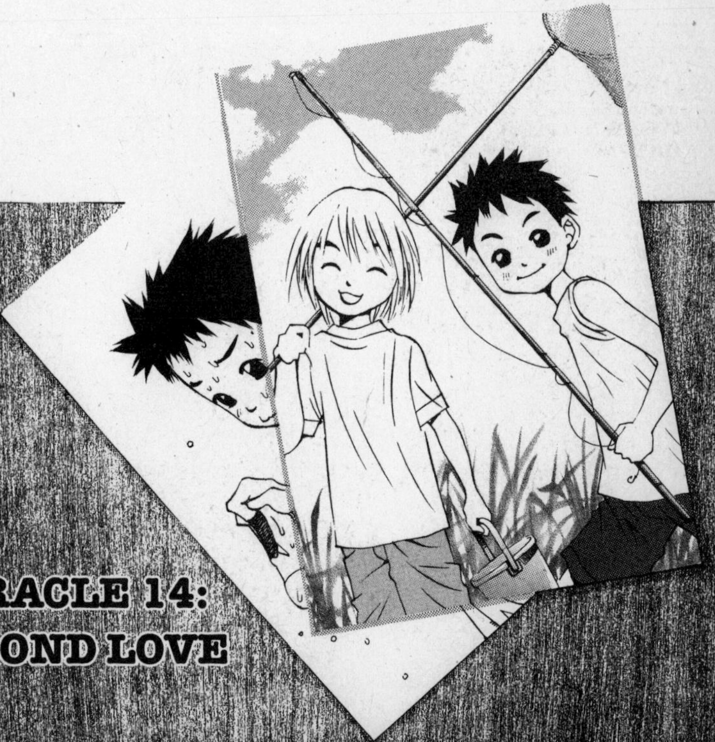

MIRACLE 14: SECOND LOVE

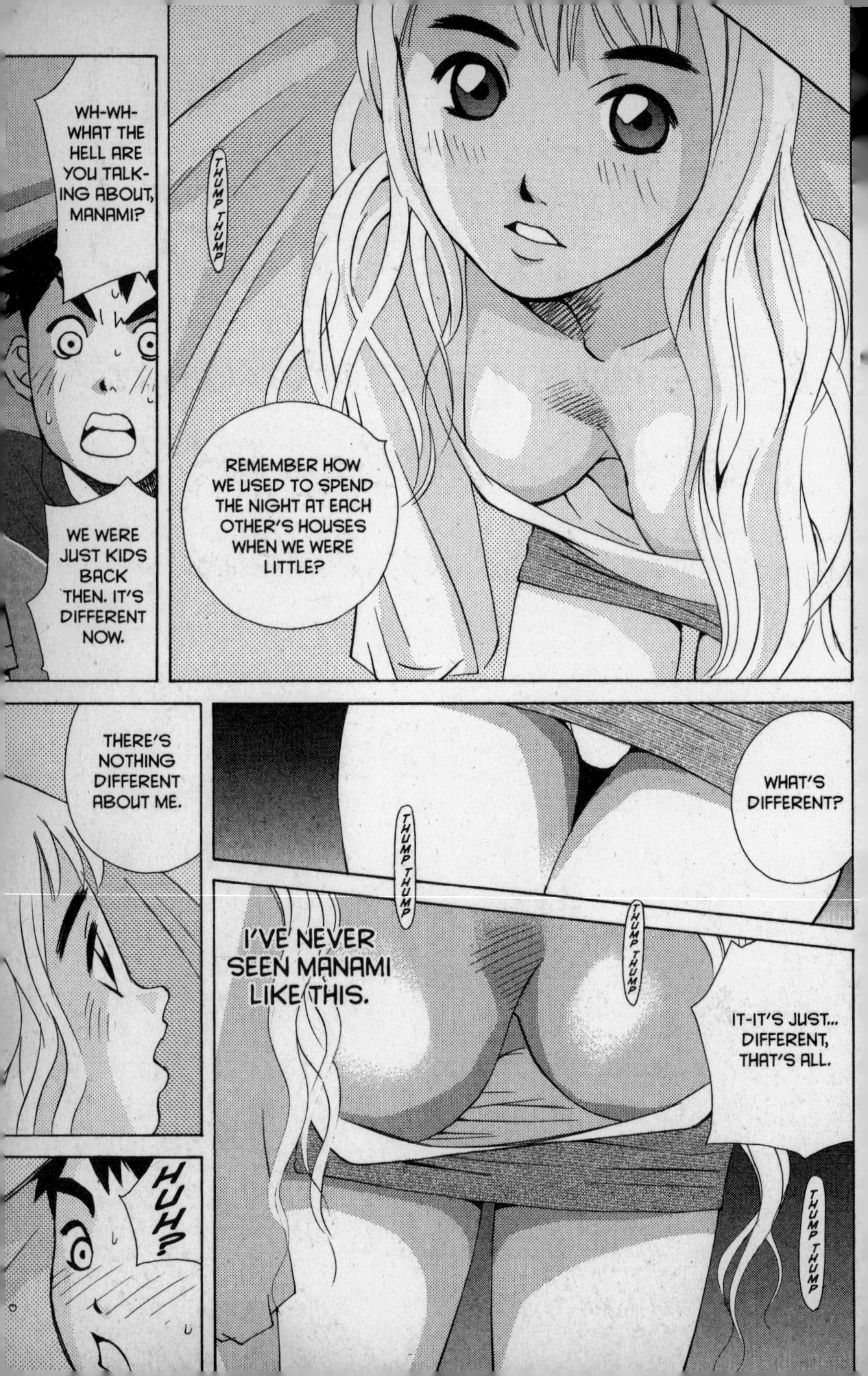
THUMP THUMP
REMEMBER HOW WE USED TO SPEND THE NIGHT AT EACH OTHER'S HOUSES WHEN WE WERE LITTLE?
WH-WH-WHAT THE HELL ARE YOU TALKING ABOUT, MANAMI?
WE WERE JUST KIDS BACK THEN. IT'S DIFFERENT NOW.
WHAT'S DIFFERENT?
THUMP THUMP
THUMP THUMP
IT-IT'S JUST... DIFFERENT, THAT'S ALL.
I'VE NEVER SEEN MANAMI LIKE THIS.
THUMP THUMP
THERE'S NOTHING DIFFERENT ABOUT ME.
HUH?

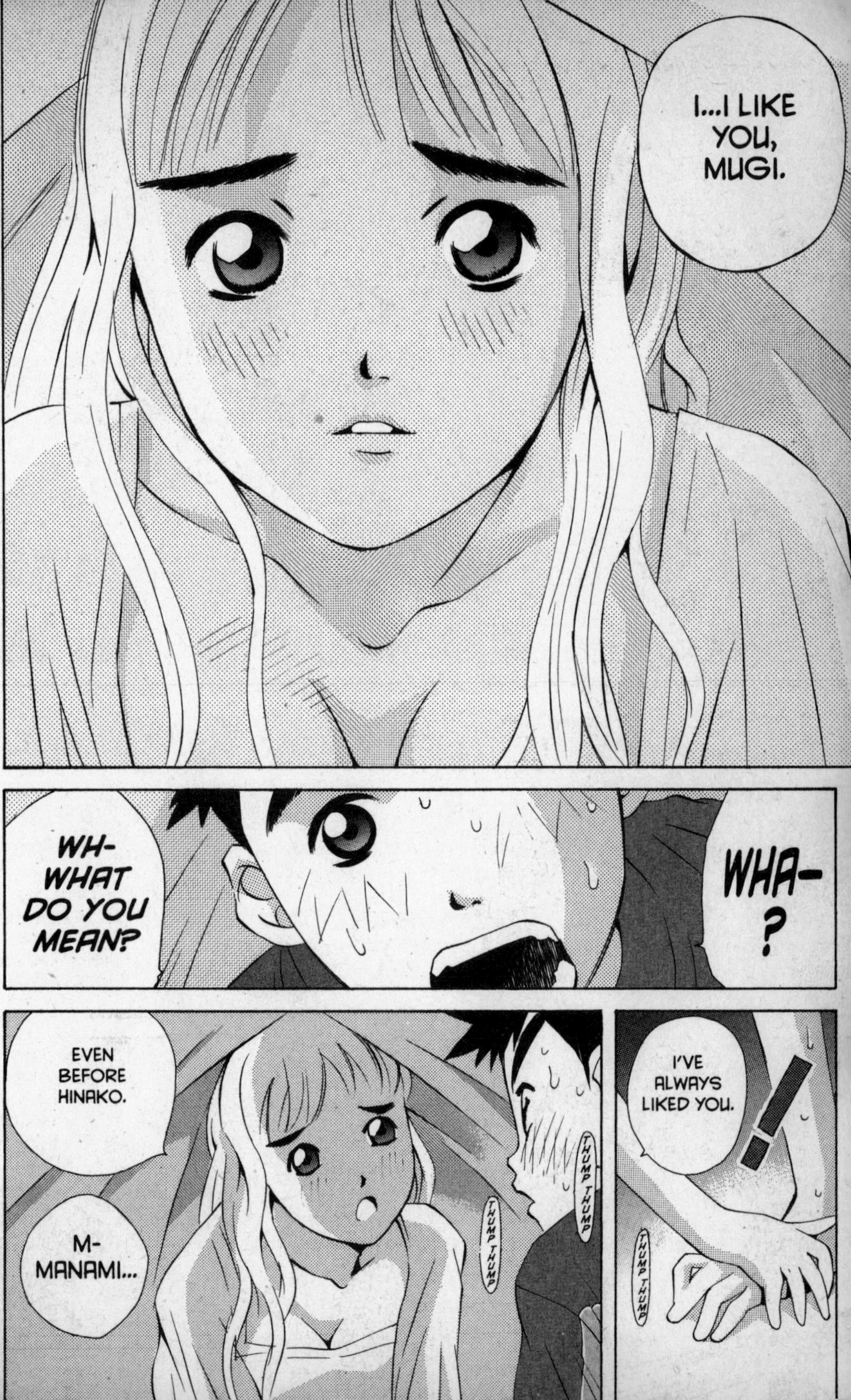
I...I LIKE YOU, MUGI.
WHA-?
WH-WHAT DO YOU MEAN?
!
I'VE ALWAYS LIKED YOU.
THUMP THUMP
THUMP THUMP
EVEN BEFORE HINAKO.
THUMP THUMP
M-MANAMI...

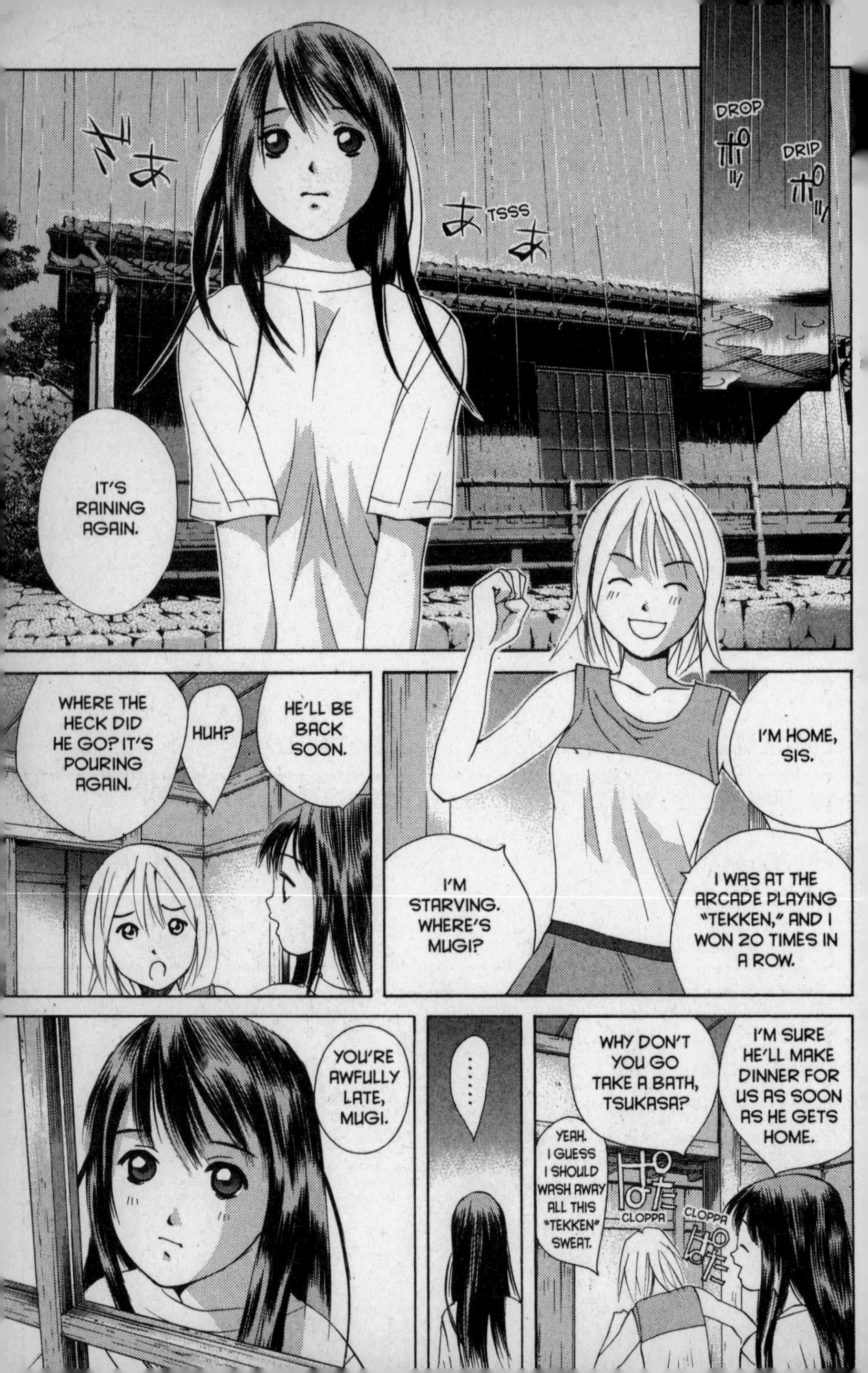
DROP
DRIP
TSSS
IT'S RAINING AGAIN.
I'M HOME, SIS.
I WAS AT THE ARCADE PLAYING "TEKKEN," AND I WON 20 TIMES IN A ROW.
I'M STARVING. WHERE'S MUGI?
HE'LL BE BACK SOON.
HUH?
WHERE THE HECK DID HE GO? IT'S POURING AGAIN.
I'M SURE HE'LL MAKE DINNER FOR US AS SOON AS HE GETS HOME.
WHY DON'T YOU GO TAKE A BATH, TSUKASA?
YEAH. I GUESS I SHOULD WASH AWAY ALL THIS "TEKKEN" SWEAT.
CLOPPA
CLOPPA
......
YOU'RE AWFULLY LATE, MUGI.

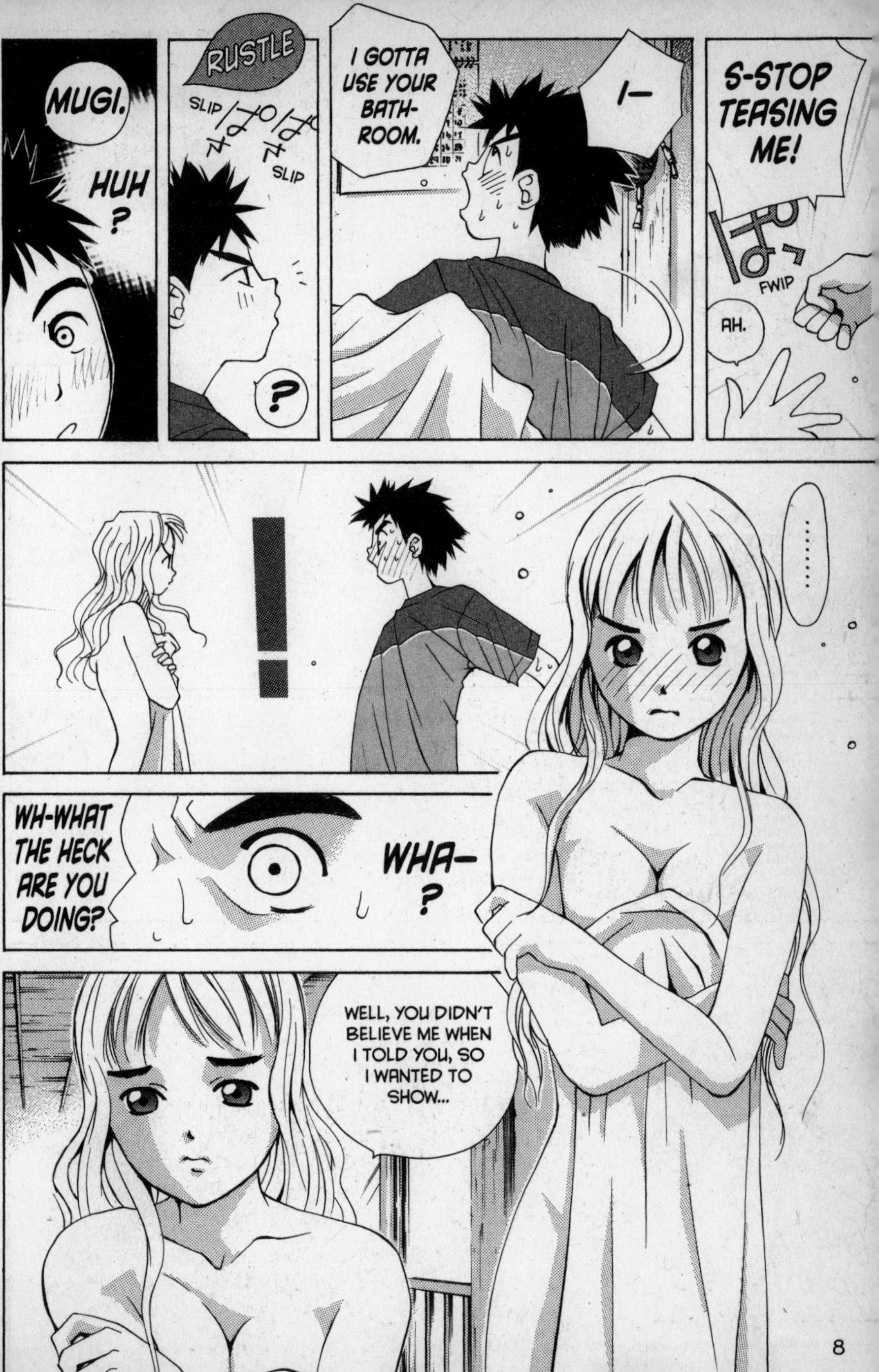
S-STOP TEASING ME!
FWIP
AH.
I—
I GOTTA USE YOUR BATHROOM.
RUSTLE
SLIP
SLIP
?
MUGI.
HUH?
......
!
WHA-?
WH-WHAT THE HECK ARE YOU DOING?
WELL, YOU DIDN'T BELIEVE ME WHEN I TOLD YOU, SO I WANTED TO SHOW...

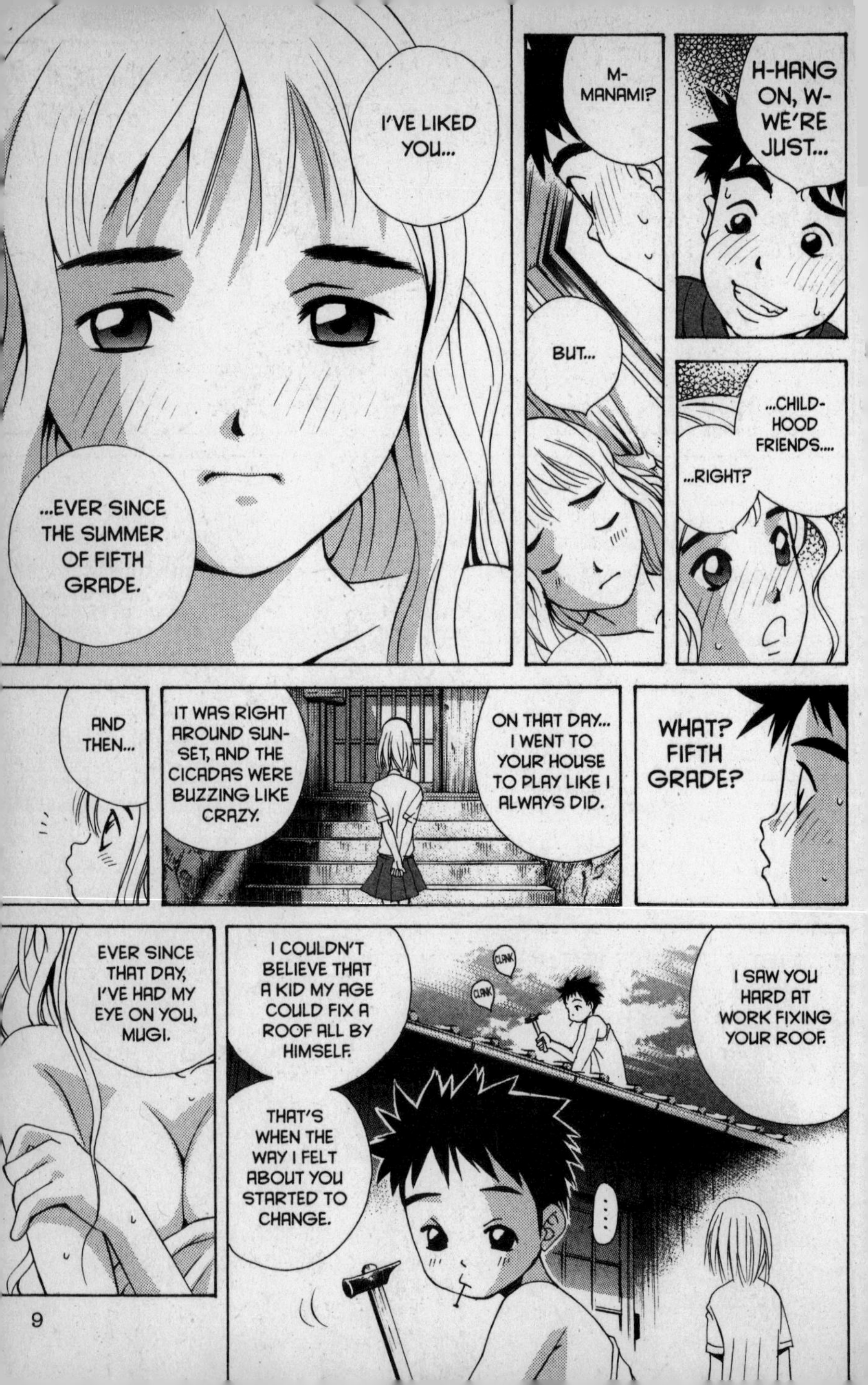
H-HANG ON, W-WE'RE JUST...
...CHILDHOOD FRIENDS....
...RIGHT?
M-MANAMI?
BUT...
I'VE LIKED YOU...
...EVER SINCE THE SUMMER OF FIFTH GRADE.
WHAT? FIFTH GRADE?
ON THAT DAY... I WENT TO YOUR HOUSE TO PLAY LIKE I ALWAYS DID.
IT WAS RIGHT AROUND SUNSET, AND THE CICADAS WERE BUZZING LIKE CRAZY.
AND THEN...
I SAW YOU HARD AT WORK FIXING YOUR ROOF.
CLANK
CLANK
I COULDN'T BELIEVE THAT A KID MY AGE COULD FIX A ROOF ALL BY HIMSELF.
THAT'S WHEN THE WAY I FELT ABOUT YOU STARTED TO CHANGE.
...
EVER SINCE THAT DAY, I'VE HAD MY EYE ON YOU, MUGI.

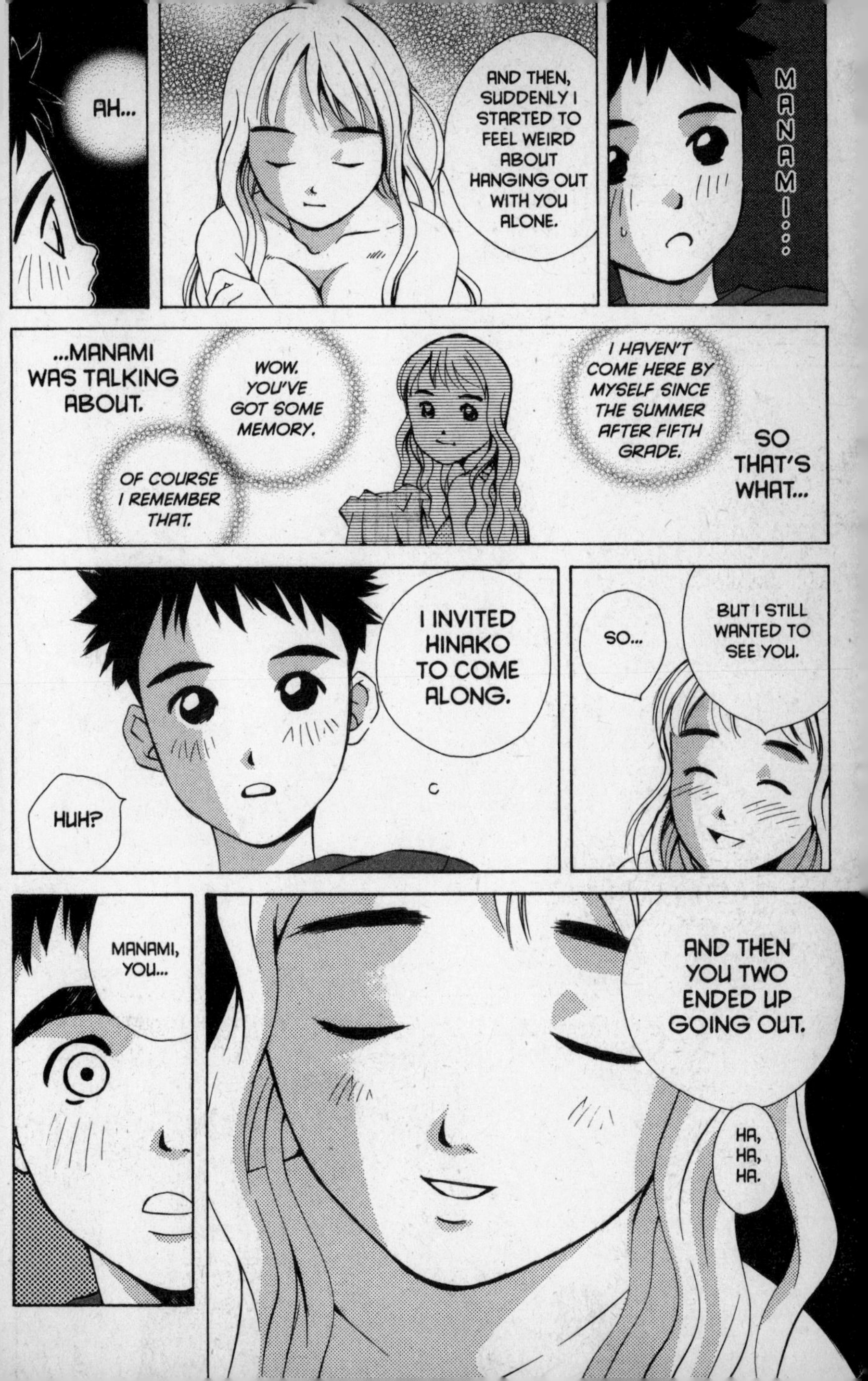
MANAMI...
AND THEN, SUDDENLY I STARTED TO FEEL WEIRD ABOUT HANGING OUT WITH YOU ALONE.
AH...
SO THAT'S WHAT...
I HAVEN'T COME HERE BY MYSELF SINCE THE SUMMER AFTER FIFTH GRADE.
WOW. YOU'VE GOT SOME MEMORY.
OF COURSE I REMEMBER THAT.
...MANAMI WAS TALKING ABOUT.
BUT I STILL WANTED TO SEE YOU.
SO...
I INVITED HINAKO TO COME ALONG.
HUH?
AND THEN YOU TWO ENDED UP GOING OUT.
HA, HA, HA.
MANAMI, YOU...

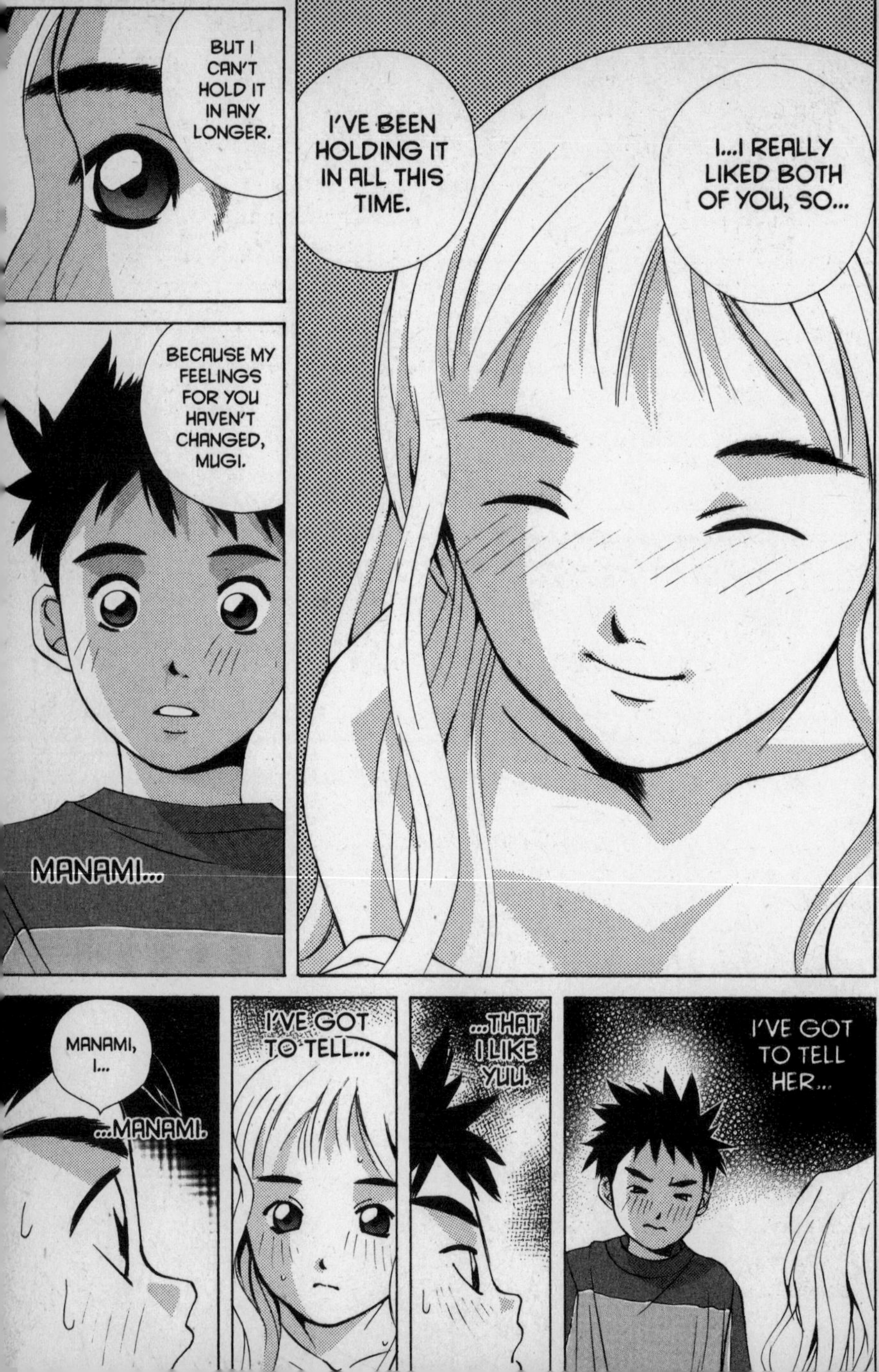
I...I REALLY LIKED BOTH OF YOU, SO...
I'VE BEEN HOLDING IT IN ALL THIS TIME.
BUT I CAN'T HOLD IT IN ANY LONGER.
BECAUSE MY FEELINGS FOR YOU HAVEN'T CHANGED, MUGI.
MANAMI...
I'VE GOT TO TELL HER...
...THAT I LIKE YUU.
I'VE GOT TO TELL...
MANAMI, I...
...MANAMI.

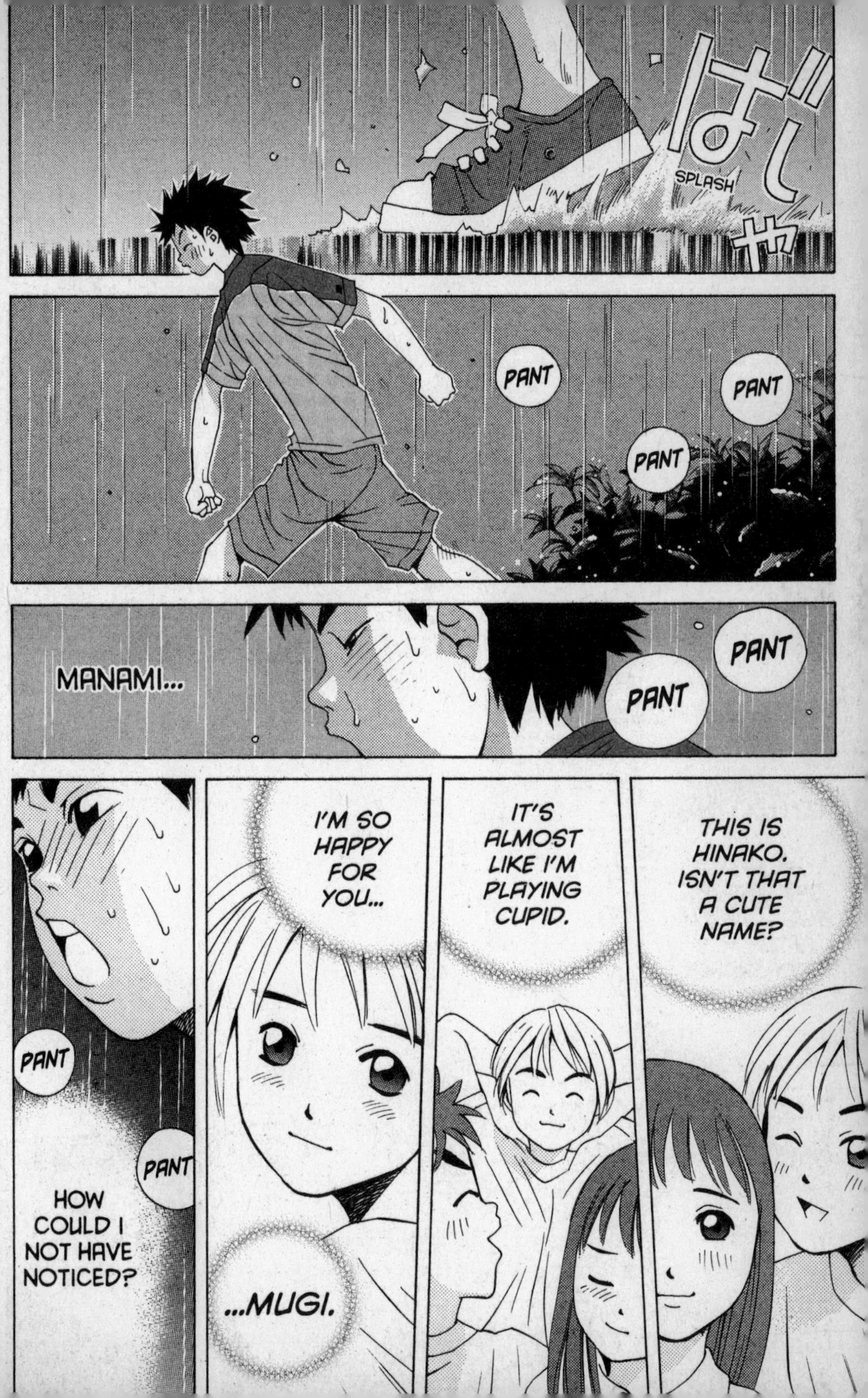
ばしゃ
SPLASH
PANT
PANT
PANT
PANT
PANT
MANAMI...
THIS IS HINAKO. ISN'T THAT A CUTE NAME?
IT'S ALMOST LIKE I'M PLAYING CUPID.
I'M SO HAPPY FOR YOU...
...MUGI.
PANT
PANT
HOW COULD I NOT HAVE NOTICED?

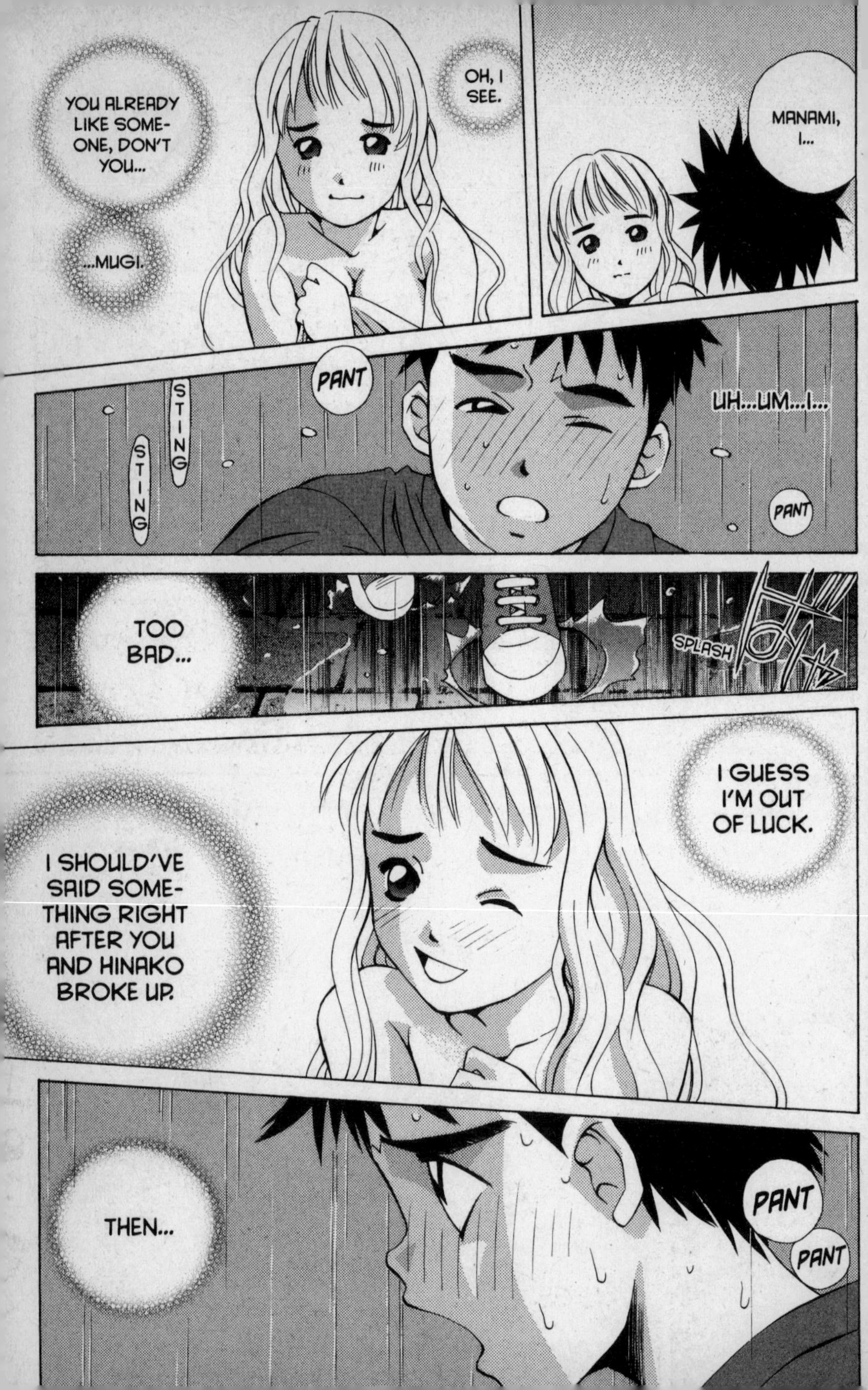
MANAMI, I...
OH, I SEE.
YOU ALREADY LIKE SOME-ONE, DON'T YOU...
...MUGI.
UH...UM...I...
PANT
PANT
STING
STING
SPLASH
TOO BAD...
I GUESS I'M OUT OF LUCK.
I SHOULD'VE SAID SOME-THING RIGHT AFTER YOU AND HINAKO BROKE UP.
PANT
PANT
THEN...

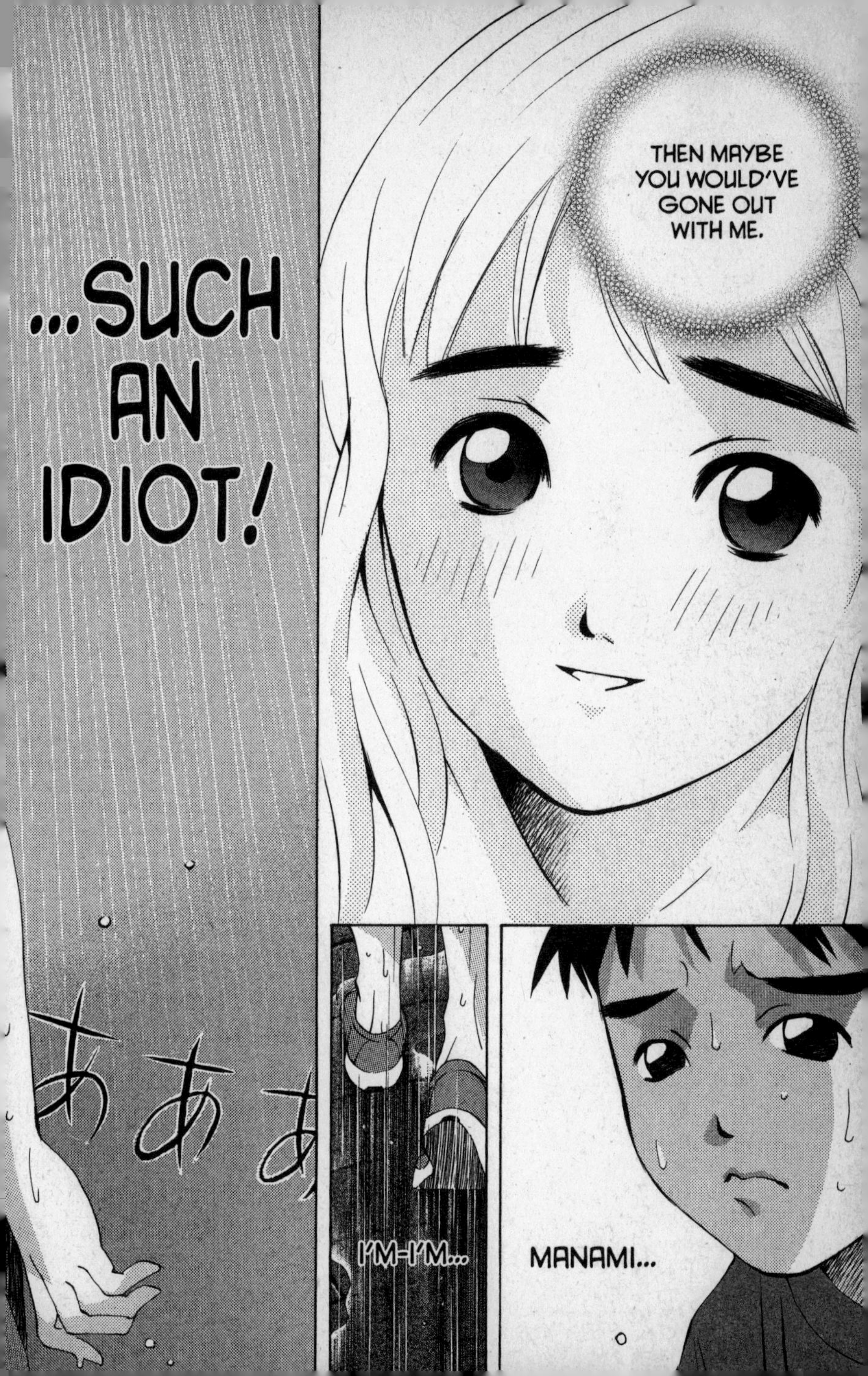
THEN MAYBE YOU WOULD'VE GONE OUT WITH ME.
MANAMI...
I'M-I'M...
...SUCH AN IDIOT!
あああ

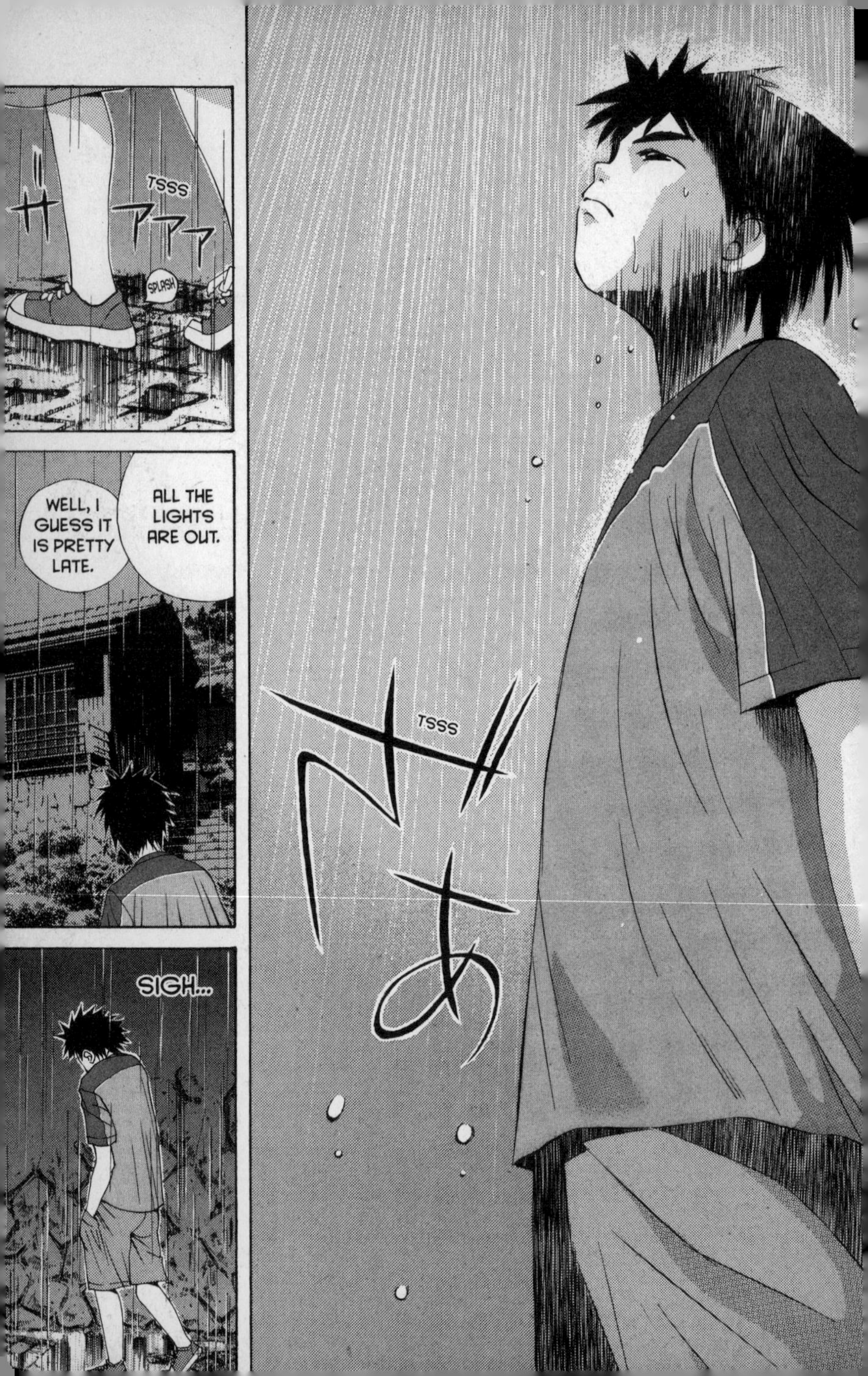
TSSS
ザあ
TSSS
ザァァァ
SPLASH
ALL THE LIGHTS ARE OUT.
WELL, I GUESS IT IS PRETTY LATE.
SIGH...

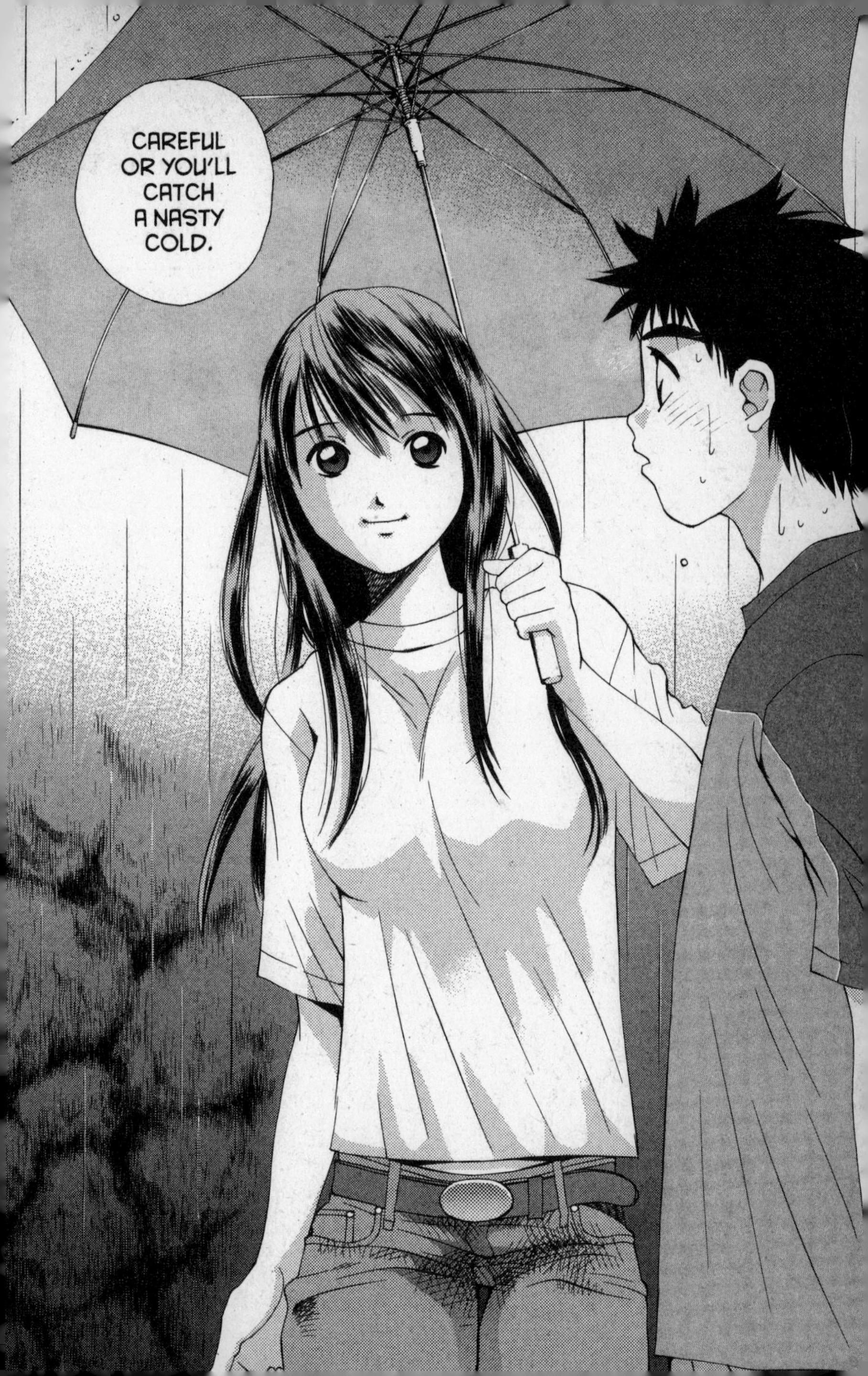
CAREFUL OR YOU'LL CATCH A NASTY COLD.

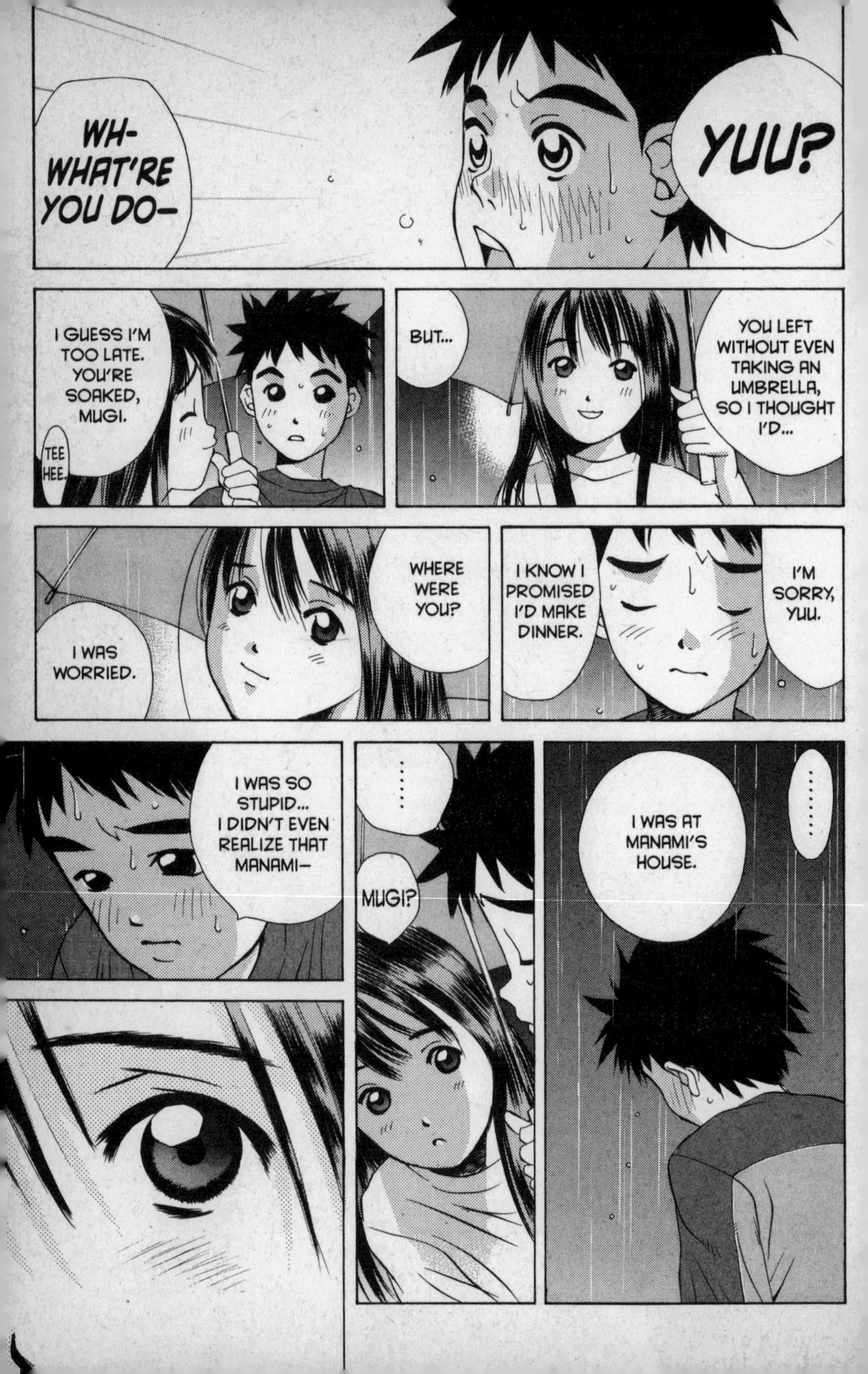
YUU?
WH- WHAT'RE YOU DO-
YOU LEFT WITHOUT EVEN TAKING AN UMBRELLA, SO I THOUGHT I'D...
BUT...
I GUESS I'M TOO LATE. YOU'RE SOAKED, MUGI.
TEE HEE.
I'M SORRY, YUU.
I KNOW I PROMISED I'D MAKE DINNER.
WHERE WERE YOU?
I WAS WORRIED.
......
I WAS AT MANAMI'S HOUSE.
......
MUGI?
I WAS SO STUPID... I DIDN'T EVEN REALIZE THAT MANAMI—

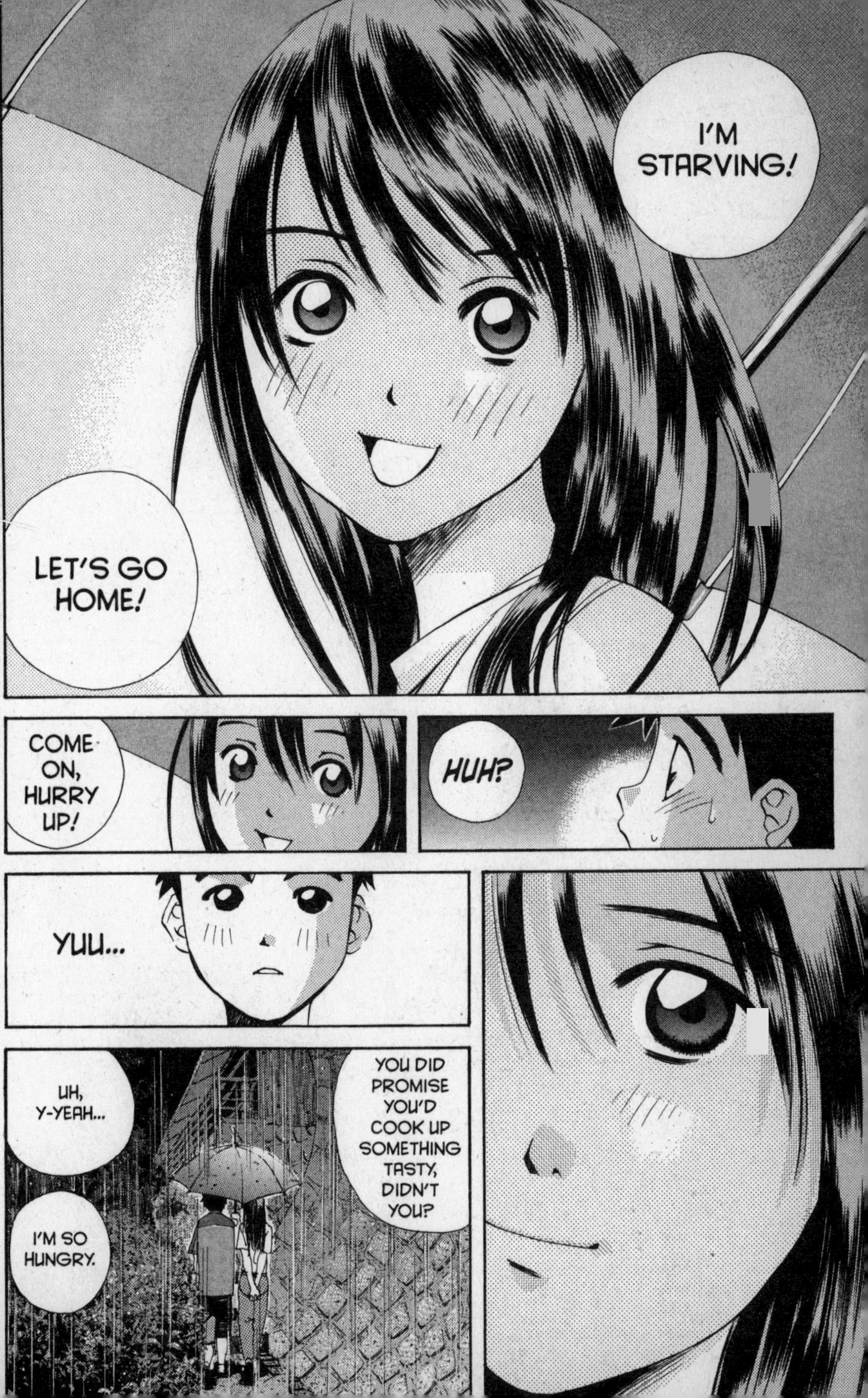
I'M STARVING!
LET'S GO HOME!
HUH?
COME ON, HURRY UP!
YUU...
YOU DID PROMISE YOU'D COOK UP SOMETHING TASTY, DIDN'T YOU?
UH, Y-YEAH...
I'M SO HUNGRY.

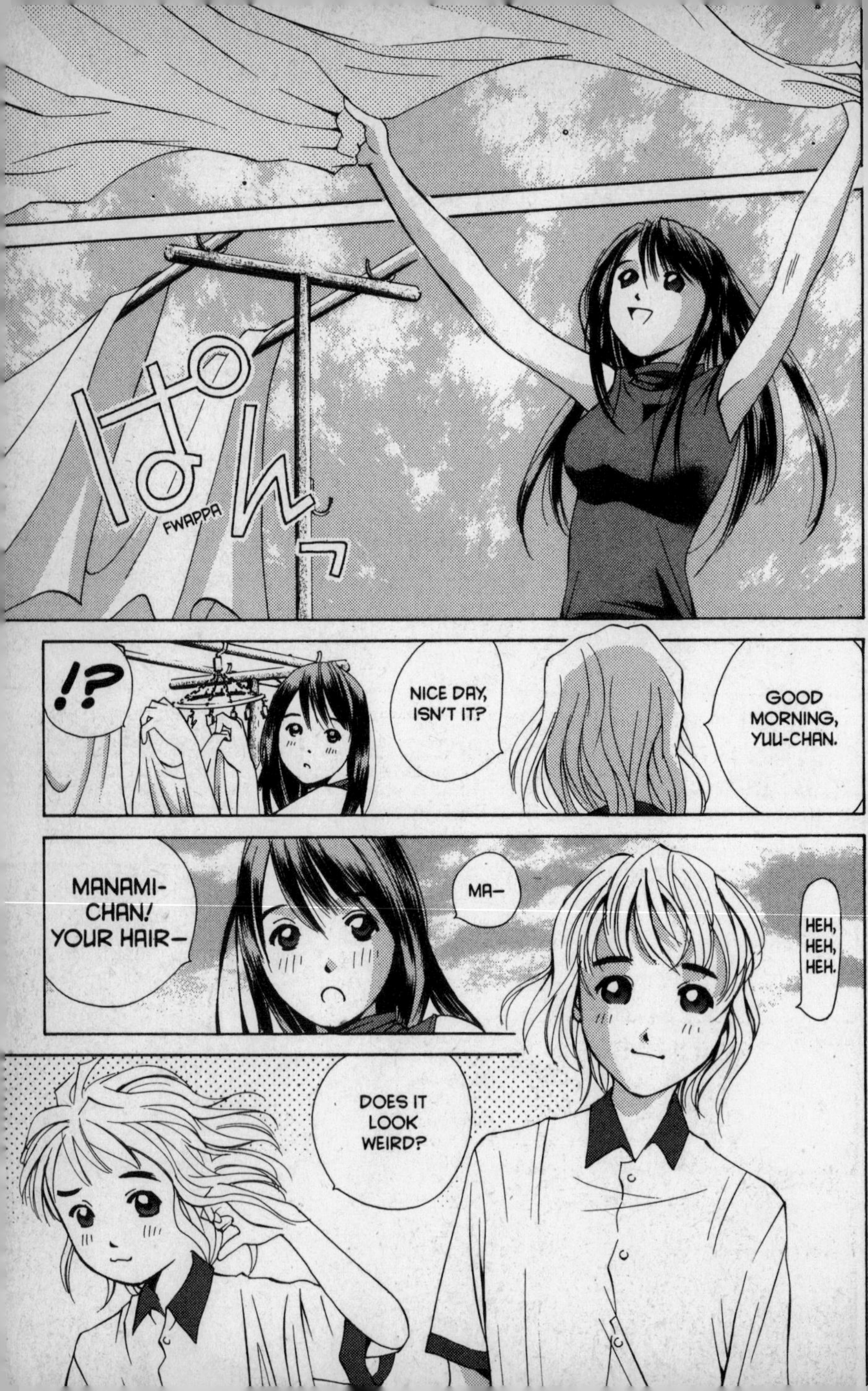
ぱんっ
FWAPPA
GOOD MORNING, YUU-CHAN.
NICE DAY, ISN'T IT?
!?
HEH, HEH, HEH.
MA—
MANAMI-CHAN! YOUR HAIR—
DOES IT LOOK WEIRD?

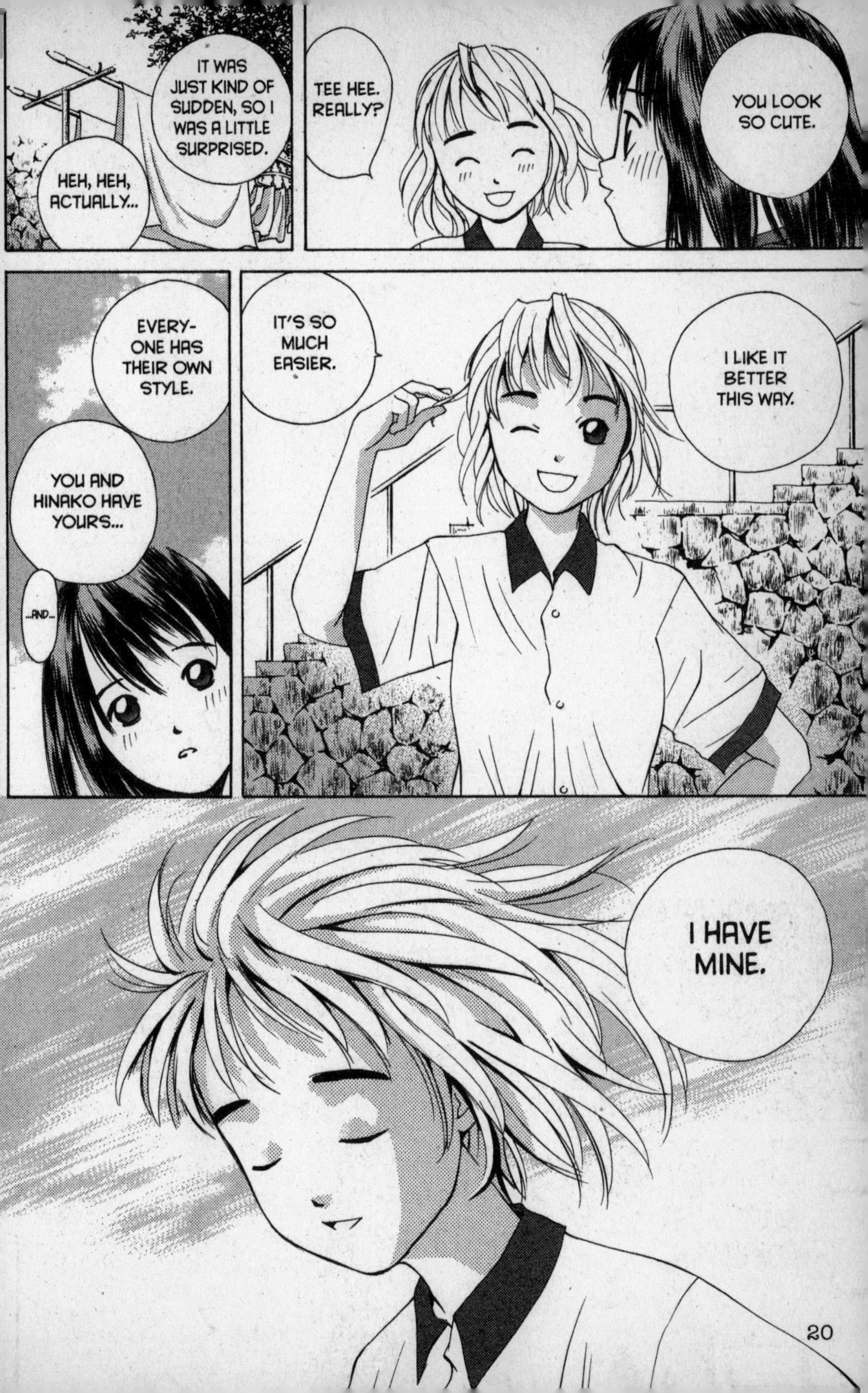
YOU LOOK SO CUTE.
TEE HEE. REALLY?
IT WAS JUST KIND OF SUDDEN, SO I WAS A LITTLE SURPRISED.
HEH, HEH, ACTUALLY...
I LIKE IT BETTER THIS WAY.
IT'S SO MUCH EASIER.
EVERY-ONE HAS THEIR OWN STYLE.
YOU AND HINAKO HAVE YOURS...
...AND...
I HAVE MINE.

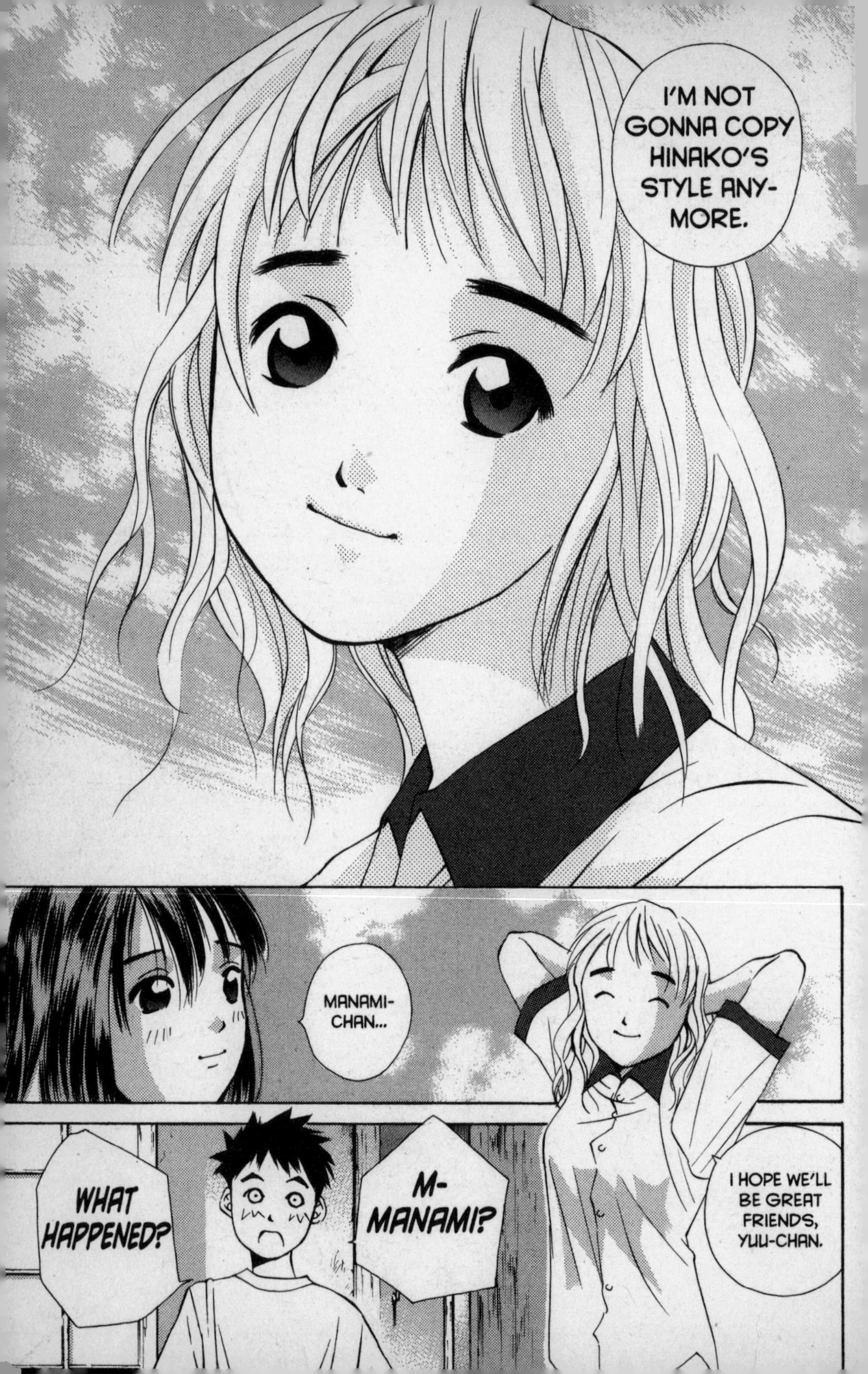
I'M NOT GONNA COPY HINAKO'S STYLE ANY-MORE.
MANAMI-CHAN...
I HOPE WE'LL BE GREAT FRIENDS, YUU-CHAN.
M-MANAMI?
WHAT HAPPENED?

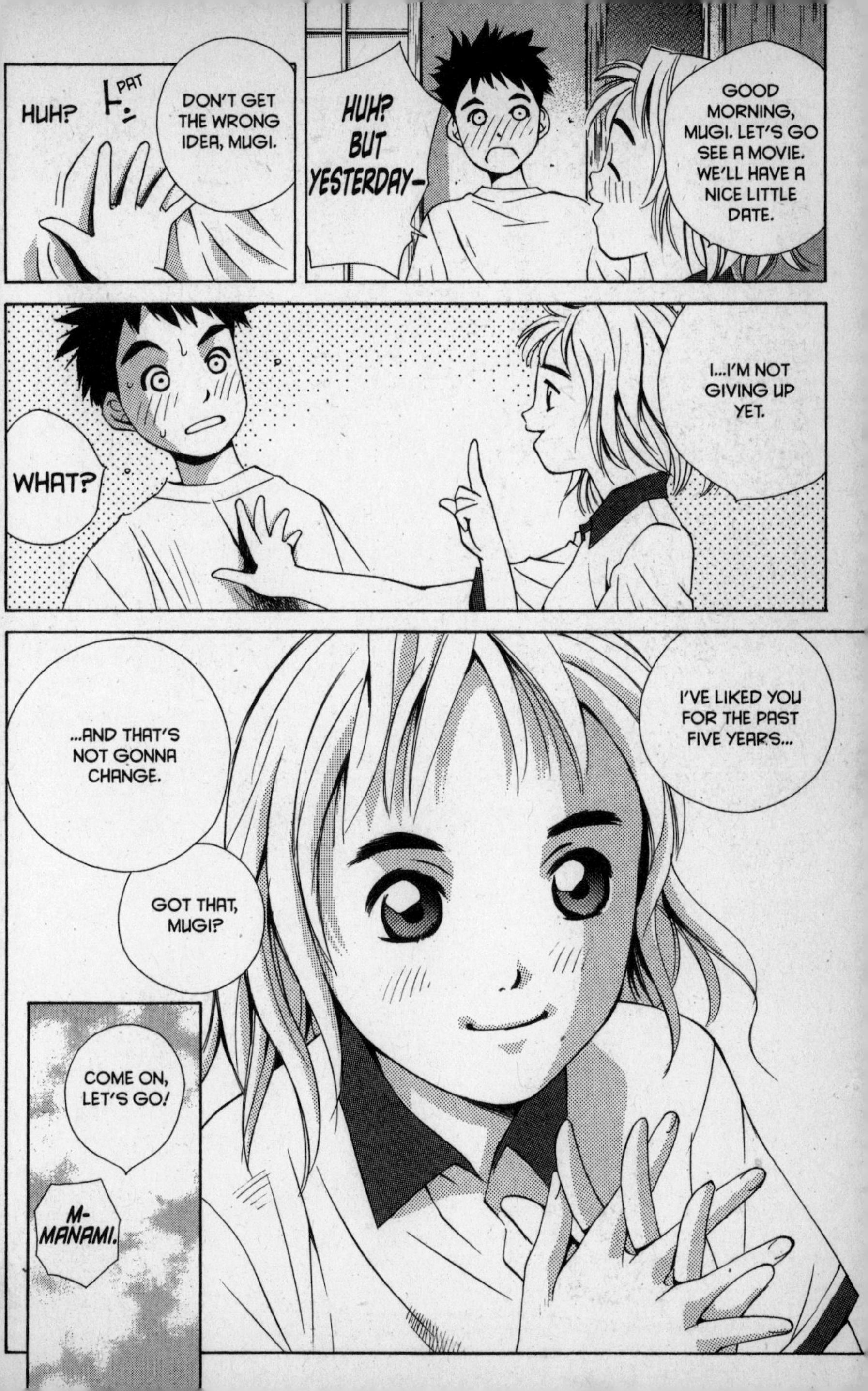
GOOD MORNING, MUGI. LET'S GO SEE A MOVIE. WE'LL HAVE A NICE LITTLE DATE.
HUH? BUT YESTERDAY—
DON'T GET THE WRONG IDEA, MUGI.
PAT
HUH?
I...I'M NOT GIVING UP YET.
WHAT?
I'VE LIKED YOU FOR THE PAST FIVE YEARS...
...AND THAT'S NOT GONNA CHANGE.
GOT THAT, MUGI?
COME ON, LET'S GO!
M-MANAMI.

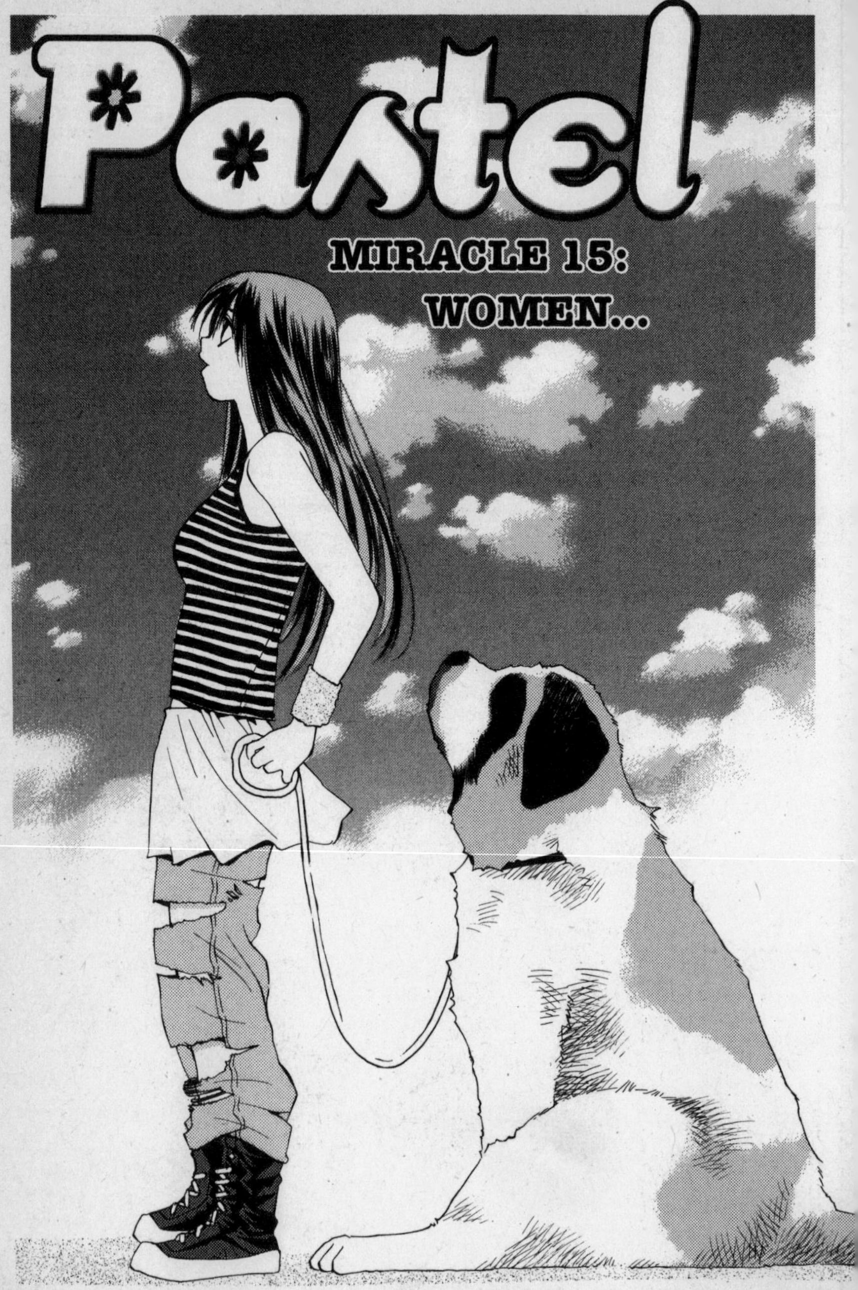
Pastel
MIRACLE 15:
WOMEN...

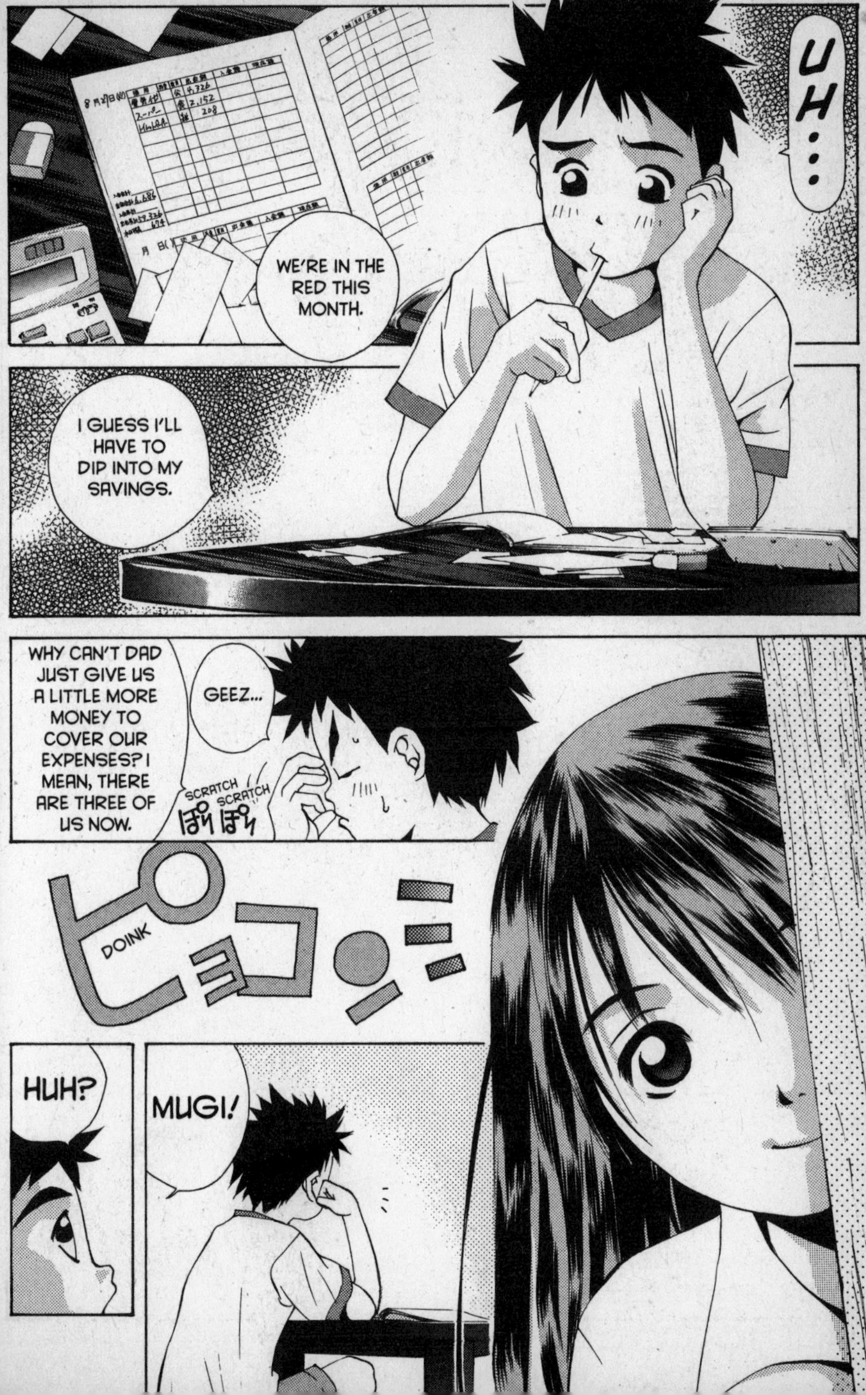
UH...
WE'RE IN THE RED THIS MONTH.
I GUESS I'LL HAVE TO DIP INTO MY SAVINGS.
ピョコン
DOINK
GEEZ...
WHY CAN'T DAD JUST GIVE US A LITTLE MORE MONEY TO COVER OUR EXPENSES? I MEAN, THERE ARE THREE OF US NOW.
ぽりぽり
SCRATCH SCRATCH
MUGI!
HUH?

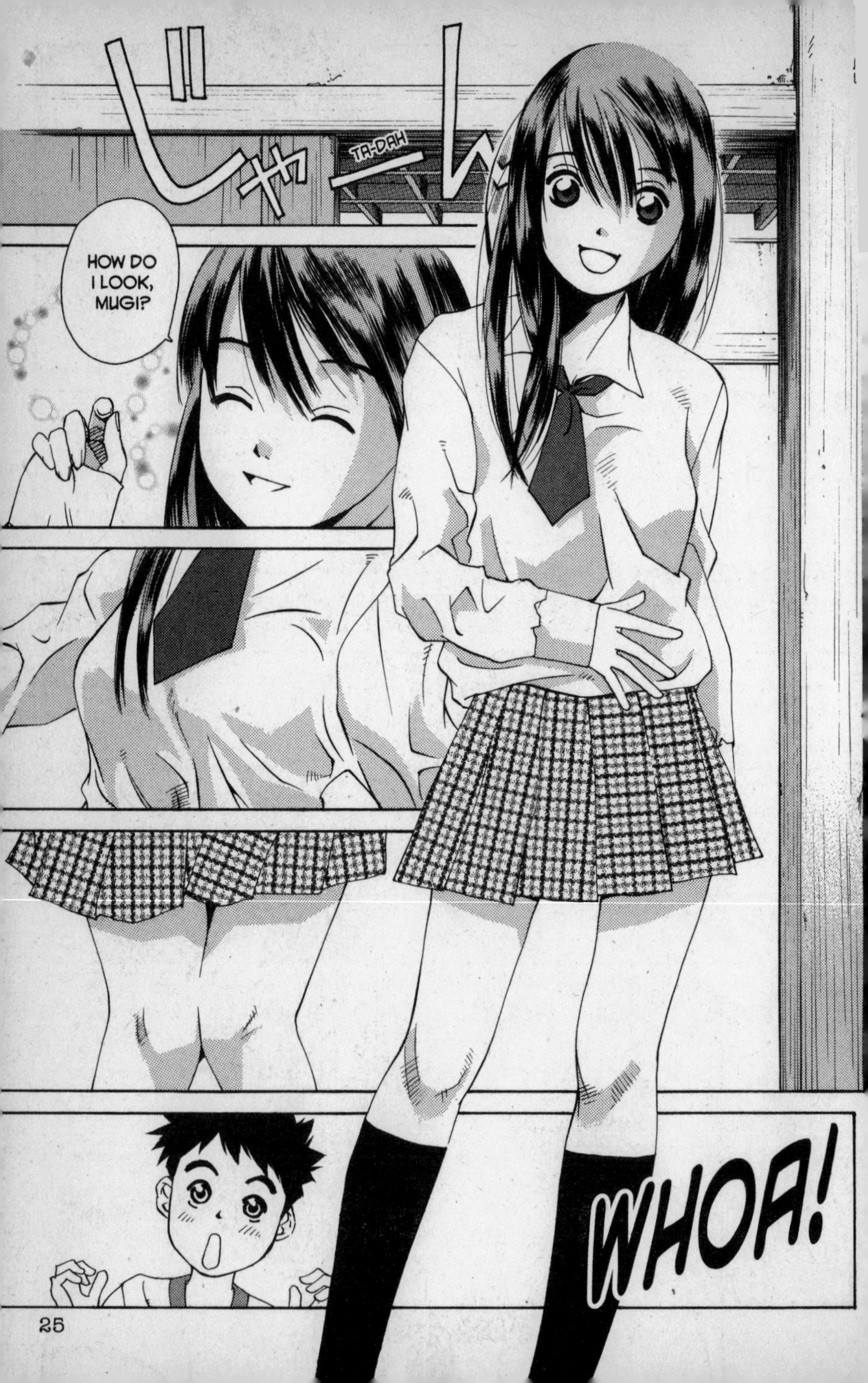
じゃーん
TA-DAH
HOW DO I LOOK, MUGI?
WHOA!

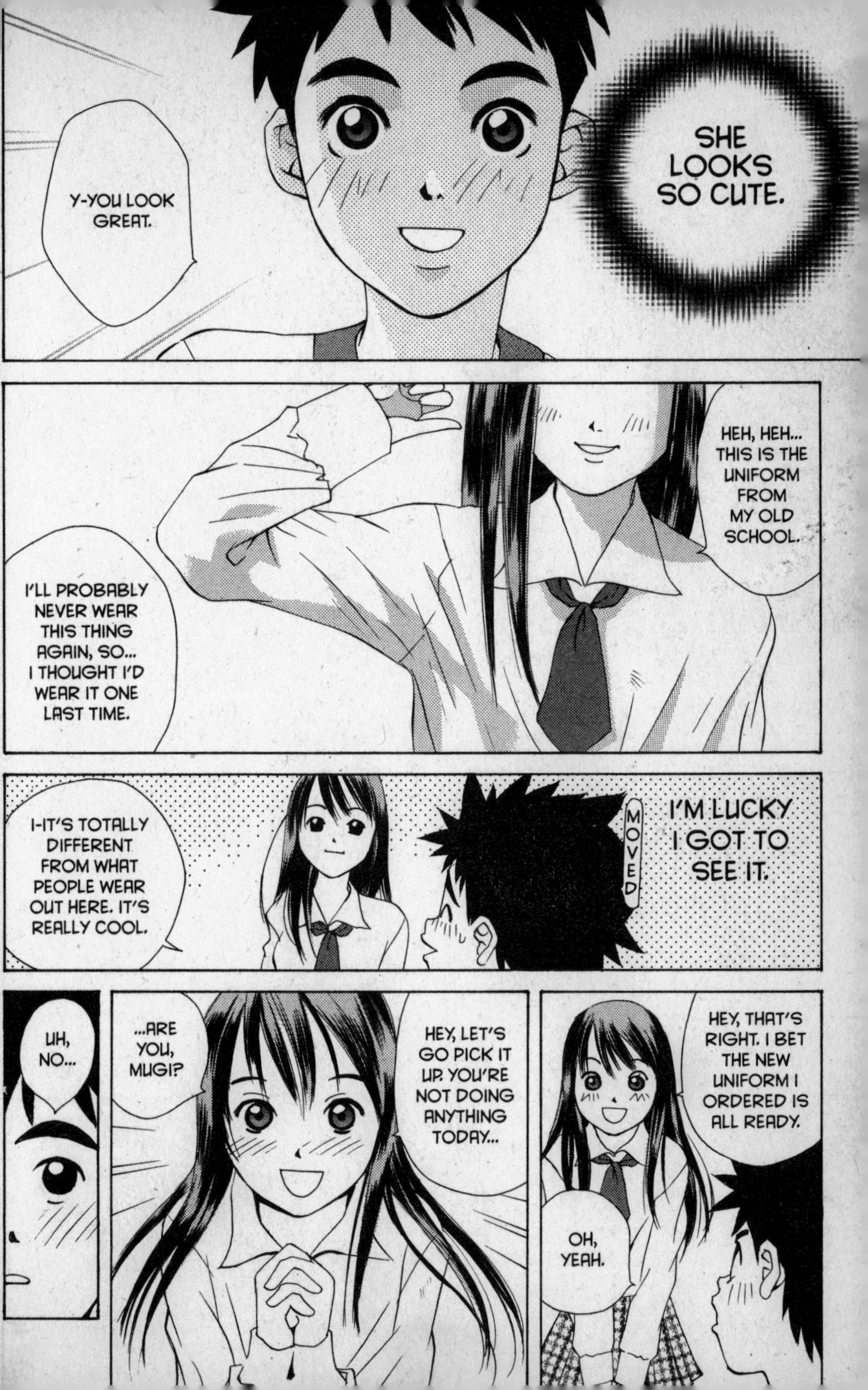
SHE LOOKS SO CUTE.
Y-YOU LOOK GREAT.
HEH, HEH... THIS IS THE UNIFORM FROM MY OLD SCHOOL.
I'LL PROBABLY NEVER WEAR THIS THING AGAIN, SO... I THOUGHT I'D WEAR IT ONE LAST TIME.
I'M LUCKY I GOT TO SEE IT.
MOVED
I-IT'S TOTALLY DIFFERENT FROM WHAT PEOPLE WEAR OUT HERE. IT'S REALLY COOL.
HEY, THAT'S RIGHT. I BET THE NEW UNIFORM I ORDERED IS ALL READY.
OH, YEAH.
HEY, LET'S GO PICK IT UP. YOU'RE NOT DOING ANYTHING TODAY...
...ARE YOU, MUGI?
UH, NO...

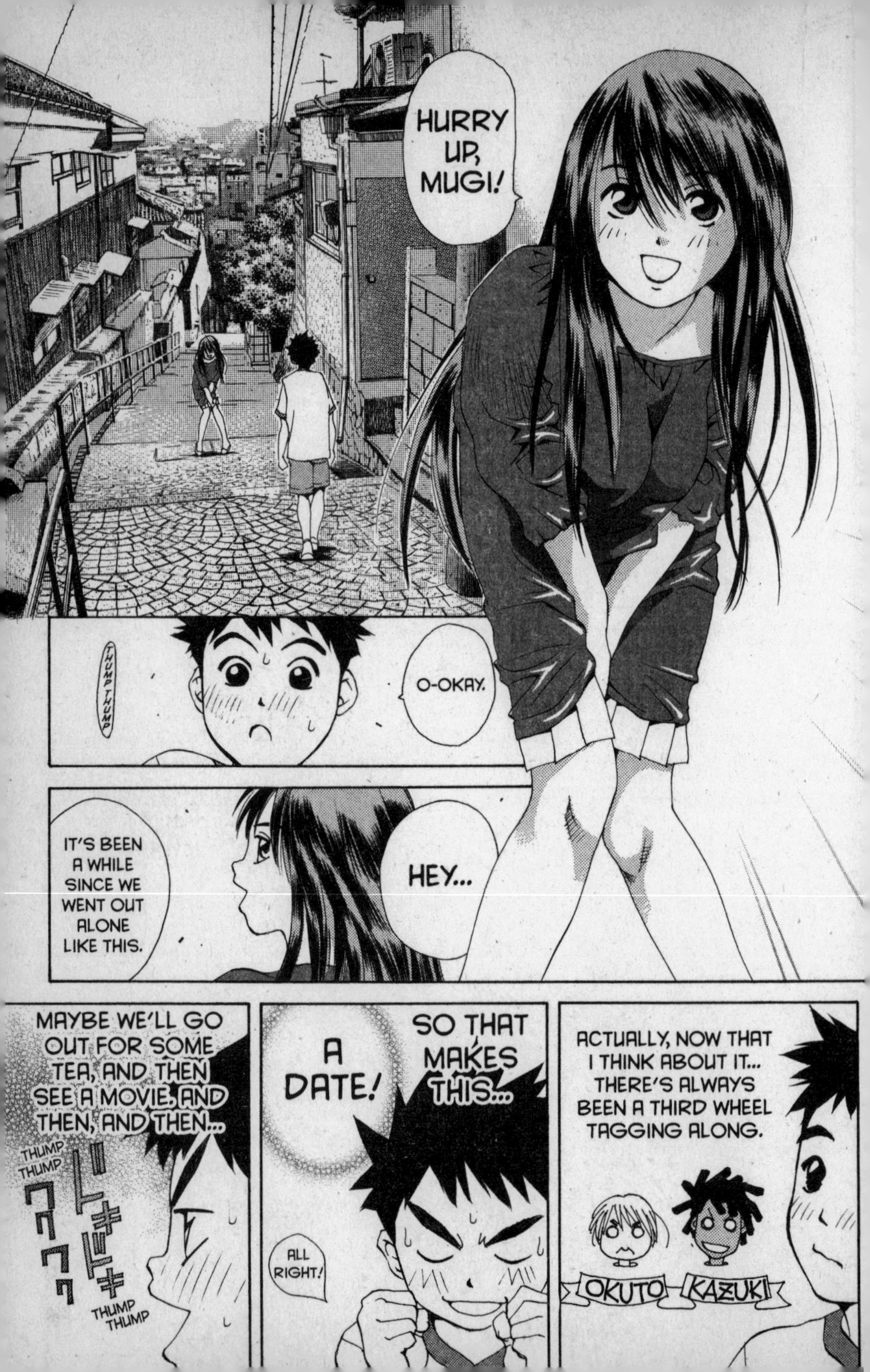
HURRY UP, MUGI!
THUMP THUMP
O-OKAY.
HEY...
IT'S BEEN A WHILE SINCE WE WENT OUT ALONE LIKE THIS.
ACTUALLY, NOW THAT I THINK ABOUT IT... THERE'S ALWAYS BEEN A THIRD WHEEL TAGGING ALONG.
KAZUKI
OKUTO
SO THAT MAKES THIS...
A DATE!
ALL RIGHT!
MAYBE WE'LL GO OUT FOR SOME TEA, AND THEN SEE A MOVIE, AND THEN, AND THEN...
ドキドキ
THUMP THUMP
ワクワク
THUMP THUMP

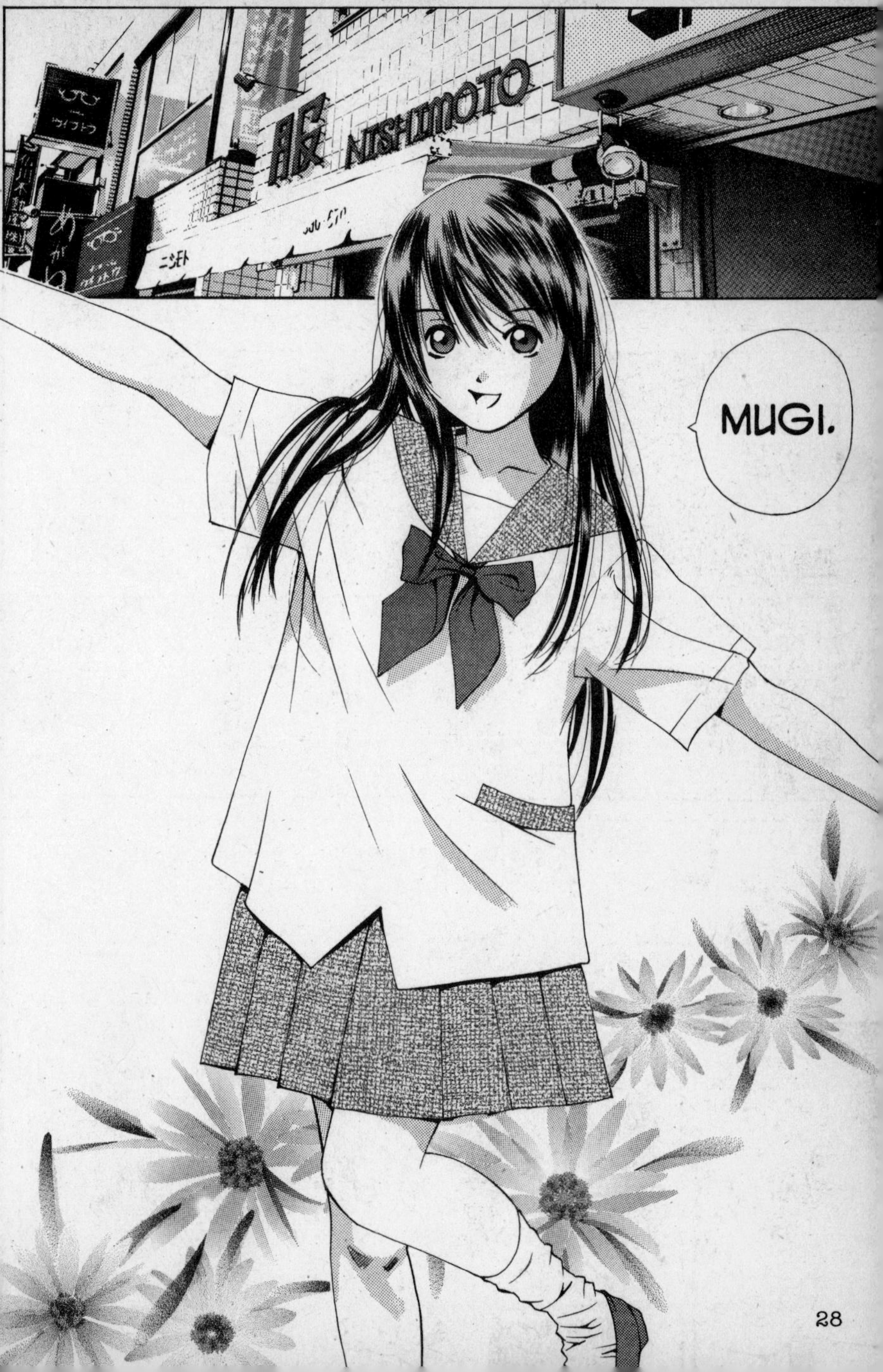
NISHIMOTO
MUGI.

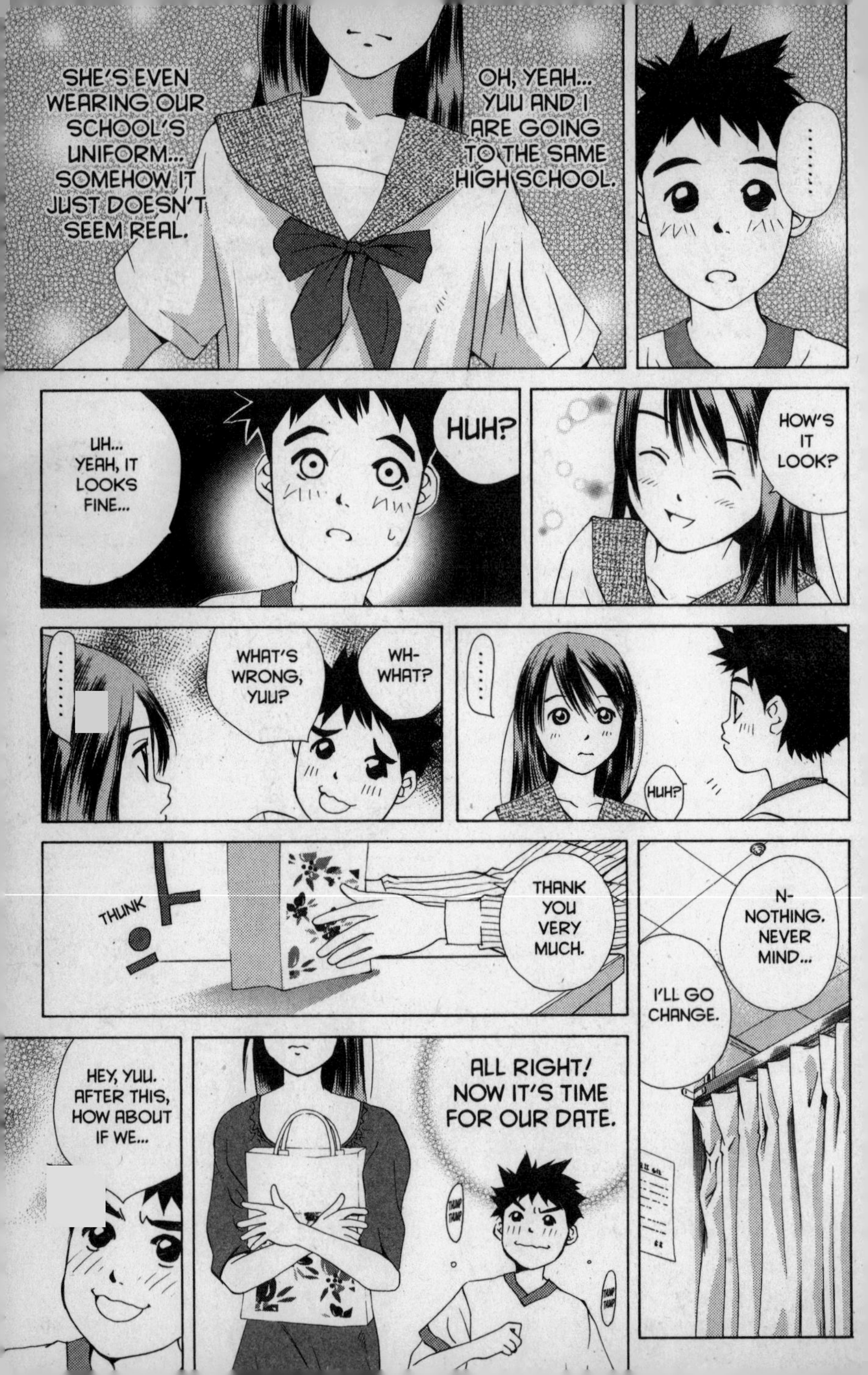
......
OH, YEAH... YUU AND I ARE GOING TO THE SAME HIGH SCHOOL.
SHE'S EVEN WEARING OUR SCHOOL'S UNIFORM... SOMEHOW IT JUST DOESN'T SEEM REAL.
HOW'S IT LOOK?
HUH?
UH... YEAH, IT LOOKS FINE...
......
HUH?
WH-WHAT?
WHAT'S WRONG, YUU?
......
N-NOTHING. NEVER MIND...
I'LL GO CHANGE.
THANK YOU VERY MUCH.
THUNK
ALL RIGHT! NOW IT'S TIME FOR OUR DATE.
THUMP THUMP
THUMP THUMP
HEY, YUU. AFTER THIS, HOW ABOUT IF WE...

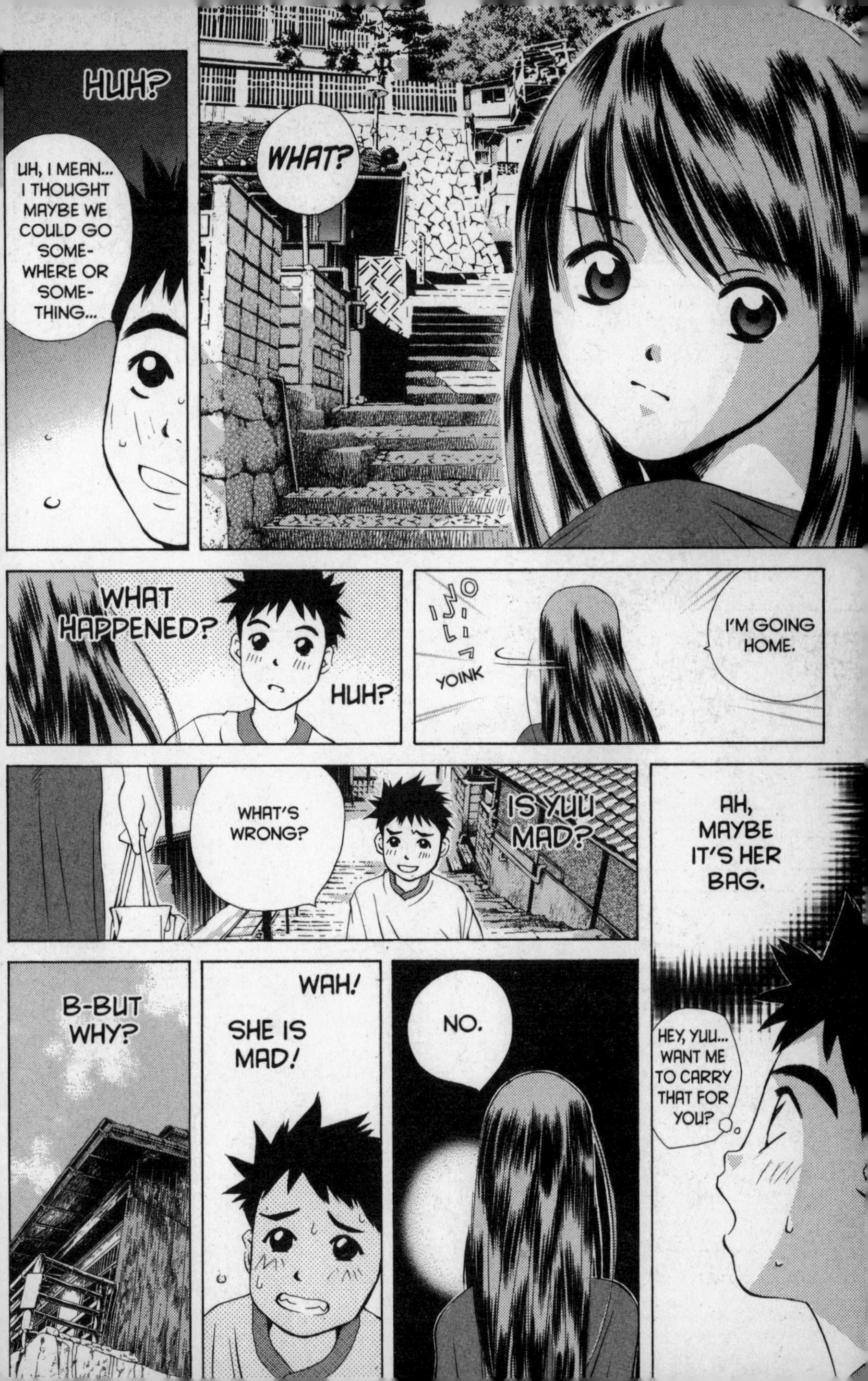
WHAT?
HUH?
UH, I MEAN... I THOUGHT MAYBE WE COULD GO SOMEWHERE OR SOMETHING...
I'M GOING HOME.
YOINK
WHAT HAPPENED?
HUH?
AH, MAYBE IT'S HER BAG.
HEY, YUU... WANT ME TO CARRY THAT FOR YOU?
IS YUU MAD?
WHAT'S WRONG?
NO.
WAH!
SHE IS MAD!
B-BUT WHY?

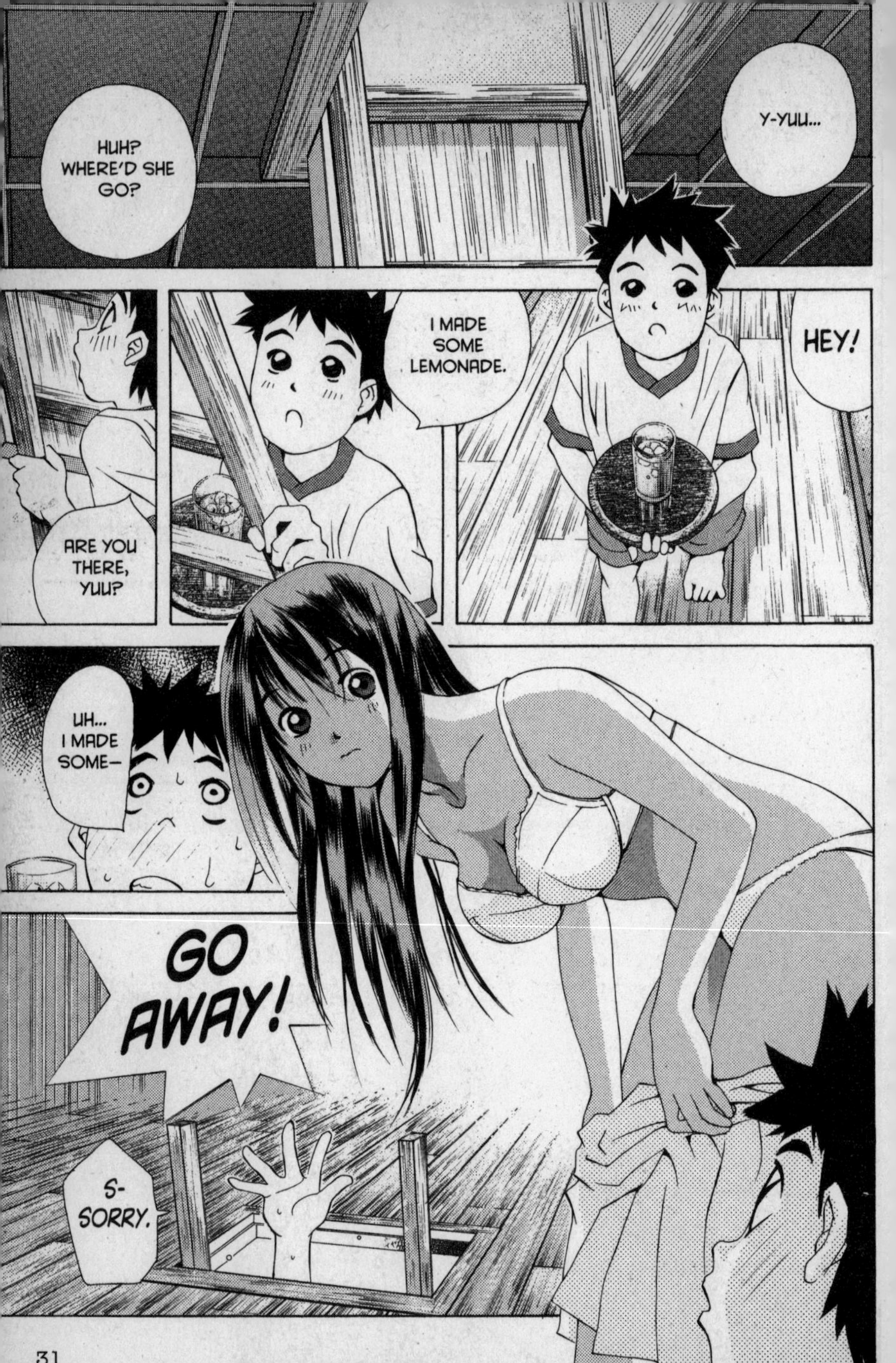
Y-YUU...
HUH? WHERE'D SHE GO?
HEY!
I MADE SOME LEMONADE.
ARE YOU THERE, YUU?
UH... I MADE SOME—
GO AWAY!
S-SORRY.

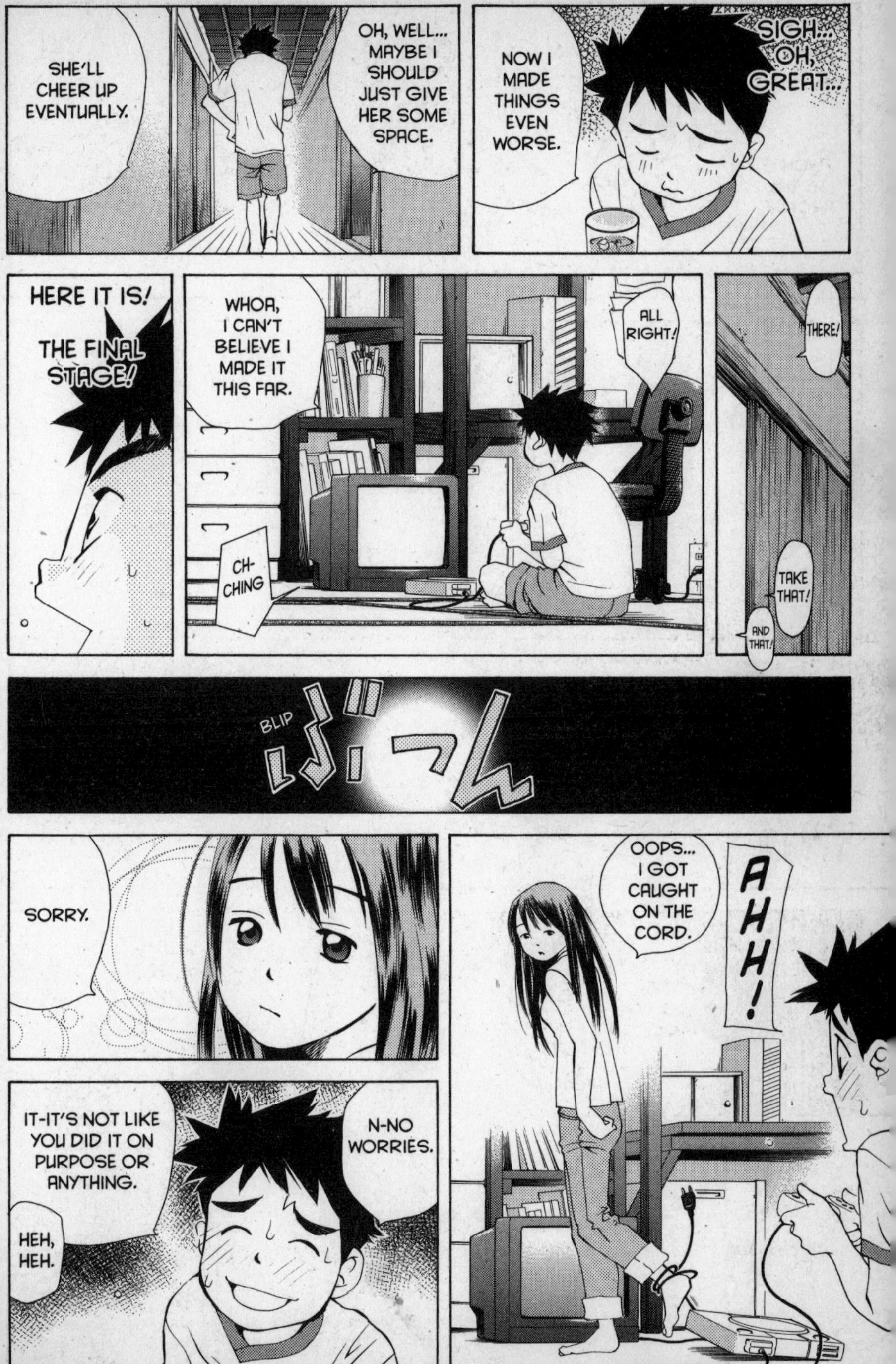
SIGH... OH, GREAT...
NOW I MADE THINGS EVEN WORSE.
OH, WELL... MAYBE I SHOULD JUST GIVE HER SOME SPACE.
SHE'LL CHEER UP EVENTUALLY.
THERE!
TAKE THAT!
AND THAT!
ALL RIGHT!
WHOA, I CAN'T BELIEVE I MADE IT THIS FAR.
CH-CHING
HERE IT IS!
THE FINAL STAGE!
BLIP
ぶつん
AHH!
OOPS... I GOT CAUGHT ON THE CORD.
SORRY.
N-NO WORRIES.
IT-IT'S NOT LIKE YOU DID IT ON PURPOSE OR ANYTHING.
HEH, HEH.

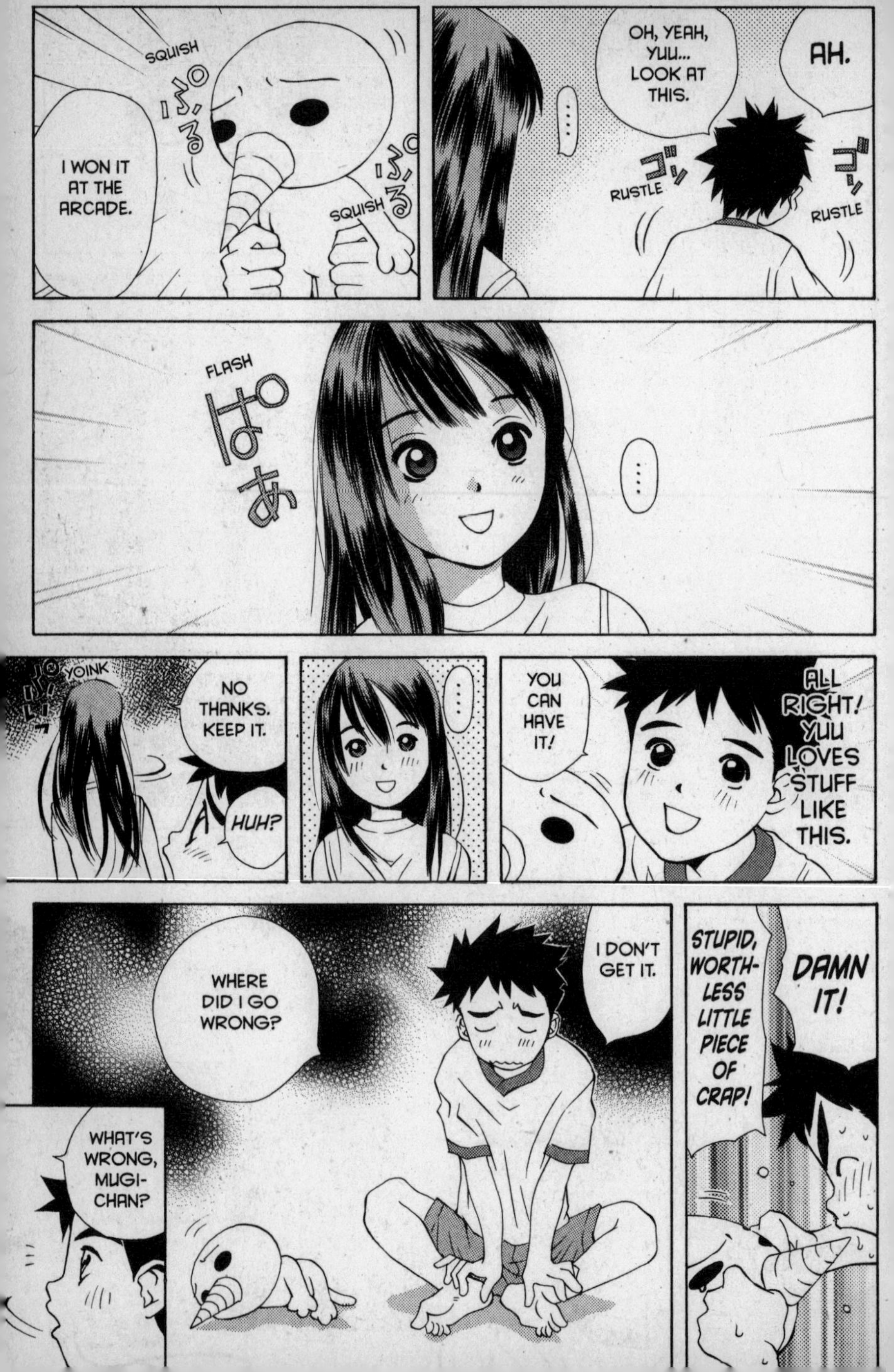
AH.
OH, YEAH, YUU... LOOK AT THIS.
.....
RUSTLE
RUSTLE
SQUISH
SQUISH
I WON IT AT THE ARCADE.
FLASH
.....
ALL RIGHT! YUU LOVES STUFF LIKE THIS.
YOU CAN HAVE IT!
.....
NO THANKS. KEEP IT.
HUH?
YOINK
DAMN IT!
STUPID, WORTHLESS LITTLE PIECE OF CRAP!
I DON'T GET IT.
WHERE DID I GO WRONG?
WHAT'S WRONG, MUGI-CHAN?

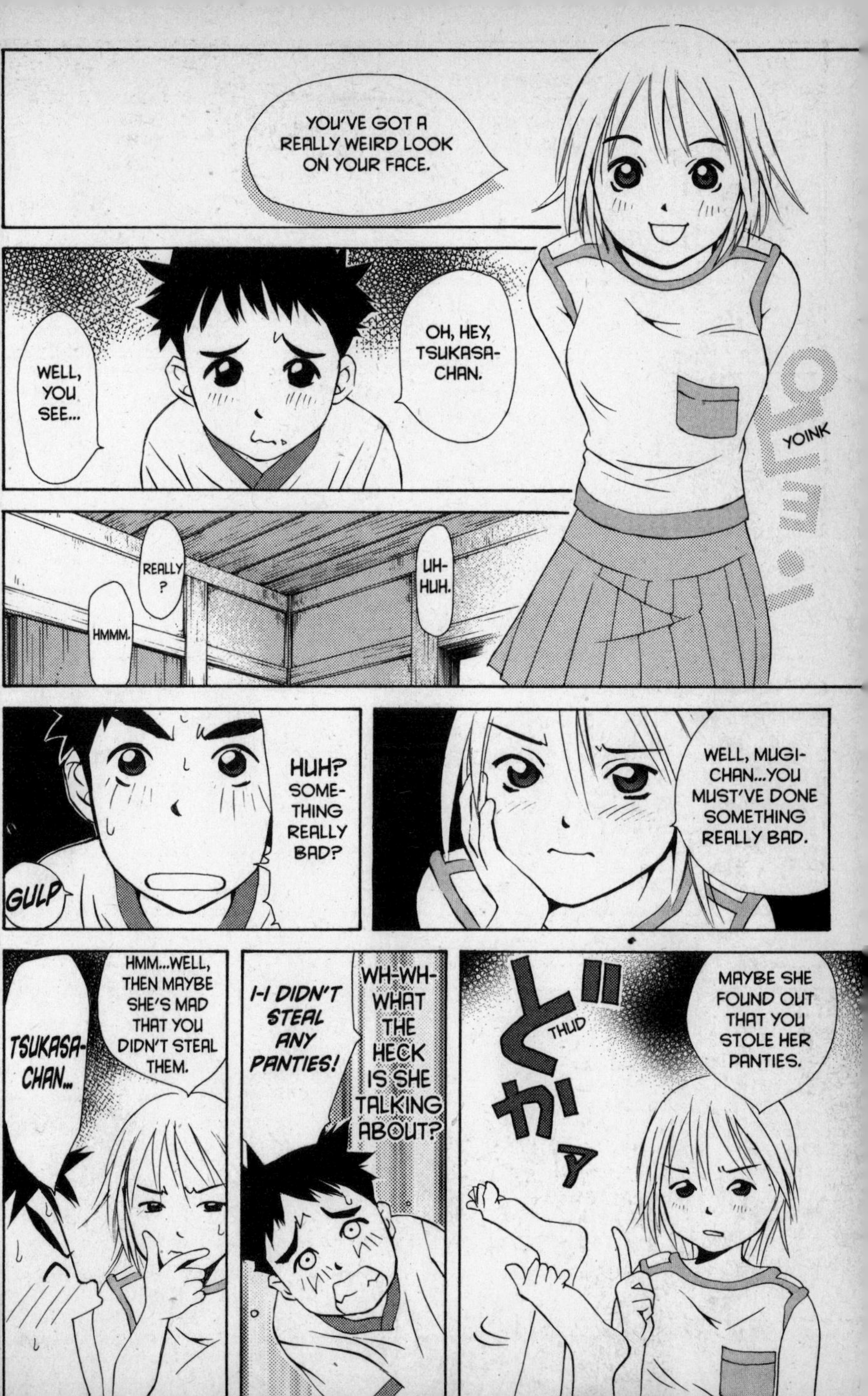
YOINK
YOU'VE GOT A REALLY WEIRD LOOK ON YOUR FACE.
OH, HEY, TSUKASA-CHAN.
WELL, YOU SEE...
UH-HUH.
REALLY?
HMMM.
WELL, MUGI-CHAN...YOU MUST'VE DONE SOMETHING REALLY BAD.
HUH? SOMETHING REALLY BAD?
GULP
MAYBE SHE FOUND OUT THAT YOU STOLE HER PANTIES.
どかァ
THUD
WH-WH-WHAT THE HECK IS SHE TALKING ABOUT?
I-I DIDN'T STEAL ANY PANTIES!
HMM...WELL, THEN MAYBE SHE'S MAD THAT YOU DIDN'T STEAL THEM.
TSUKASA-CHAN...

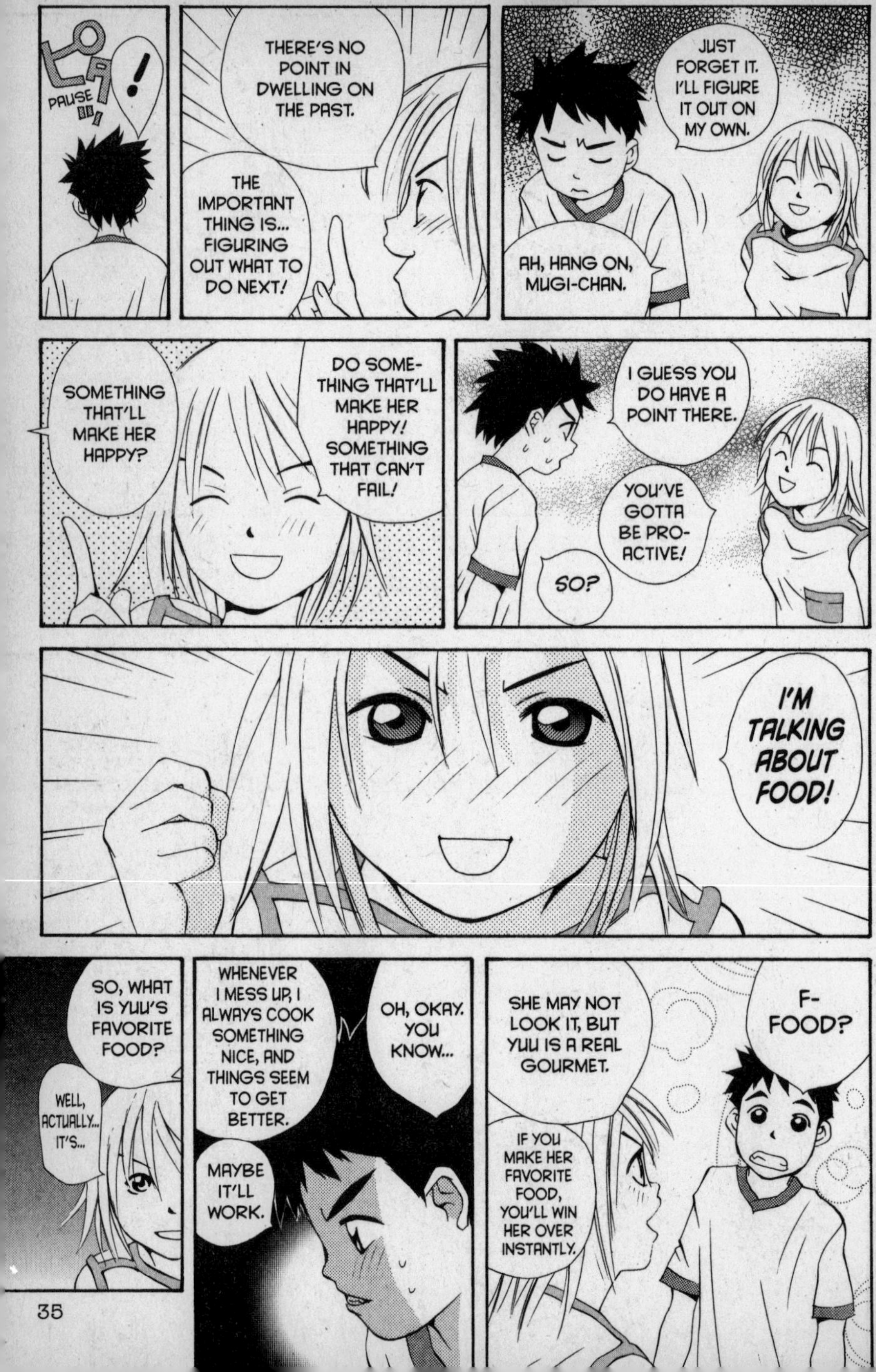
JUST FORGET IT. I'LL FIGURE IT OUT ON MY OWN.
AH, HANG ON, MUGI-CHAN.
THERE'S NO POINT IN DWELLING ON THE PAST.
THE IMPORTANT THING IS... FIGURING OUT WHAT TO DO NEXT!
PAUSE
!
I GUESS YOU DO HAVE A POINT THERE.
YOU'VE GOTTA BE PRO-ACTIVE!
SO?
DO SOME-THING THAT'LL MAKE HER HAPPY! SOMETHING THAT CAN'T FAIL!
SOMETHING THAT'LL MAKE HER HAPPY?
I'M TALKING ABOUT FOOD!
F-FOOD?
SHE MAY NOT LOOK IT, BUT YUU IS A REAL GOURMET.
IF YOU MAKE HER FAVORITE FOOD, YOU'LL WIN HER OVER INSTANTLY.
OH, OKAY. YOU KNOW...
WHENEVER I MESS UP, I ALWAYS COOK SOMETHING NICE, AND THINGS SEEM TO GET BETTER.
MAYBE IT'LL WORK.
SO, WHAT IS YUU'S FAVORITE FOOD?
WELL, ACTUALLY... IT'S...

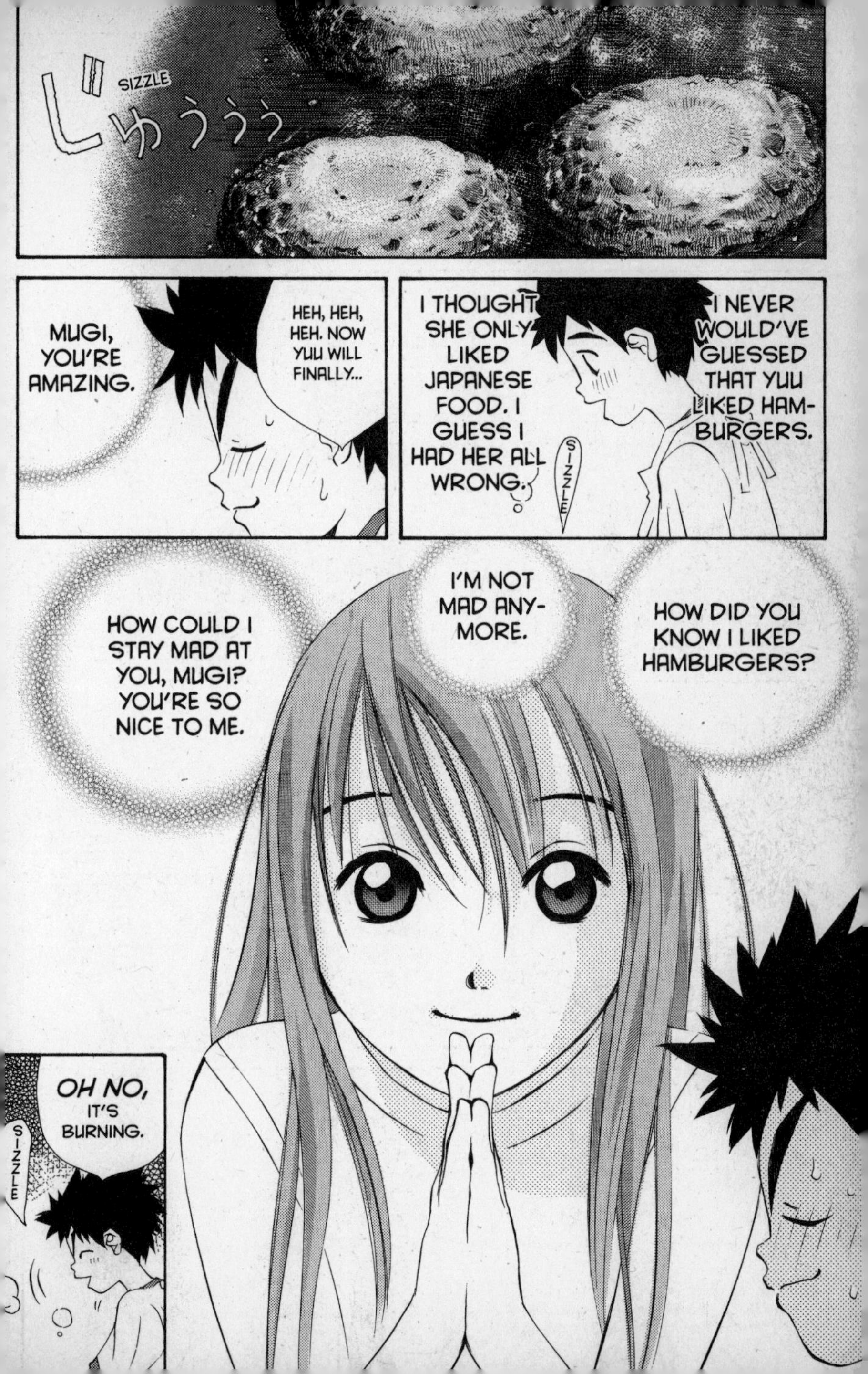
じゅううう
SIZZLE
I NEVER WOULD'VE GUESSED THAT YUU LIKED HAM-BURGERS.
I THOUGHT SHE ONLY LIKED JAPANESE FOOD. I GUESS I HAD HER ALL WRONG.
SIZZLE
HEH, HEH, HEH. NOW YUU WILL FINALLY...
MUGI, YOU'RE AMAZING.
HOW DID YOU KNOW I LIKED HAMBURGERS?
I'M NOT MAD ANY-MORE.
HOW COULD I STAY MAD AT YOU, MUGI? YOU'RE SO NICE TO ME.
OH NO, IT'S BURNING.
SIZZLE

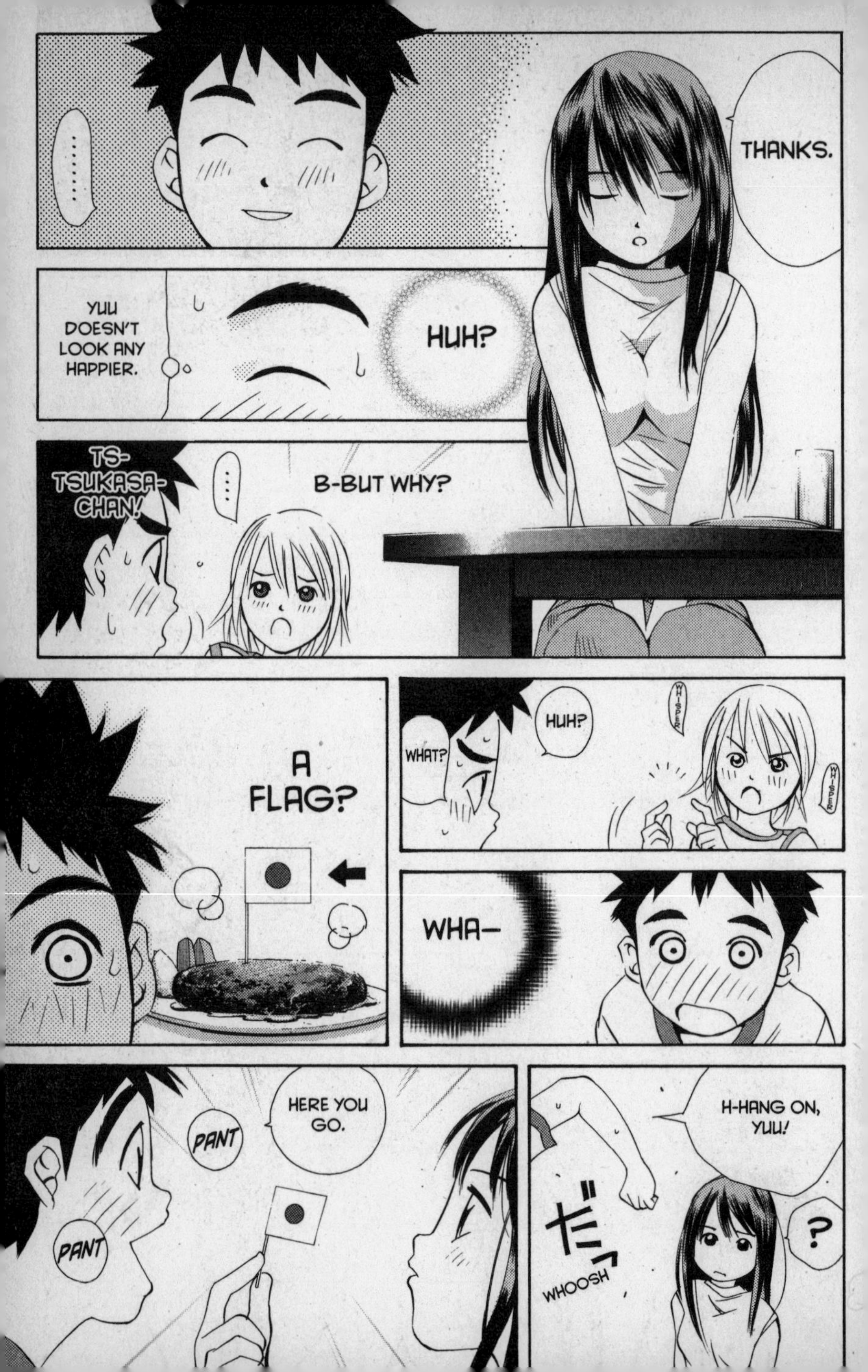
THANKS.
......
HUH?
YUU DOESN'T LOOK ANY HAPPIER.
B-BUT WHY?
....
TS-TSUKASA-CHAN!
WHISPER
WHISPER
HUH?
WHAT?
WHA-
A FLAG?
H-HANG ON, YUU!
?
ダッ
WHOOSH
HERE YOU GO.
PANT
PANT

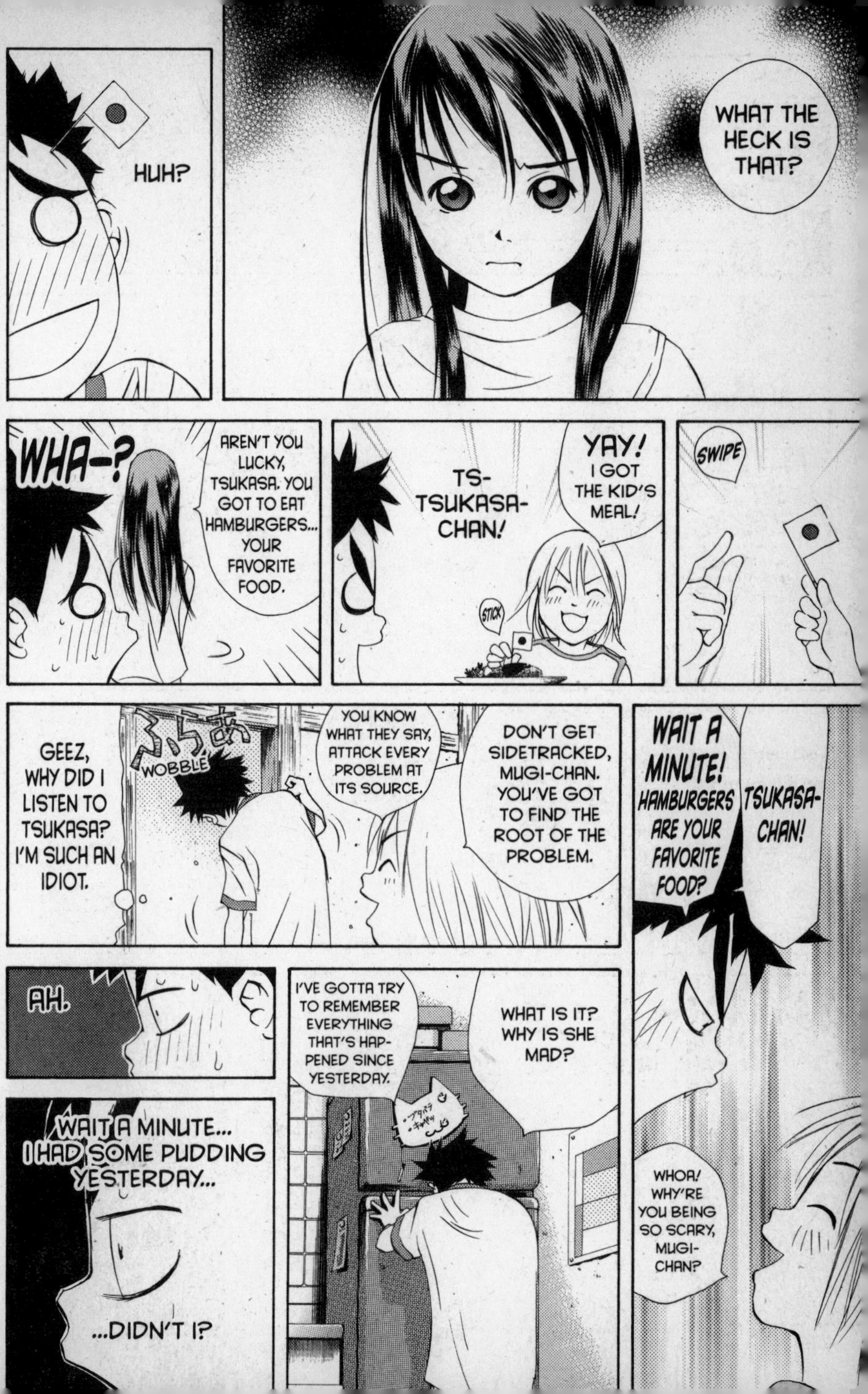
WHAT THE HECK IS THAT?
HUH?
SWIPE
YAY! I GOT THE KID'S MEAL!
STICK
TS-TSUKASA-CHAN!
AREN'T YOU LUCKY, TSUKASA. YOU GOT TO EAT HAMBURGERS... YOUR FAVORITE FOOD.
WHA-?
WAIT A MINUTE! HAMBURGERS ARE YOUR FAVORITE FOOD?
TSUKASA-CHAN!
WHOA! WHY'RE YOU BEING SO SCARY, MUGI-CHAN?
DON'T GET SIDETRACKED, MUGI-CHAN. YOU'VE GOT TO FIND THE ROOT OF THE PROBLEM.
YOU KNOW WHAT THEY SAY, ATTACK EVERY PROBLEM AT ITS SOURCE.
WOBBLE
GEEZ, WHY DID I LISTEN TO TSUKASA? I'M SUCH AN IDIOT.
WHAT IS IT? WHY IS SHE MAD?
I'VE GOTTA TRY TO REMEMBER EVERYTHING THAT'S HAPPENED SINCE YESTERDAY.
AH.
WAIT A MINUTE... I HAD SOME PUDDING YESTERDAY...
...DIDN'T I?

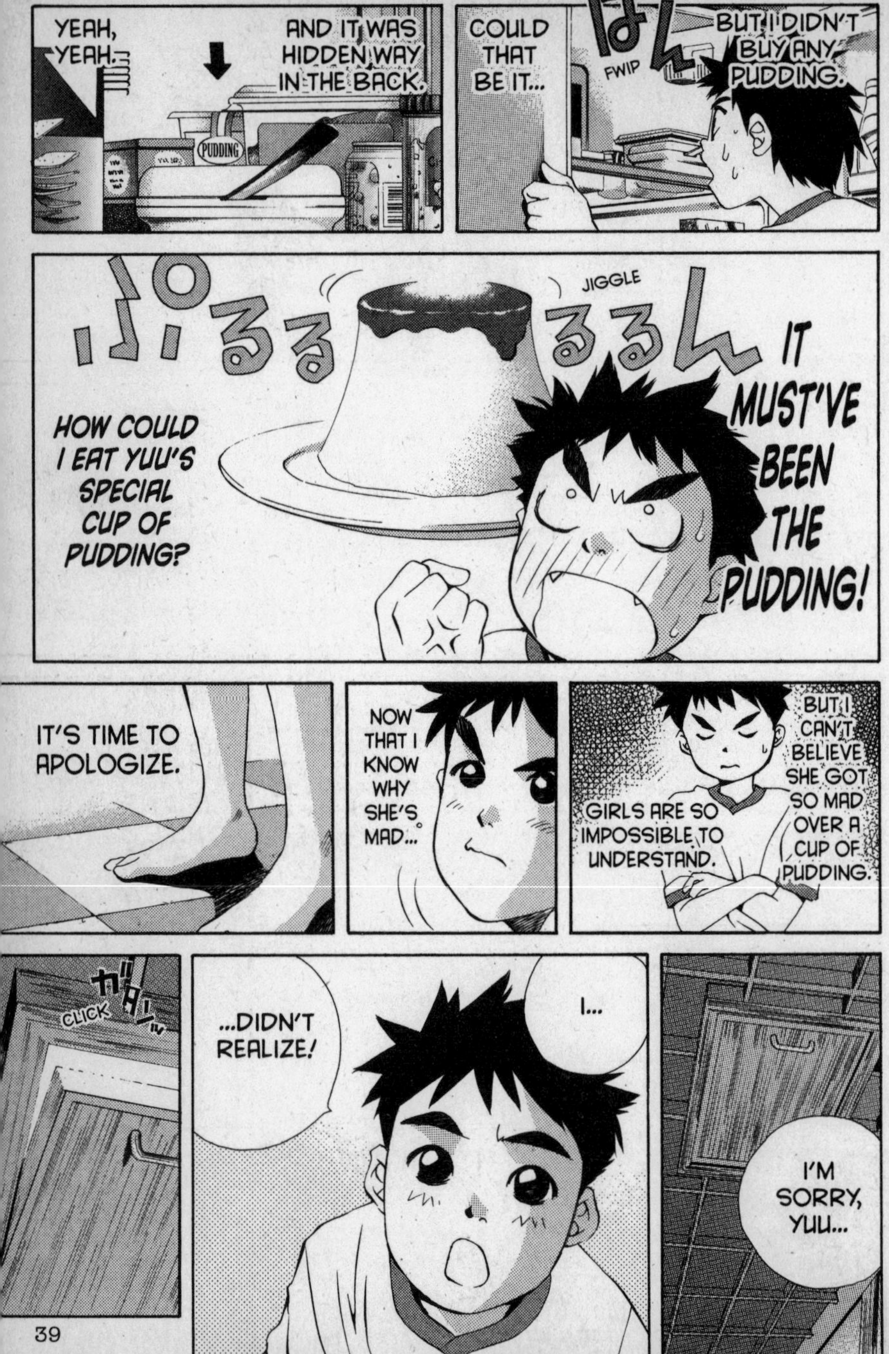

ばん
FWIP
BUT I DIDN'T BUY ANY PUDDING.
COULD THAT BE IT...
AND IT WAS HIDDEN WAY IN THE BACK.
YEAH, YEAH.
PUDDING
IT MUST'VE BEEN THE PUDDING!
ぷるるるるん
JIGGLE
HOW COULD I EAT YUU'S SPECIAL CUP OF PUDDING?
BUT I CAN'T BELIEVE SHE GOT SO MAD OVER A CUP OF PUDDING.
GIRLS ARE SO IMPOSSIBLE TO UNDERSTAND.
NOW THAT I KNOW WHY SHE'S MAD...
IT'S TIME TO APOLOGIZE.
I'M SORRY, YUU...
I...
...DIDN'T REALIZE!
ガタン
CLICK

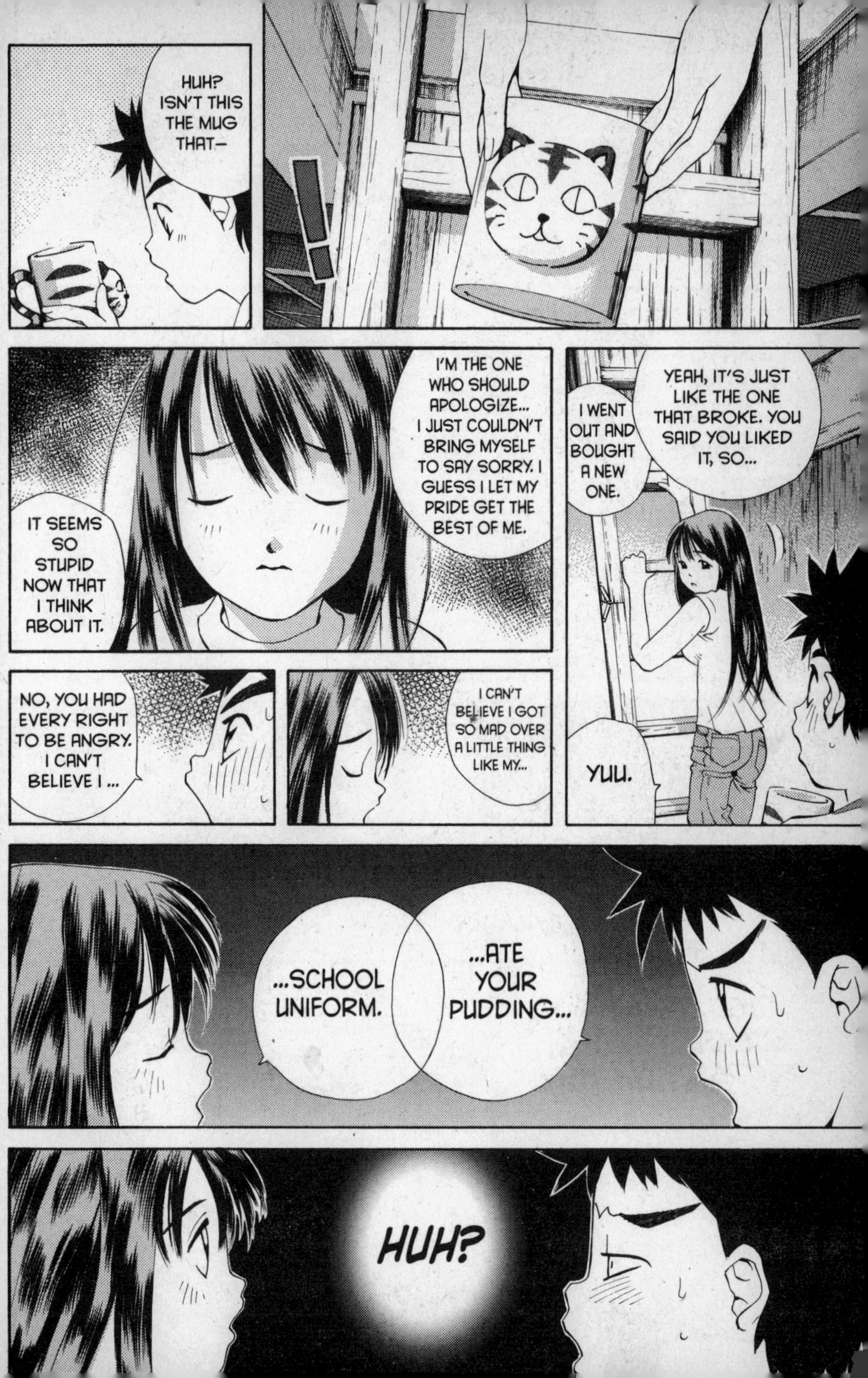
HUH? ISN'T THIS THE MUG THAT—
YEAH, IT'S JUST LIKE THE ONE THAT BROKE. YOU SAID YOU LIKED IT, SO...
I WENT OUT AND BOUGHT A NEW ONE.
YUU.
I'M THE ONE WHO SHOULD APOLOGIZE... I JUST COULDN'T BRING MYSELF TO SAY SORRY. I GUESS I LET MY PRIDE GET THE BEST OF ME.
IT SEEMS SO STUPID NOW THAT I THINK ABOUT IT.
I CAN'T BELIEVE I GOT SO MAD OVER A LITTLE THING LIKE MY...
NO, YOU HAD EVERY RIGHT TO BE ANGRY. I CAN'T BELIEVE I ...
...ATE YOUR PUDDING...
...SCHOOL UNIFORM.
HUH?

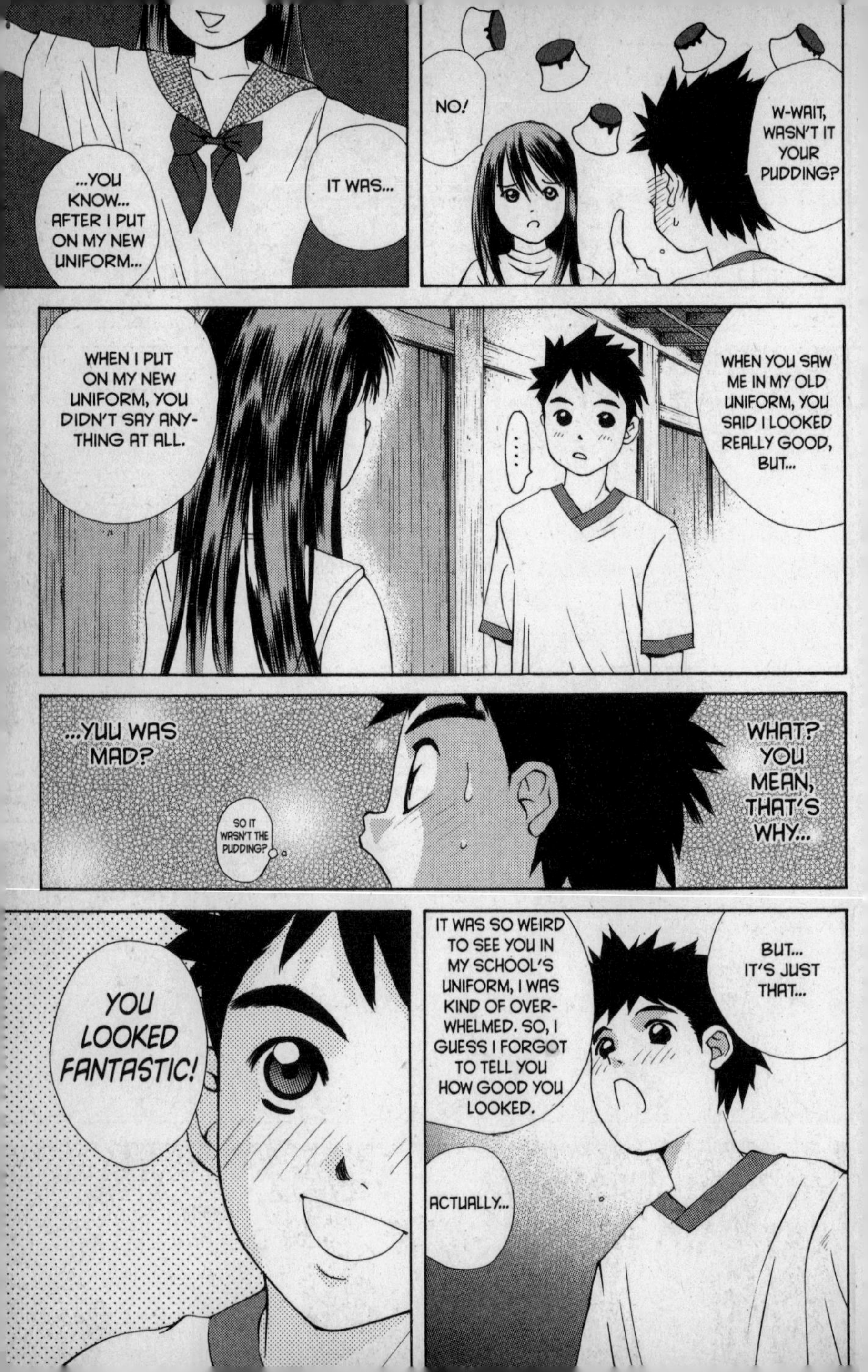
W-WAIT, WASN'T IT YOUR PUDDING?
NO!
IT WAS...
...YOU KNOW... AFTER I PUT ON MY NEW UNIFORM...
WHEN YOU SAW ME IN MY OLD UNIFORM, YOU SAID I LOOKED REALLY GOOD, BUT...
....
WHEN I PUT ON MY NEW UNIFORM, YOU DIDN'T SAY ANY-THING AT ALL.
WHAT? YOU MEAN, THAT'S WHY...
SO IT WASN'T THE PUDDING?
...YUU WAS MAD?
BUT... IT'S JUST THAT...
IT WAS SO WEIRD TO SEE YOU IN MY SCHOOL'S UNIFORM, I WAS KIND OF OVER-WHELMED. SO, I GUESS I FORGOT TO TELL YOU HOW GOOD YOU LOOKED.
ACTUALLY...
YOU LOOKED FANTASTIC!

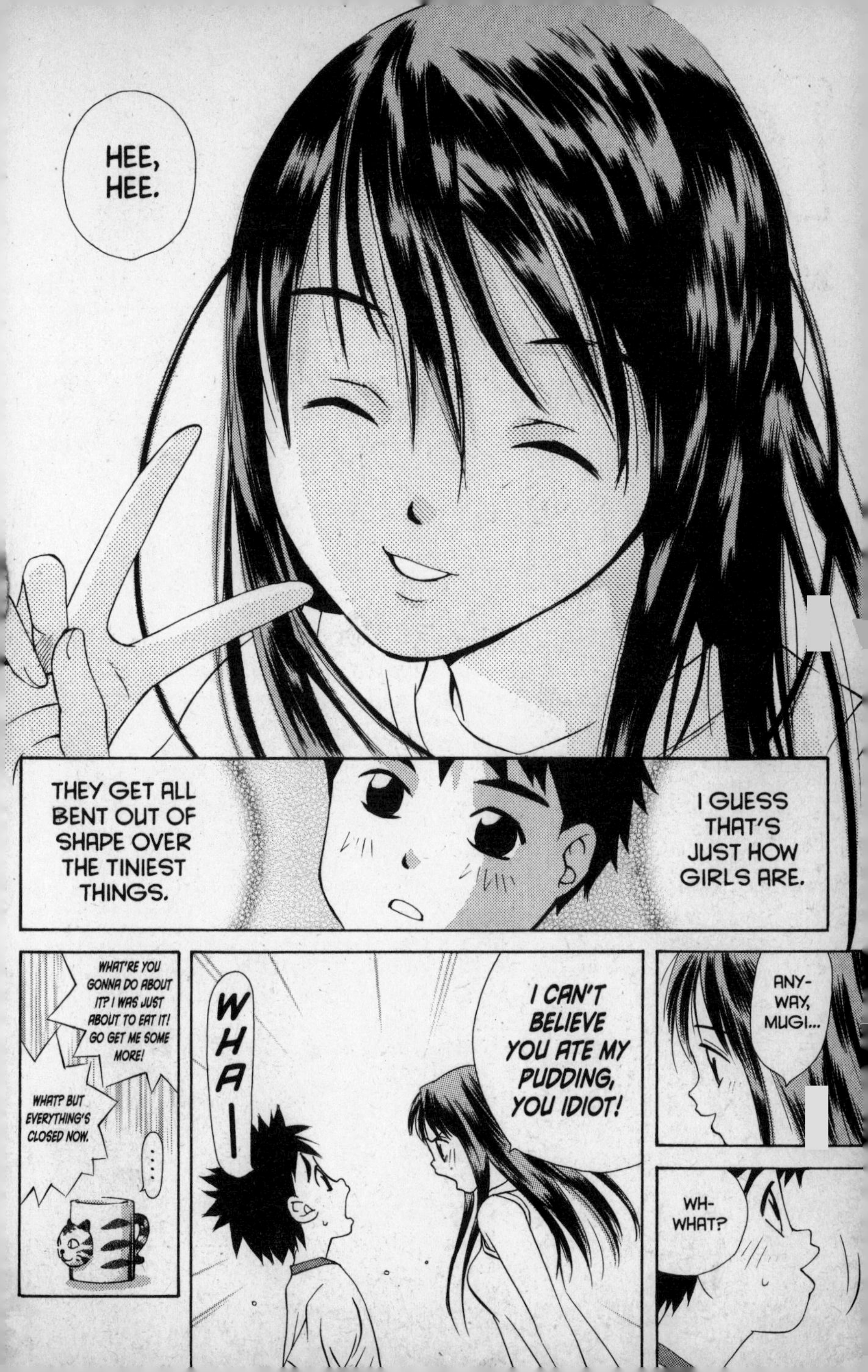
HEE, HEE.
I GUESS THAT'S JUST HOW GIRLS ARE.
THEY GET ALL BENT OUT OF SHAPE OVER THE TINIEST THINGS.
ANY-WAY, MUGI...
WH-WHAT?
I CAN'T BELIEVE YOU ATE MY PUDDING, YOU IDIOT!
WHA!
WHAT'RE YOU GONNA DO ABOUT IT? I WAS JUST ABOUT TO EAT IT! GO GET ME SOME MORE!
WHAT? BUT EVERYTHING'S CLOSED NOW.
.....

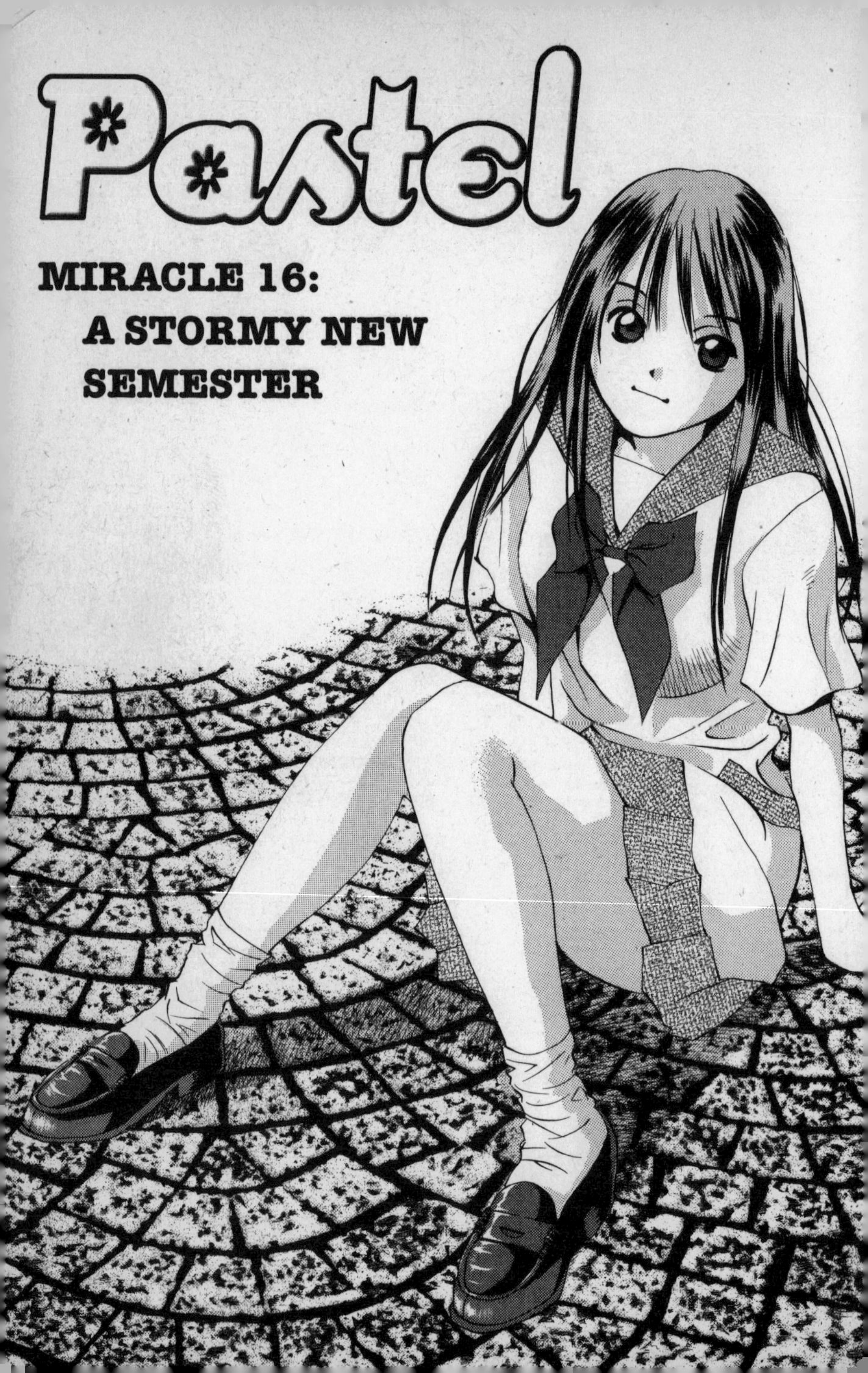
Pastel
MIRACLE 16:
A STORMY NEW
SEMESTER

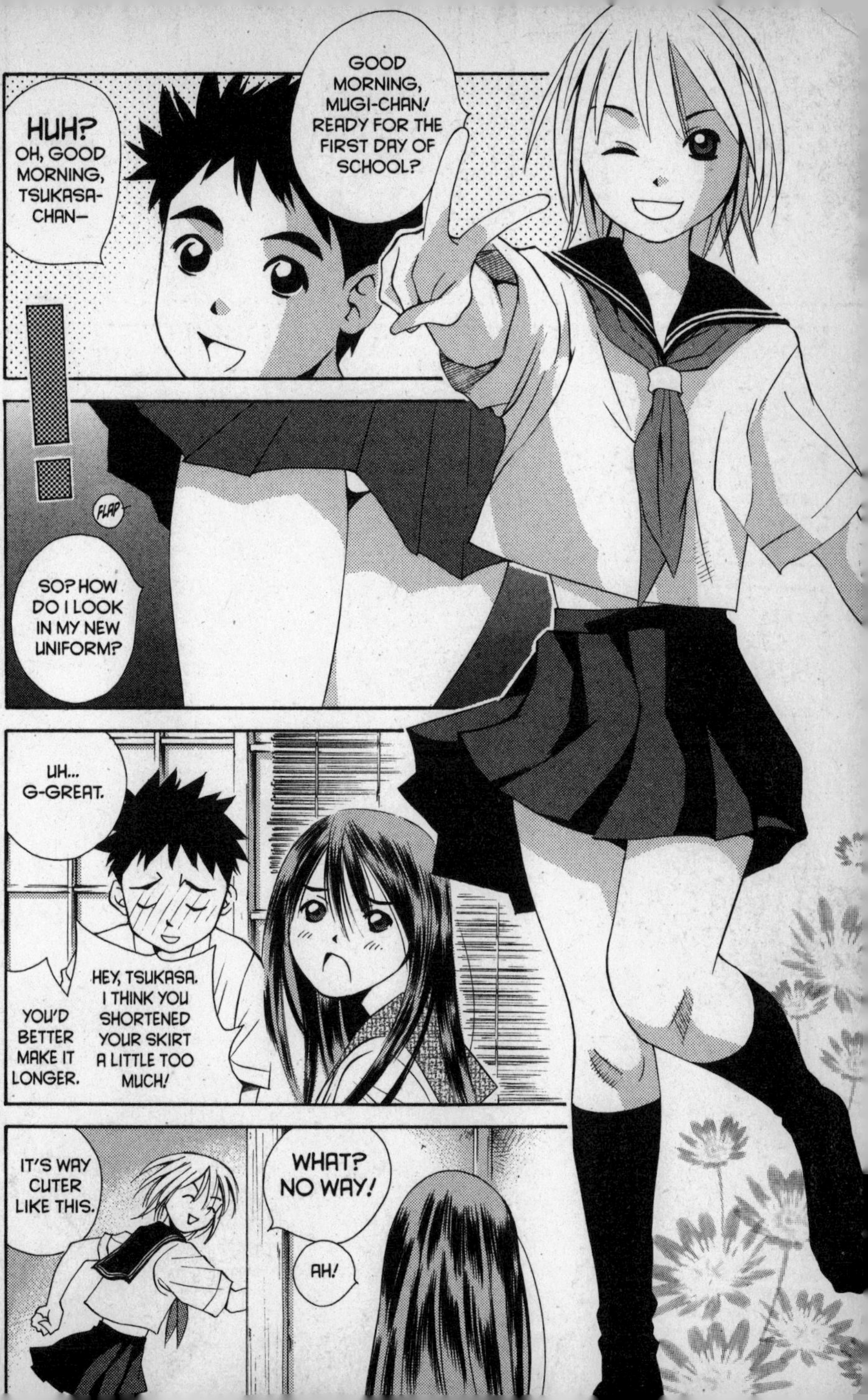
GOOD MORNING, MUGI-CHAN! READY FOR THE FIRST DAY OF SCHOOL?
HUH? OH, GOOD MORNING, TSUKASA-CHAN—
!
FLAP
SO? HOW DO I LOOK IN MY NEW UNIFORM?
UH... G-GREAT.
HEY, TSUKASA. I THINK YOU SHORTENED YOUR SKIRT A LITTLE TOO MUCH!
YOU'D BETTER MAKE IT LONGER.
WHAT? NO WAY!
IT'S WAY CUTER LIKE THIS.
AH!

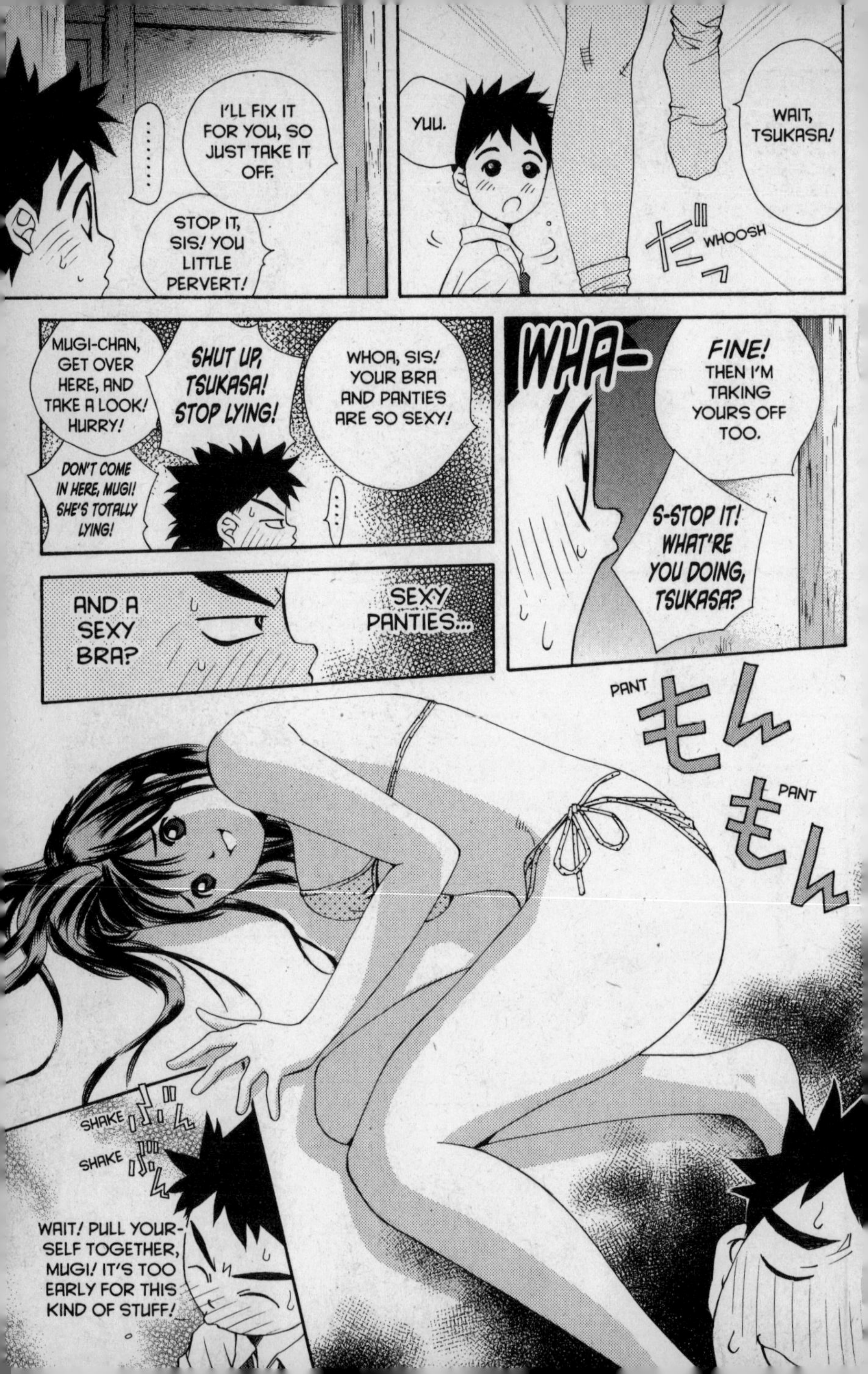
WAIT, TSUKASA!
WHOOSH
YUU.
I'LL FIX IT FOR YOU, SO JUST TAKE IT OFF.
......
STOP IT, SIS! YOU LITTLE PERVERT!
FINE! THEN I'M TAKING YOURS OFF TOO.
WHA-
S-STOP IT! WHAT'RE YOU DOING, TSUKASA?
WHOA, SIS! YOUR BRA AND PANTIES ARE SO SEXY!
SHUT UP, TSUKASA! STOP LYING!
MUGI-CHAN, GET OVER HERE, AND TAKE A LOOK! HURRY!
....
DON'T COME IN HERE, MUGI! SHE'S TOTALLY LYING!
SEXY PANTIES...
AND A SEXY BRA?
PANT
PANT
SHAKE
SHAKE
WAIT! PULL YOUR-SELF TOGETHER, MUGI! IT'S TOO EARLY FOR THIS KIND OF STUFF!

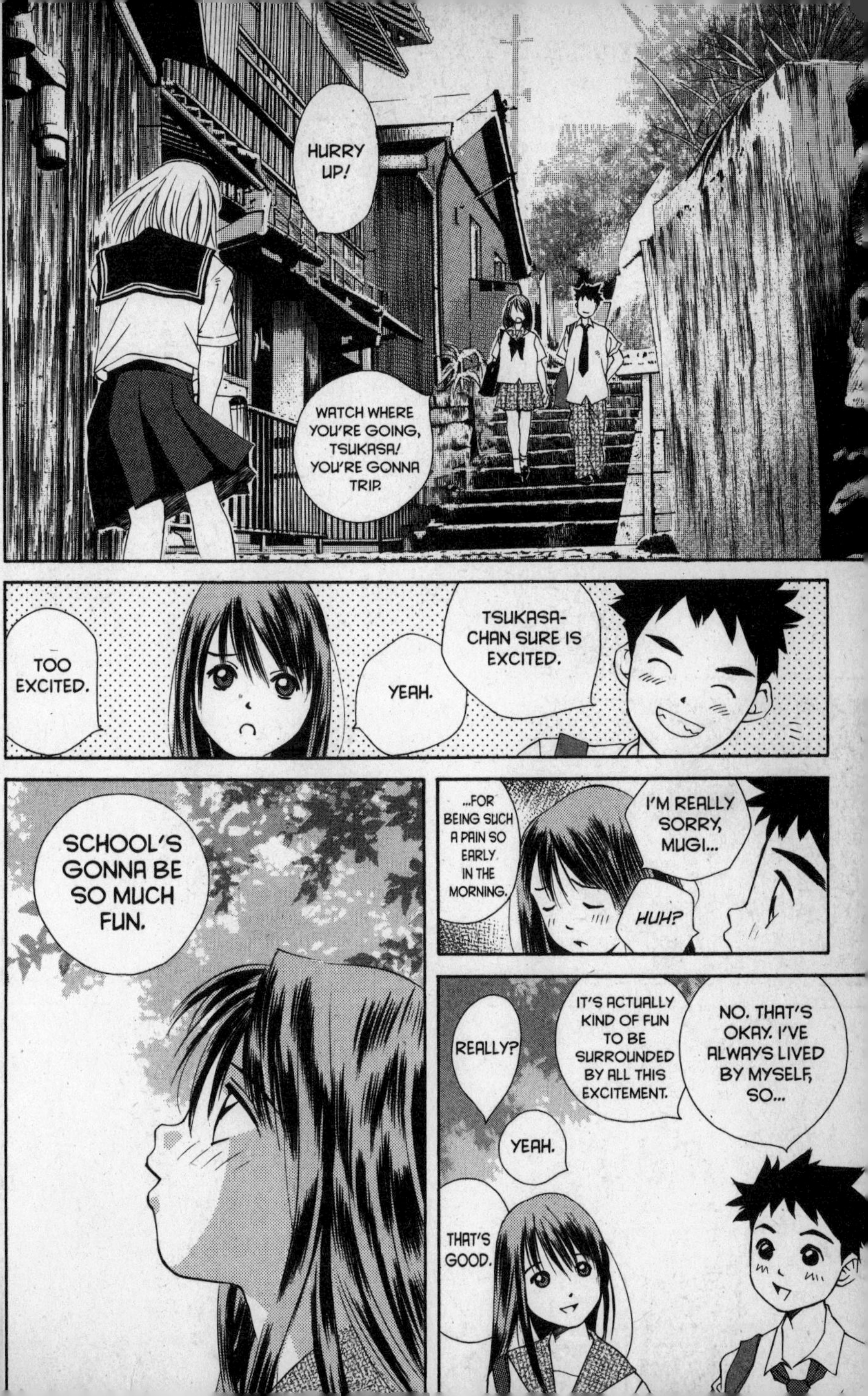
HURRY UP!
WATCH WHERE YOU'RE GOING, TSUKASA! YOU'RE GONNA TRIP.
TSUKASA-CHAN SURE IS EXCITED.
YEAH.
TOO EXCITED.
I'M REALLY SORRY, MUGI...
...FOR BEING SUCH A PAIN SO EARLY IN THE MORNING.
HUH?
NO. THAT'S OKAY. I'VE ALWAYS LIVED BY MYSELF, SO...
IT'S ACTUALLY KIND OF FUN TO BE SURROUNDED BY ALL THIS EXCITEMENT.
REALLY?
YEAH.
THAT'S GOOD.
SCHOOL'S GONNA BE SO MUCH FUN.

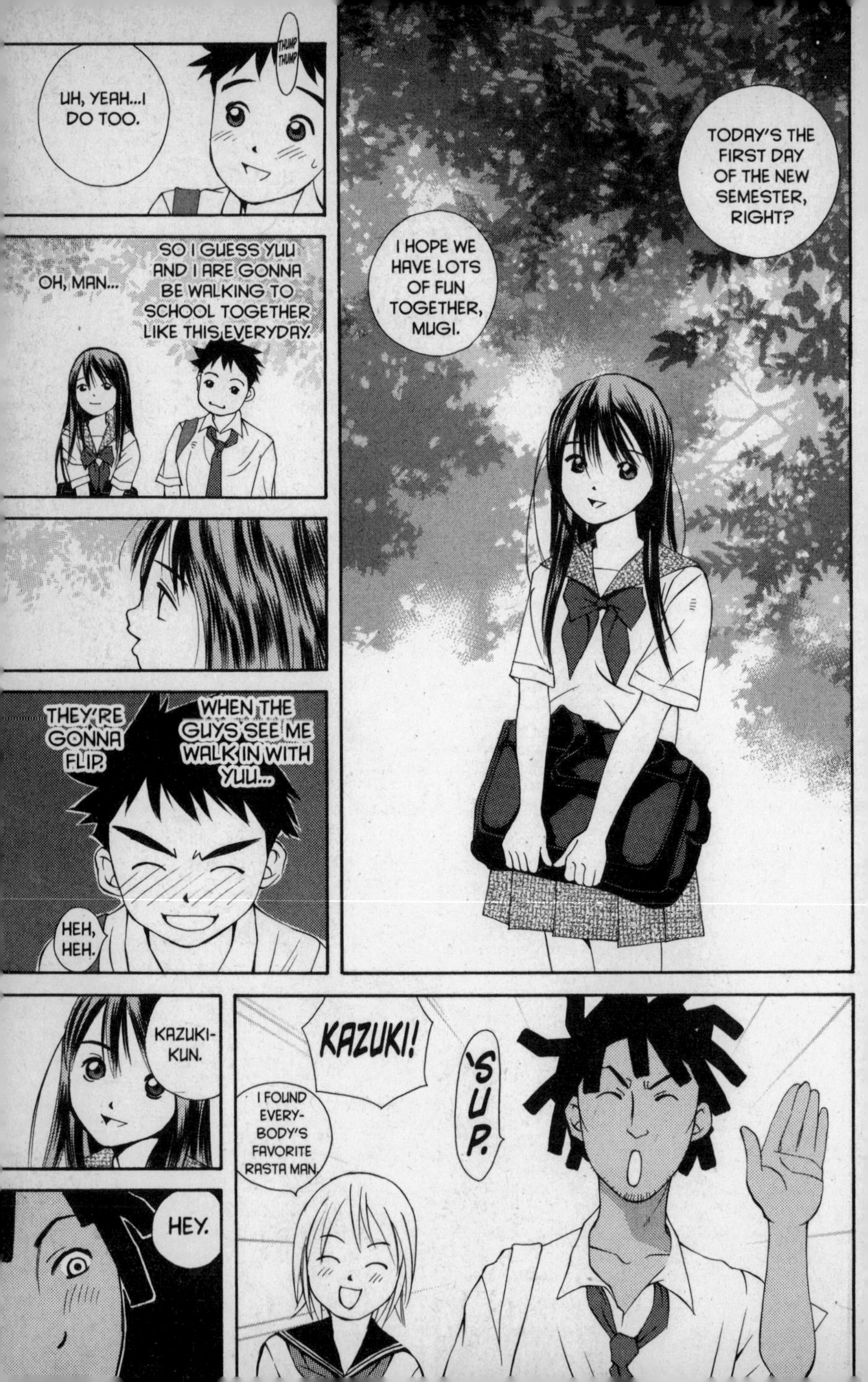
TODAY'S THE FIRST DAY OF THE NEW SEMESTER, RIGHT?
I HOPE WE HAVE LOTS OF FUN TOGETHER, MUGI.
THUMP THUMP
UH, YEAH...I DO TOO.
SO I GUESS YUU AND I ARE GONNA BE WALKING TO SCHOOL TOGETHER LIKE THIS EVERYDAY.
OH, MAN...
WHEN THE GUYS SEE ME WALK IN WITH YUU...
THEY'RE GONNA FLIP.
HEH, HEH.
KAZUKI!
'SUP.
I FOUND EVERY-BODY'S FAVORITE RASTA MAN.
KAZUKI-KUN.
HEY.

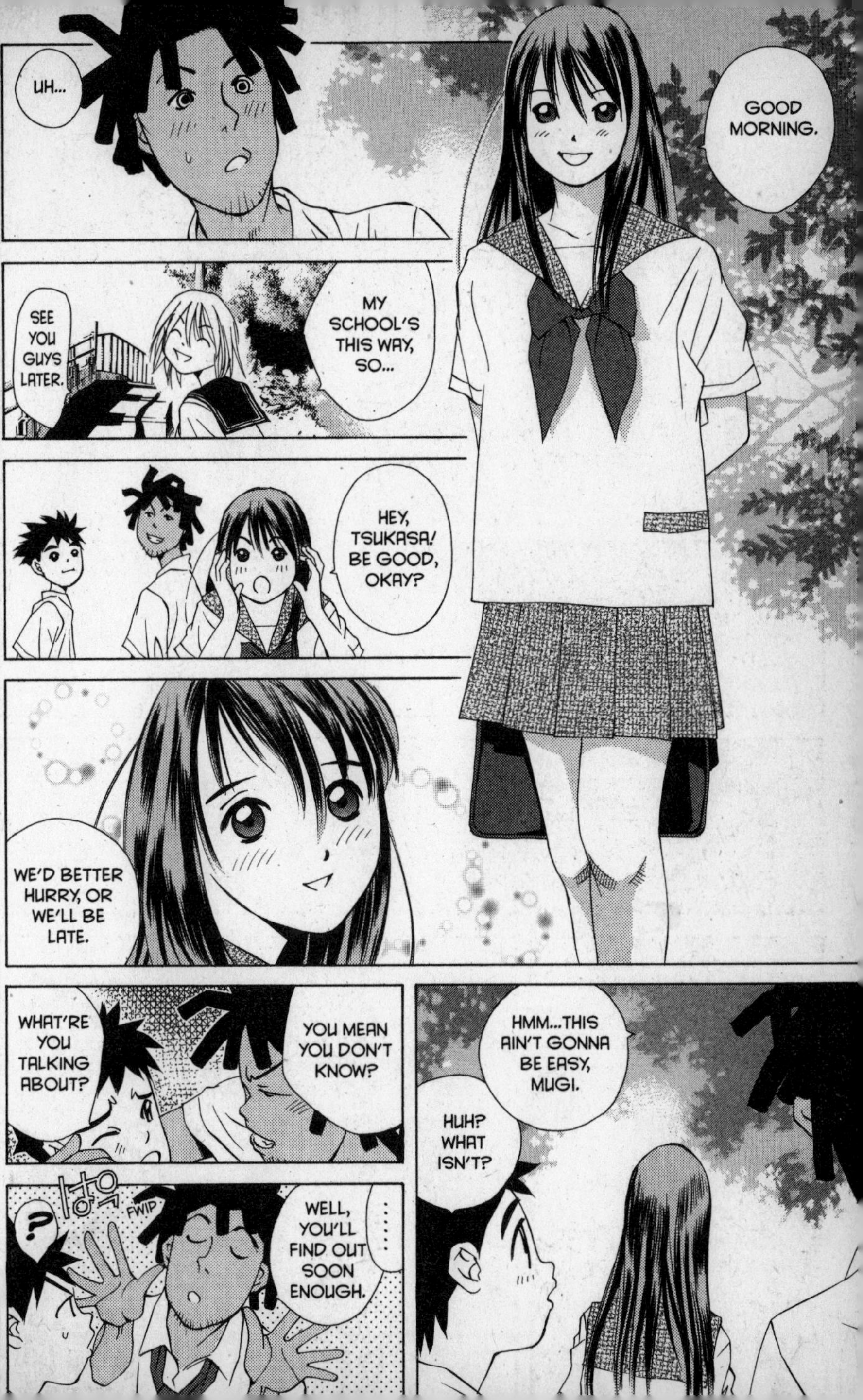
GOOD MORNING.
UH...
MY SCHOOL'S THIS WAY, SO...
SEE YOU GUYS LATER.
HEY, TSUKASA! BE GOOD, OKAY?
WE'D BETTER HURRY, OR WE'LL BE LATE.
HMM...THIS AIN'T GONNA BE EASY, MUGI.
HUH? WHAT ISN'T?
YOU MEAN YOU DON'T KNOW?
WHAT'RE YOU TALKING ABOUT?
......
WELL, YOU'LL FIND OUT SOON ENOUGH.
FWIP
?

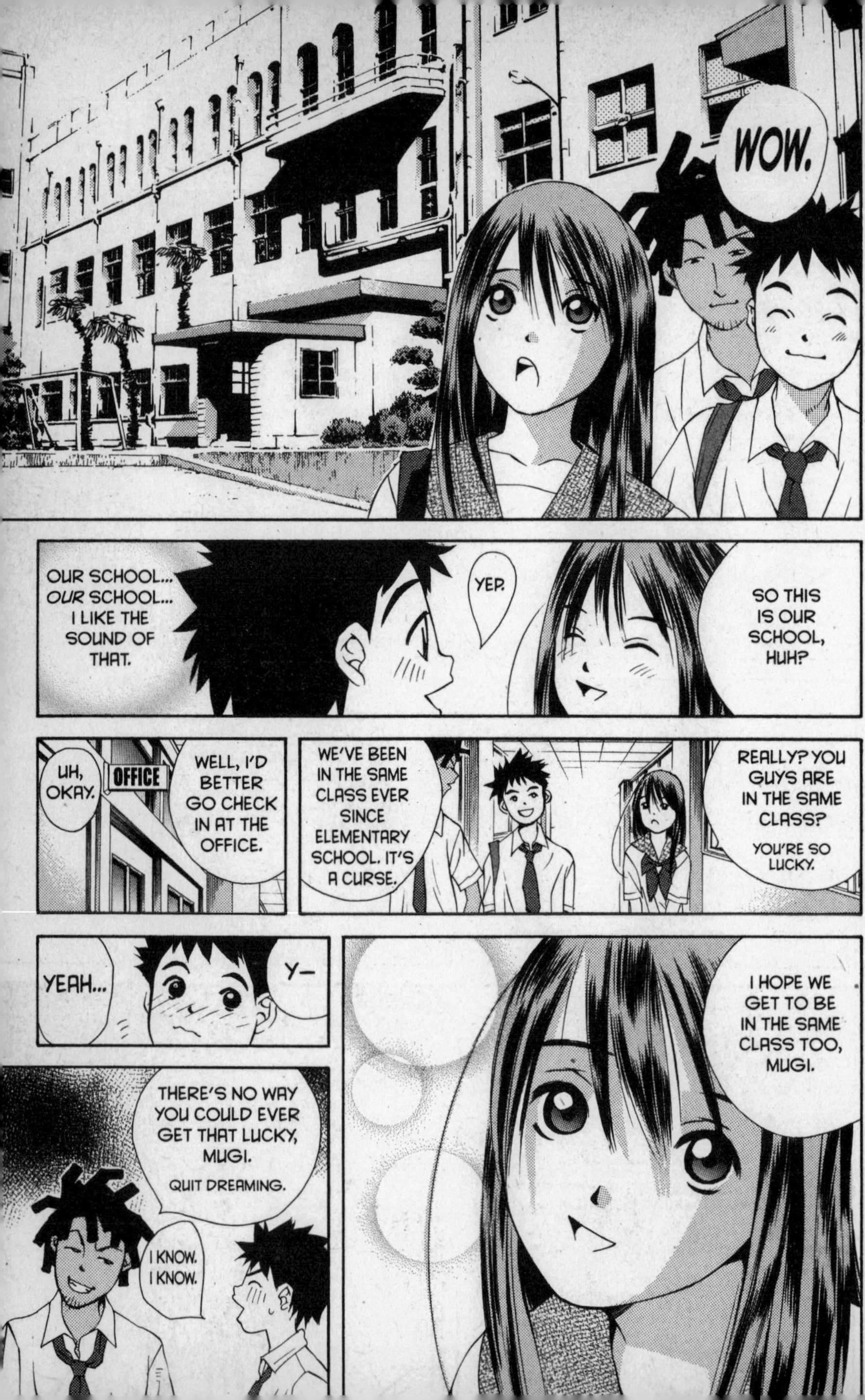
WOW.
SO THIS IS OUR SCHOOL, HUH?
YEP.
OUR SCHOOL... OUR SCHOOL... I LIKE THE SOUND OF THAT.
REALLY? YOU GUYS ARE IN THE SAME CLASS?
YOU'RE SO LUCKY.
WE'VE BEEN IN THE SAME CLASS EVER SINCE ELEMENTARY SCHOOL. IT'S A CURSE.
WELL, I'D BETTER GO CHECK IN AT THE OFFICE.
OFFICE
UH, OKAY.
I HOPE WE GET TO BE IN THE SAME CLASS TOO, MUGI.
Y—
YEAH...
THERE'S NO WAY YOU COULD EVER GET THAT LUCKY, MUGI.
QUIT DREAMING.
I KNOW. I KNOW.

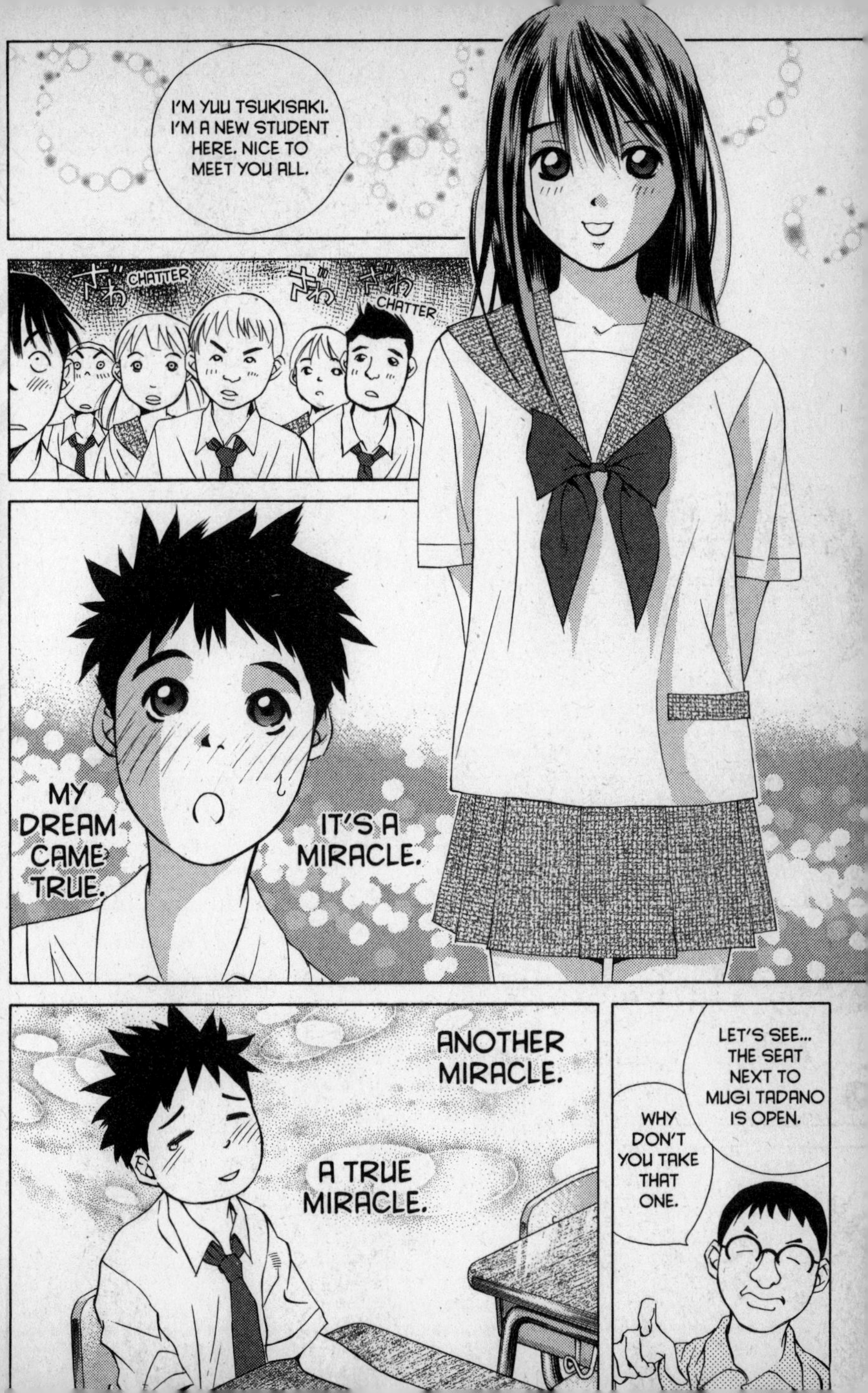
I'M YUU TSUKISAKI. I'M A NEW STUDENT HERE. NICE TO MEET YOU ALL.
ざわ ざわ CHATTER
ざわ CHATTER
IT'S A MIRACLE.
MY DREAM CAME TRUE.
LET'S SEE... THE SEAT NEXT TO MUGI TADANO IS OPEN.
WHY DON'T YOU TAKE THAT ONE.
ANOTHER MIRACLE.
A TRUE MIRACLE.

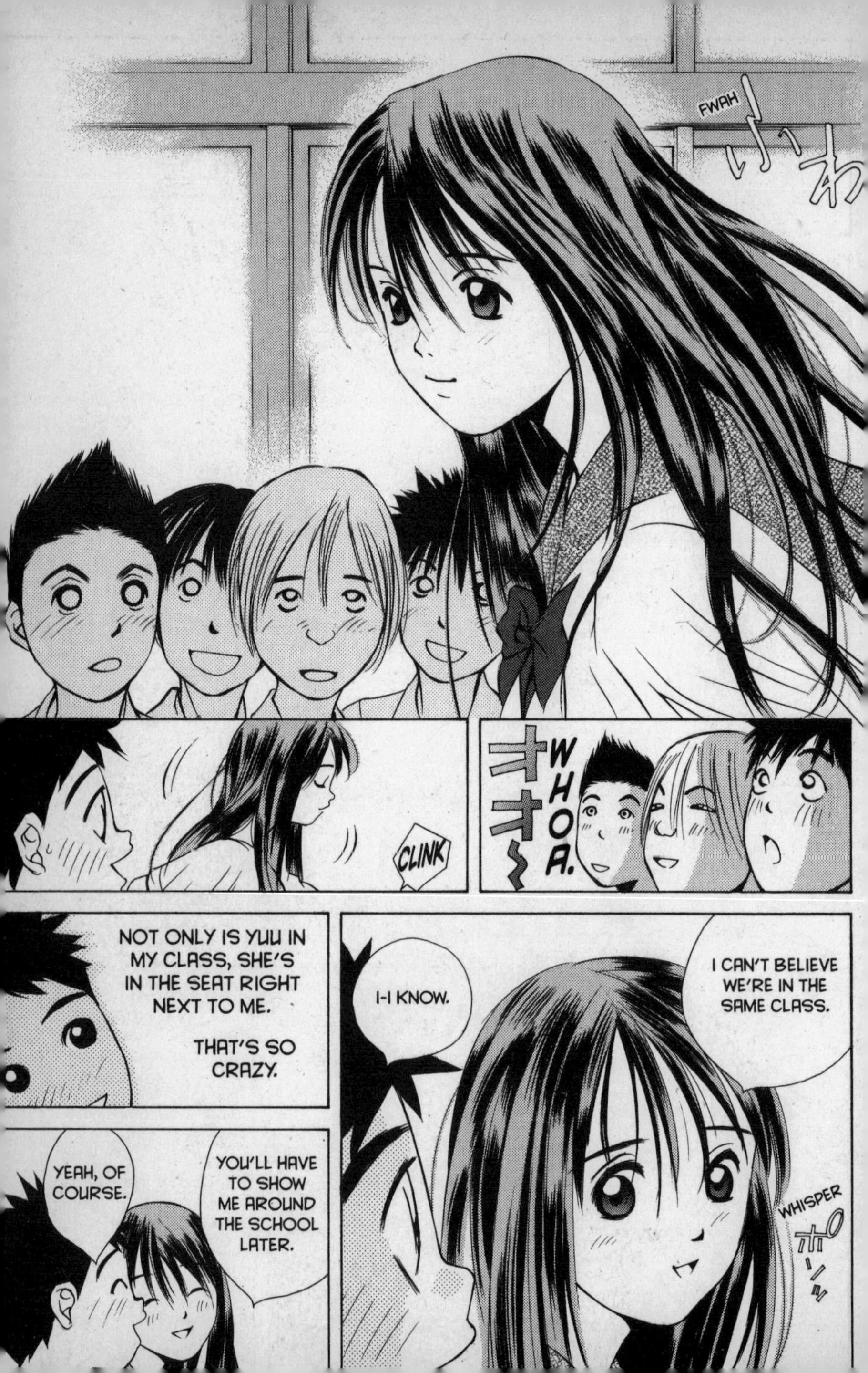
FWAH
ふわ
WHOA.
オオ~
CLINK
I CAN'T BELIEVE WE'RE IN THE SAME CLASS.
I-I KNOW.
WHISPER
NOT ONLY IS YUU IN MY CLASS, SHE'S IN THE SEAT RIGHT NEXT TO ME.
THAT'S SO CRAZY.
YOU'LL HAVE TO SHOW ME AROUND THE SCHOOL LATER.
YEAH, OF COURSE.

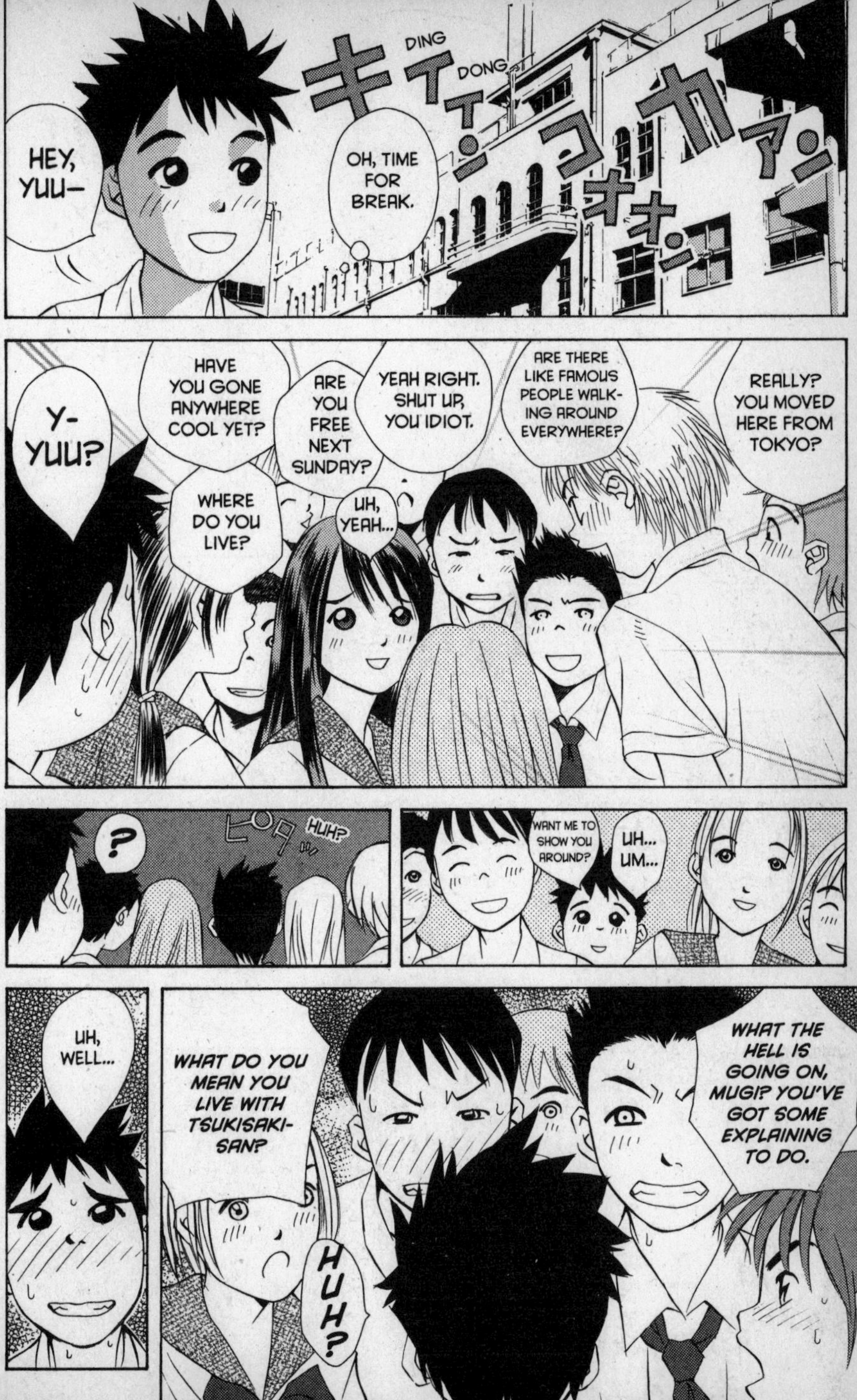
DING
DONG
OH, TIME FOR BREAK.
HEY, YUU—
REALLY? YOU MOVED HERE FROM TOKYO?
ARE THERE LIKE FAMOUS PEOPLE WALK-ING AROUND EVERYWHERE?
YEAH RIGHT. SHUT UP, YOU IDIOT.
ARE YOU FREE NEXT SUNDAY?
UH, YEAH...
HAVE YOU GONE ANYWHERE COOL YET?
WHERE DO YOU LIVE?
Y-YUU?
WANT ME TO SHOW YOU AROUND?
UH... UM...
HUH?
?
WHAT THE HELL IS GOING ON, MUGI? YOU'VE GOT SOME EXPLAINING TO DO.
WHAT DO YOU MEAN YOU LIVE WITH TSUKISAKI-SAN?
HUH?
UH, WELL...

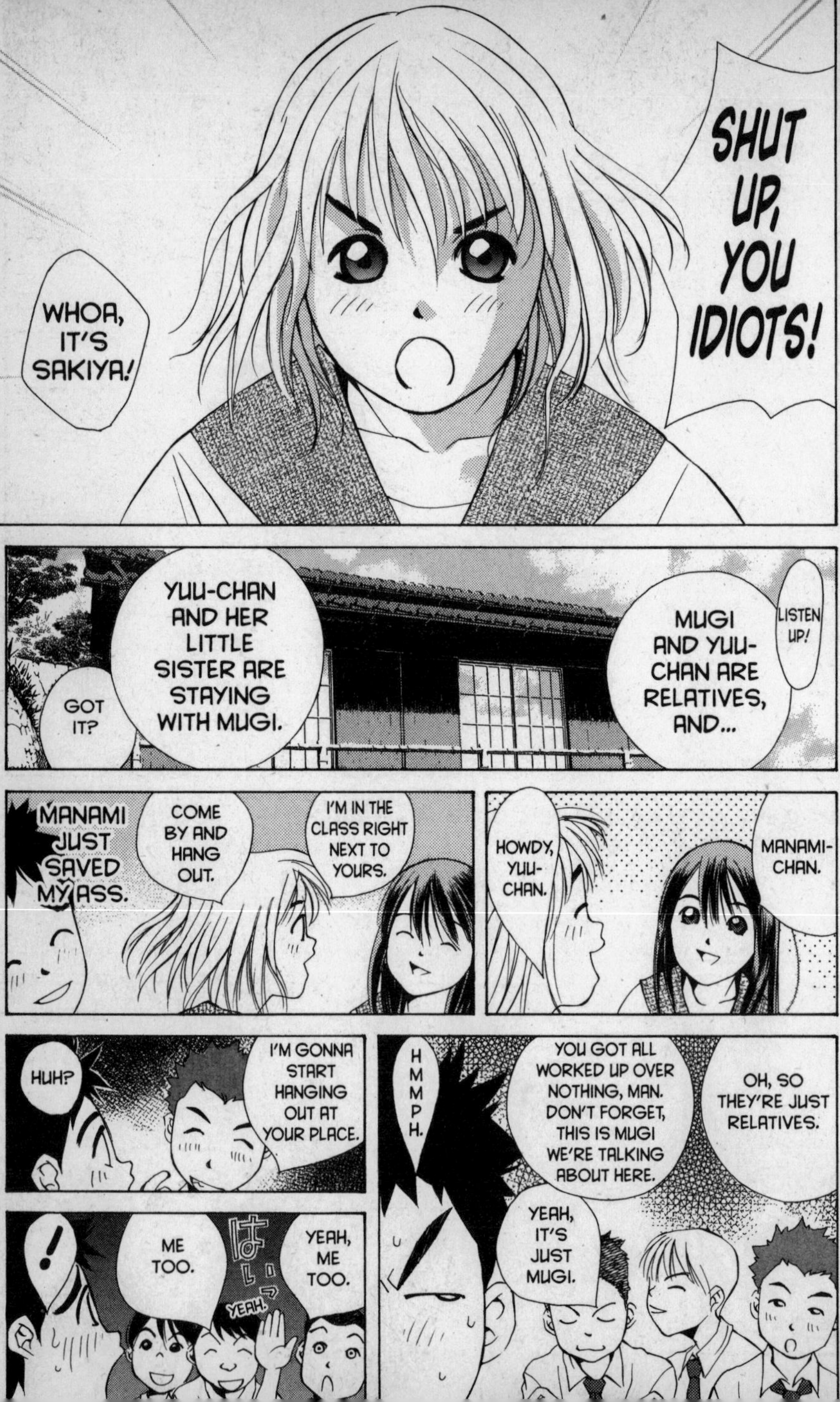
SHUT UP, YOU IDIOTS!
WHOA, IT'S SAKIYA!
LISTEN UP!
MUGI AND YUU-CHAN ARE RELATIVES, AND...
YUU-CHAN AND HER LITTLE SISTER ARE STAYING WITH MUGI.
GOT IT?
MANAMI-CHAN.
HOWDY, YUU-CHAN.
I'M IN THE CLASS RIGHT NEXT TO YOURS.
COME BY AND HANG OUT.
MANAMI JUST SAVED MY ASS.
OH, SO THEY'RE JUST RELATIVES.
YOU GOT ALL WORKED UP OVER NOTHING, MAN. DON'T FORGET, THIS IS MUGI WE'RE TALKING ABOUT HERE.
HMMPH.
YEAH, IT'S JUST MUGI.
I'M GONNA START HANGING OUT AT YOUR PLACE.
HUH?
YEAH, ME TOO.
はい
YEAH.
ME TOO.
!

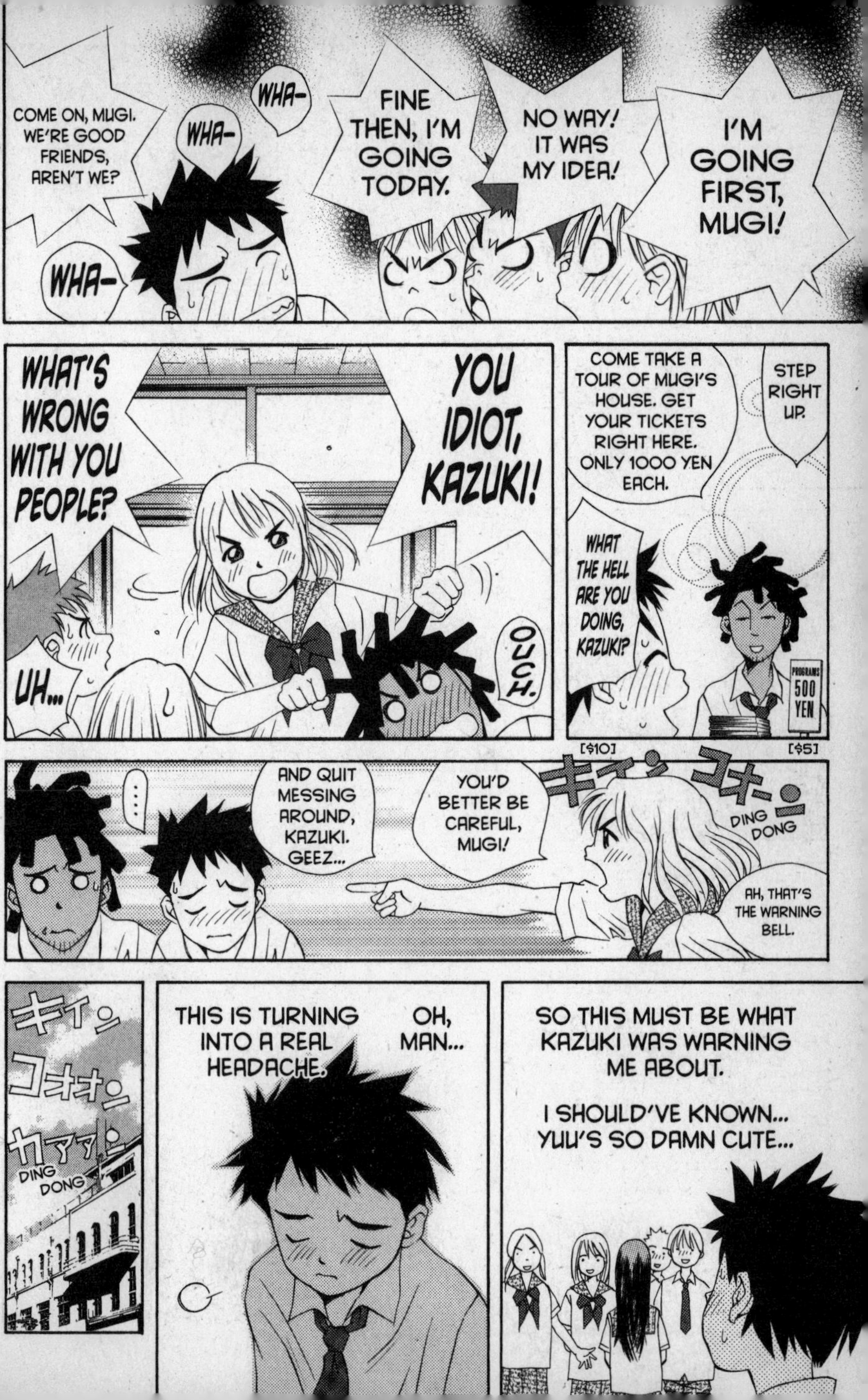
I'M GOING FIRST, MUGI!
NO WAY! IT WAS MY IDEA!
FINE THEN, I'M GOING TODAY.
WHA-
WHA-
COME ON, MUGI. WE'RE GOOD FRIENDS, AREN'T WE?
WHA-
STEP RIGHT UP.
COME TAKE A TOUR OF MUGI'S HOUSE. GET YOUR TICKETS RIGHT HERE. ONLY 1000 YEN EACH.
WHAT THE HELL ARE YOU DOING, KAZUKI?
PROGRAMS 500 YEN
[$5]
[$10]
YOU IDIOT, KAZUKI!
OUCH.
WHAT'S WRONG WITH YOU PEOPLE?
UH...
DING DONG
AH, THAT'S THE WARNING BELL.
YOU'D BETTER BE CAREFUL, MUGI!
AND QUIT MESSING AROUND, KAZUKI. GEEZ...
....
SO THIS MUST BE WHAT KAZUKI WAS WARNING ME ABOUT.
I SHOULD'VE KNOWN... YUU'S SO DAMN CUTE...
OH, MAN...
THIS IS TURNING INTO A REAL HEADACHE.
DING DONG

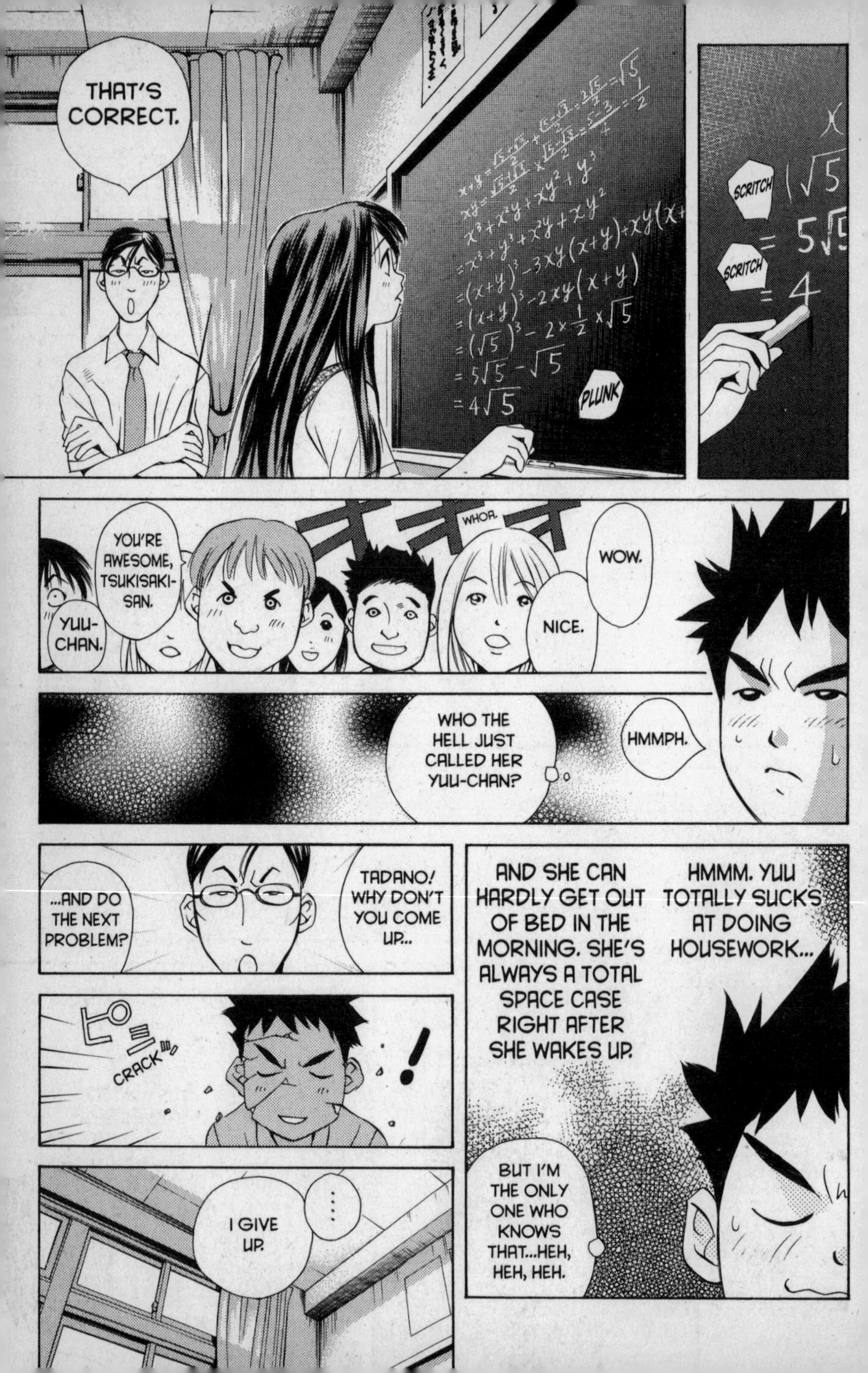
SCRITCH
SCRITCH
PLUNK
THAT'S CORRECT.
WOW.
NICE.
WHOA.
YOU'RE AWESOME, TSUKISAKI-SAN.
YUU-CHAN.
HMMPH.
WHO THE HELL JUST CALLED HER YUU-CHAN?
HMMM. YUU TOTALLY SUCKS AT DOING HOUSEWORK...
AND SHE CAN HARDLY GET OUT OF BED IN THE MORNING. SHE'S ALWAYS A TOTAL SPACE CASE RIGHT AFTER SHE WAKES UP.
BUT I'M THE ONLY ONE WHO KNOWS THAT...HEH, HEH, HEH.
TADANO! WHY DON'T YOU COME UP...
...AND DO THE NEXT PROBLEM?
CRACK
!
....
I GIVE UP.

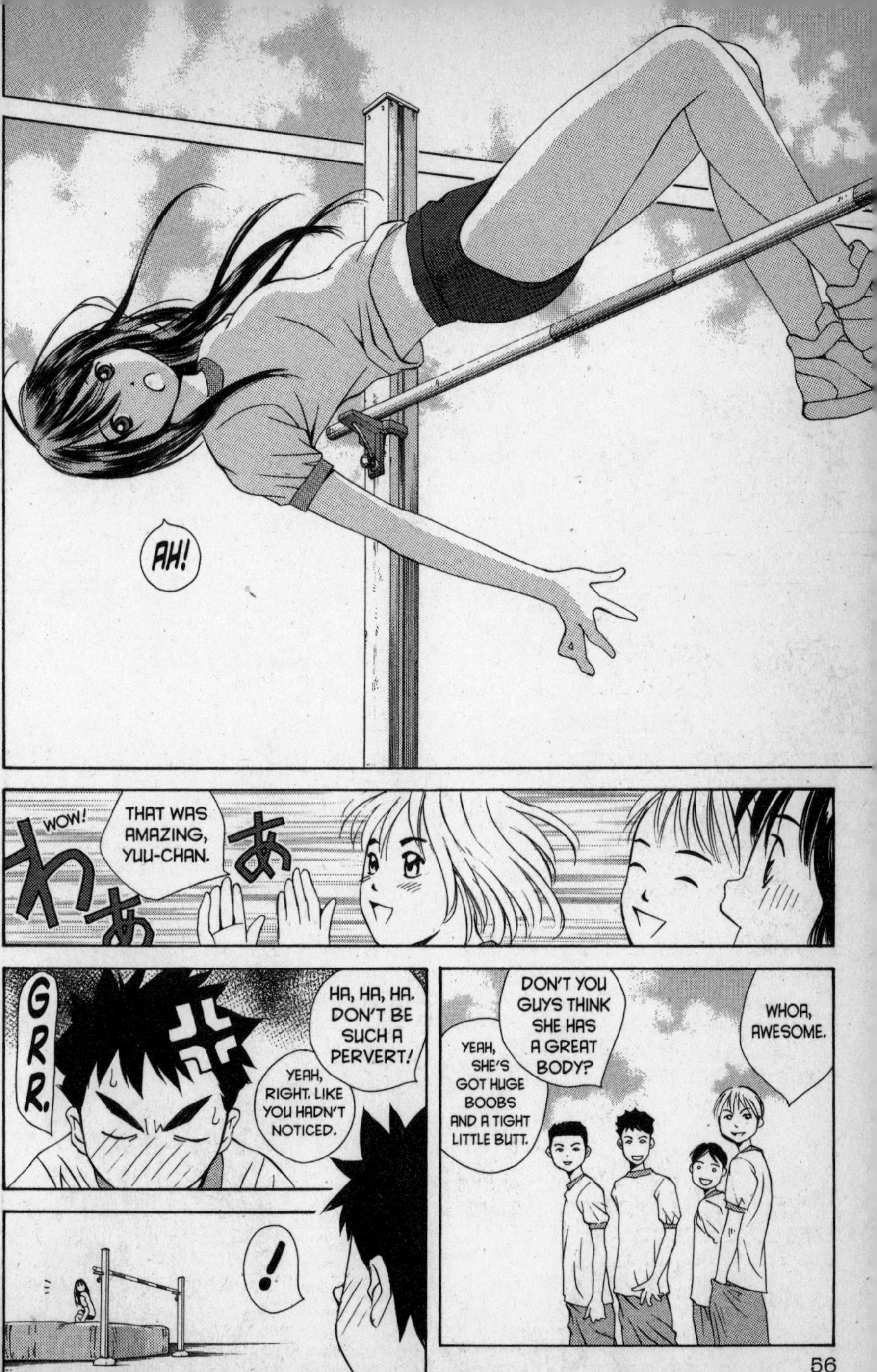
AH!
WOW!
THAT WAS AMAZING, YUU-CHAN.
わぁあ
WHOA, AWESOME.
DON'T YOU GUYS THINK SHE HAS A GREAT BODY?
YEAH, SHE'S GOT HUGE BOOBS AND A TIGHT LITTLE BUTT.
HA, HA, HA. DON'T BE SUCH A PERVERT!
YEAH, RIGHT. LIKE YOU HADN'T NOTICED.
GRR.
!

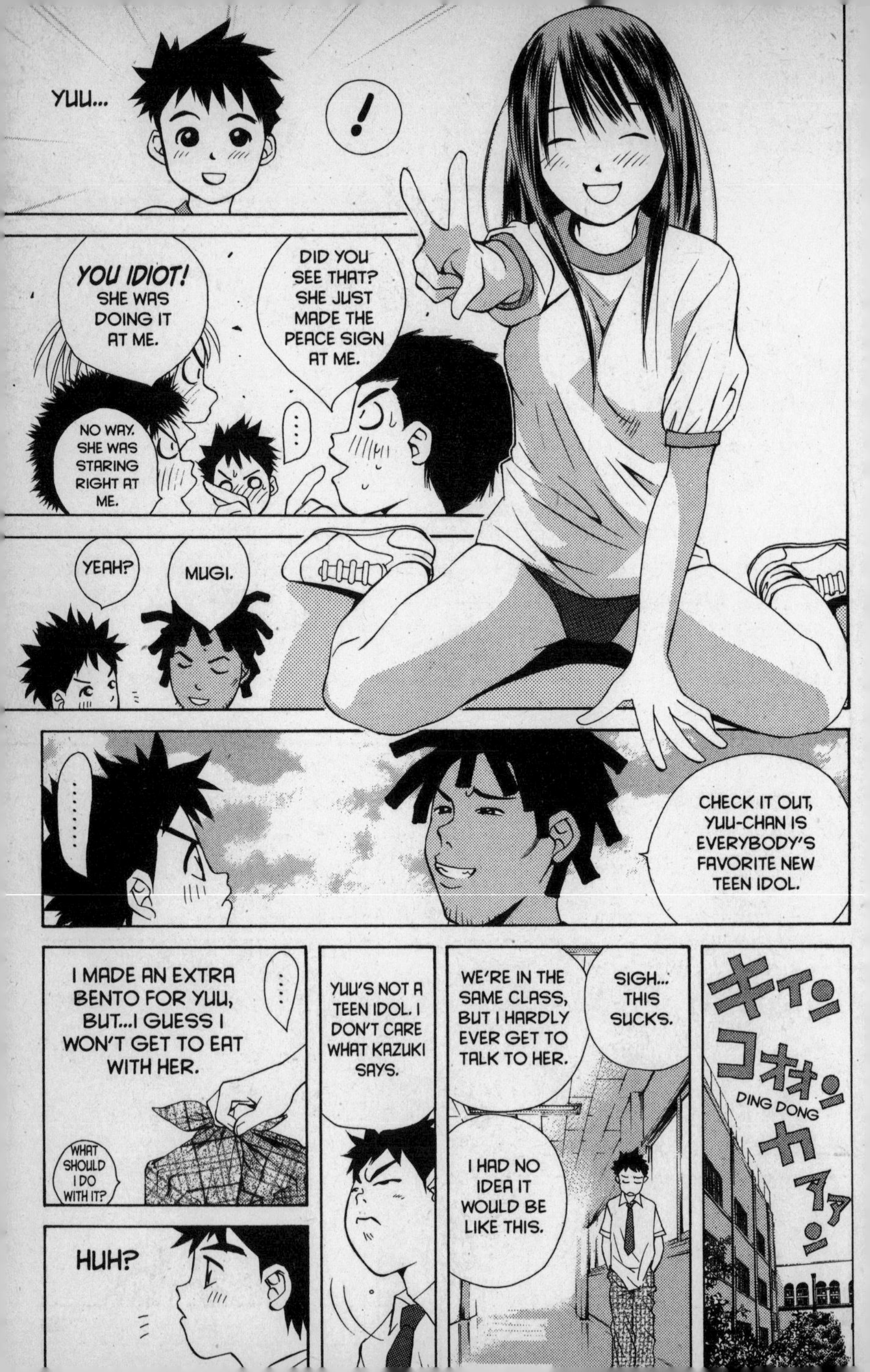
!
YUU...
DID YOU SEE THAT? SHE JUST MADE THE PEACE SIGN AT ME.
YOU IDIOT! SHE WAS DOING IT AT ME.
.....
NO WAY. SHE WAS STARING RIGHT AT ME.
MUGI.
YEAH?
CHECK IT OUT, YUU-CHAN IS EVERYBODY'S FAVORITE NEW TEEN IDOL.
....
キィンコォンカァン
DING DONG
SIGH... THIS SUCKS.
WE'RE IN THE SAME CLASS, BUT I HARDLY EVER GET TO TALK TO HER.
I HAD NO IDEA IT WOULD BE LIKE THIS.
YUU'S NOT A TEEN IDOL. I DON'T CARE WHAT KAZUKI SAYS.
I MADE AN EXTRA BENTO FOR YUU, BUT...I GUESS I WON'T GET TO EAT WITH HER.
.....
WHAT SHOULD I DO WITH IT?
HUH?

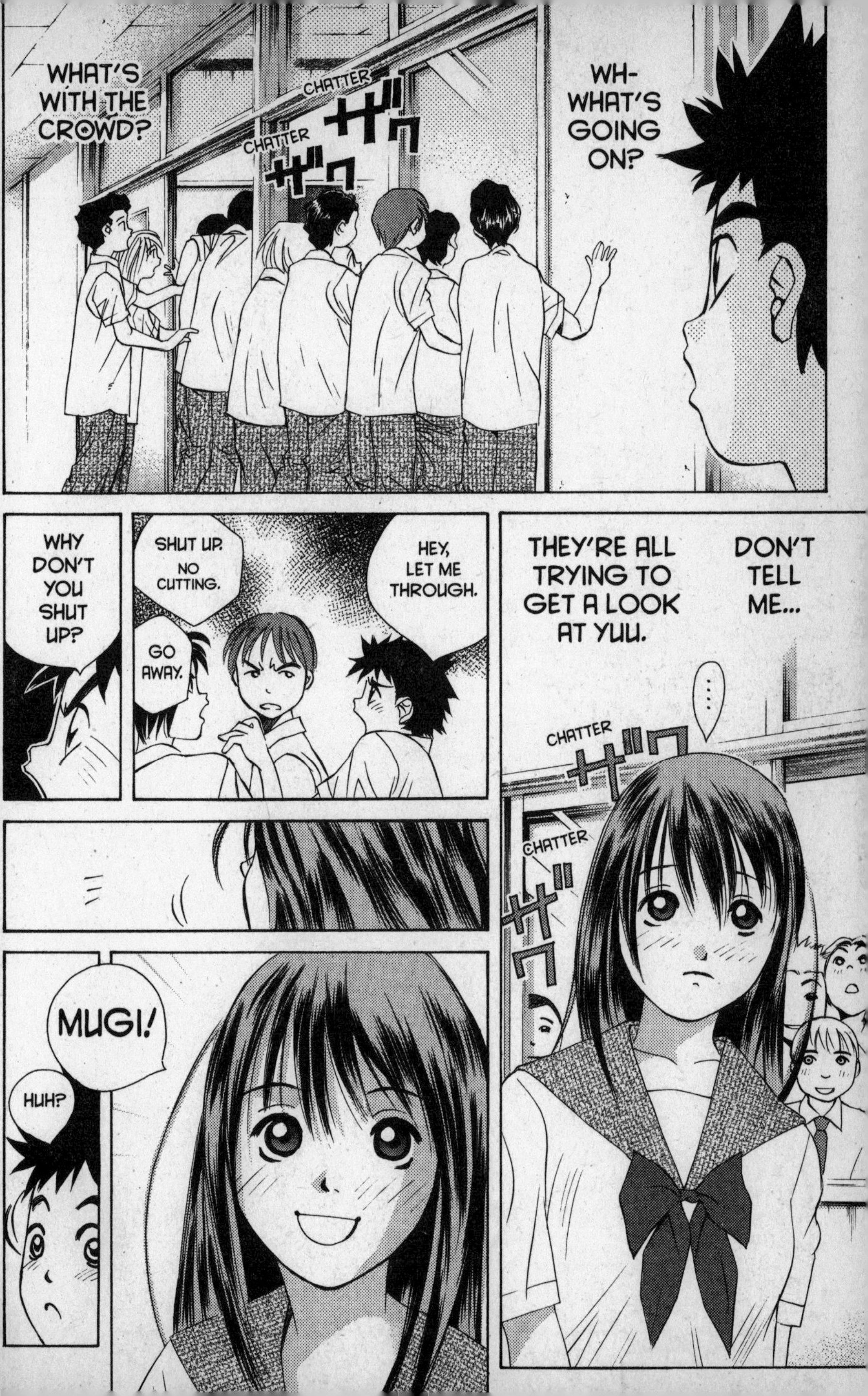
WH- WHAT'S GOING ON?
WHAT'S WITH THE CROWD?
CHATTER
ザワ
CHATTER
ザワ
DON'T TELL ME...
THEY'RE ALL TRYING TO GET A LOOK AT YUU.
...
CHATTER
ザワ
CHATTER
ザワ
HEY, LET ME THROUGH.
SHUT UP. NO CUTTING.
GO AWAY.
WHY DON'T YOU SHUT UP?
MUGI!
HUH?

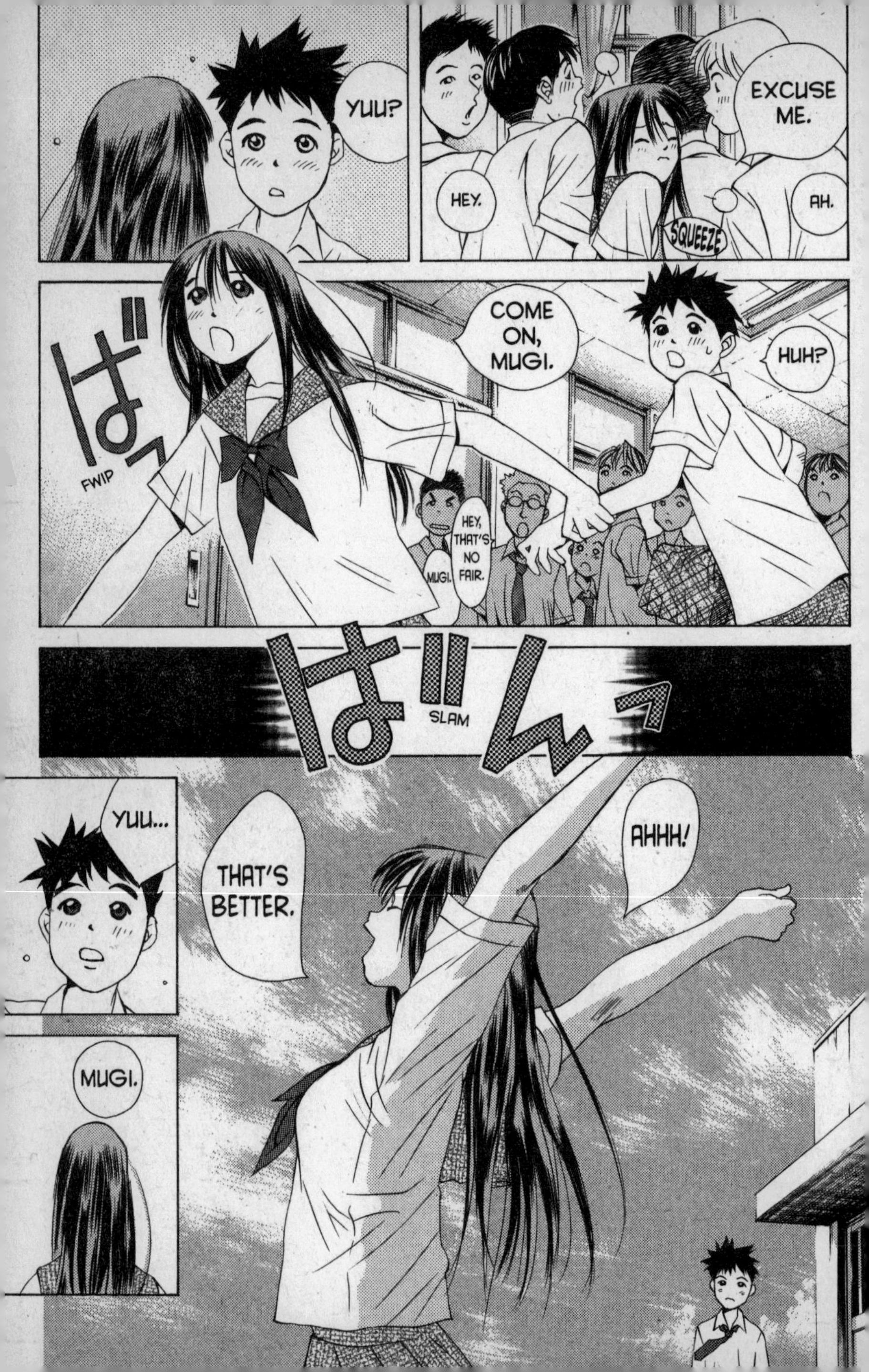
EXCUSE ME.
AH.
SQUEEZE
HEY.
YUU?
HUH?
COME ON, MUGI.
HEY, THAT'S NO FAIR.
MUGI.
ばっ
FWIP
ばんっ
SLAM
AHHH!
THAT'S BETTER.
YUU...
MUGI.

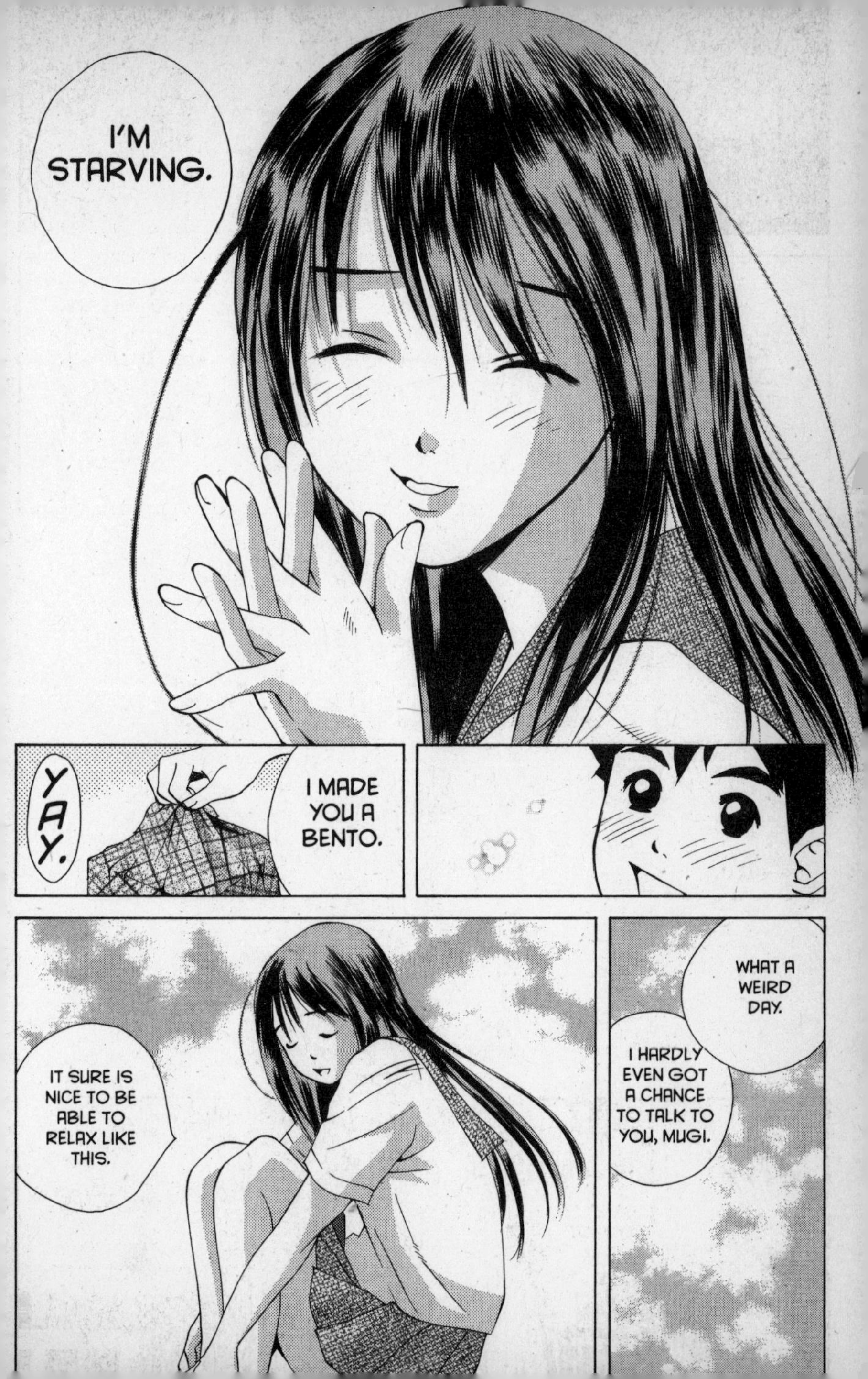
I'M STARVING.
I MADE YOU A BENTO.
YAY.
WHAT A WEIRD DAY.
I HARDLY EVEN GOT A CHANCE TO TALK TO YOU, MUGI.
IT SURE IS NICE TO BE ABLE TO RELAX LIKE THIS.

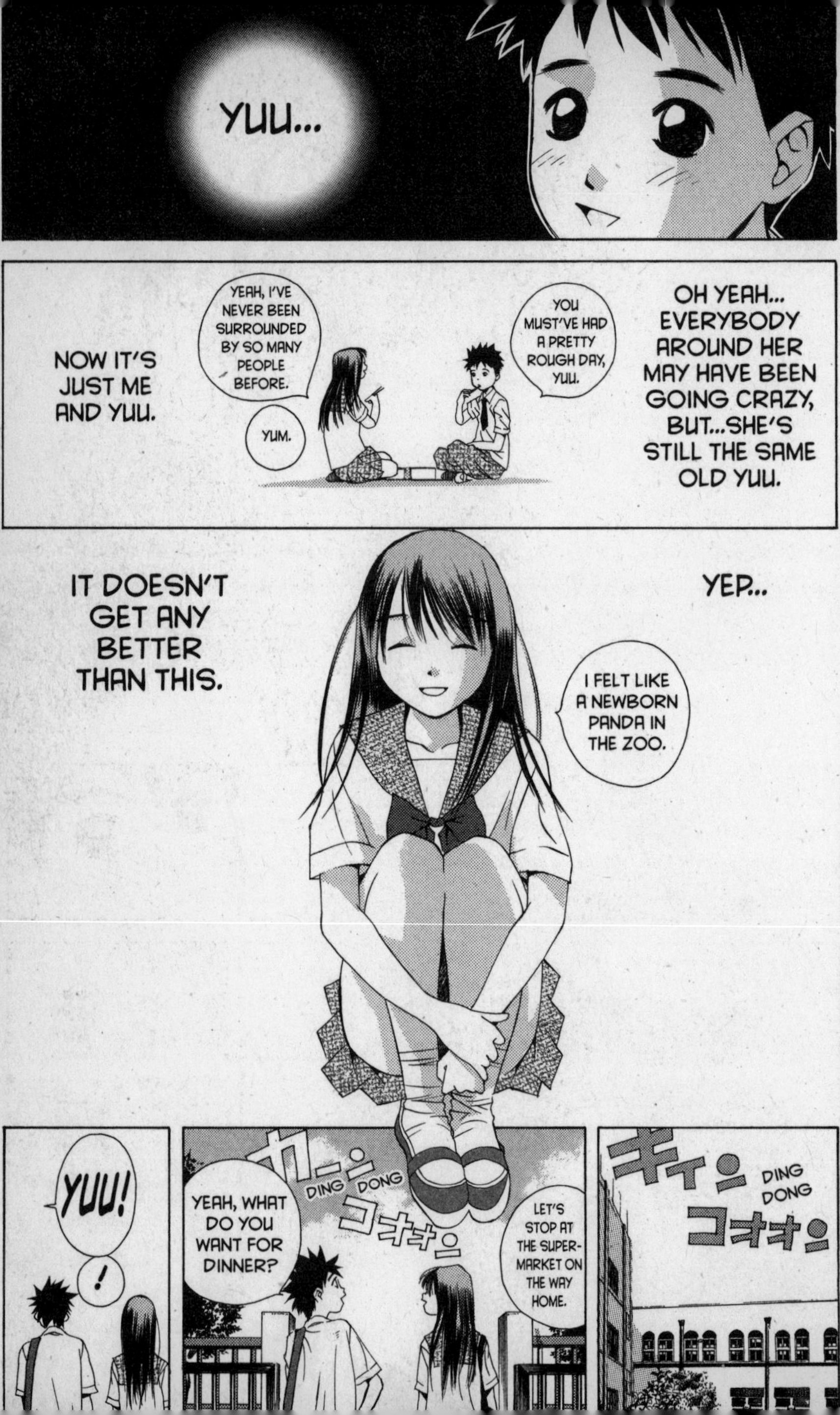
YUU...
OH YEAH... EVERYBODY AROUND HER MAY HAVE BEEN GOING CRAZY, BUT...SHE'S STILL THE SAME OLD YUU.
YOU MUST'VE HAD A PRETTY ROUGH DAY, YUU.
YEAH, I'VE NEVER BEEN SURROUNDED BY SO MANY PEOPLE BEFORE.
YUM.
NOW IT'S JUST ME AND YUU.
YEP...
I FELT LIKE A NEWBORN PANDA IN THE ZOO.
IT DOESN'T GET ANY BETTER THAN THIS.
DING DONG
LET'S STOP AT THE SUPER-MARKET ON THE WAY HOME.
YEAH, WHAT DO YOU WANT FOR DINNER?
DING DONG
YUU!
!

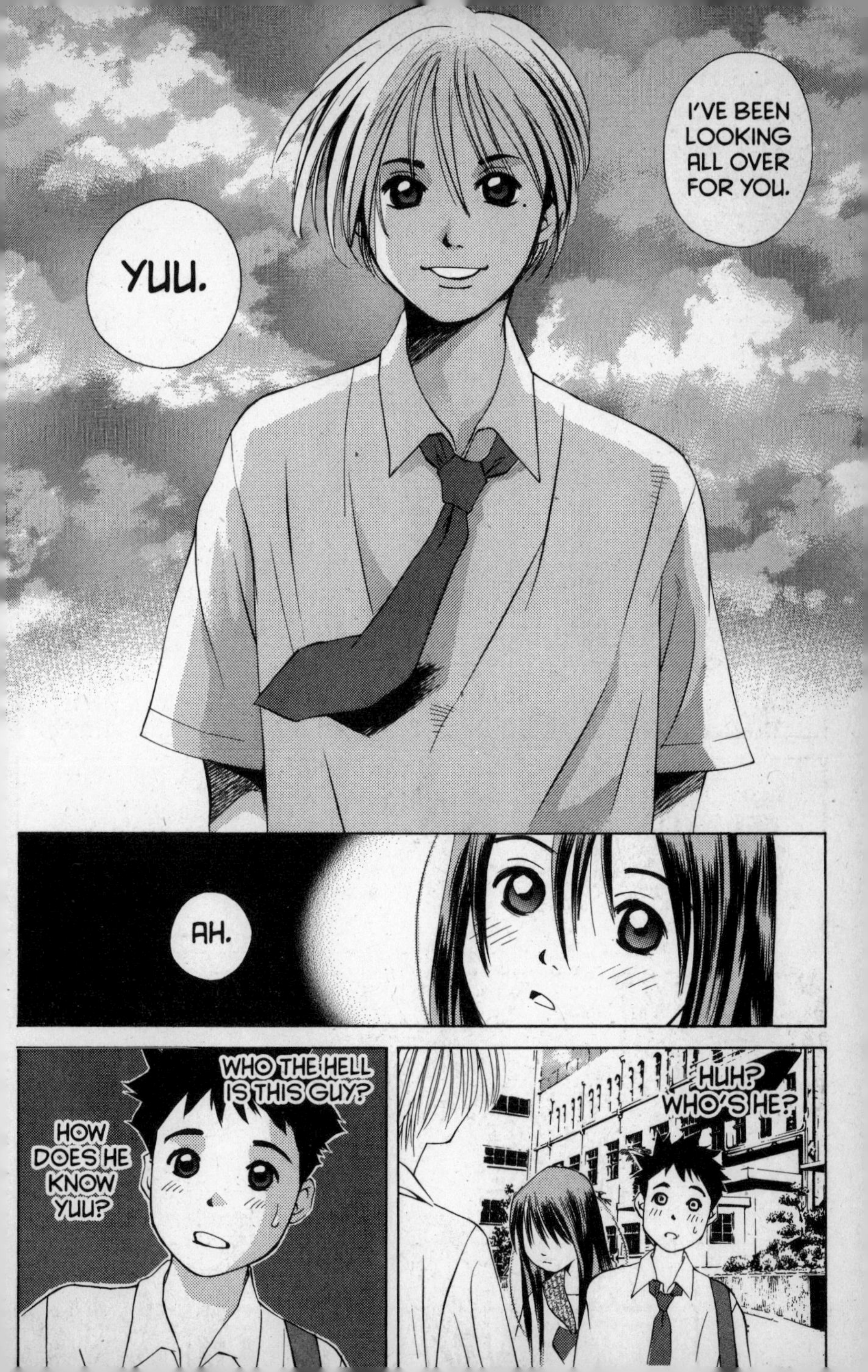
I'VE BEEN LOOKING ALL OVER FOR YOU.
YUU.
AH.
HUH? WHO'S HE?
WHO THE HELL IS THIS GUY?
HOW DOES HE KNOW YUU?

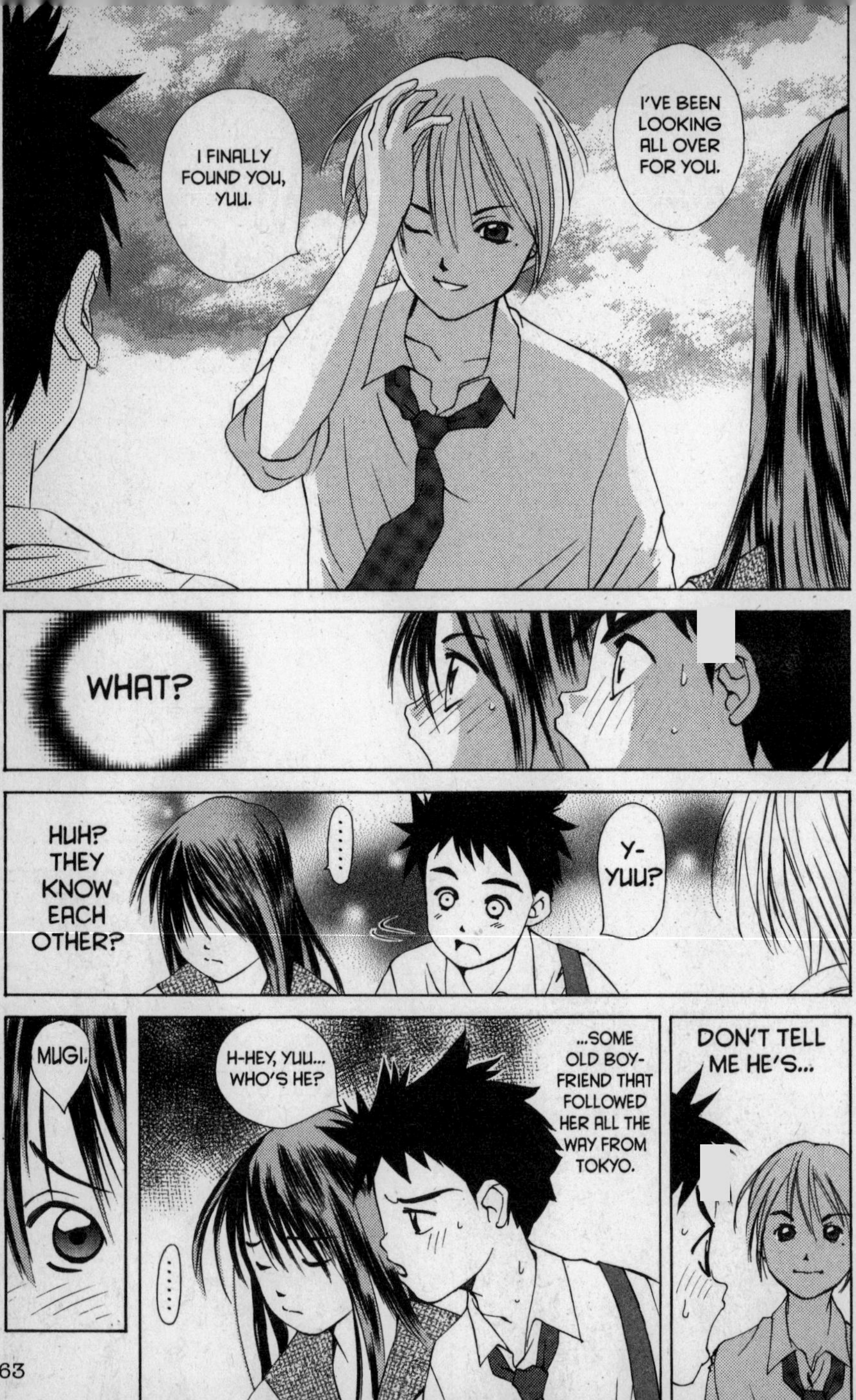
I'VE BEEN LOOKING ALL OVER FOR YOU.
I FINALLY FOUND YOU, YUU.
WHAT?
Y-YUU?
......
HUH? THEY KNOW EACH OTHER?
DON'T TELL ME HE'S...
...SOME OLD BOY-FRIEND THAT FOLLOWED HER ALL THE WAY FROM TOKYO.
H-HEY, YUU... WHO'S HE?
......
MUGI.

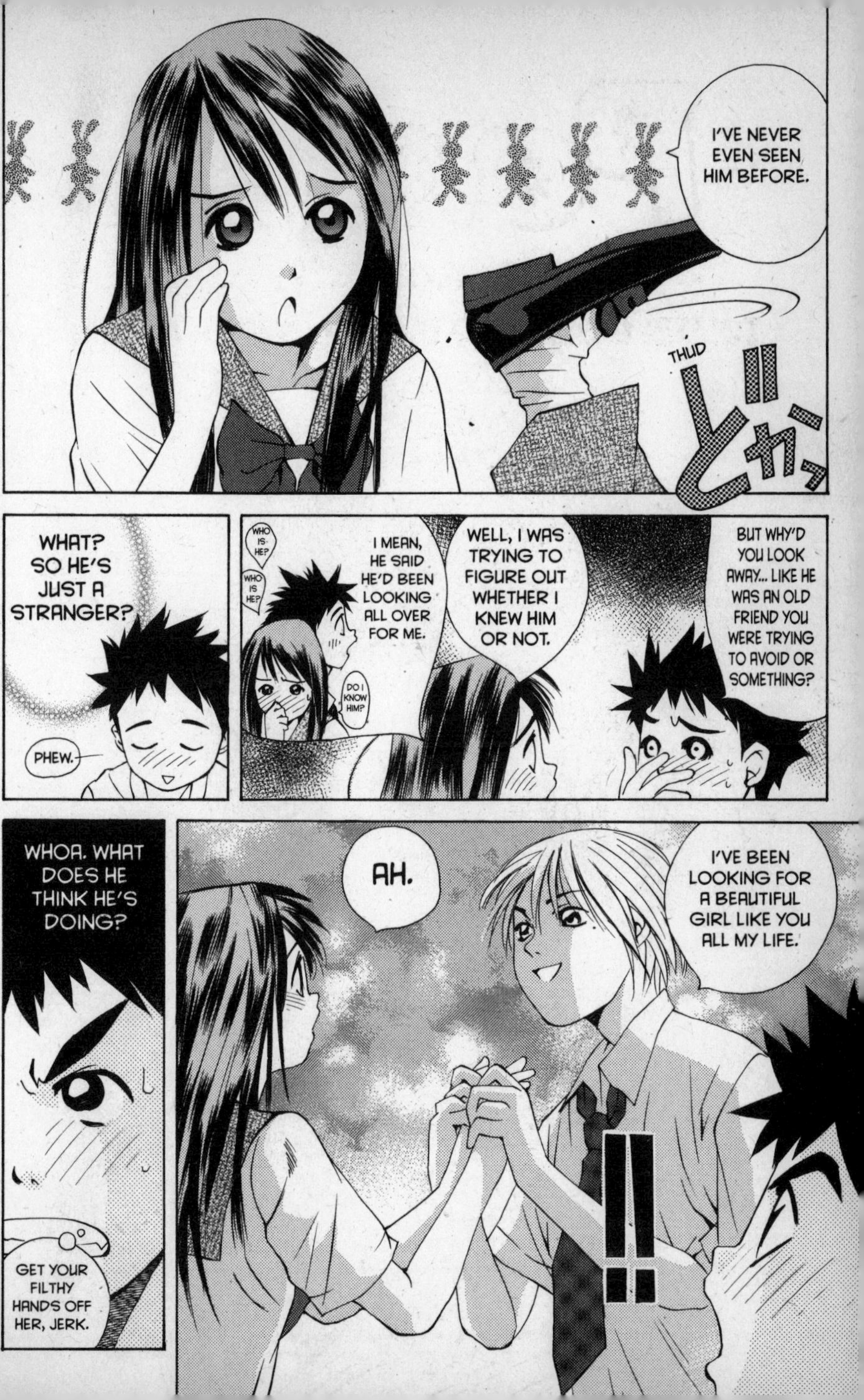
I'VE NEVER EVEN SEEN HIM BEFORE.
THUD
どかっ
BUT WHY'D YOU LOOK AWAY... LIKE HE WAS AN OLD FRIEND YOU WERE TRYING TO AVOID OR SOMETHING?
WELL, I WAS TRYING TO FIGURE OUT WHETHER I KNEW HIM OR NOT.
I MEAN, HE SAID HE'D BEEN LOOKING ALL OVER FOR ME.
WHO IS HE?
WHO IS HE?
DO I KNOW HIM?
WHAT? SO HE'S JUST A STRANGER?
PHEW.
I'VE BEEN LOOKING FOR A BEAUTIFUL GIRL LIKE YOU ALL MY LIFE.
AH.
!!
WHOA. WHAT DOES HE THINK HE'S DOING?
GET YOUR FILTHY HANDS OFF HER, JERK.

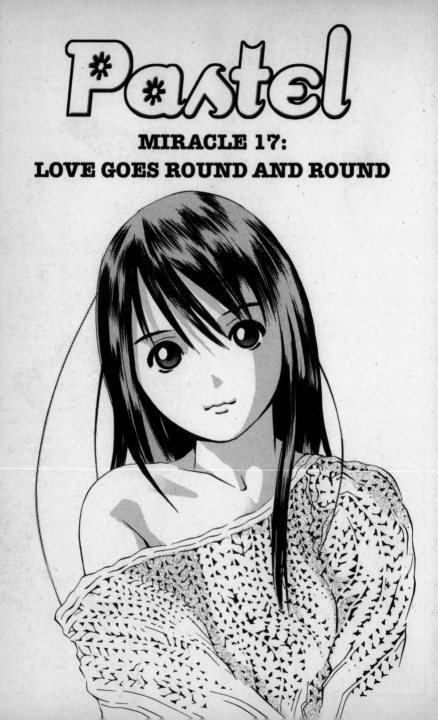

Pastel

MIRACLE 17:
LOVE GOES ROUND AND ROUND

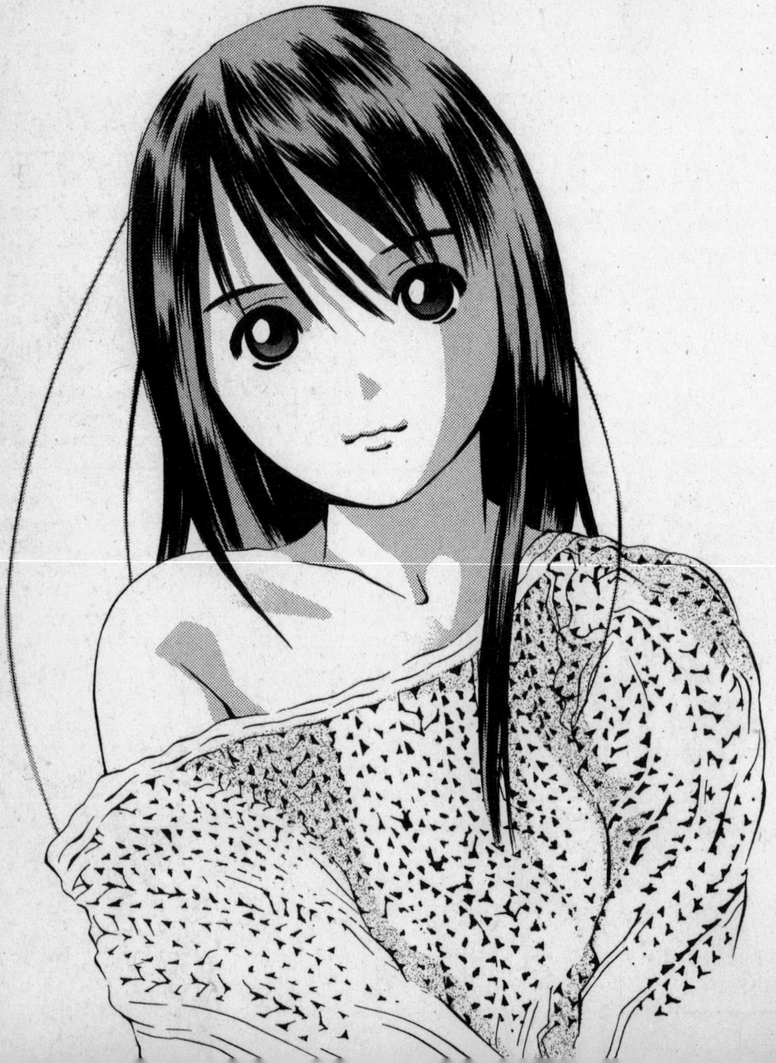

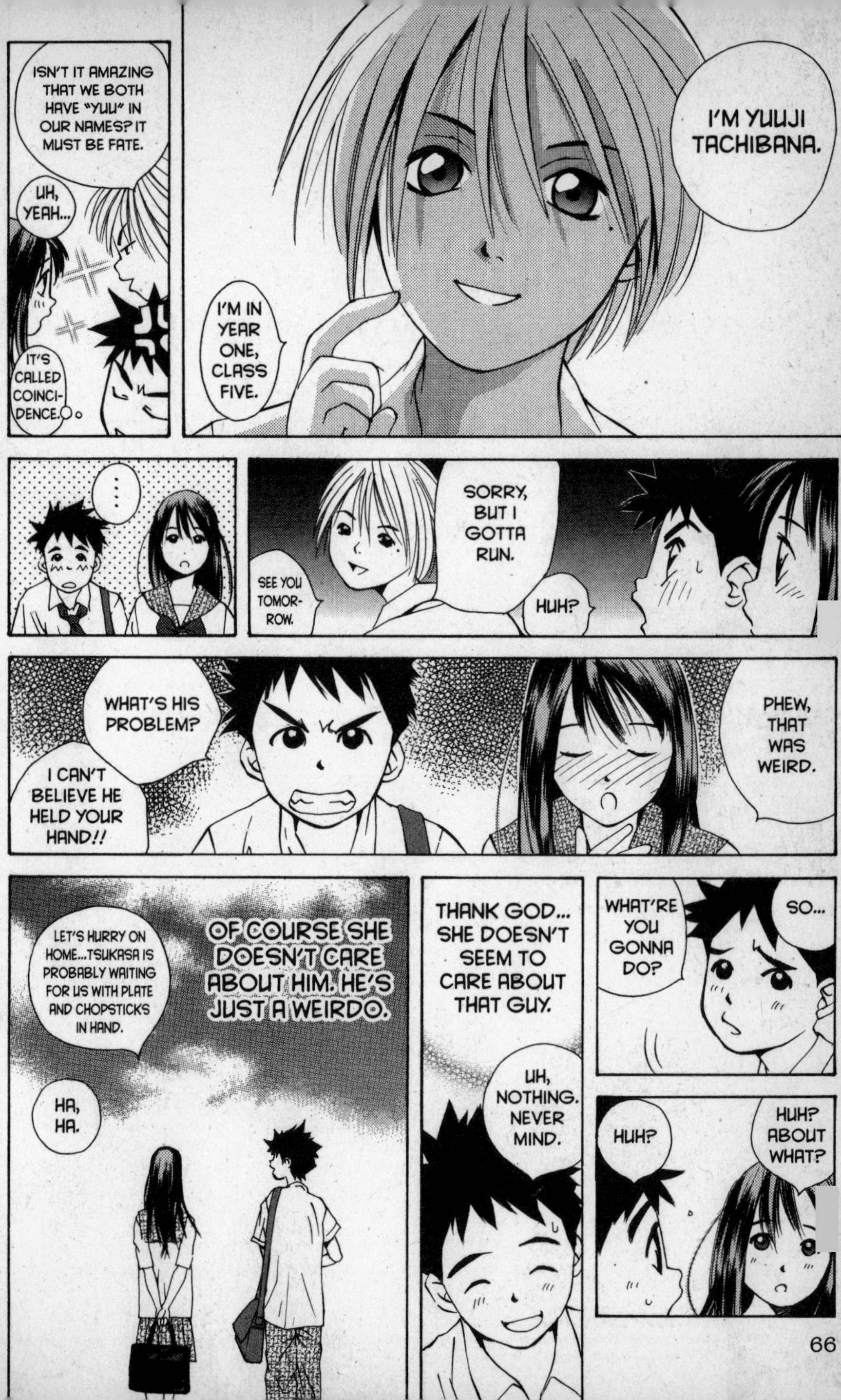
I'M YUUJI TACHIBANA.
I'M IN YEAR ONE, CLASS FIVE.
ISN'T IT AMAZING THAT WE BOTH HAVE "YUU" IN OUR NAMES? IT MUST BE FATE.
UH, YEAH...
IT'S CALLED COINCIDENCE.
SORRY, BUT I GOTTA RUN.
HUH?
SEE YOU TOMORROW.
...
PHEW, THAT WAS WEIRD.
WHAT'S HIS PROBLEM?
I CAN'T BELIEVE HE HELD YOUR HAND!!
SO...
WHAT'RE YOU GONNA DO?
HUH? ABOUT WHAT?
HUH?
THANK GOD... SHE DOESN'T SEEM TO CARE ABOUT THAT GUY.
UH, NOTHING. NEVER MIND.
OF COURSE SHE DOESN'T CARE ABOUT HIM. HE'S JUST A WEIRDO.
LET'S HURRY ON HOME...TSUKASA IS PROBABLY WAITING FOR US WITH PLATE AND CHOPSTICKS IN HAND.
HA, HA.

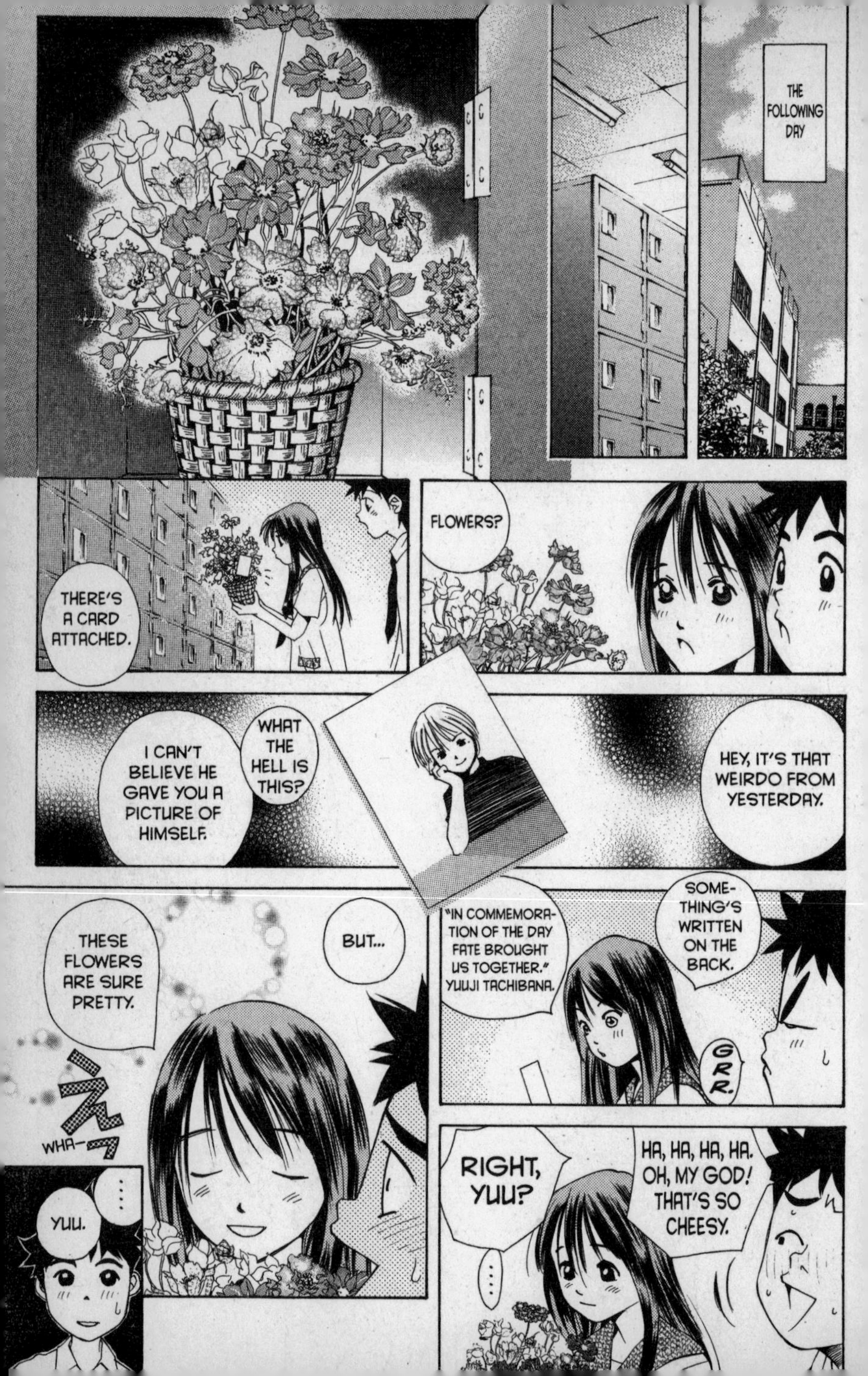
THE FOLLOWING DAY
FLOWERS?
THERE'S A CARD ATTACHED.
HEY, IT'S THAT WEIRDO FROM YESTERDAY.
WHAT THE HELL IS THIS?
I CAN'T BELIEVE HE GAVE YOU A PICTURE OF HIMSELF.
SOME-THING'S WRITTEN ON THE BACK.
"IN COMMEMORA-TION OF THE DAY FATE BROUGHT US TOGETHER." YUUJI TACHIBANA.
GRR.
HA, HA, HA, HA. OH, MY GOD! THAT'S SO CHEESY.
RIGHT, YUU?
...
BUT...
THESE FLOWERS ARE SURE PRETTY.
WHA-
....
YUU.

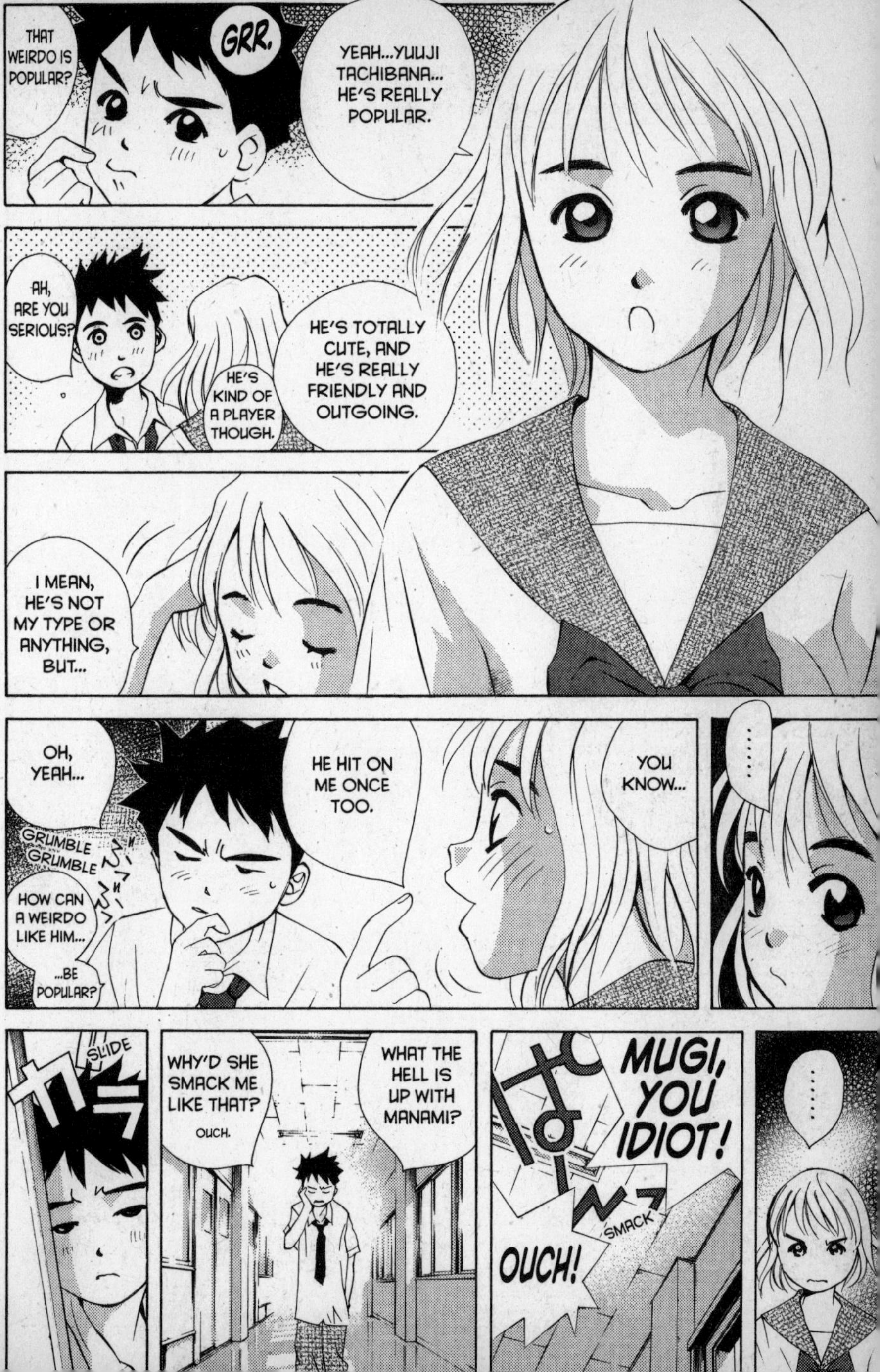
YEAH...YUUJI TACHIBANA... HE'S REALLY POPULAR.
GRR.
THAT WEIRDO IS POPULAR?
HE'S TOTALLY CUTE, AND HE'S REALLY FRIENDLY AND OUTGOING.
HE'S KIND OF A PLAYER THOUGH.
AH, ARE YOU SERIOUS?
I MEAN, HE'S NOT MY TYPE OR ANYTHING, BUT...
......
YOU KNOW...
HE HIT ON ME ONCE TOO.
OH, YEAH...
GRUMBLE GRUMBLE
HOW CAN A WEIRDO LIKE HIM...
...BE POPULAR?
......
MUGI, YOU IDIOT!
SMACK
OUCH!
WHAT THE HELL IS UP WITH MANAMI?
WHY'D SHE SMACK ME LIKE THAT?
OUCH.
SLIDE

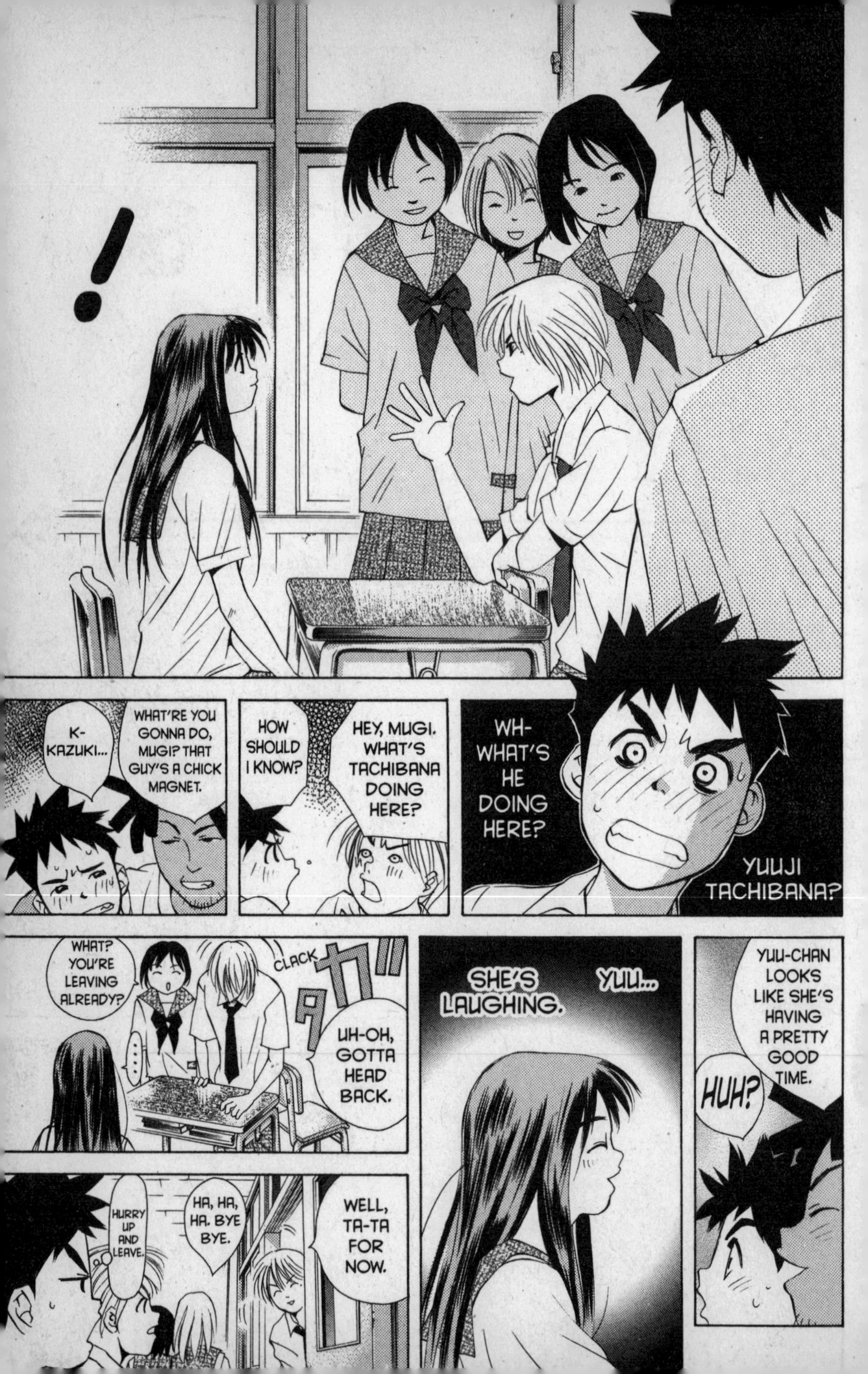
!
WH- WHAT'S HE DOING HERE?
YUUJI TACHIBANA?
HEY, MUGI. WHAT'S TACHIBANA DOING HERE?
HOW SHOULD I KNOW?
WHAT'RE YOU GONNA DO, MUGI? THAT GUY'S A CHICK MAGNET.
K-KAZUKI...
YUU-CHAN LOOKS LIKE SHE'S HAVING A PRETTY GOOD TIME.
HUH?
YUU...
SHE'S LAUGHING.
CLACK
UH-OH, GOTTA HEAD BACK.
WHAT? YOU'RE LEAVING ALREADY?
...
WELL, TA-TA FOR NOW.
HA, HA, HA. BYE BYE.
HURRY UP AND LEAVE.

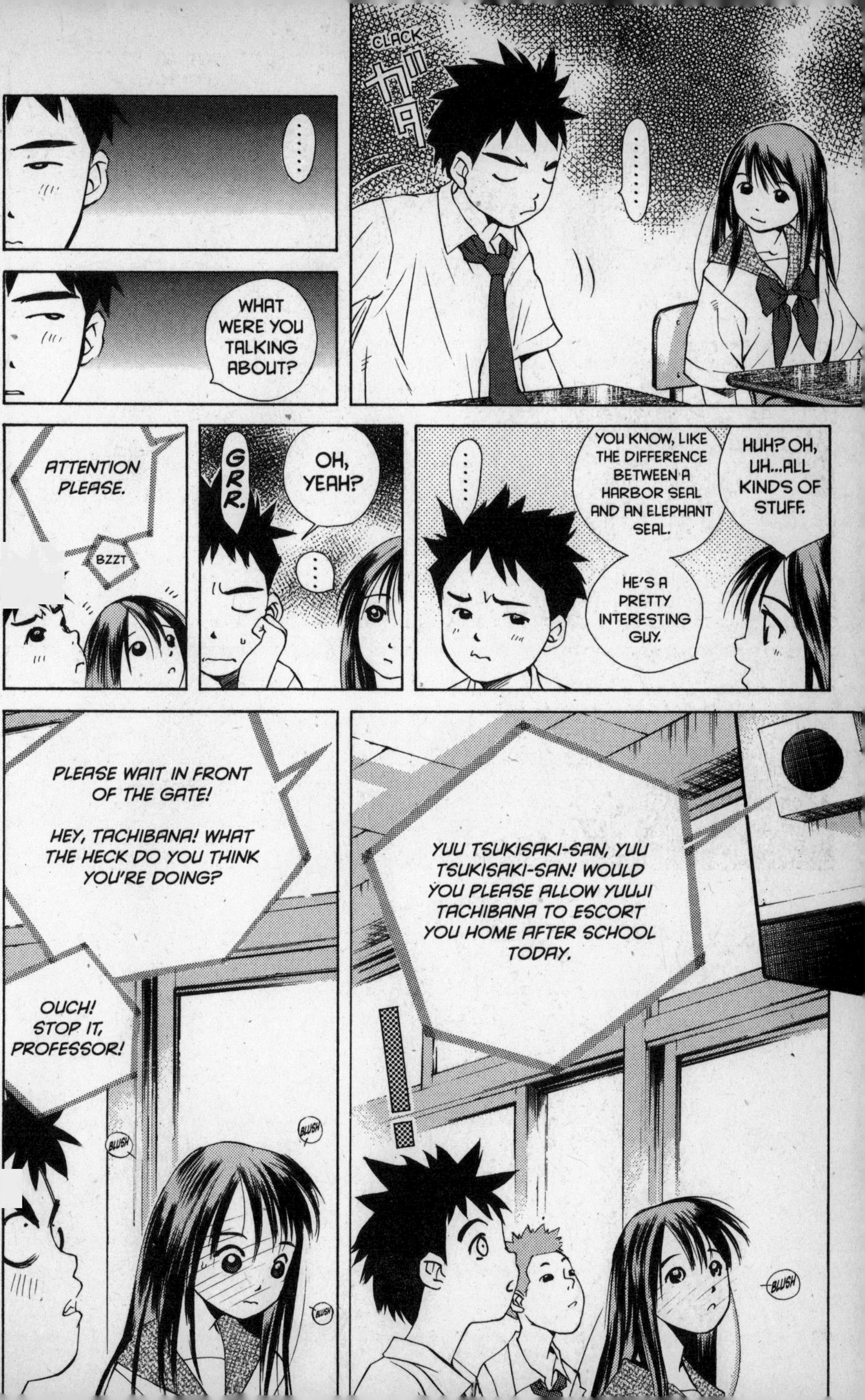
CLACK
......
......
WHAT WERE YOU TALKING ABOUT?
HUH? OH, UH...ALL KINDS OF STUFF.
YOU KNOW, LIKE THE DIFFERENCE BETWEEN A HARBOR SEAL AND AN ELEPHANT SEAL.
HE'S A PRETTY INTERESTING GUY.
......
GRR.
OH, YEAH?
...
ATTENTION PLEASE.
BZZT
YUU TSUKISAKI-SAN, YUU TSUKISAKI-SAN! WOULD YOU PLEASE ALLOW YUUJI TACHIBANA TO ESCORT YOU HOME AFTER SCHOOL TODAY.
!
BLUSH
PLEASE WAIT IN FRONT OF THE GATE!
HEY, TACHIBANA! WHAT THE HECK DO YOU THINK YOU'RE DOING?
OUCH! STOP IT, PROFESSOR!
BLUSH
BLUSH
BLUSH

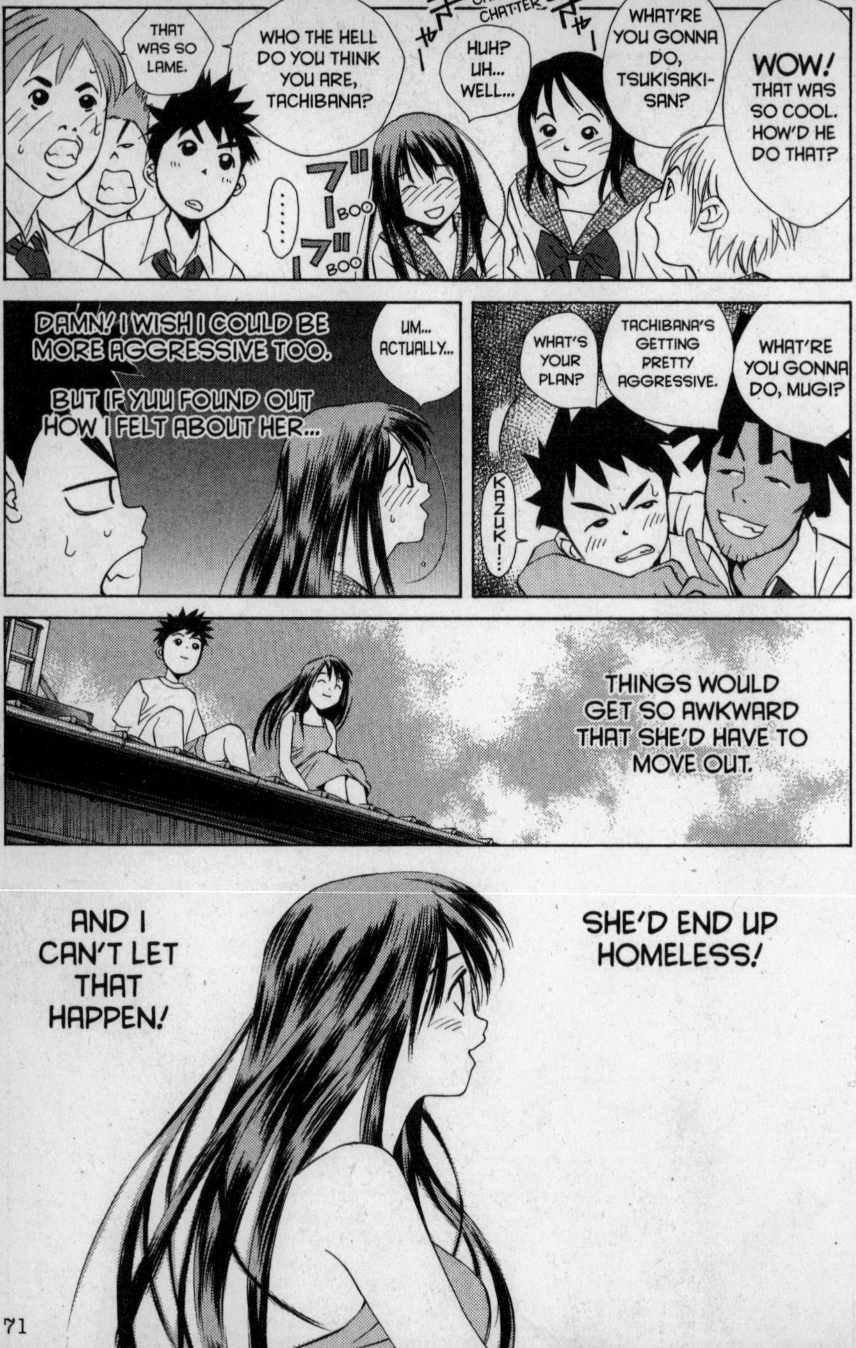
WOW! THAT WAS SO COOL. HOW'D HE DO THAT?
WHAT'RE YOU GONNA DO, TSUKISAKI-SAN?
CHATTER CHATTER
HUH? UH... WELL...
WHO THE HELL DO YOU THINK YOU ARE, TACHIBANA?
THAT WAS SO LAME.
BOO BOO
......
WHAT'RE YOU GONNA DO, MUGI?
TACHIBANA'S GETTING PRETTY AGGRESSIVE.
WHAT'S YOUR PLAN?
KAZUKI...!
UM... ACTUALLY...
DAMN! I WISH I COULD BE MORE AGGRESSIVE TOO.
BUT IF YUU FOUND OUT HOW I FELT ABOUT HER...
THINGS WOULD GET SO AWKWARD THAT SHE'D HAVE TO MOVE OUT.
SHE'D END UP HOMELESS!
AND I CAN'T LET THAT HAPPEN!

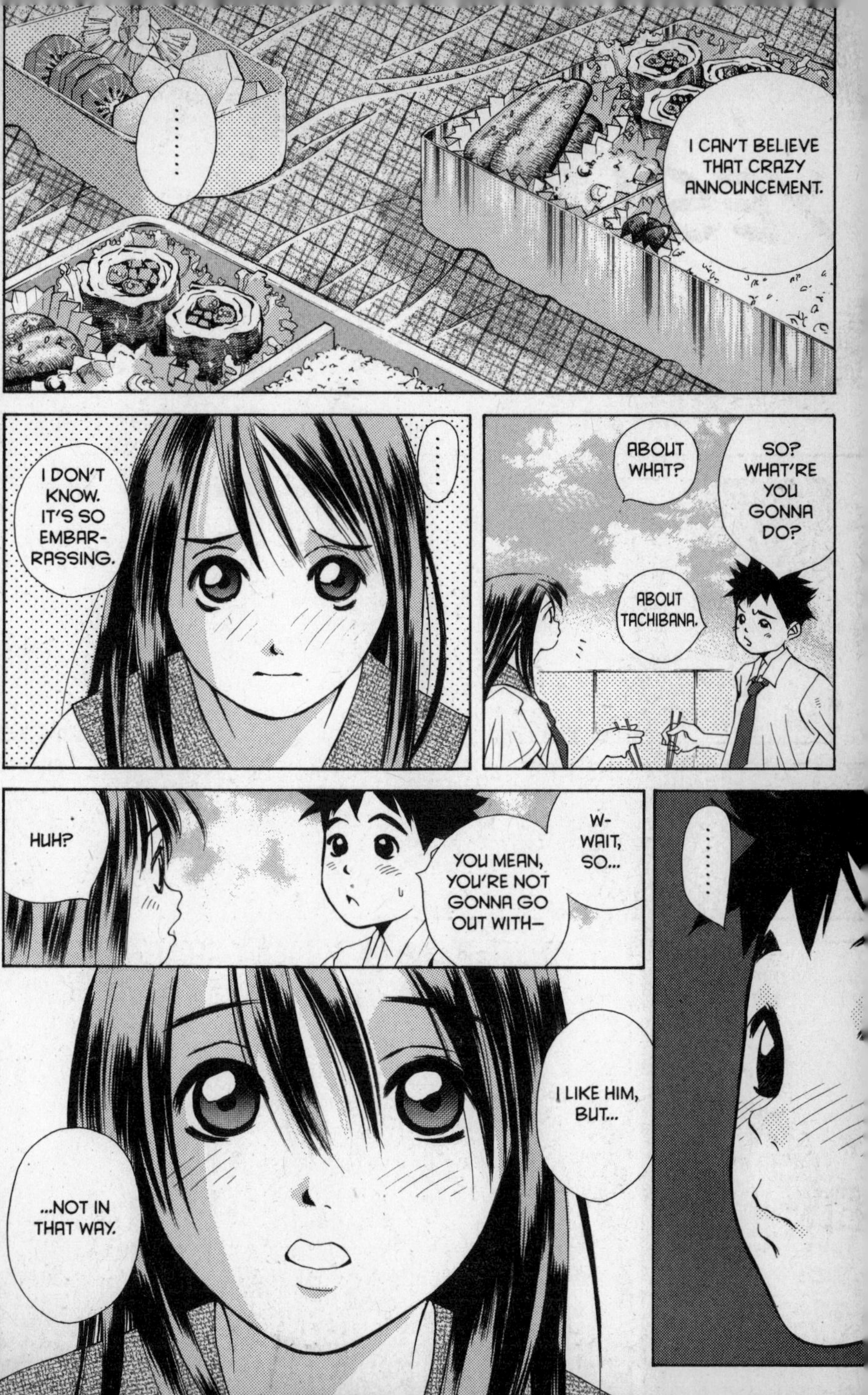
I CAN'T BELIEVE THAT CRAZY ANNOUNCEMENT.
......
SO? WHAT'RE YOU GONNA DO?
ABOUT WHAT?
ABOUT TACHIBANA.
......
I DON'T KNOW. IT'S SO EMBARRASSING.
......
W-WAIT, SO...
YOU MEAN, YOU'RE NOT GONNA GO OUT WITH—
HUH?
I LIKE HIM, BUT...
...NOT IN THAT WAY.

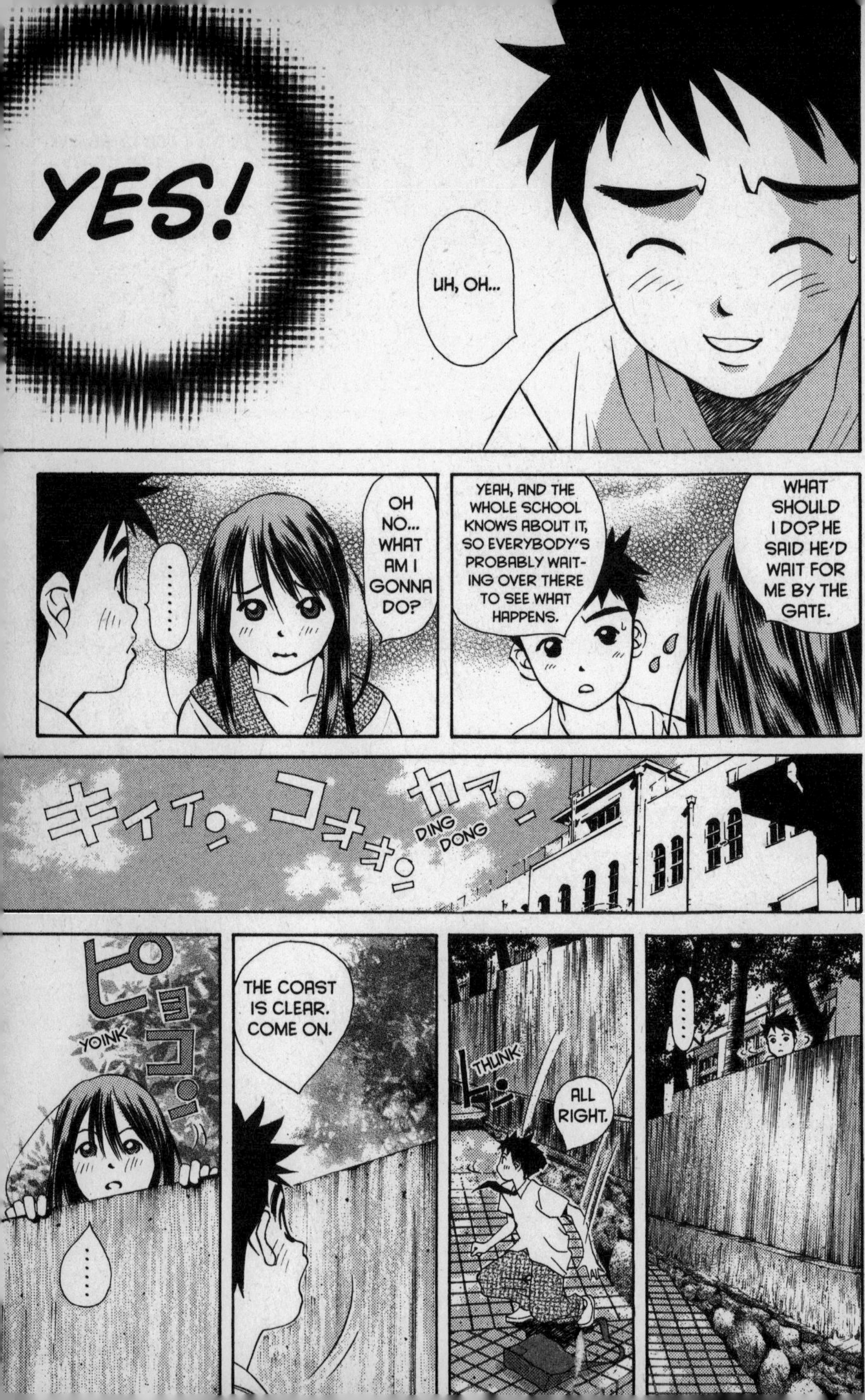
UH, OH...
YES!
WHAT SHOULD I DO? HE SAID HE'D WAIT FOR ME BY THE GATE.
YEAH, AND THE WHOLE SCHOOL KNOWS ABOUT IT, SO EVERYBODY'S PROBABLY WAIT-ING OVER THERE TO SEE WHAT HAPPENS.
OH NO... WHAT AM I GONNA DO?
......
DING DONG
......
ALL RIGHT.
THUNK
THE COAST IS CLEAR. COME ON.
YOINK
......

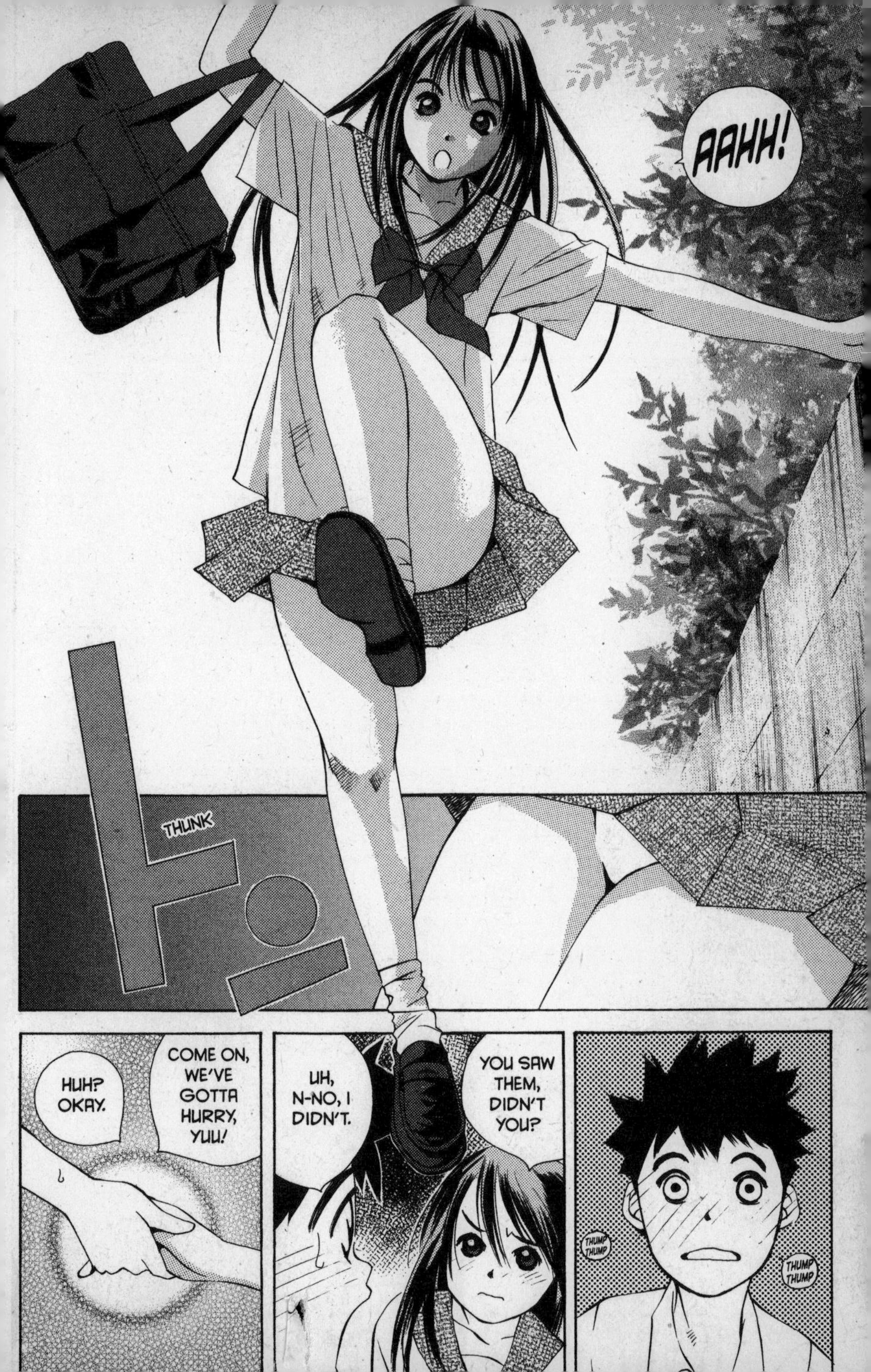
AAHH!
THUNK
THUMP THUMP
THUMP THUMP
YOU SAW THEM, DIDN'T YOU?
UH, N-NO, I DIDN'T.
COME ON, WE'VE GOTTA HURRY, YUU!
HUH? OKAY.

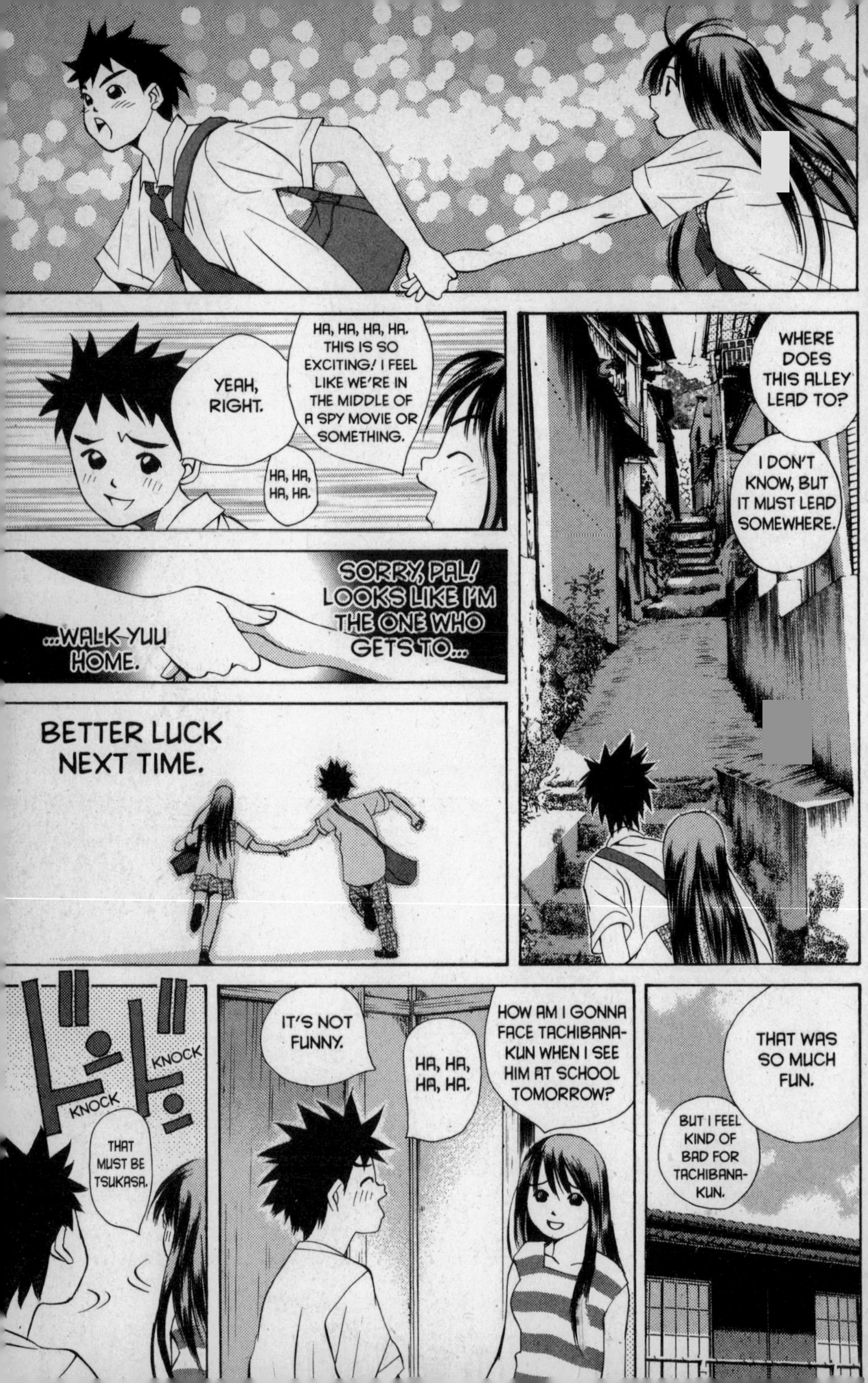
WHERE DOES THIS ALLEY LEAD TO?
I DON'T KNOW, BUT IT MUST LEAD SOMEWHERE.
HA, HA, HA, HA. THIS IS SO EXCITING! I FEEL LIKE WE'RE IN THE MIDDLE OF A SPY MOVIE OR SOMETHING.
YEAH, RIGHT.
HA, HA, HA, HA.
SORRY, PAL! LOOKS LIKE I'M THE ONE WHO GETS TO...
...WALK YUU HOME.
BETTER LUCK NEXT TIME.
THAT WAS SO MUCH FUN.
BUT I FEEL KIND OF BAD FOR TACHIBANA-KUN.
HOW AM I GONNA FACE TACHIBANA-KUN WHEN I SEE HIM AT SCHOOL TOMORROW?
HA, HA, HA, HA.
IT'S NOT FUNNY.
KNOCK
KNOCK
THAT MUST BE TSUKASA.

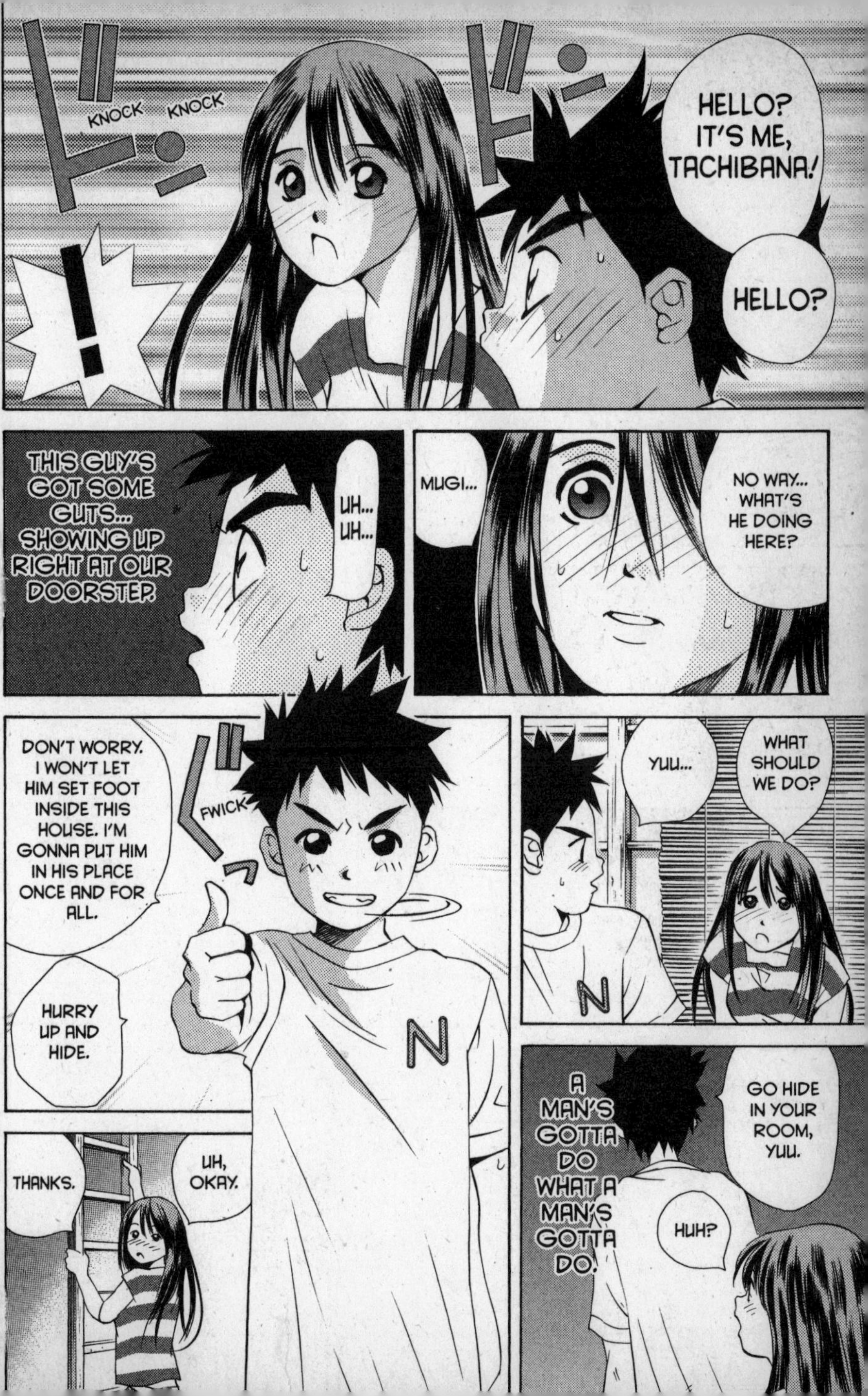
HELLO? IT'S ME, TACHIBANA!
HELLO?
KNOCK KNOCK
!
NO WAY... WHAT'S HE DOING HERE?
MUGI...
UH... UH...
THIS GUY'S GOT SOME GUTS... SHOWING UP RIGHT AT OUR DOORSTEP.
WHAT SHOULD WE DO?
YUU...
GO HIDE IN YOUR ROOM, YUU.
A MAN'S GOTTA DO WHAT A MAN'S GOTTA DO.
HUH?
DON'T WORRY. I WON'T LET HIM SET FOOT INSIDE THIS HOUSE. I'M GONNA PUT HIM IN HIS PLACE ONCE AND FOR ALL.
FWICK
HURRY UP AND HIDE.
UH, OKAY.
THANKS.

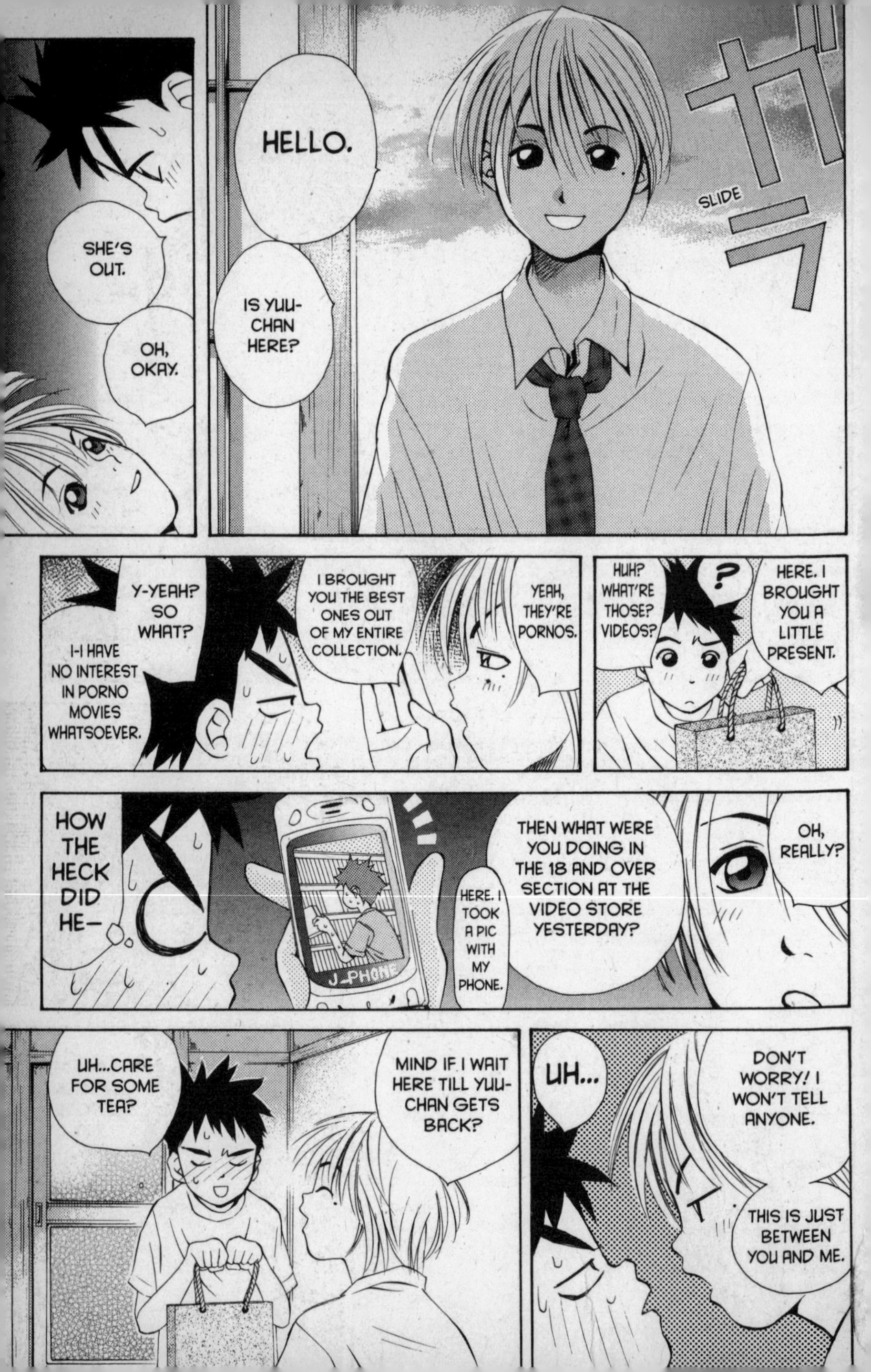
ガラ
SLIDE
HELLO.
IS YUU-CHAN HERE?
SHE'S OUT.
OH, OKAY.
HERE. I BROUGHT YOU A LITTLE PRESENT.
?
HUH? WHAT'RE THOSE? VIDEOS?
YEAH, THEY'RE PORNOS.
I BROUGHT YOU THE BEST ONES OUT OF MY ENTIRE COLLECTION.
Y-YEAH? SO WHAT?
I-I HAVE NO INTEREST IN PORNO MOVIES WHATSOEVER.
OH, REALLY?
THEN WHAT WERE YOU DOING IN THE 18 AND OVER SECTION AT THE VIDEO STORE YESTERDAY?
HERE. I TOOK A PIC WITH MY PHONE.
J-PHONE
HOW THE HECK DID HE—
DON'T WORRY! I WON'T TELL ANYONE.
THIS IS JUST BETWEEN YOU AND ME.
UH...
MIND IF I WAIT HERE TILL YUU-CHAN GETS BACK?
UH...CARE FOR SOME TEA?

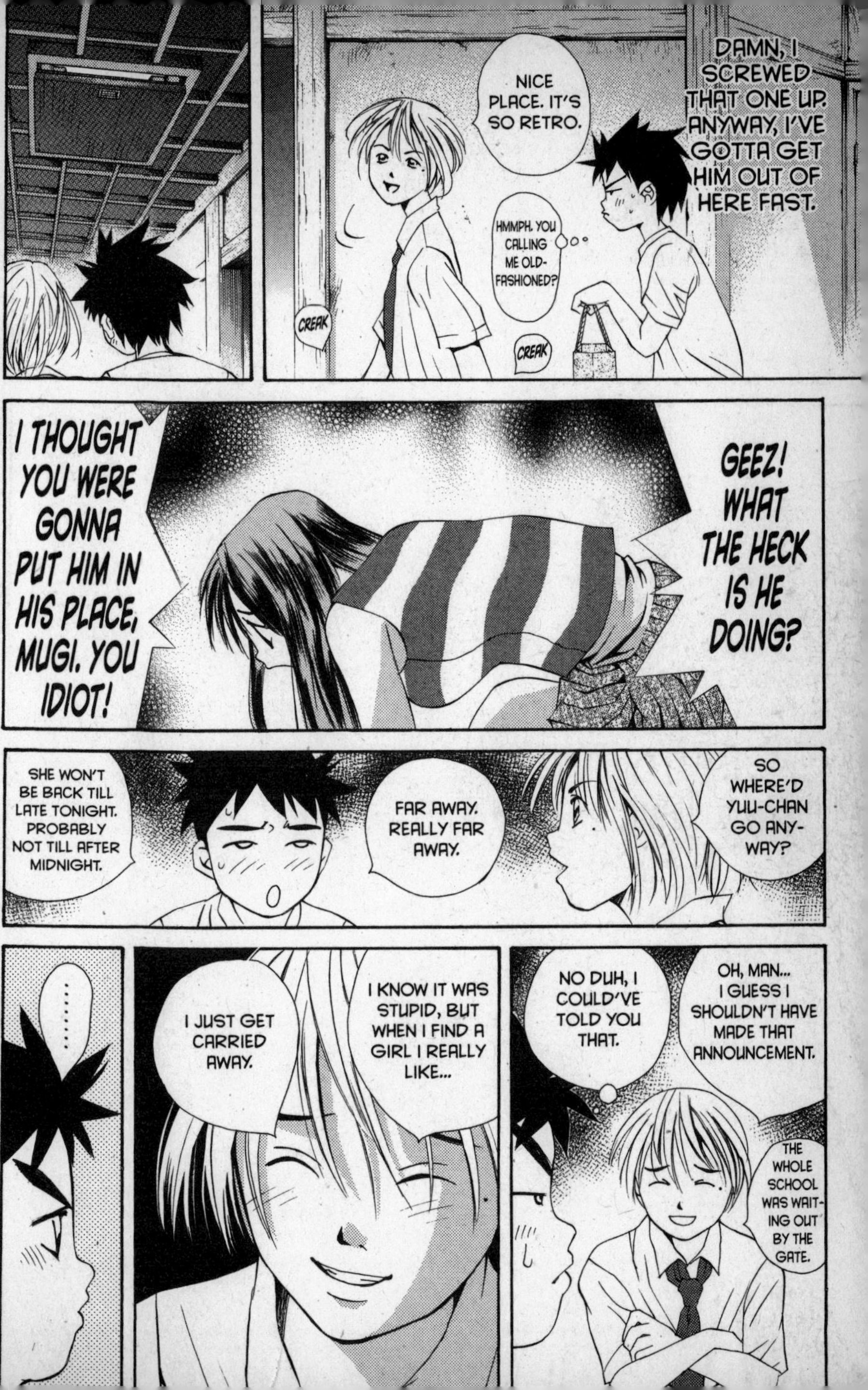
DAMN, I SCREWED THAT ONE UP. ANYWAY, I'VE GOTTA GET HIM OUT OF HERE FAST.
NICE PLACE. IT'S SO RETRO.
HMMPH. YOU CALLING ME OLD-FASHIONED?
CREAK
CREAK
GEEZ! WHAT THE HECK IS HE DOING?
I THOUGHT YOU WERE GONNA PUT HIM IN HIS PLACE, MUGI. YOU IDIOT!
SO WHERE'D YUU-CHAN GO ANY-WAY?
FAR AWAY. REALLY FAR AWAY.
SHE WON'T BE BACK TILL LATE TONIGHT. PROBABLY NOT TILL AFTER MIDNIGHT.
OH, MAN... I GUESS I SHOULDN'T HAVE MADE THAT ANNOUNCEMENT.
NO DUH, I COULD'VE TOLD YOU THAT.
THE WHOLE SCHOOL WAS WAIT-ING OUT BY THE GATE.
I KNOW IT WAS STUPID, BUT WHEN I FIND A GIRL I REALLY LIKE...
I JUST GET CARRIED AWAY.
....

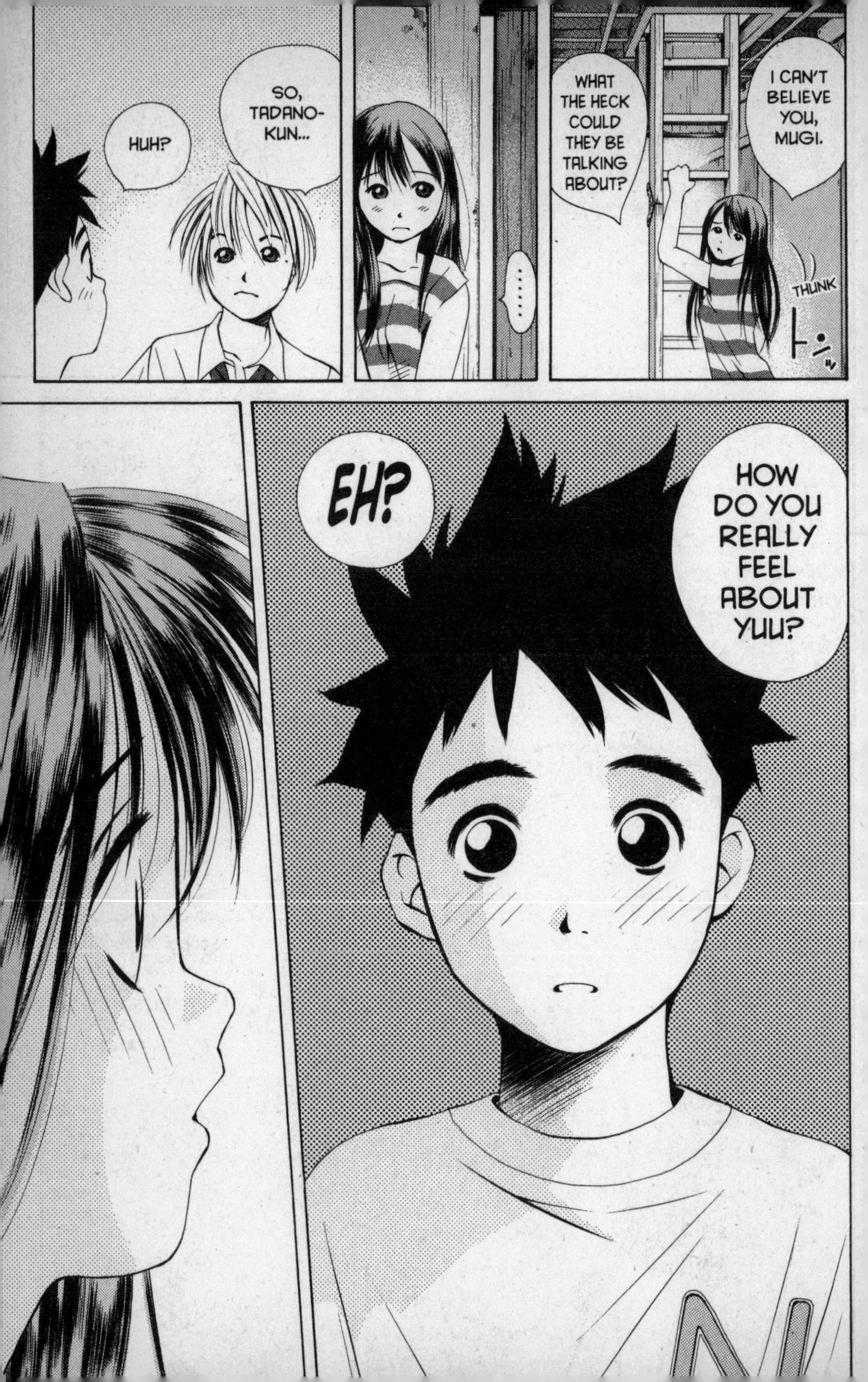
I CAN'T BELIEVE YOU, MUGI.
WHAT THE HECK COULD THEY BE TALKING ABOUT?
THUNK
......
SO, TADANO-KUN...
HUH?
HOW DO YOU REALLY FEEL ABOUT YUU?
EH?

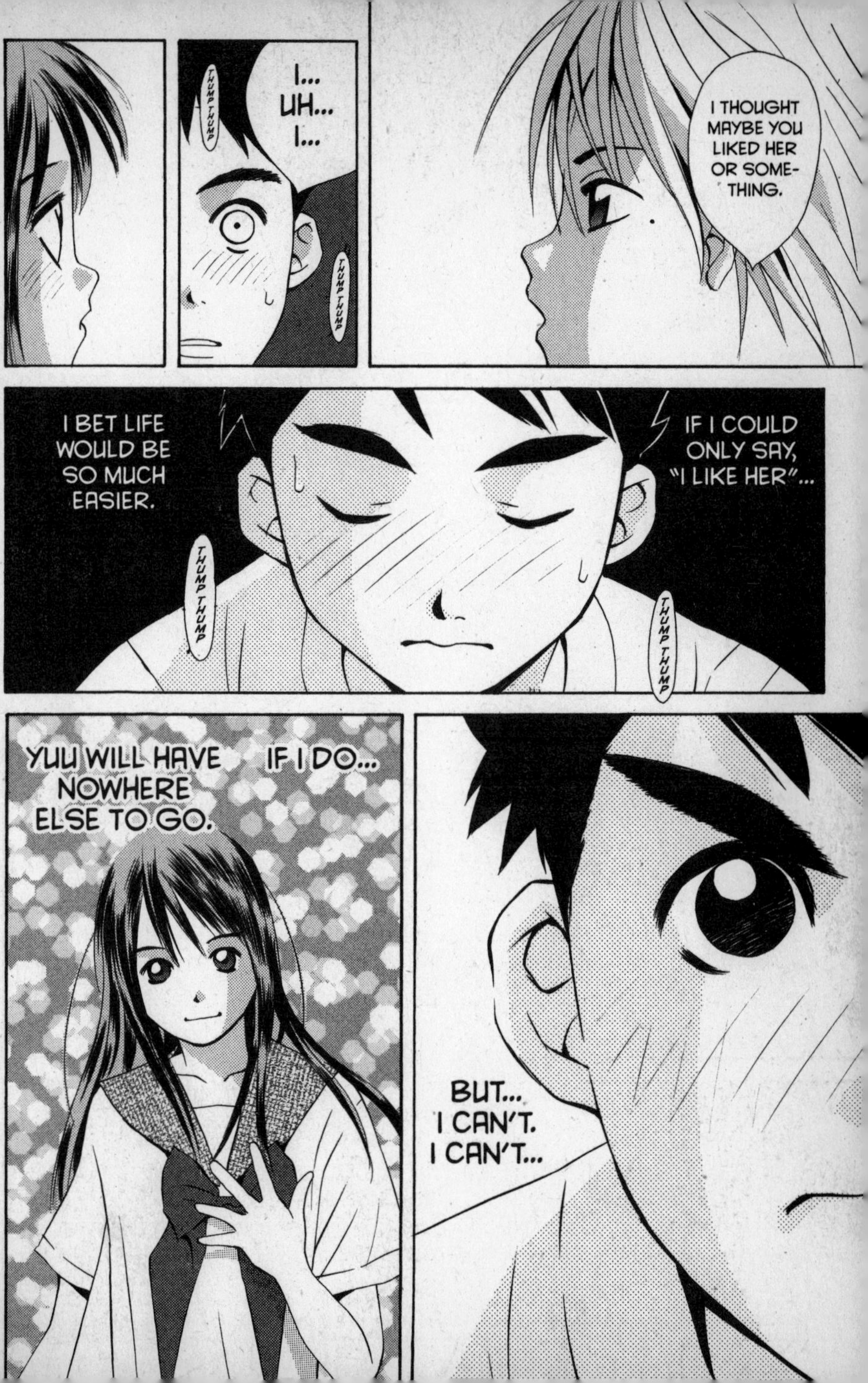
I THOUGHT MAYBE YOU LIKED HER OR SOME-THING.
I... UH... I...
THUMP THUMP
THUMP THUMP
IF I COULD ONLY SAY, "I LIKE HER"...
THUMP THUMP
I BET LIFE WOULD BE SO MUCH EASIER.
THUMP THUMP
BUT... I CAN'T. I CAN'T...
IF I DO...
YUU WILL HAVE NOWHERE ELSE TO GO.

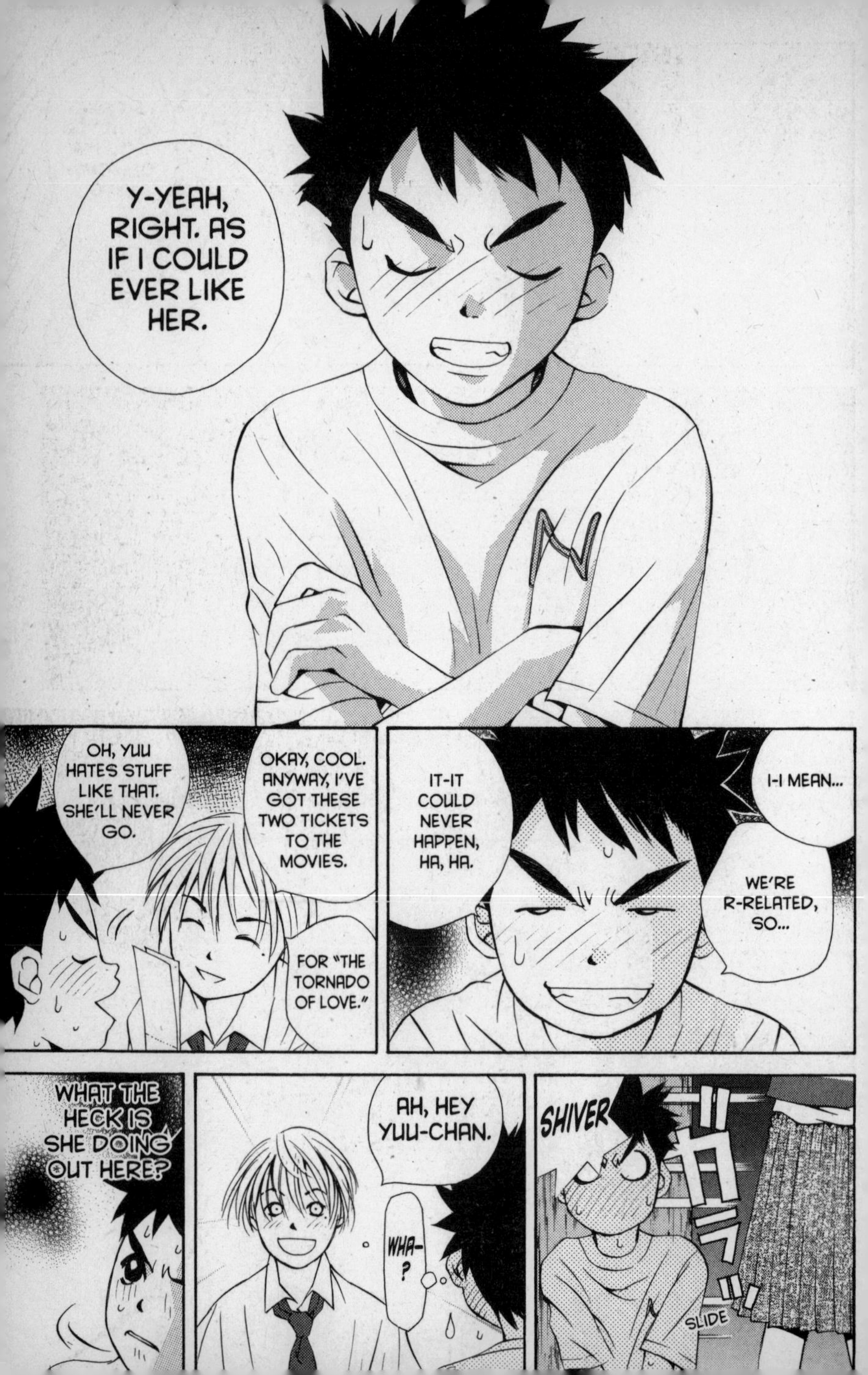
Y-YEAH, RIGHT. AS IF I COULD EVER LIKE HER.
I-I MEAN...
IT-IT COULD NEVER HAPPEN, HA, HA.
WE'RE R-RELATED, SO...
OKAY, COOL. ANYWAY, I'VE GOT THESE TWO TICKETS TO THE MOVIES.
FOR "THE TORNADO OF LOVE."
OH, YUU HATES STUFF LIKE THAT. SHE'LL NEVER GO.
SHIVER
ガラッ
SLIDE
AH, HEY YUU-CHAN.
WHA-?
WHAT THE HECK IS SHE DOING OUT HERE?

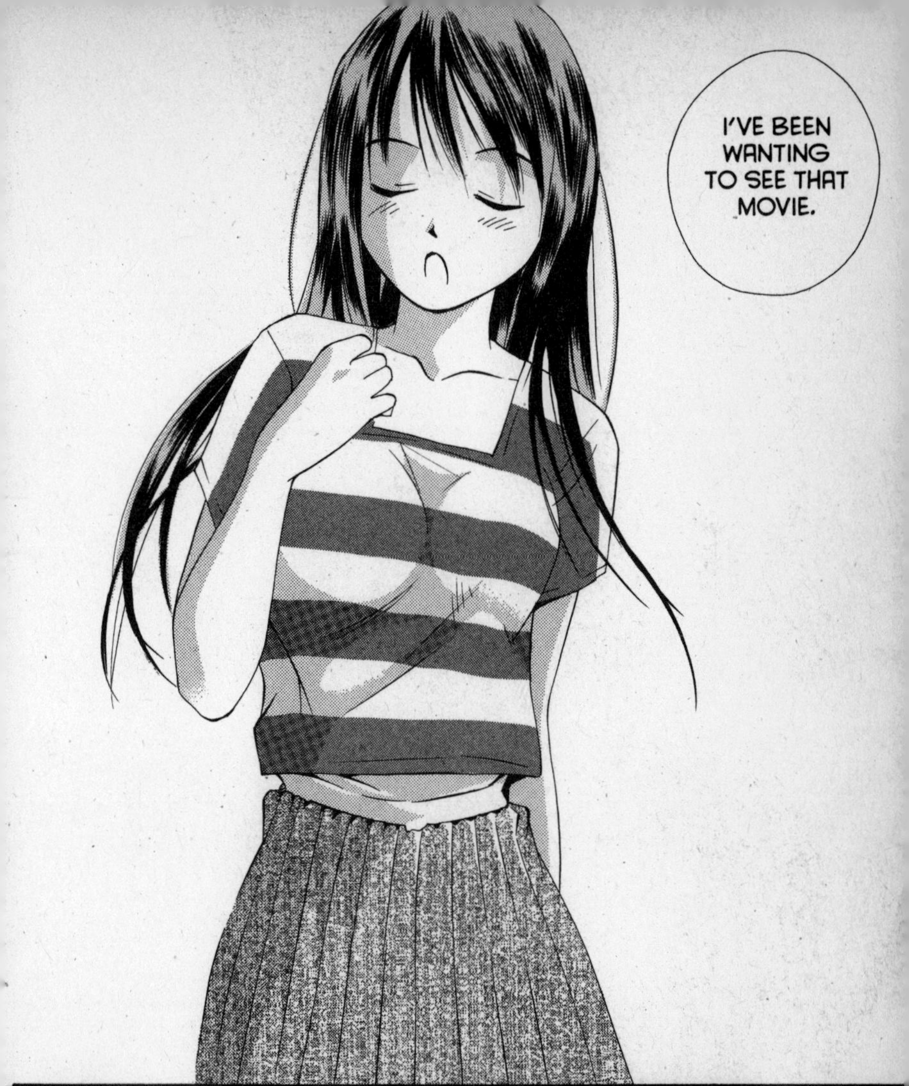
I'VE BEEN WANTING TO SEE THAT MOVIE.

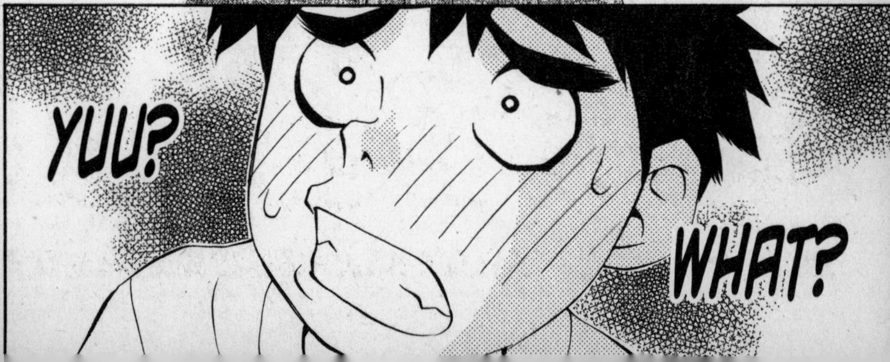
WHAT?
YUU?

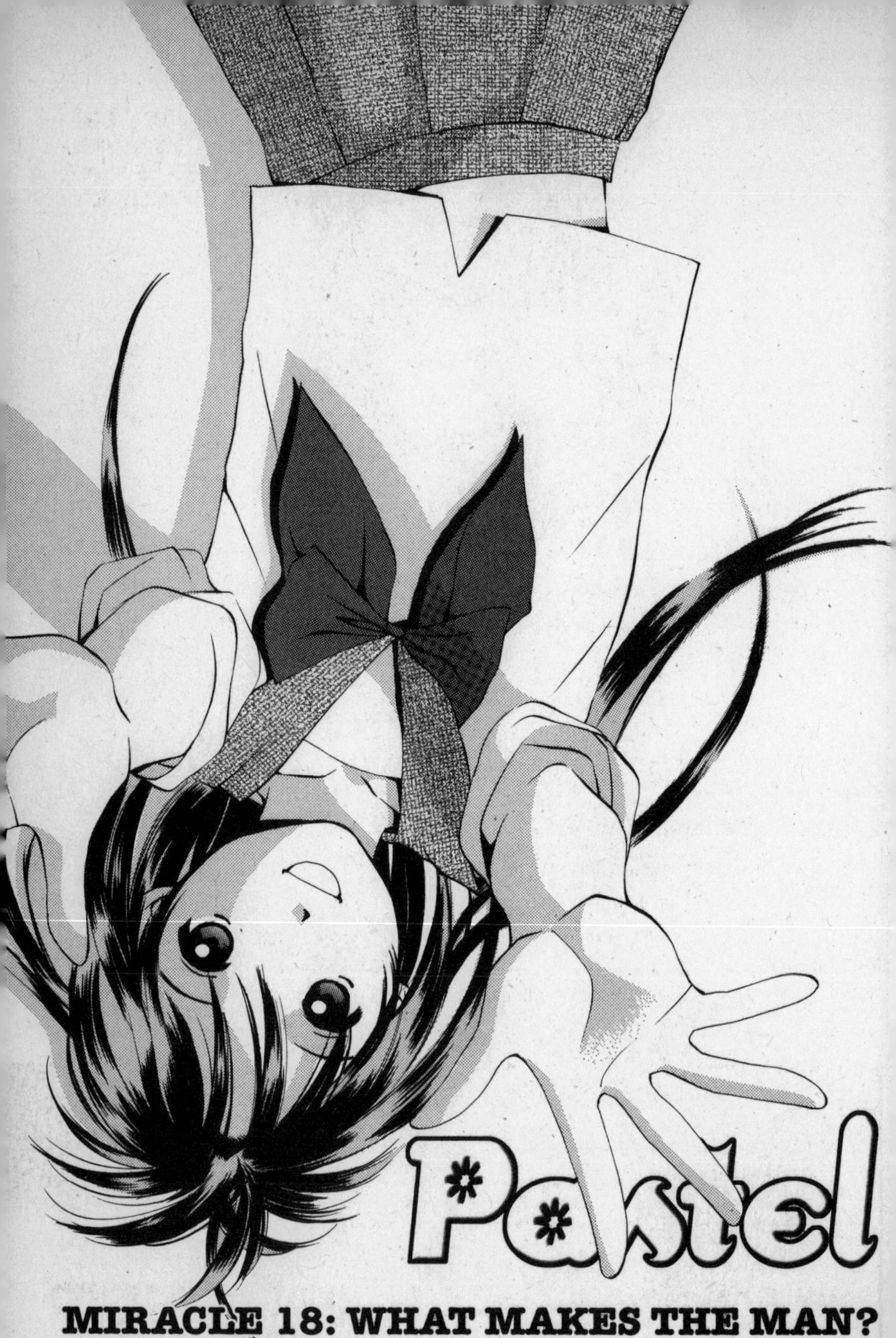
Pastel

MIRACLE 18: WHAT MAKES THE MAN?

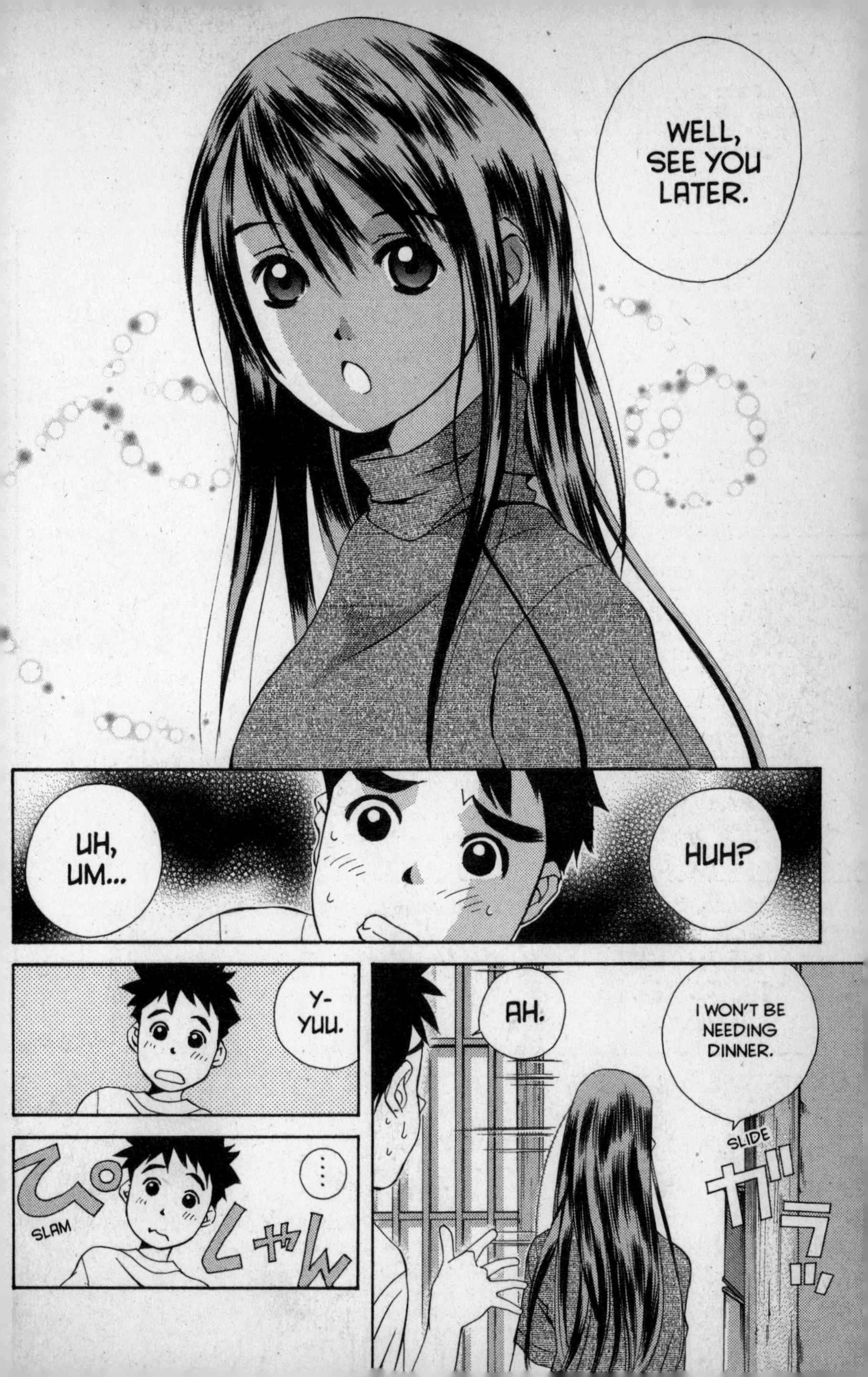
WELL, SEE YOU LATER.
HUH?
UH, UM...
I WON'T BE NEEDING DINNER.
AH.
SLIDE
ガラッ
Y-YUU.
...
ぴしゃん
SLAM

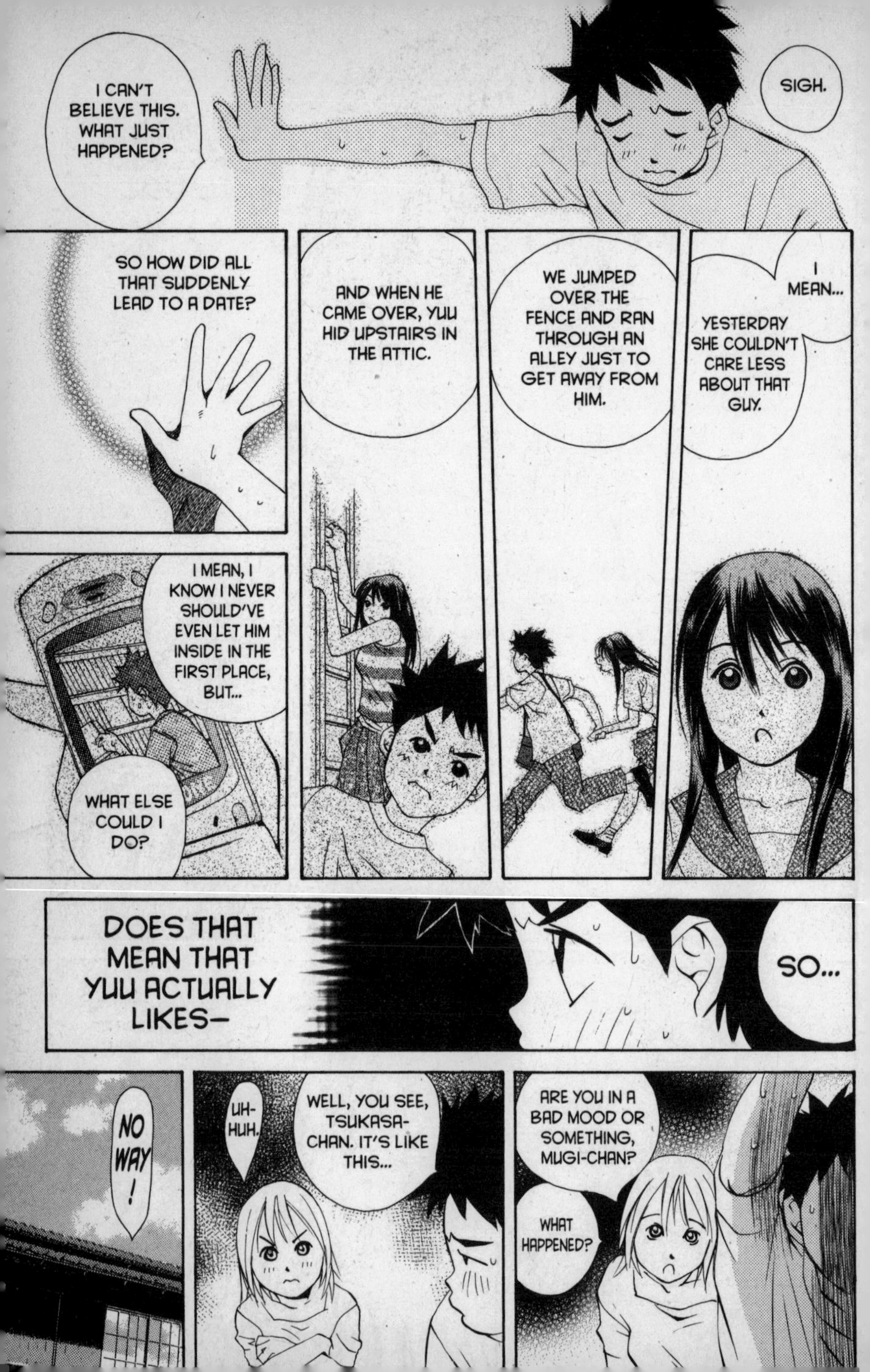
SIGH.
I CAN'T BELIEVE THIS. WHAT JUST HAPPENED?
I MEAN...
YESTERDAY SHE COULDN'T CARE LESS ABOUT THAT GUY.
WE JUMPED OVER THE FENCE AND RAN THROUGH AN ALLEY JUST TO GET AWAY FROM HIM.
AND WHEN HE CAME OVER, YUU HID UPSTAIRS IN THE ATTIC.
SO HOW DID ALL THAT SUDDENLY LEAD TO A DATE?
I MEAN, I KNOW I NEVER SHOULD'VE EVEN LET HIM INSIDE IN THE FIRST PLACE, BUT...
WHAT ELSE COULD I DO?
SO...
DOES THAT MEAN THAT YUU ACTUALLY LIKES—
ARE YOU IN A BAD MOOD OR SOMETHING, MUGI-CHAN?
WHAT HAPPENED?
WELL, YOU SEE, TSUKASA-CHAN. IT'S LIKE THIS...
UH-HUH.
NO WAY!

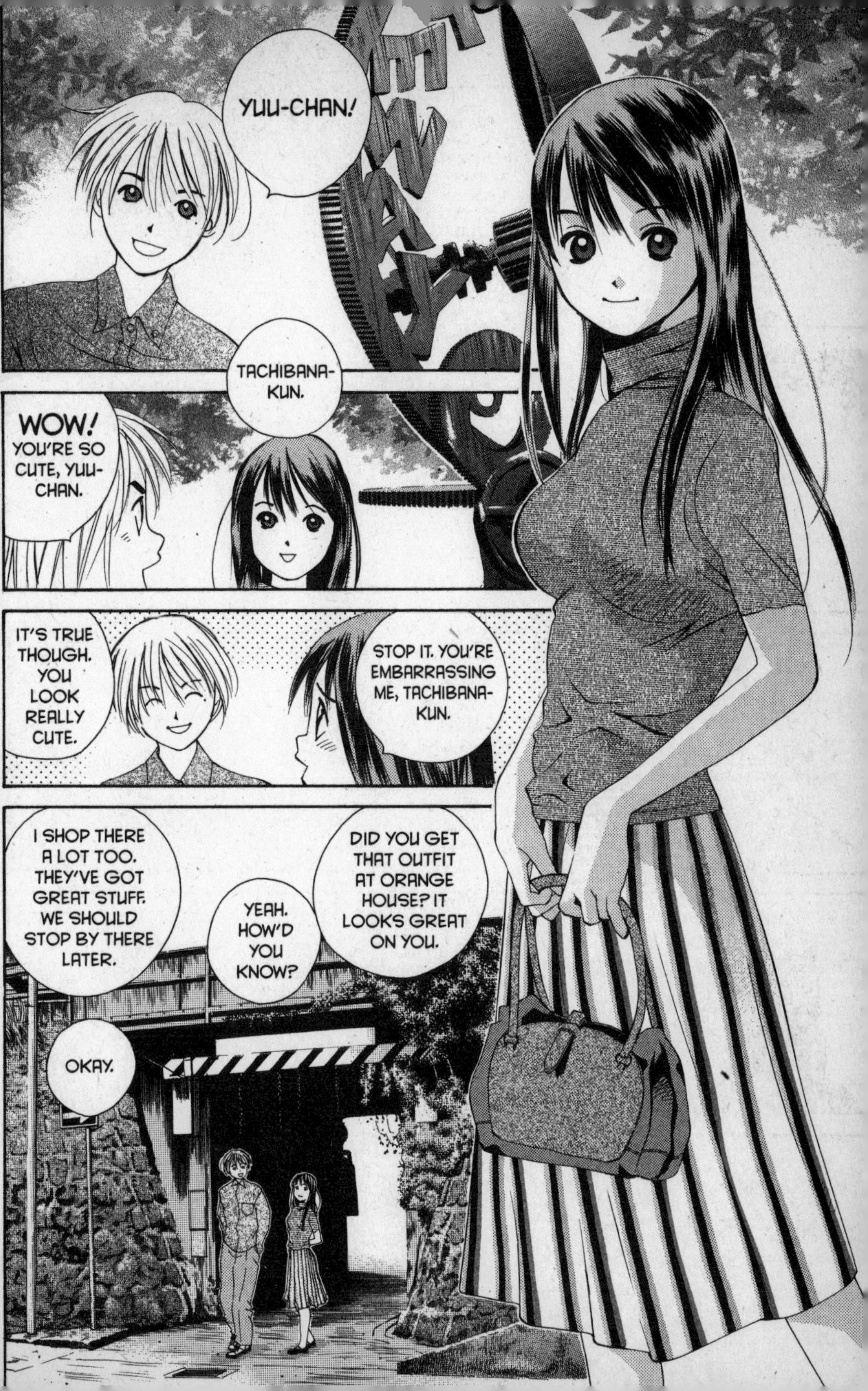
YUU-CHAN!
TACHIBANA-KUN.
WOW! YOU'RE SO CUTE, YUU-CHAN.
STOP IT. YOU'RE EMBARRASSING ME, TACHIBANA-KUN.
IT'S TRUE THOUGH. YOU LOOK REALLY CUTE.
DID YOU GET THAT OUTFIT AT ORANGE HOUSE? IT LOOKS GREAT ON YOU.
YEAH. HOW'D YOU KNOW?
I SHOP THERE A LOT TOO. THEY'VE GOT GREAT STUFF. WE SHOULD STOP BY THERE LATER.
OKAY.

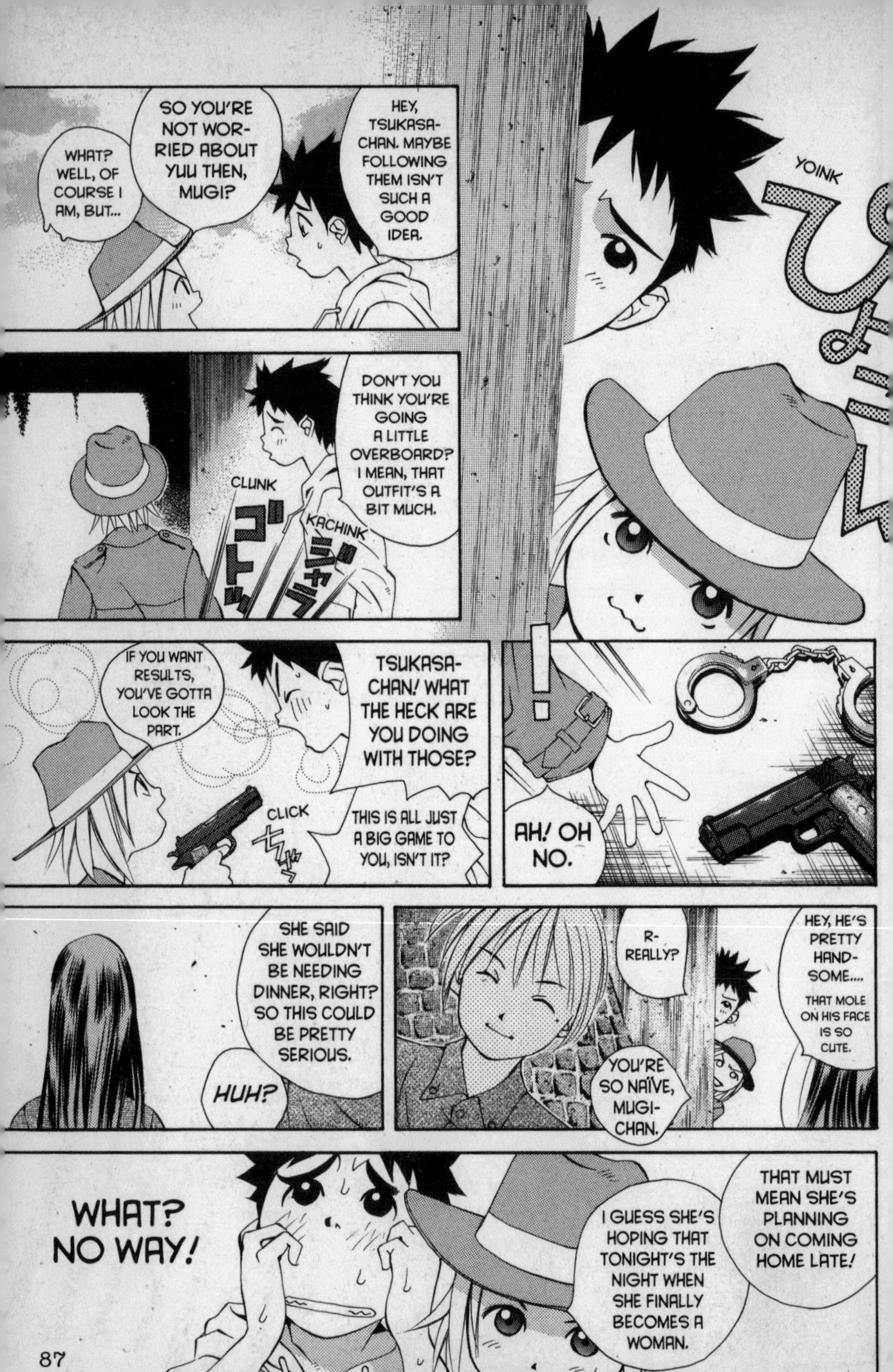
YOINK
HEY, TSUKASA-CHAN. MAYBE FOLLOWING THEM ISN'T SUCH A GOOD IDEA.
SO YOU'RE NOT WOR-RIED ABOUT YUU THEN, MUGI?
WHAT? WELL, OF COURSE I AM, BUT...
DON'T YOU THINK YOU'RE GOING A LITTLE OVERBOARD? I MEAN, THAT OUTFIT'S A BIT MUCH.
KACHINK
CLUNK
AH! OH NO.
TSUKASA-CHAN! WHAT THE HECK ARE YOU DOING WITH THOSE?
THIS IS ALL JUST A BIG GAME TO YOU, ISN'T IT?
IF YOU WANT RESULTS, YOU'VE GOTTA LOOK THE PART.
CLICK
HEY, HE'S PRETTY HAND-SOME....
THAT MOLE ON HIS FACE IS SO CUTE.
R-REALLY?
YOU'RE SO NAÏVE, MUGI-CHAN.
SHE SAID SHE WOULDN'T BE NEEDING DINNER, RIGHT? SO THIS COULD BE PRETTY SERIOUS.
HUH?
THAT MUST MEAN SHE'S PLANNING ON COMING HOME LATE!
I GUESS SHE'S HOPING THAT TONIGHT'S THE NIGHT WHEN SHE FINALLY BECOMES A WOMAN.
WHAT? NO WAY!

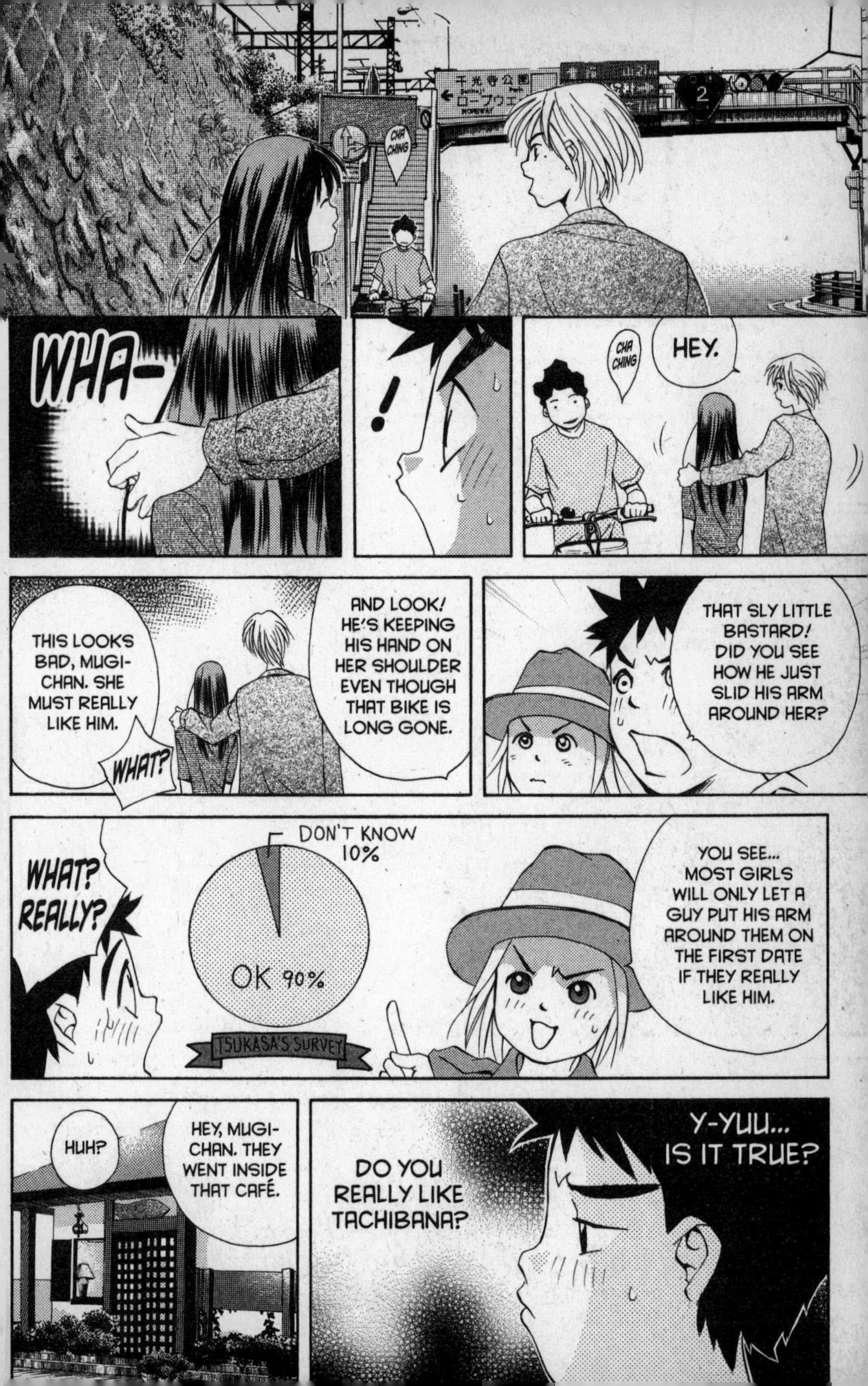
CHA CHING
CHA CHING
HEY.
!
WHA-
THAT SLY LITTLE BASTARD! DID YOU SEE HOW HE JUST SLID HIS ARM AROUND HER?
AND LOOK! HE'S KEEPING HIS HAND ON HER SHOULDER EVEN THOUGH THAT BIKE IS LONG GONE.
THIS LOOKS BAD, MUGI-CHAN. SHE MUST REALLY LIKE HIM.
WHAT?
YOU SEE... MOST GIRLS WILL ONLY LET A GUY PUT HIS ARM AROUND THEM ON THE FIRST DATE IF THEY REALLY LIKE HIM.
DON'T KNOW 10%
OK 90%
TSUKASA'S SURVEY
WHAT? REALLY?
Y-YUU... IS IT TRUE?
DO YOU REALLY LIKE TACHIBANA?
HEY, MUGI-CHAN. THEY WENT INSIDE THAT CAFÉ.
HUH?

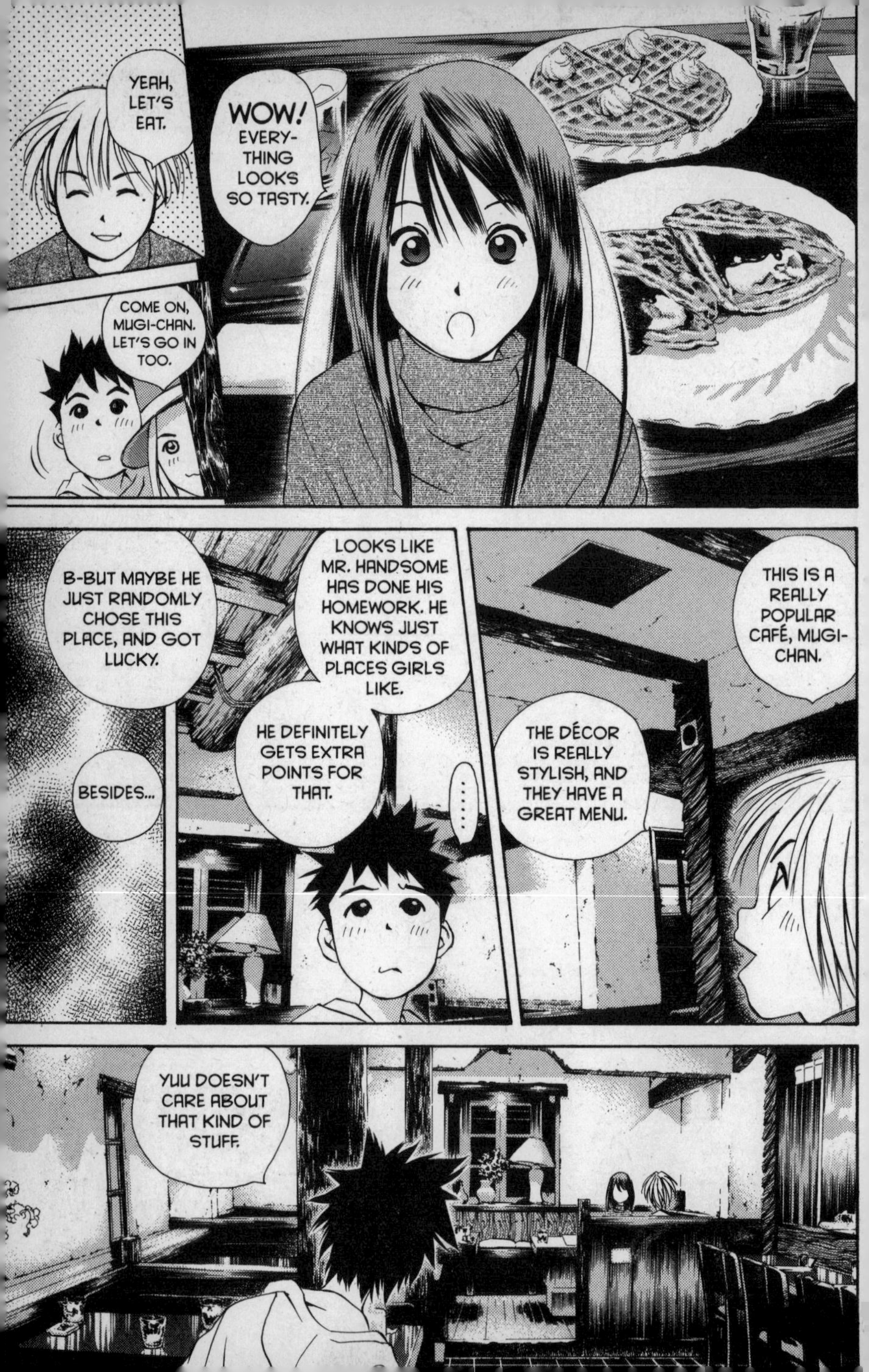

WOW! EVERYTHING LOOKS SO TASTY.
YEAH, LET'S EAT.
COME ON, MUGI-CHAN. LET'S GO IN TOO.
THIS IS A REALLY POPULAR CAFÉ, MUGI-CHAN.
THE DÉCOR IS REALLY STYLISH, AND THEY HAVE A GREAT MENU.
......
LOOKS LIKE MR. HANDSOME HAS DONE HIS HOMEWORK. HE KNOWS JUST WHAT KINDS OF PLACES GIRLS LIKE.
HE DEFINITELY GETS EXTRA POINTS FOR THAT.
B-BUT MAYBE HE JUST RANDOMLY CHOSE THIS PLACE, AND GOT LUCKY.
BESIDES...
YUU DOESN'T CARE ABOUT THAT KIND OF STUFF.

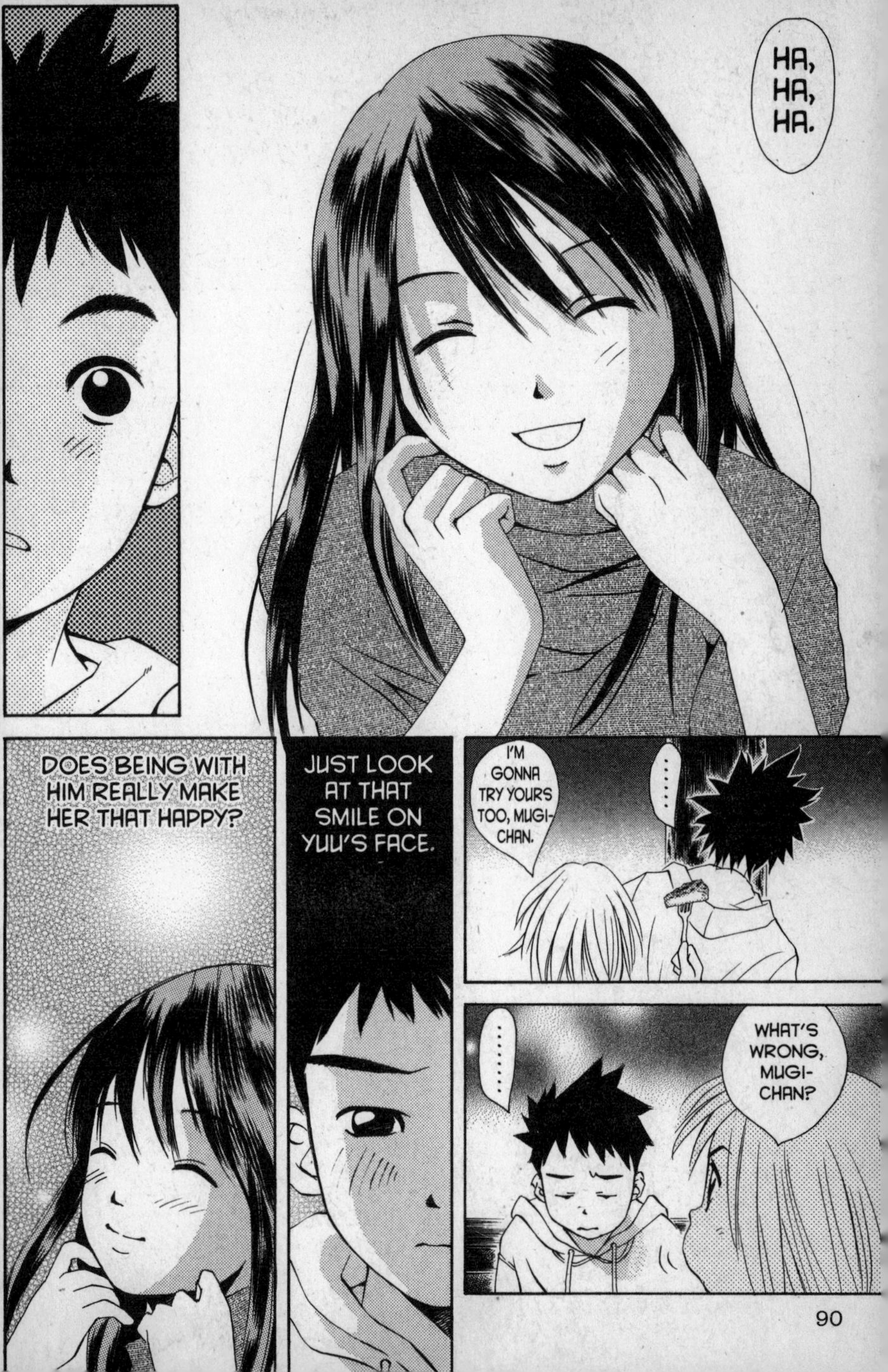
HA, HA, HA.
......
I'M GONNA TRY YOURS TOO, MUGI-CHAN.
WHAT'S WRONG, MUGI-CHAN?
......
JUST LOOK AT THAT SMILE ON YUU'S FACE.
DOES BEING WITH HIM REALLY MAKE HER THAT HAPPY?

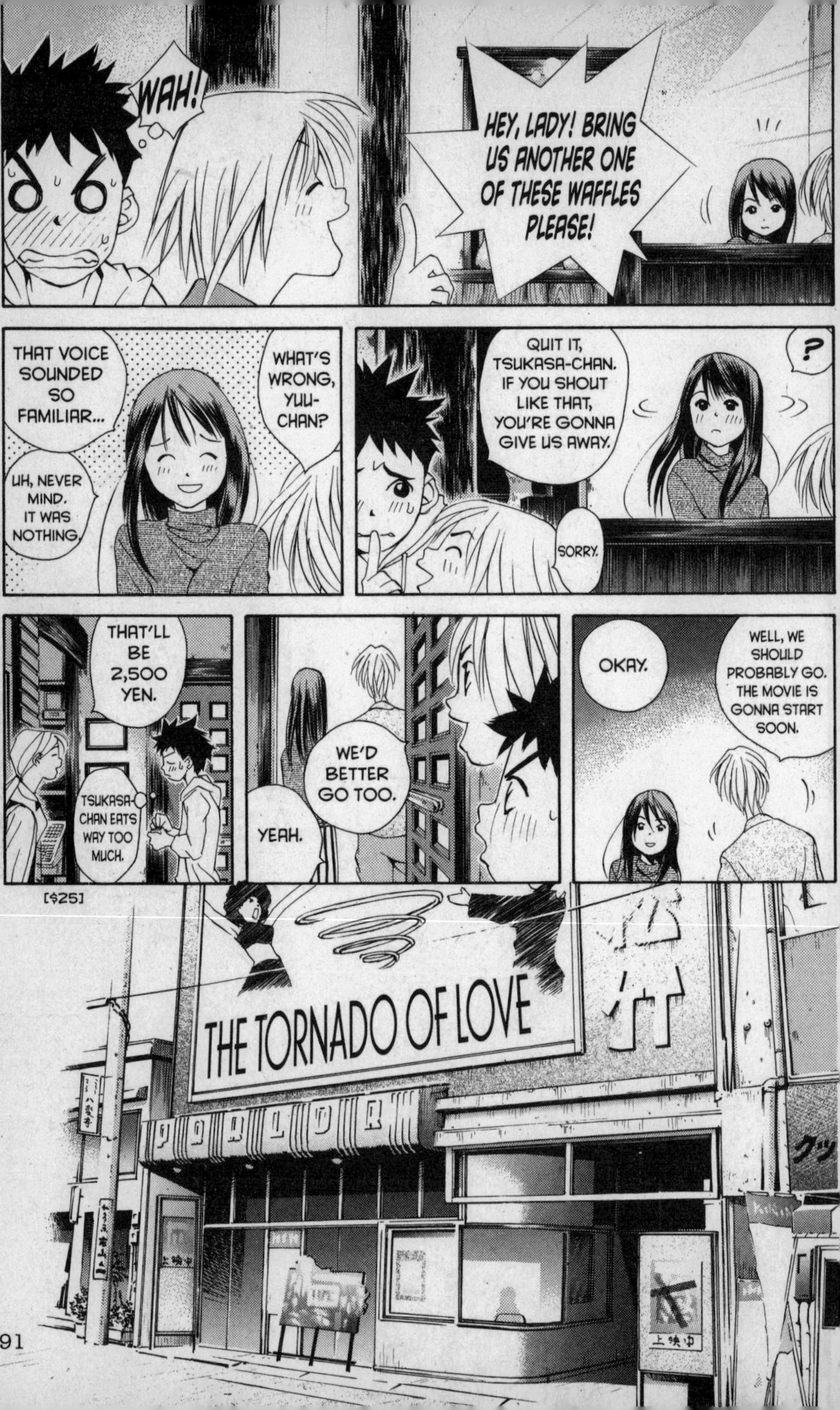
HEY, LADY! BRING US ANOTHER ONE OF THESE WAFFLES PLEASE!
WAH!
?
QUIT IT, TSUKASA-CHAN. IF YOU SHOUT LIKE THAT, YOU'RE GONNA GIVE US AWAY.
SORRY.
WHAT'S WRONG, YUU-CHAN?
THAT VOICE SOUNDED SO FAMILIAR...
UH, NEVER MIND. IT WAS NOTHING.
WELL, WE SHOULD PROBABLY GO. THE MOVIE IS GONNA START SOON.
OKAY.
WE'D BETTER GO TOO.
YEAH.
THAT'LL BE 2,500 YEN.
TSUKASA-CHAN EATS WAY TOO MUCH.
[$25]
THE TORNADO OF LOVE
上映中

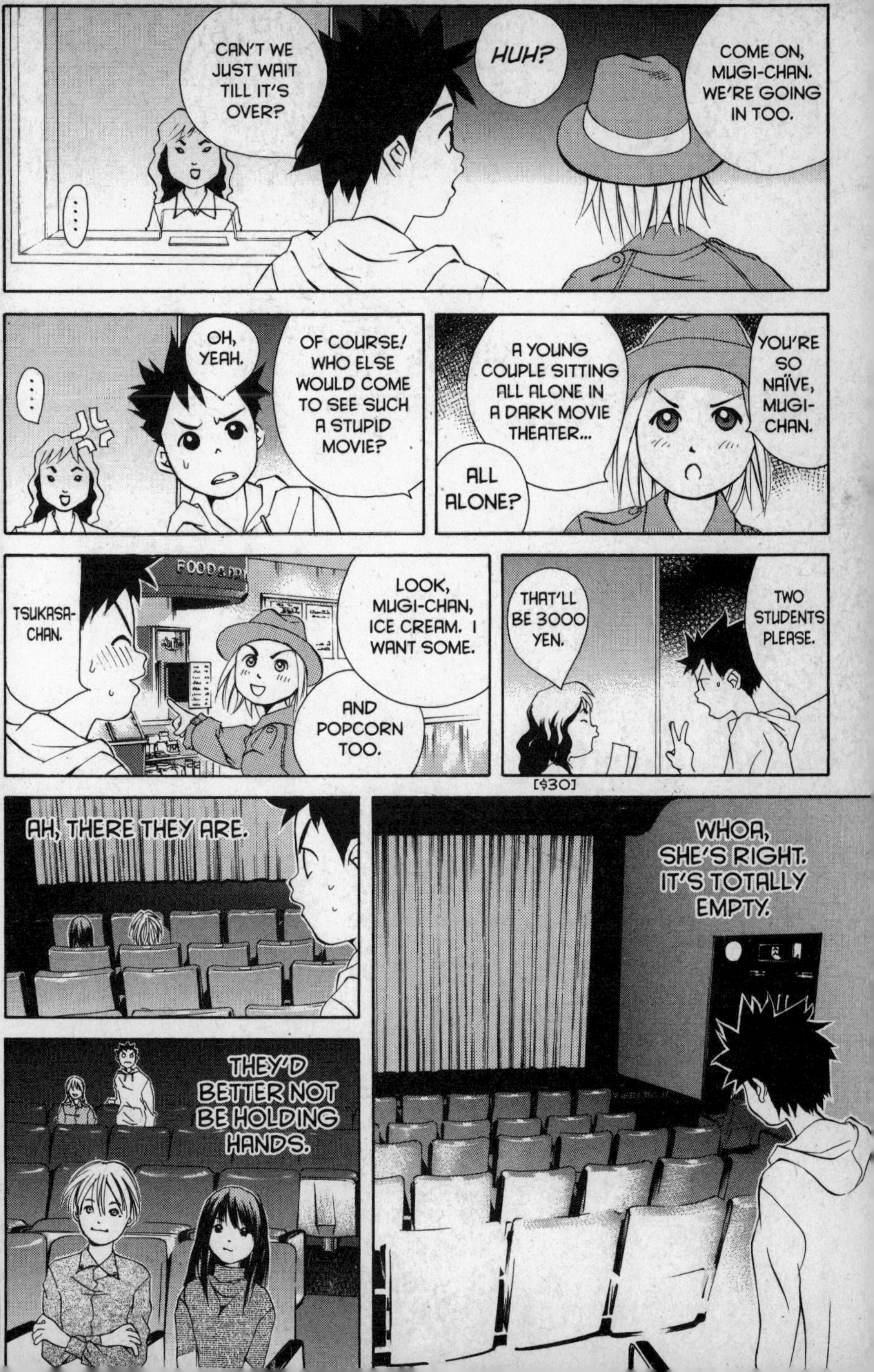
COME ON, MUGI-CHAN. WE'RE GOING IN TOO.
HUH?
CAN'T WE JUST WAIT TILL IT'S OVER?
.....
YOU'RE SO NAÏVE, MUGI-CHAN.
A YOUNG COUPLE SITTING ALL ALONE IN A DARK MOVIE THEATER...
ALL ALONE?
OF COURSE! WHO ELSE WOULD COME TO SEE SUCH A STUPID MOVIE?
OH, YEAH.
.....
TWO STUDENTS PLEASE.
THAT'LL BE 3000 YEN.
[$30]
LOOK, MUGI-CHAN, ICE CREAM. I WANT SOME.
AND POPCORN TOO.
TSUKASA-CHAN.
WHOA, SHE'S RIGHT. IT'S TOTALLY EMPTY.
AH, THERE THEY ARE.
THEY'D BETTER NOT BE HOLDING HANDS.

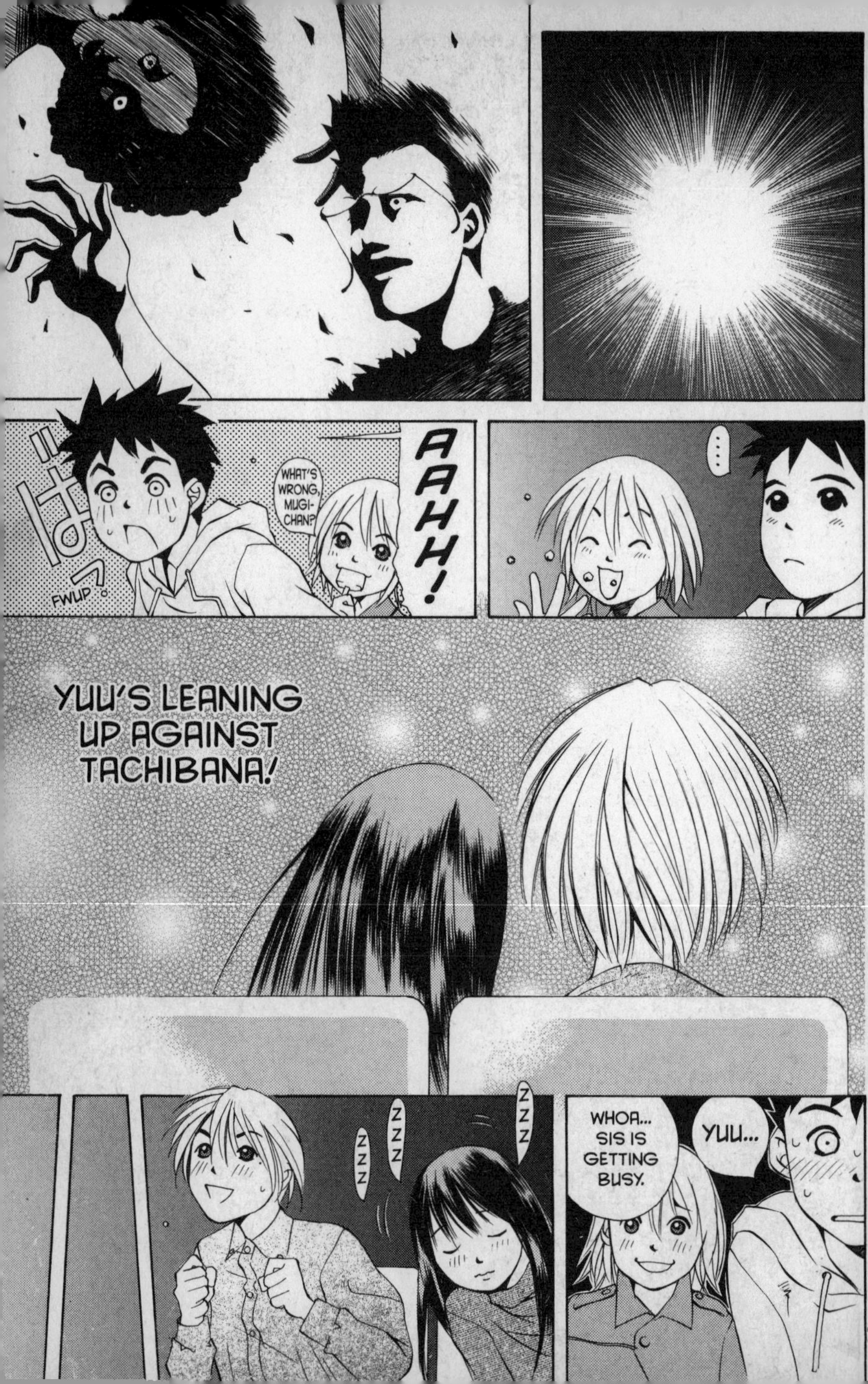
...
AAHH!
WHAT'S WRONG, MUGI-CHAN?
FWUP
YUU'S LEANING UP AGAINST TACHIBANA!
YUU...
WHOA... SIS IS GETTING BUSY.
ZZZ
ZZZ
ZZZ

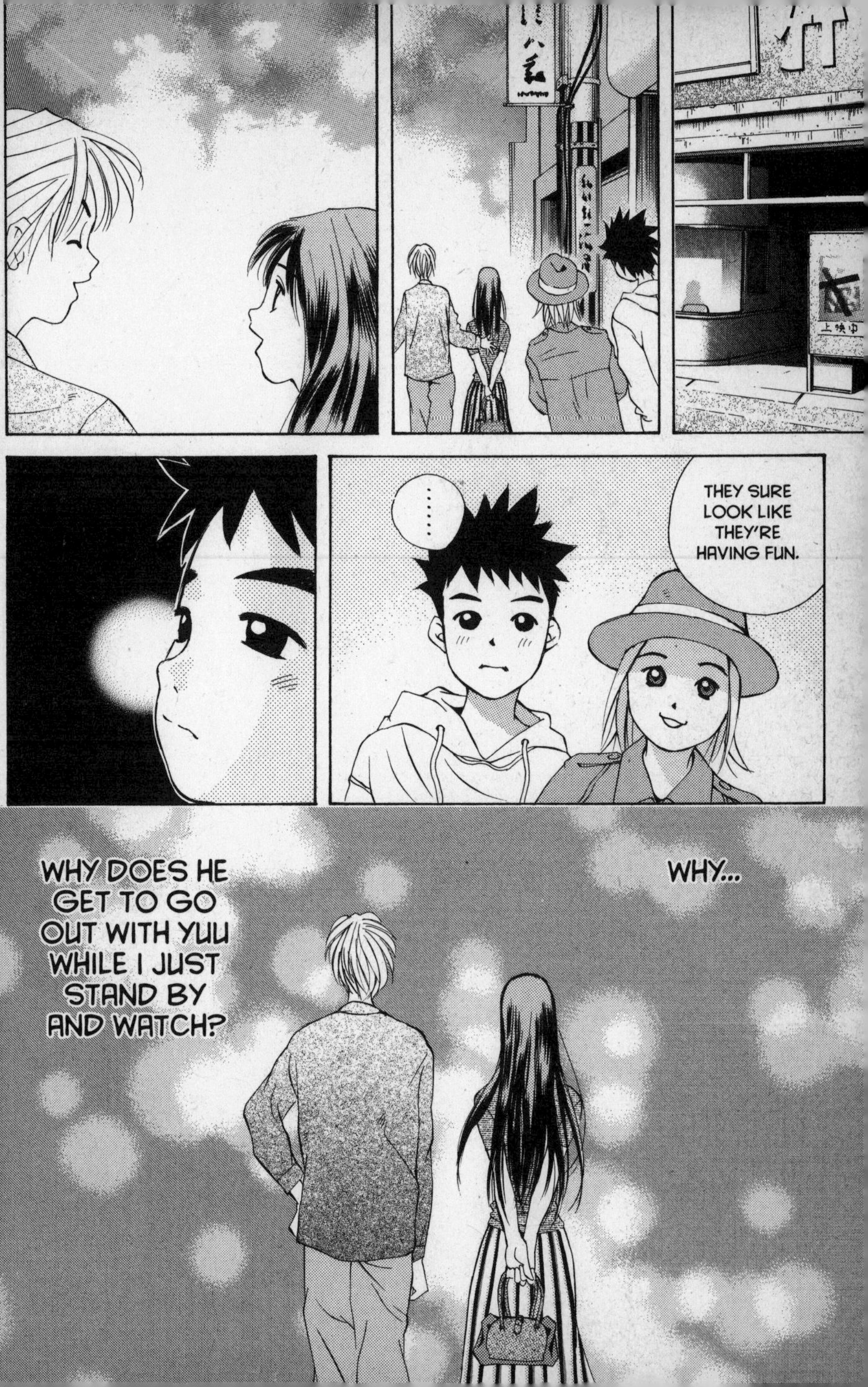
THEY SURE LOOK LIKE THEY'RE HAVING FUN.
......
WHY...
WHY DOES HE GET TO GO OUT WITH YUU WHILE I JUST STAND BY AND WATCH?

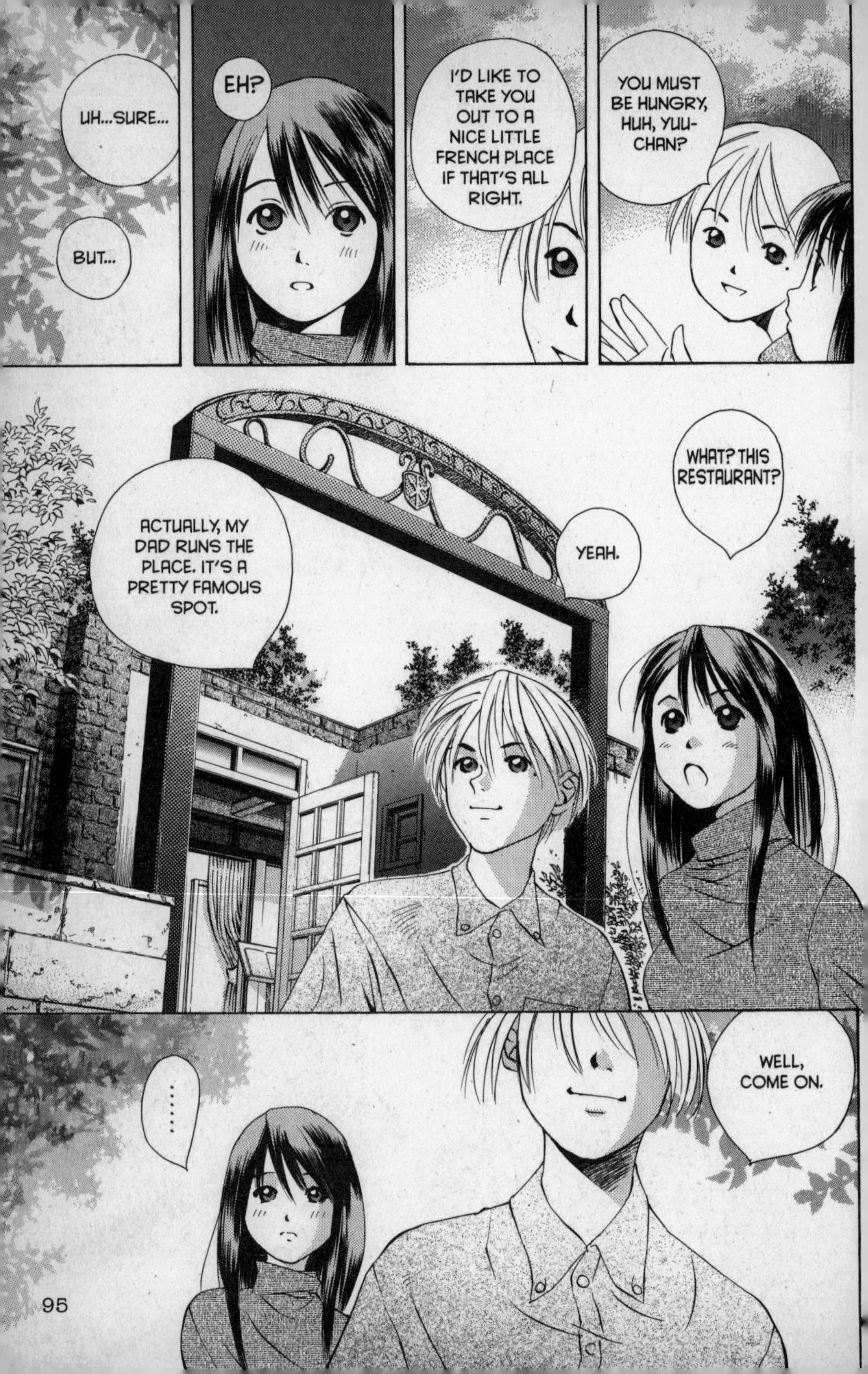
YOU MUST BE HUNGRY, HUH, YUU-CHAN?
I'D LIKE TO TAKE YOU OUT TO A NICE LITTLE FRENCH PLACE IF THAT'S ALL RIGHT.
EH?
UH...SURE...
BUT...
WHAT? THIS RESTAURANT?
YEAH.
ACTUALLY, MY DAD RUNS THE PLACE. IT'S A PRETTY FAMOUS SPOT.
WELL, COME ON.
......

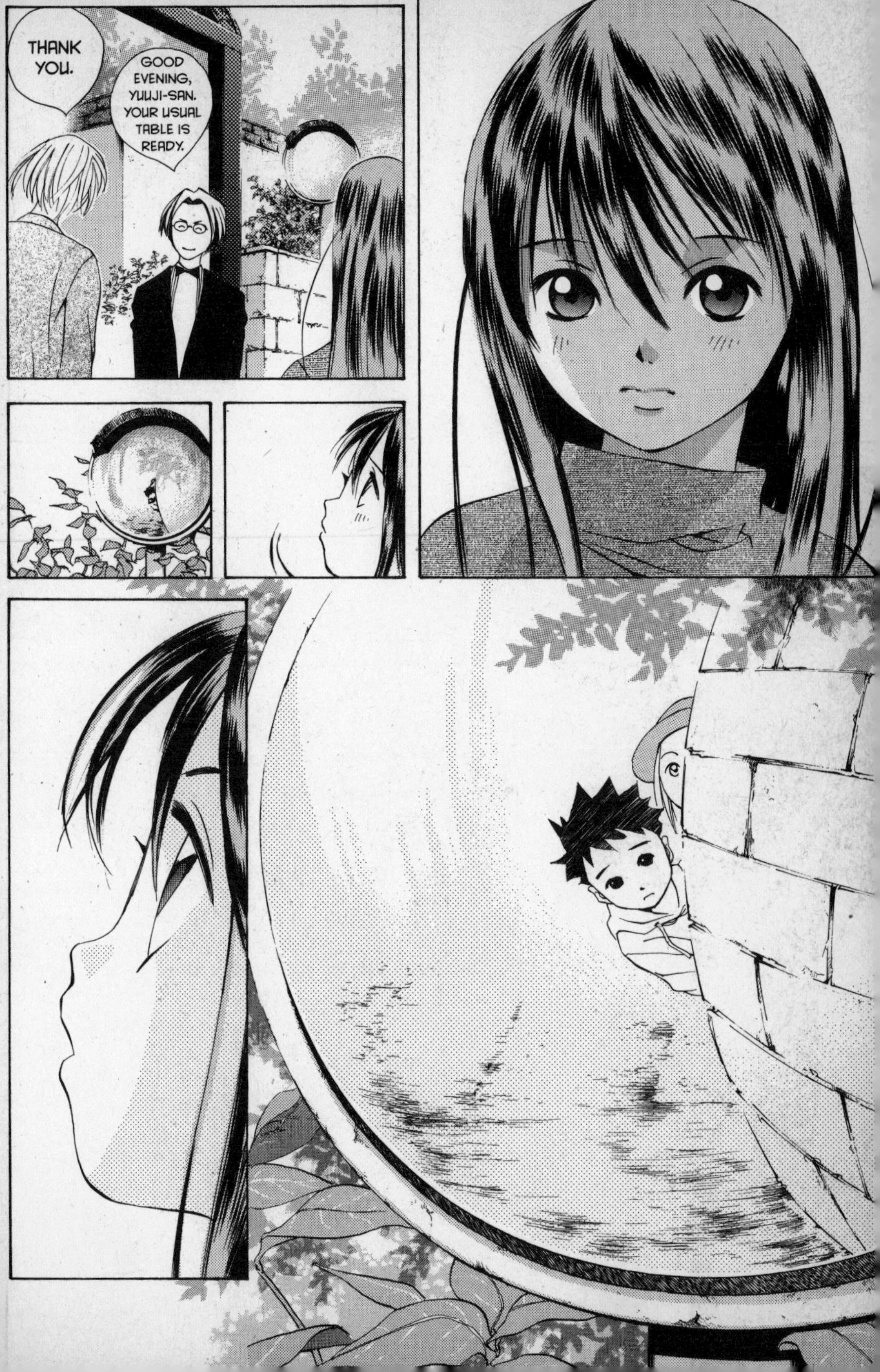
GOOD EVENING, YUUJI-SAN. YOUR USUAL TABLE IS READY.
THANK YOU.

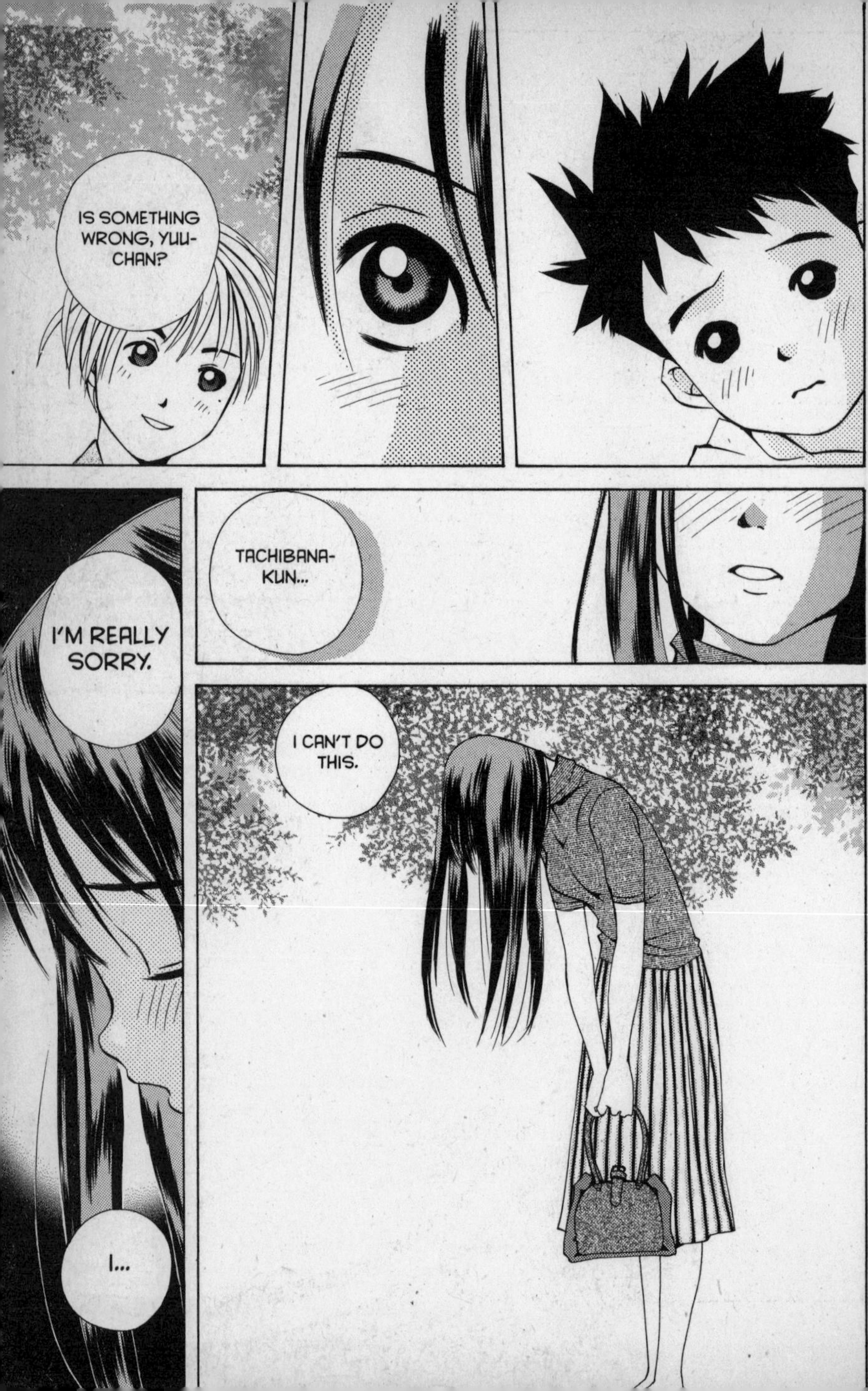
IS SOMETHING WRONG, YUU-CHAN?
TACHIBANA-KUN...
I CAN'T DO THIS.
I'M REALLY SORRY.
I...

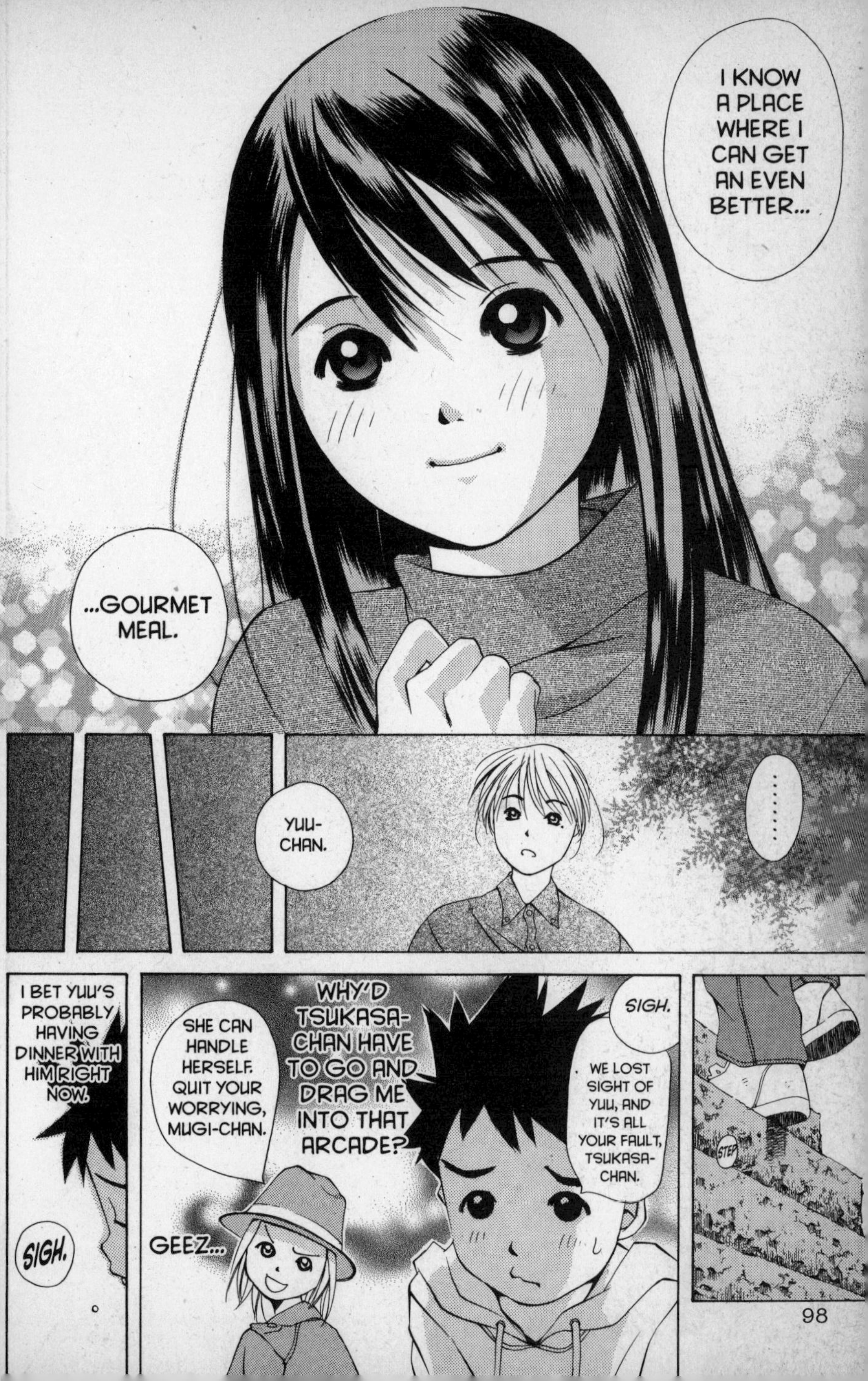
I KNOW A PLACE WHERE I CAN GET AN EVEN BETTER...
...GOURMET MEAL.
......
YUU-CHAN.
STEP
SIGH.
WE LOST SIGHT OF YUU, AND IT'S ALL YOUR FAULT, TSUKASA-CHAN.
WHY'D TSUKASA-CHAN HAVE TO GO AND DRAG ME INTO THAT ARCADE?
SHE CAN HANDLE HERSELF. QUIT YOUR WORRYING, MUGI-CHAN.
GEEZ...
I BET YUU'S PROBABLY HAVING DINNER WITH HIM RIGHT NOW.
SIGH.

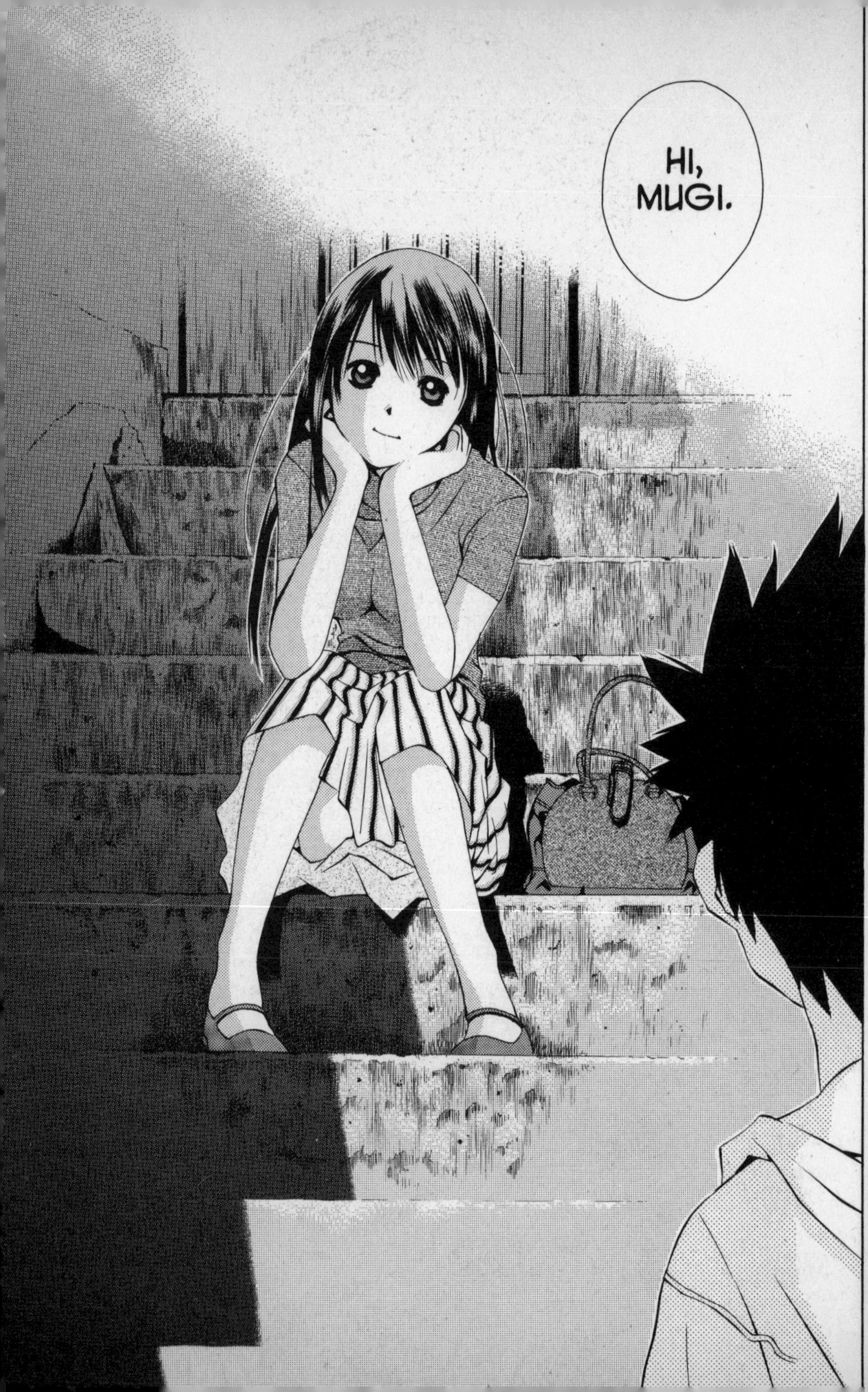
HI, MUGI.

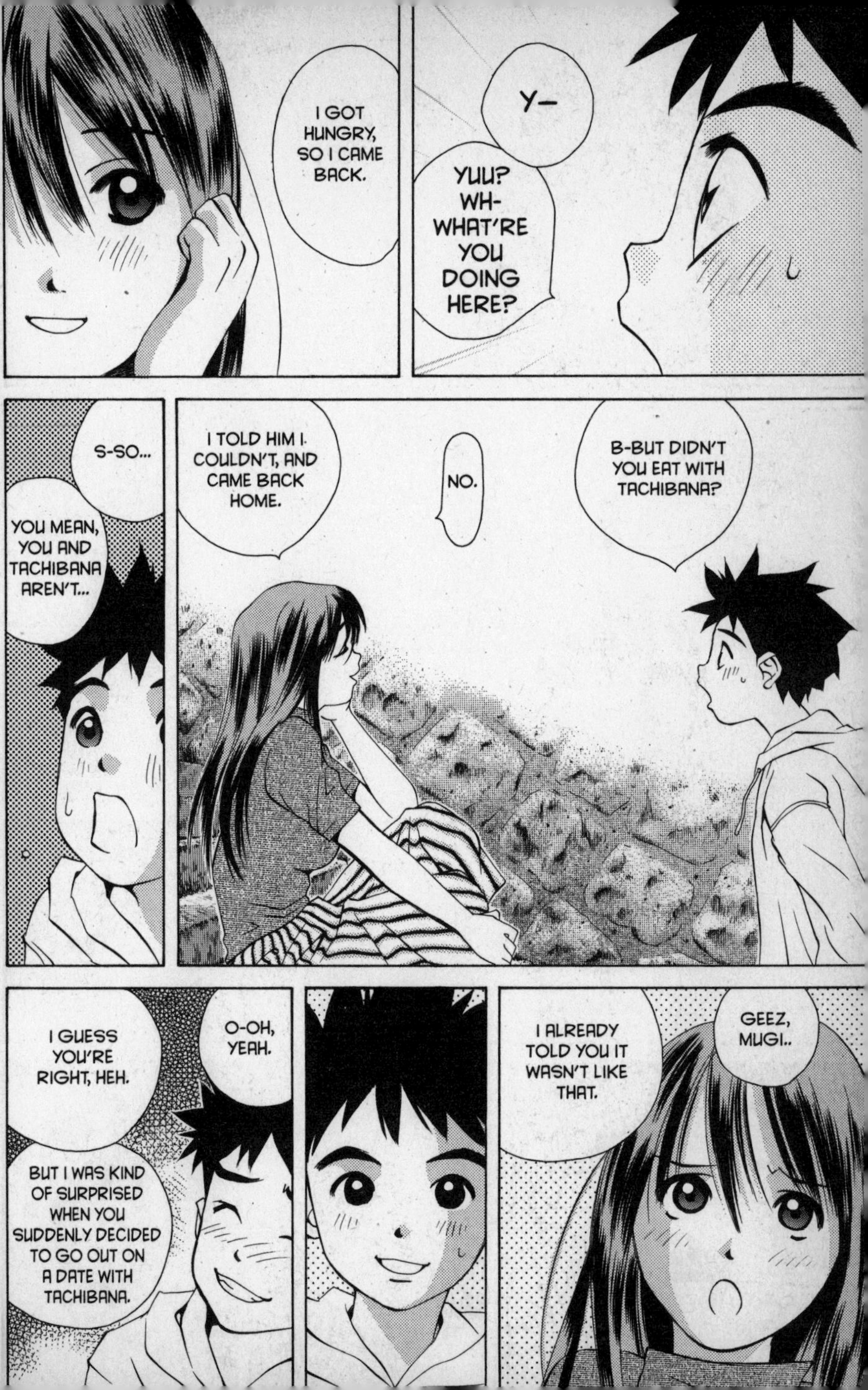
Y—
YUU? WH-WHAT'RE YOU DOING HERE?
I GOT HUNGRY, SO I CAME BACK.
B-BUT DIDN'T YOU EAT WITH TACHIBANA?
NO.
I TOLD HIM I COULDN'T, AND CAME BACK HOME.
S-SO...
YOU MEAN, YOU AND TACHIBANA AREN'T...
GEEZ, MUGI..
I ALREADY TOLD YOU IT WASN'T LIKE THAT.
O-OH, YEAH.
I GUESS YOU'RE RIGHT, HEH.
BUT I WAS KIND OF SURPRISED WHEN YOU SUDDENLY DECIDED TO GO OUT ON A DATE WITH TACHIBANA.

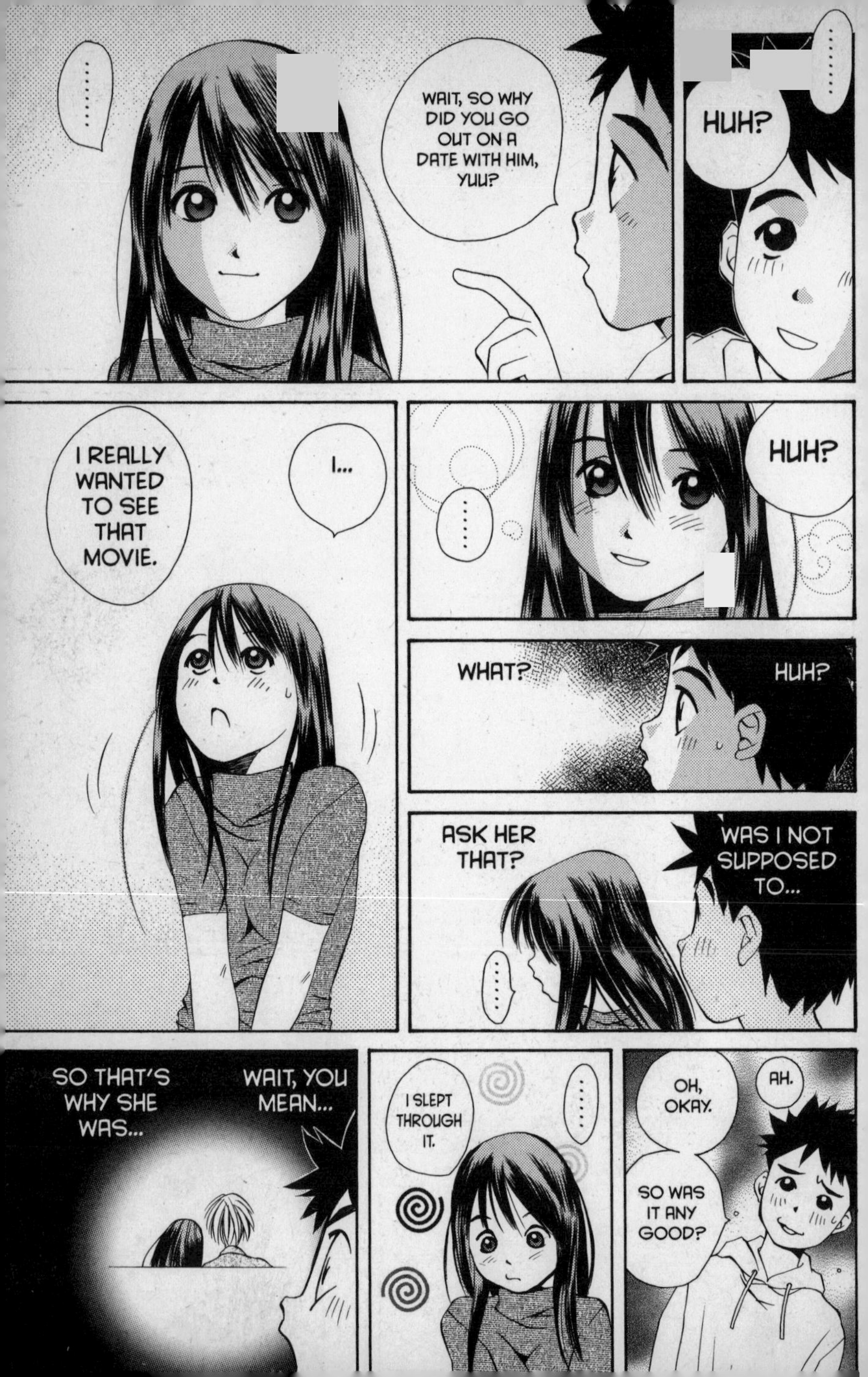
......
HUH?
WAIT, SO WHY DID YOU GO OUT ON A DATE WITH HIM, YUU?
......
HUH?
......
HUH?
WHAT?
WAS I NOT SUPPOSED TO...
ASK HER THAT?
......
I...
I REALLY WANTED TO SEE THAT MOVIE.
AH.
OH, OKAY.
SO WAS IT ANY GOOD?
......
I SLEPT THROUGH IT.
WAIT, YOU MEAN...
SO THAT'S WHY SHE WAS...

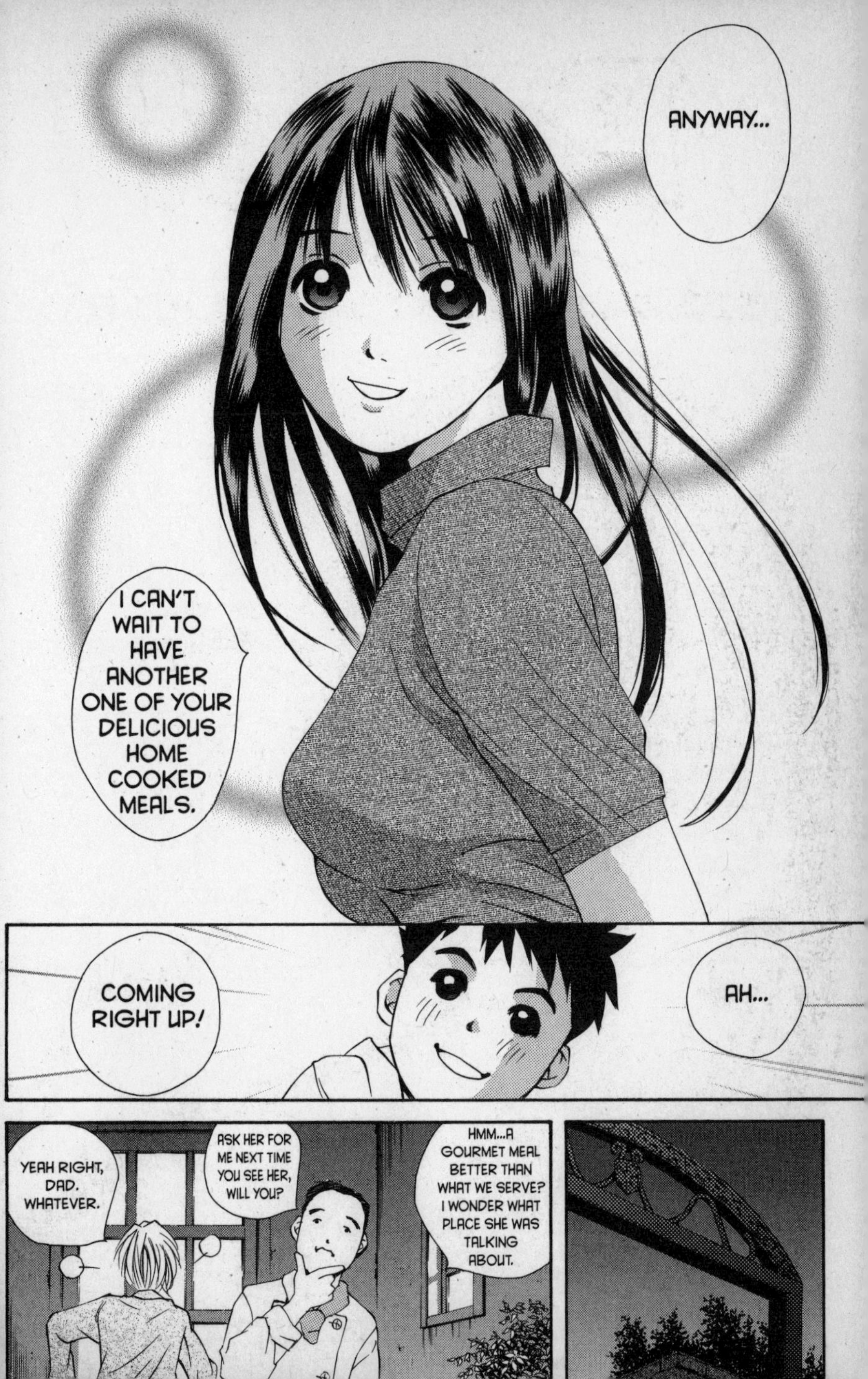
ANYWAY...
I CAN'T WAIT TO HAVE ANOTHER ONE OF YOUR DELICIOUS HOME COOKED MEALS.
AH...
COMING RIGHT UP!
HMM...A GOURMET MEAL BETTER THAN WHAT WE SERVE? I WONDER WHAT PLACE SHE WAS TALKING ABOUT.
ASK HER FOR ME NEXT TIME YOU SEE HER, WILL YOU?
YEAH RIGHT, DAD. WHATEVER.

Pastel

MIRACLE 19:
THE DATING OBSTACLE COURSE

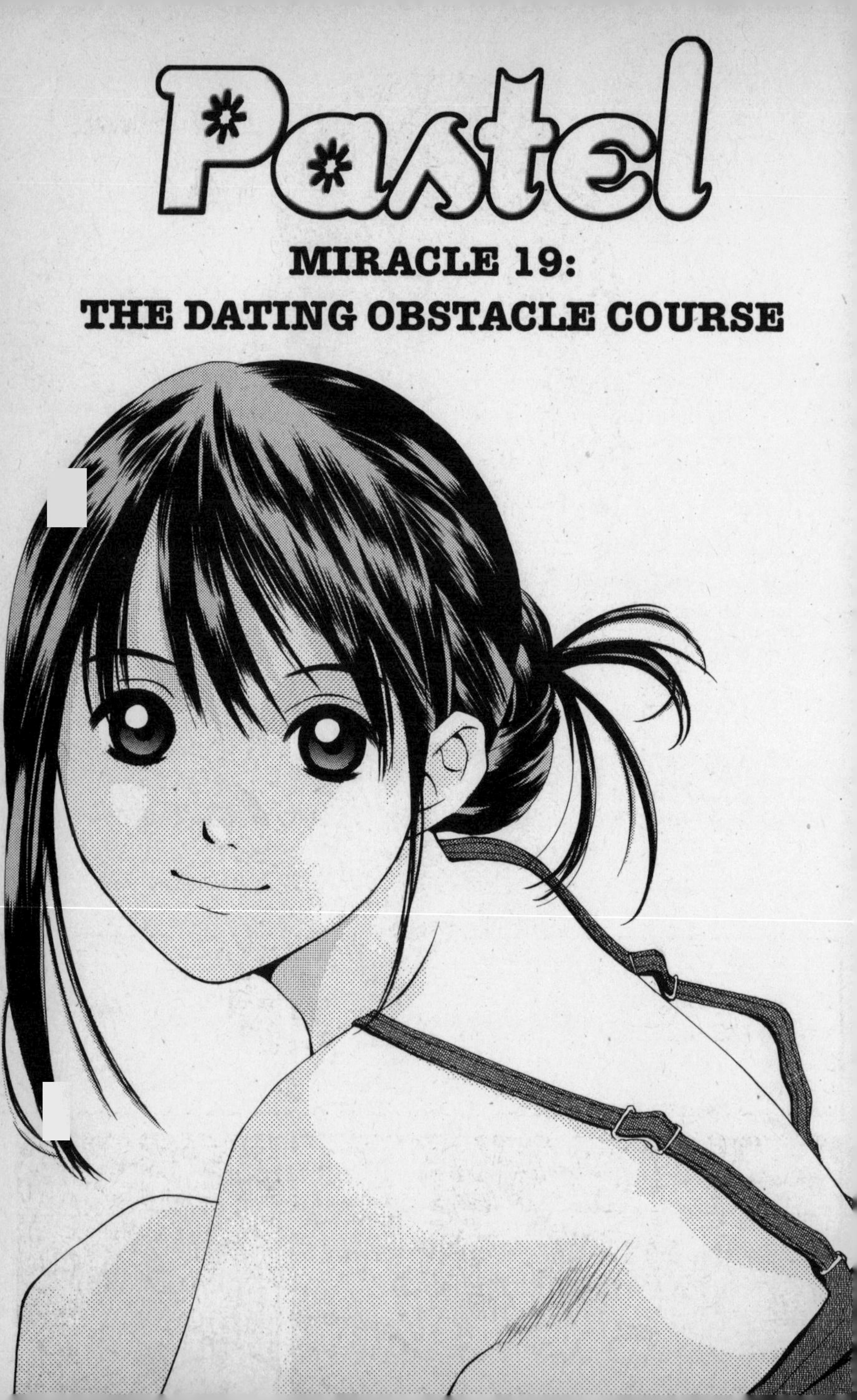

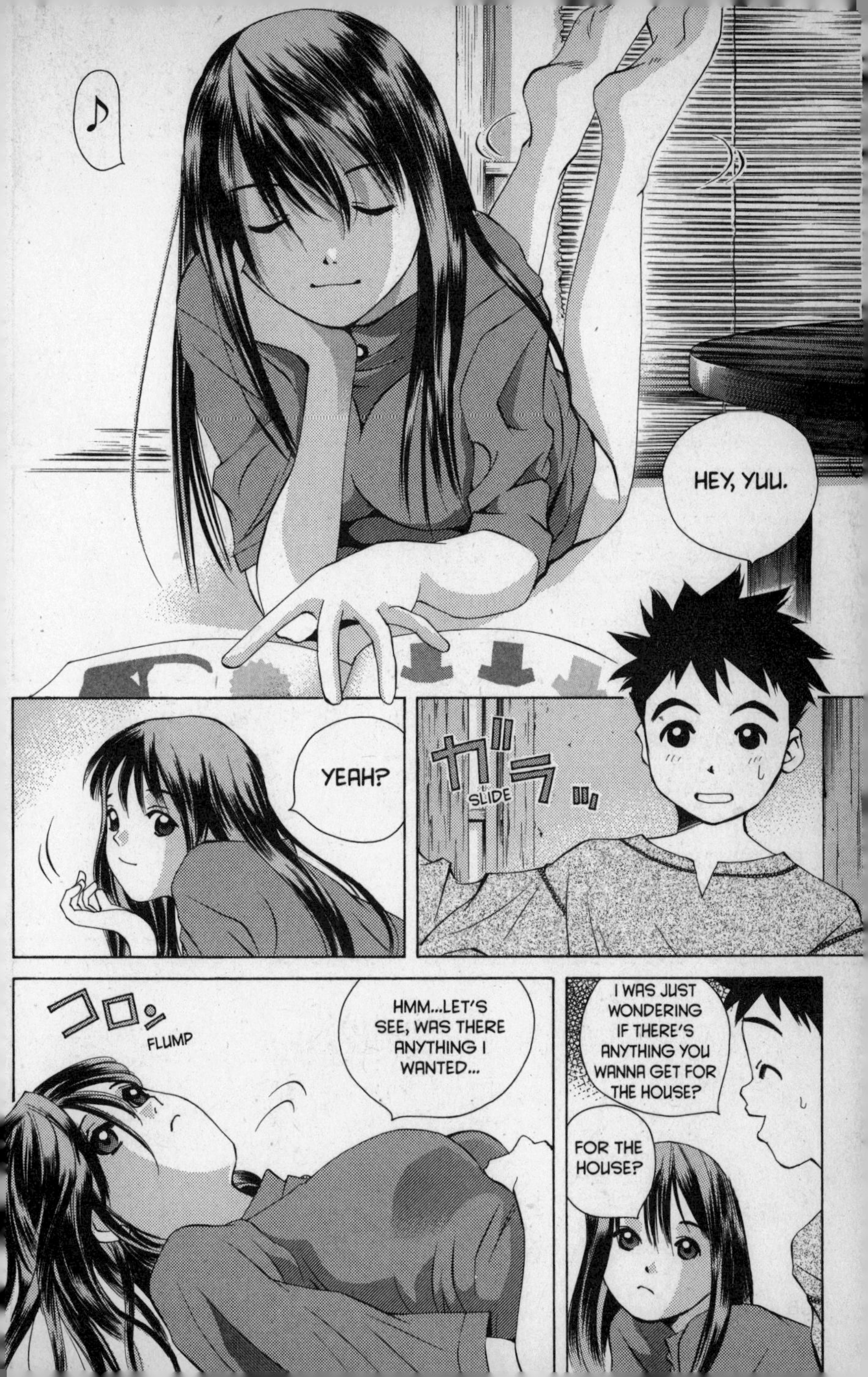
♪
HEY, YUU.
ガラ
SLIDE
YEAH?
I WAS JUST WONDERING IF THERE'S ANYTHING YOU WANNA GET FOR THE HOUSE?
FOR THE HOUSE?
HMM...LET'S SEE, WAS THERE ANYTHING I WANTED...
コロン
FLUMP

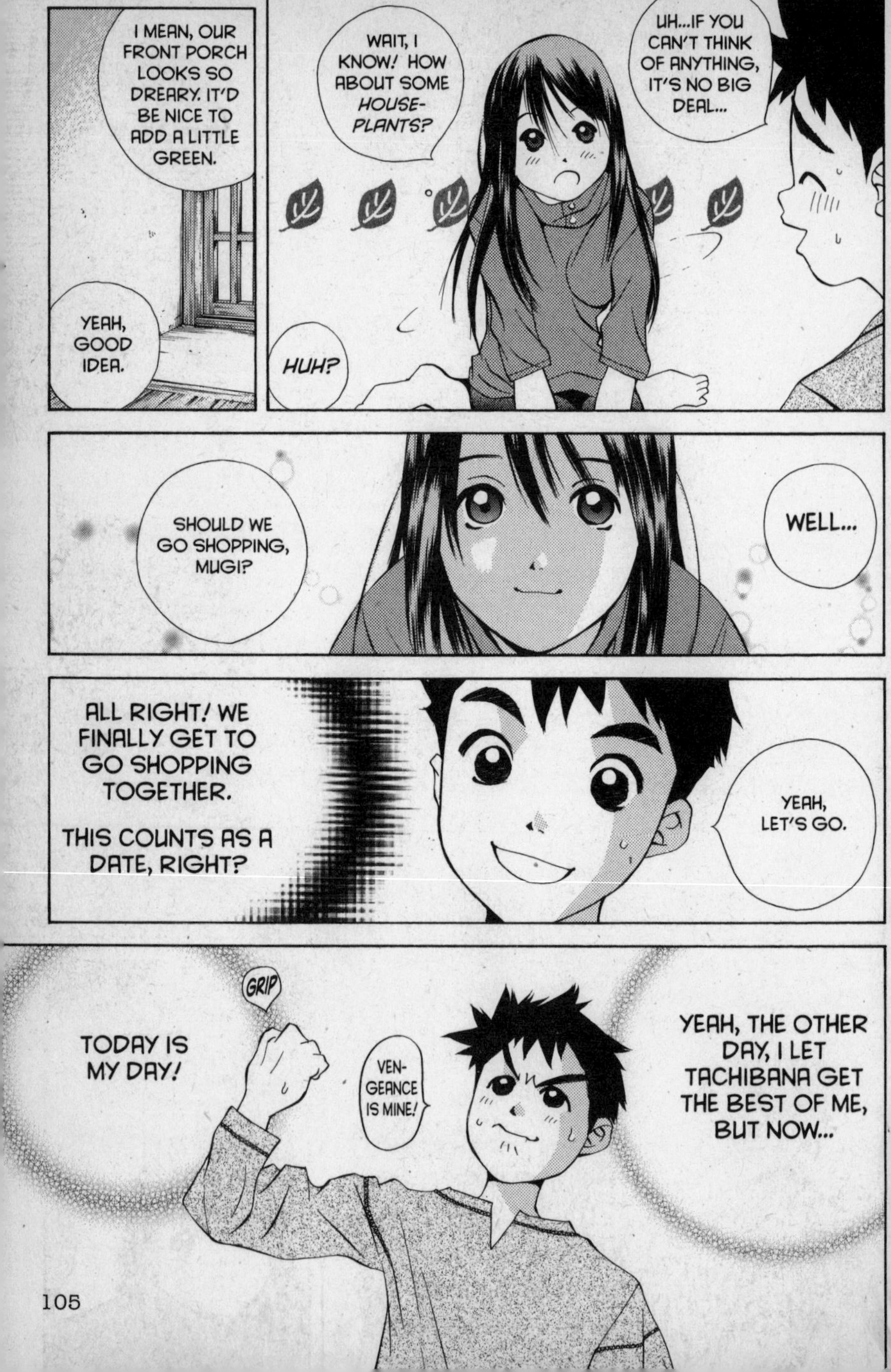
UH...IF YOU CAN'T THINK OF ANYTHING, IT'S NO BIG DEAL...
WAIT, I KNOW! HOW ABOUT SOME *HOUSE-PLANTS?*
HUH?
I MEAN, OUR FRONT PORCH LOOKS SO DREARY. IT'D BE NICE TO ADD A LITTLE GREEN.
YEAH, GOOD IDEA.
WELL...
SHOULD WE GO SHOPPING, MUGI?
YEAH, LET'S GO.
ALL RIGHT! WE FINALLY GET TO GO SHOPPING TOGETHER.
THIS COUNTS AS A DATE, RIGHT?
YEAH, THE OTHER DAY, I LET TACHIBANA GET THE BEST OF ME, BUT NOW...
VEN-GEANCE IS MINE!
GRIP
TODAY IS MY DAY!

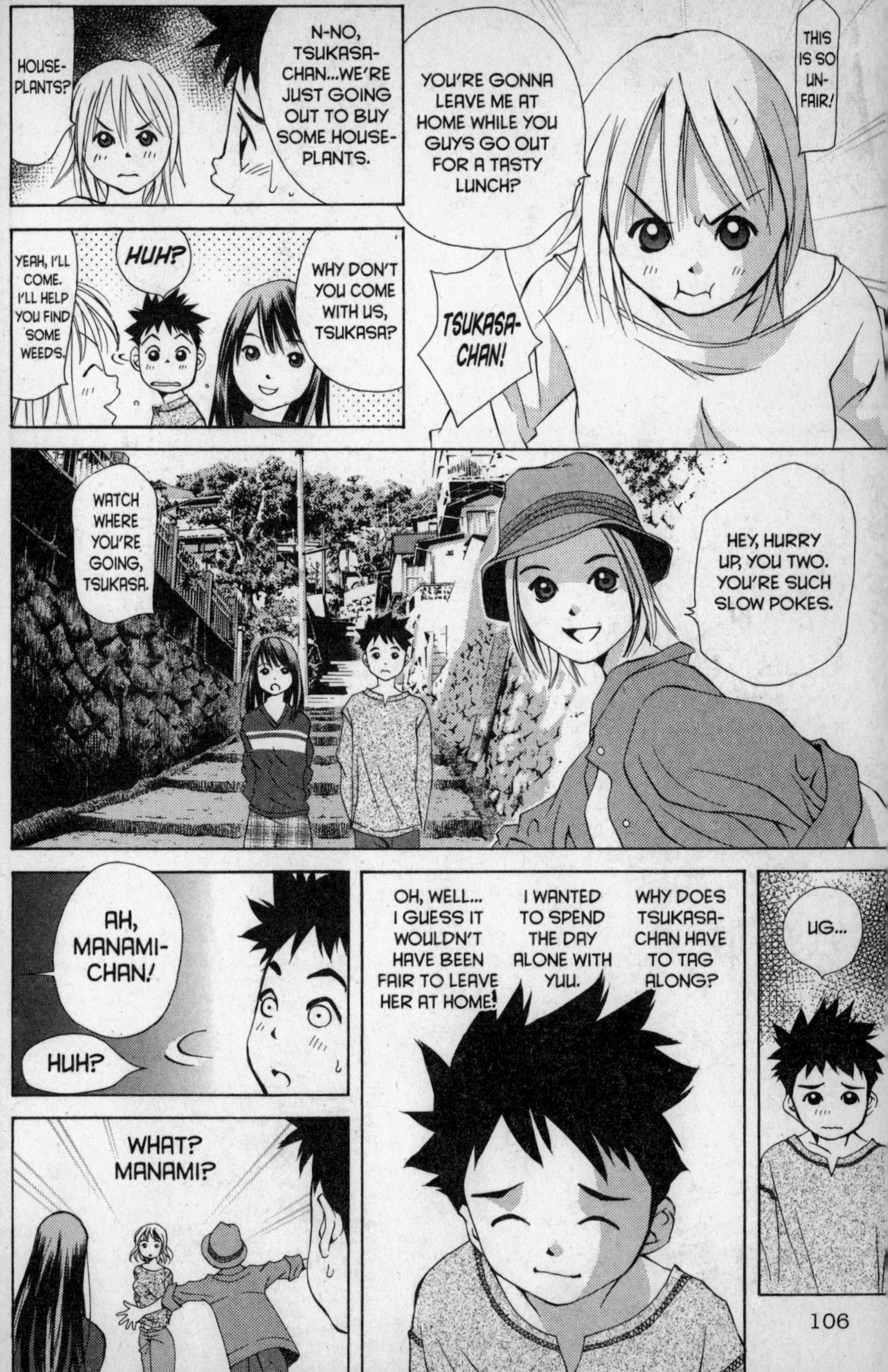
THIS IS SO UN-FAIR!
YOU'RE GONNA LEAVE ME AT HOME WHILE YOU GUYS GO OUT FOR A TASTY LUNCH?
TSUKASA-CHAN!
N-NO, TSUKASA-CHAN...WE'RE JUST GOING OUT TO BUY SOME HOUSE-PLANTS.
HOUSE-PLANTS?
WHY DON'T YOU COME WITH US, TSUKASA?
HUH?
YEAH, I'LL COME. I'LL HELP YOU FIND SOME WEEDS.
HEY, HURRY UP, YOU TWO. YOU'RE SUCH SLOW POKES.
WATCH WHERE YOU'RE GOING, TSUKASA.
UG...
WHY DOES TSUKASA-CHAN HAVE TO TAG ALONG?
I WANTED TO SPEND THE DAY ALONE WITH YUU.
OH, WELL... I GUESS IT WOULDN'T HAVE BEEN FAIR TO LEAVE HER AT HOME!
AH, MANAMI-CHAN!
HUH?
WHAT? MANAMI?

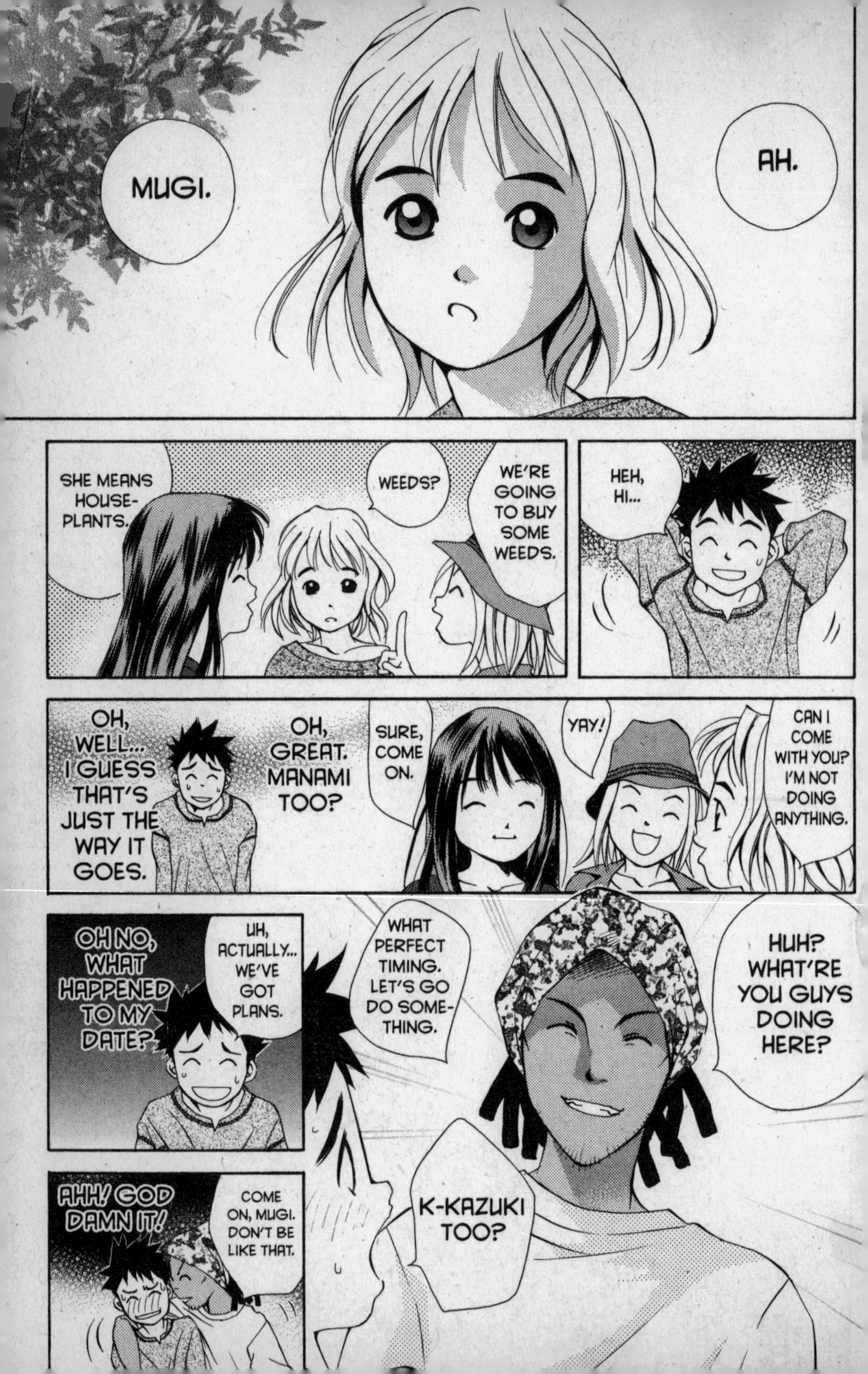
AH.
MUGI.
HEH, HI...
WE'RE GOING TO BUY SOME WEEDS.
WEEDS?
SHE MEANS HOUSE-PLANTS.
CAN I COME WITH YOU? I'M NOT DOING ANYTHING.
YAY!
SURE, COME ON.
OH, GREAT. MANAMI TOO?
OH, WELL... I GUESS THAT'S JUST THE WAY IT GOES.
HUH? WHAT'RE YOU GUYS DOING HERE?
WHAT PERFECT TIMING. LET'S GO DO SOME-THING.
K-KAZUKI TOO?
UH, ACTUALLY... WE'VE GOT PLANS.
OH NO, WHAT HAPPENED TO MY DATE?
COME ON, MUGI. DON'T BE LIKE THAT.
AHH! GOD DAMN IT!

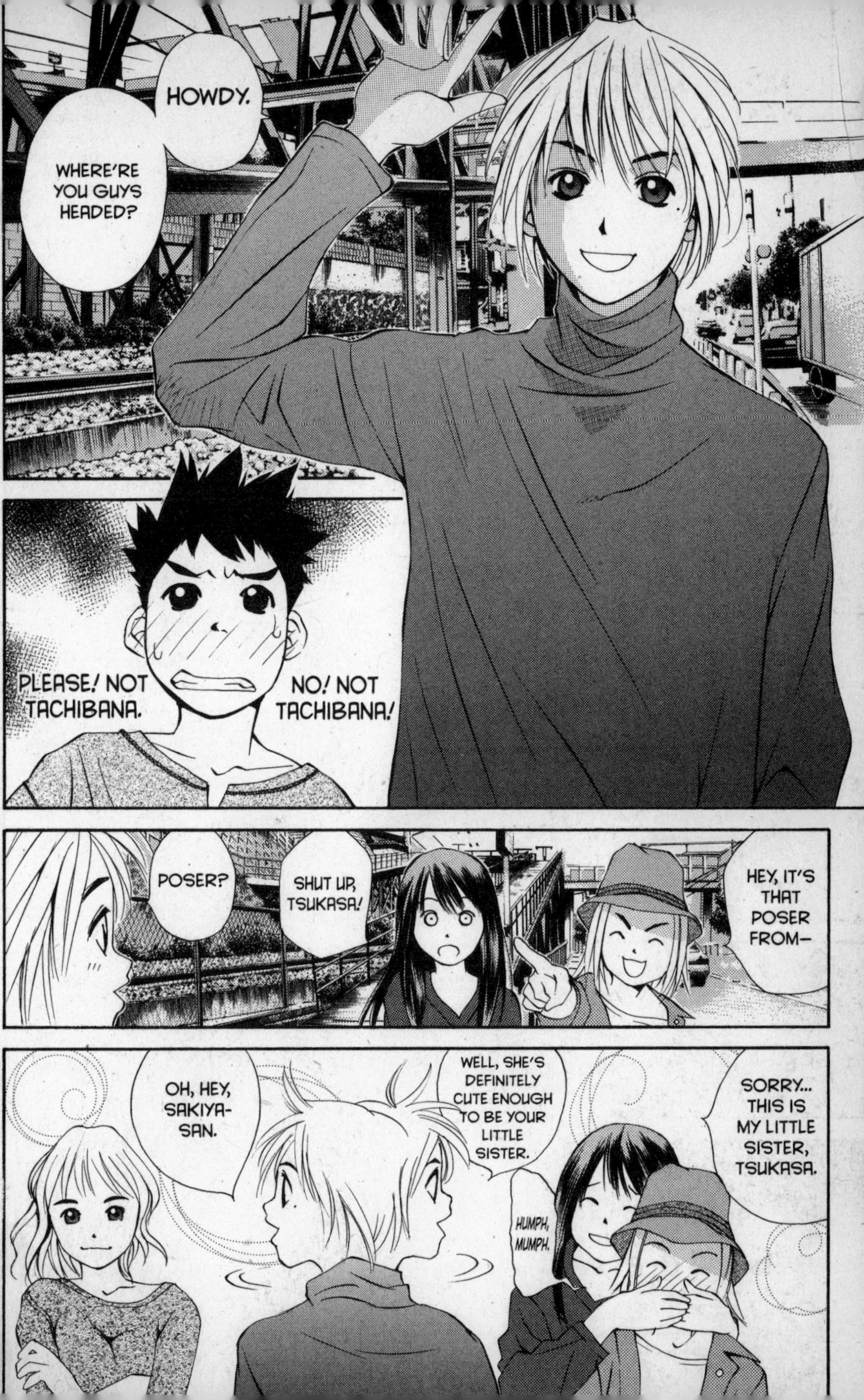
HOWDY.
WHERE'RE YOU GUYS HEADED?
NO! NOT TACHIBANA!
PLEASE! NOT TACHIBANA.
HEY, IT'S THAT POSER FROM—
SHUT UP, TSUKASA!
POSER?
SORRY... THIS IS MY LITTLE SISTER, TSUKASA.
HUMPH, MUMPH.
WELL, SHE'S DEFINITELY CUTE ENOUGH TO BE YOUR LITTLE SISTER.
OH, HEY, SAKIYA-SAN.

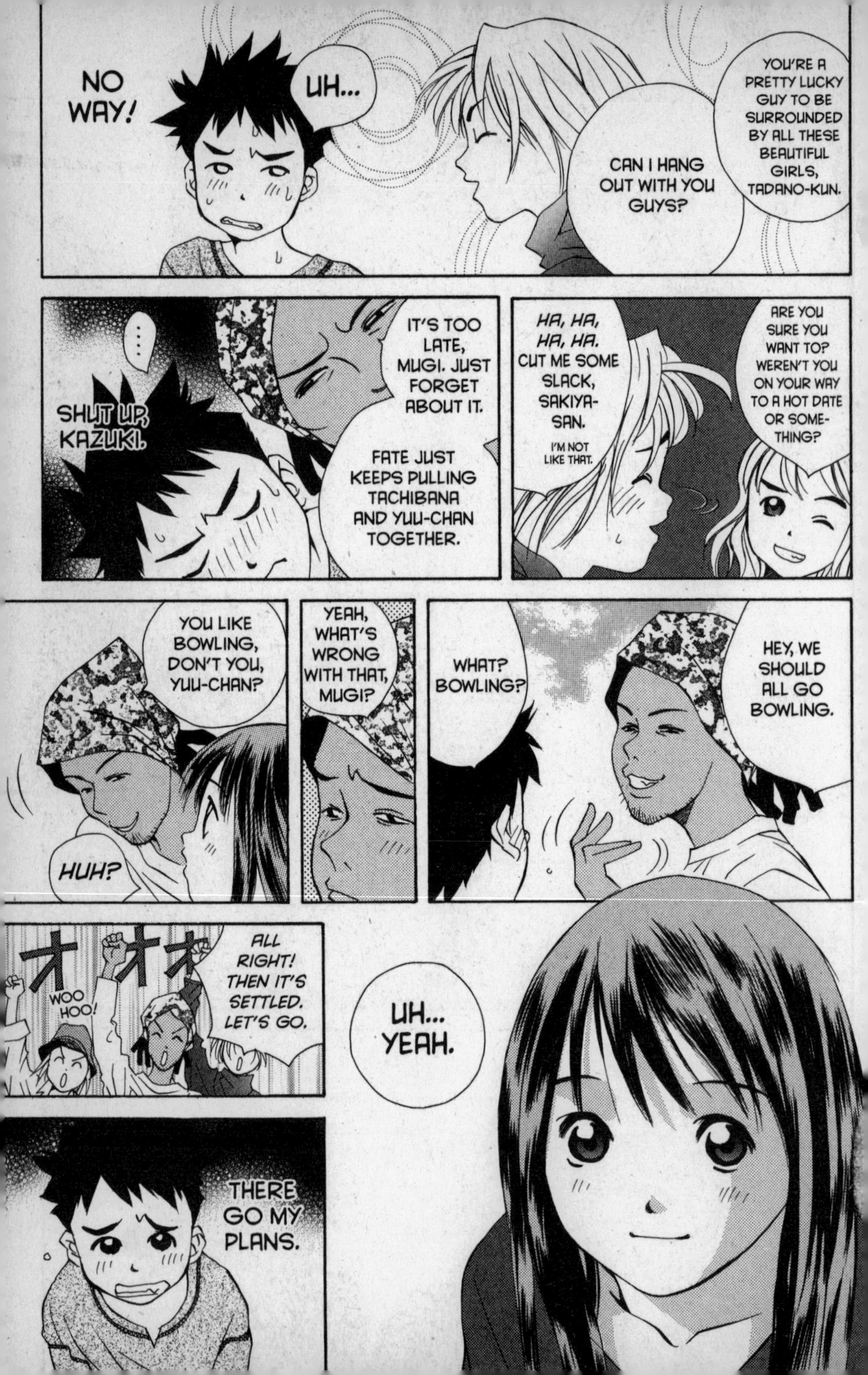
YOU'RE A PRETTY LUCKY GUY TO BE SURROUNDED BY ALL THESE BEAUTIFUL GIRLS, TADANO-KUN.
CAN I HANG OUT WITH YOU GUYS?
UH...
NO WAY!
ARE YOU SURE YOU WANT TO? WEREN'T YOU ON YOUR WAY TO A HOT DATE OR SOME-THING?
HA, HA, HA, HA. CUT ME SOME SLACK, SAKIYA-SAN.
I'M NOT LIKE THAT.
IT'S TOO LATE, MUGI. JUST FORGET ABOUT IT.
FATE JUST KEEPS PULLING TACHIBANA AND YUU-CHAN TOGETHER.
...
SHUT UP, KAZUKI.
HEY, WE SHOULD ALL GO BOWLING.
WHAT? BOWLING?
YEAH, WHAT'S WRONG WITH THAT, MUGI?
YOU LIKE BOWLING, DON'T YOU, YUU-CHAN?
HUH?
UH... YEAH.
ALL RIGHT! THEN IT'S SETTLED. LET'S GO.
オオ
WOO HOO!
THERE GO MY PLANS.

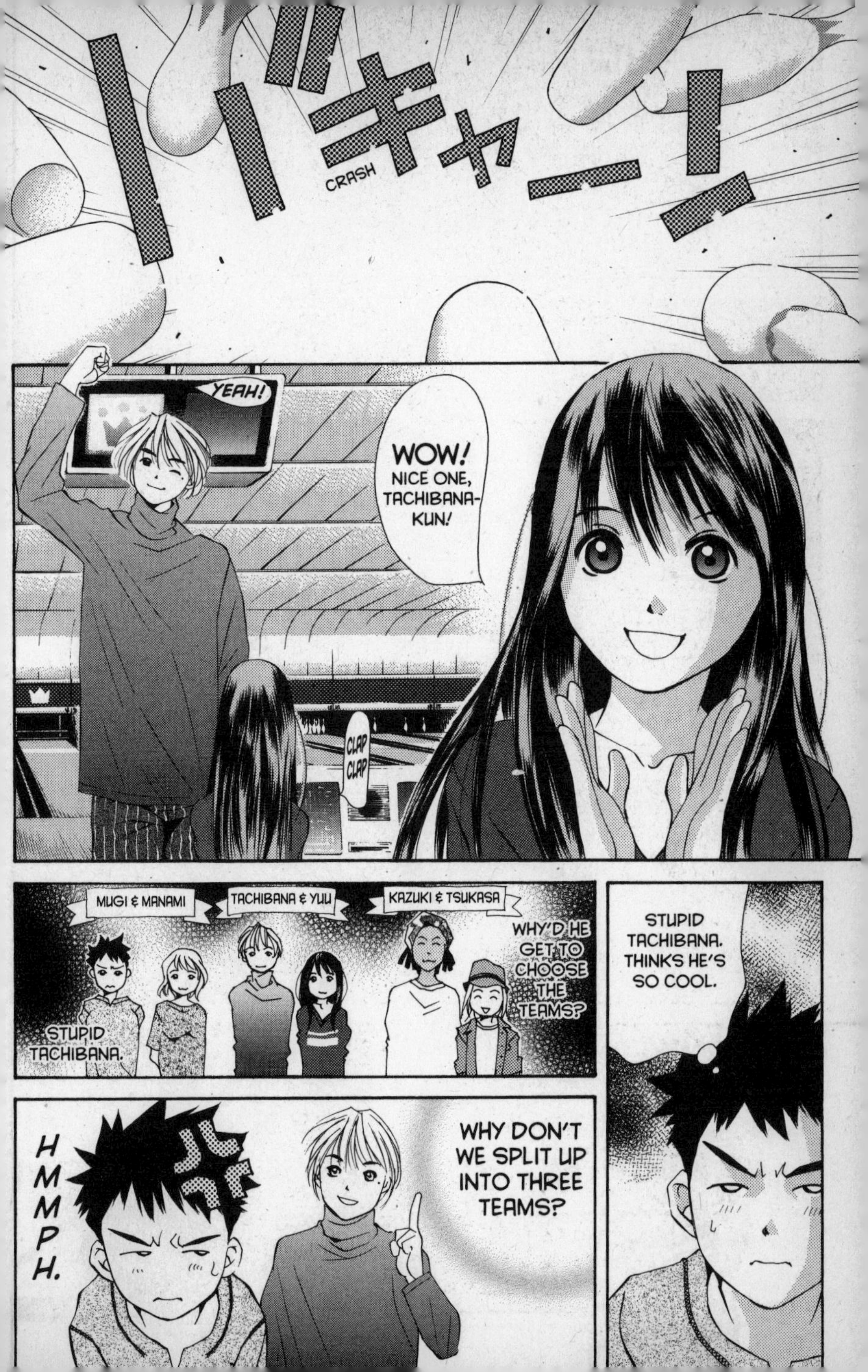
CRASH
WOW! NICE ONE, TACHIBANA-KUN!
YEAH!
CLAP CLAP
STUPID TACHIBANA. THINKS HE'S SO COOL.
KAZUKI & TSUKASA
TACHIBANA & YUU
MUGI & MANAMI
WHY'D HE GET TO CHOOSE THE TEAMS?
STUPID TACHIBANA.
WHY DON'T WE SPLIT UP INTO THREE TEAMS?
HMMPH.

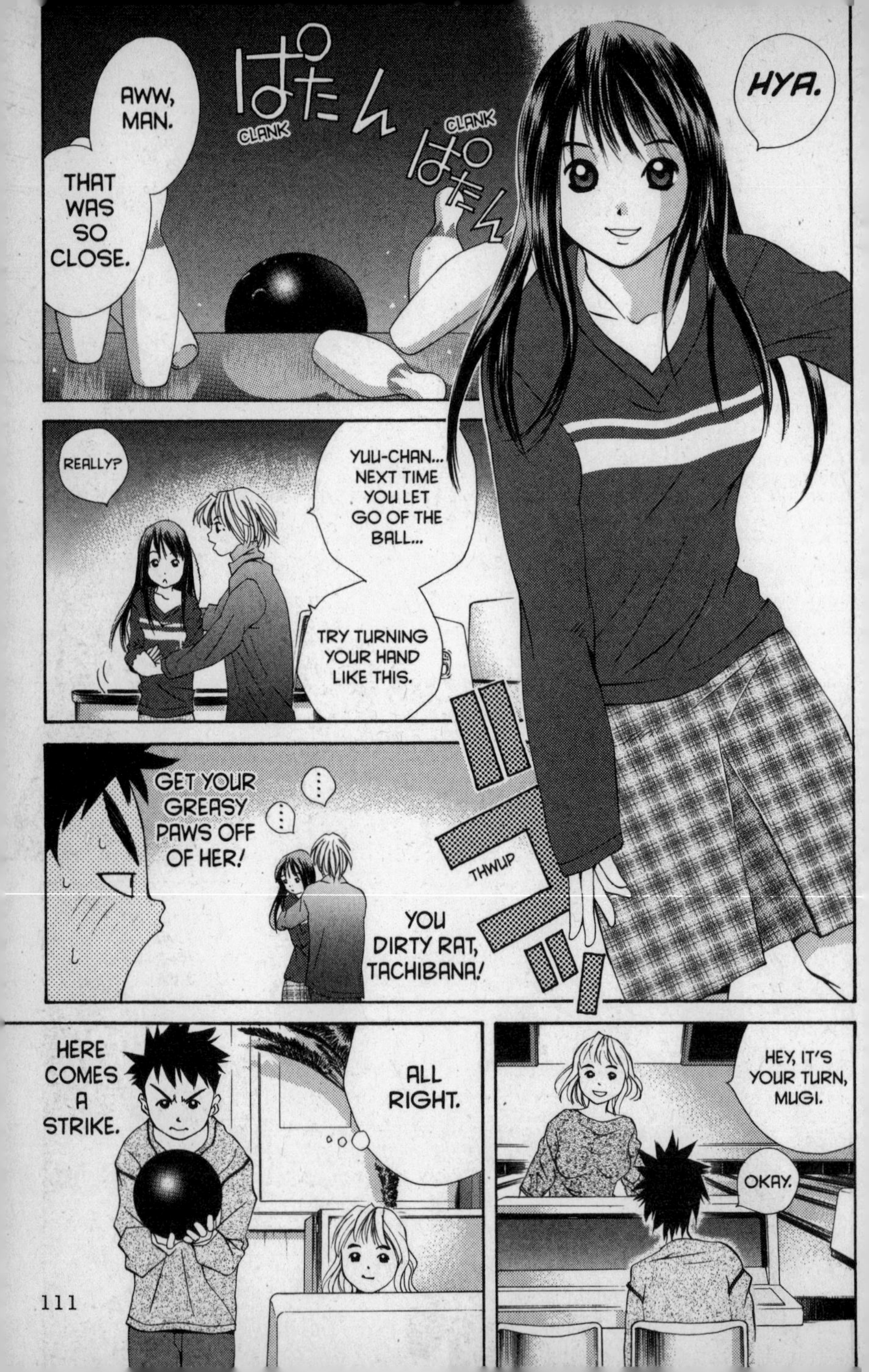
HYA.
THWUP
ぱたん
CLANK
ぱたん
CLANK
AWW, MAN.
THAT WAS SO CLOSE.
YUU-CHAN... NEXT TIME YOU LET GO OF THE BALL...
TRY TURNING YOUR HAND LIKE THIS.
REALLY?
...
...
GET YOUR GREASY PAWS OFF OF HER!
YOU DIRTY RAT, TACHIBANA!
HEY, IT'S YOUR TURN, MUGI.
OKAY.
ALL RIGHT.
HERE COMES A STRIKE.

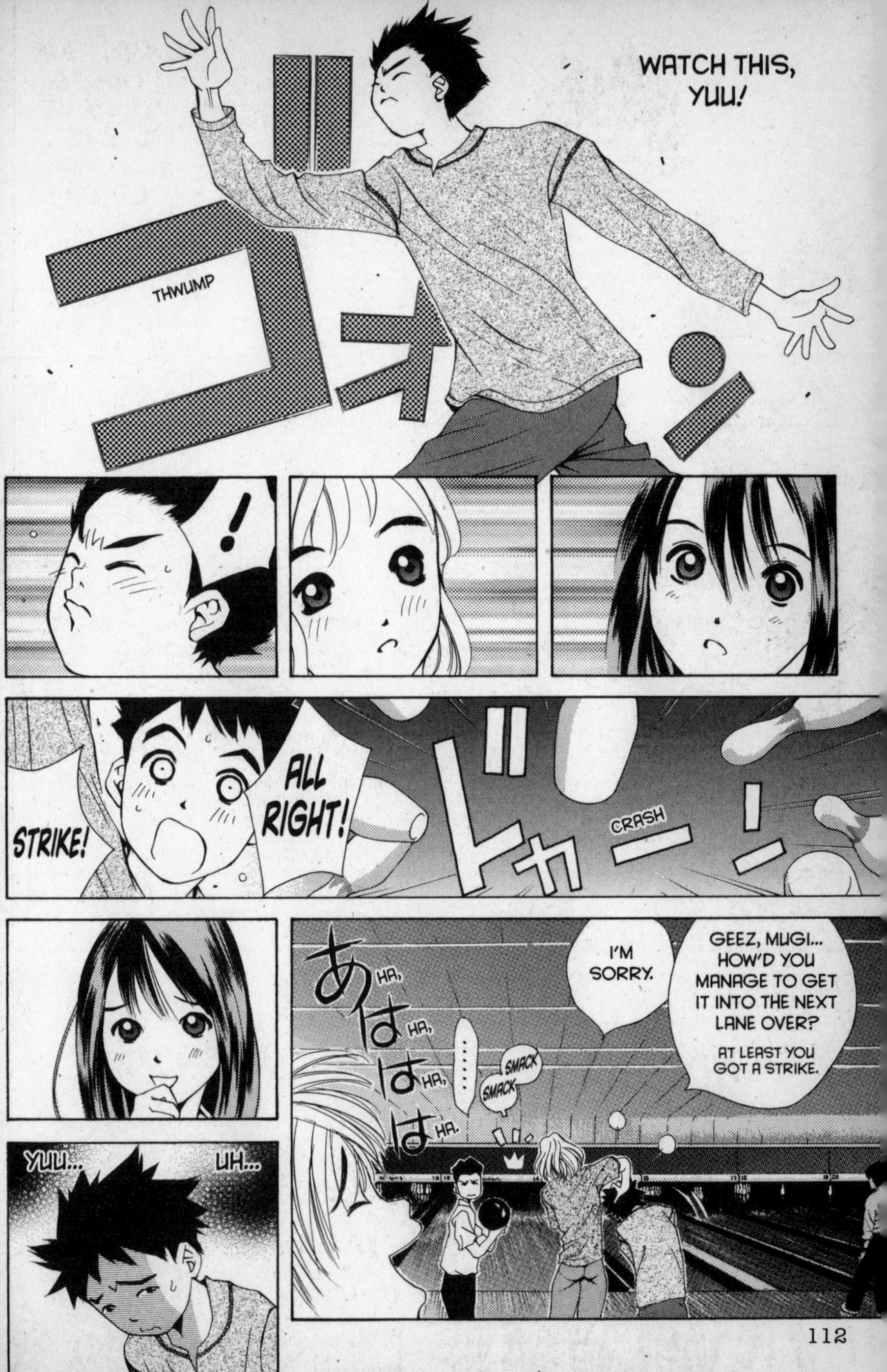
WATCH THIS, YUU!
THWUMP
!
CRASH
ALL RIGHT!
STRIKE!
GEEZ, MUGI... HOW'D YOU MANAGE TO GET IT INTO THE NEXT LANE OVER?
AT LEAST YOU GOT A STRIKE.
I'M SORRY.
HA, HA, HA, HA.
......
SMACK
SMACK
UH...
YUU...

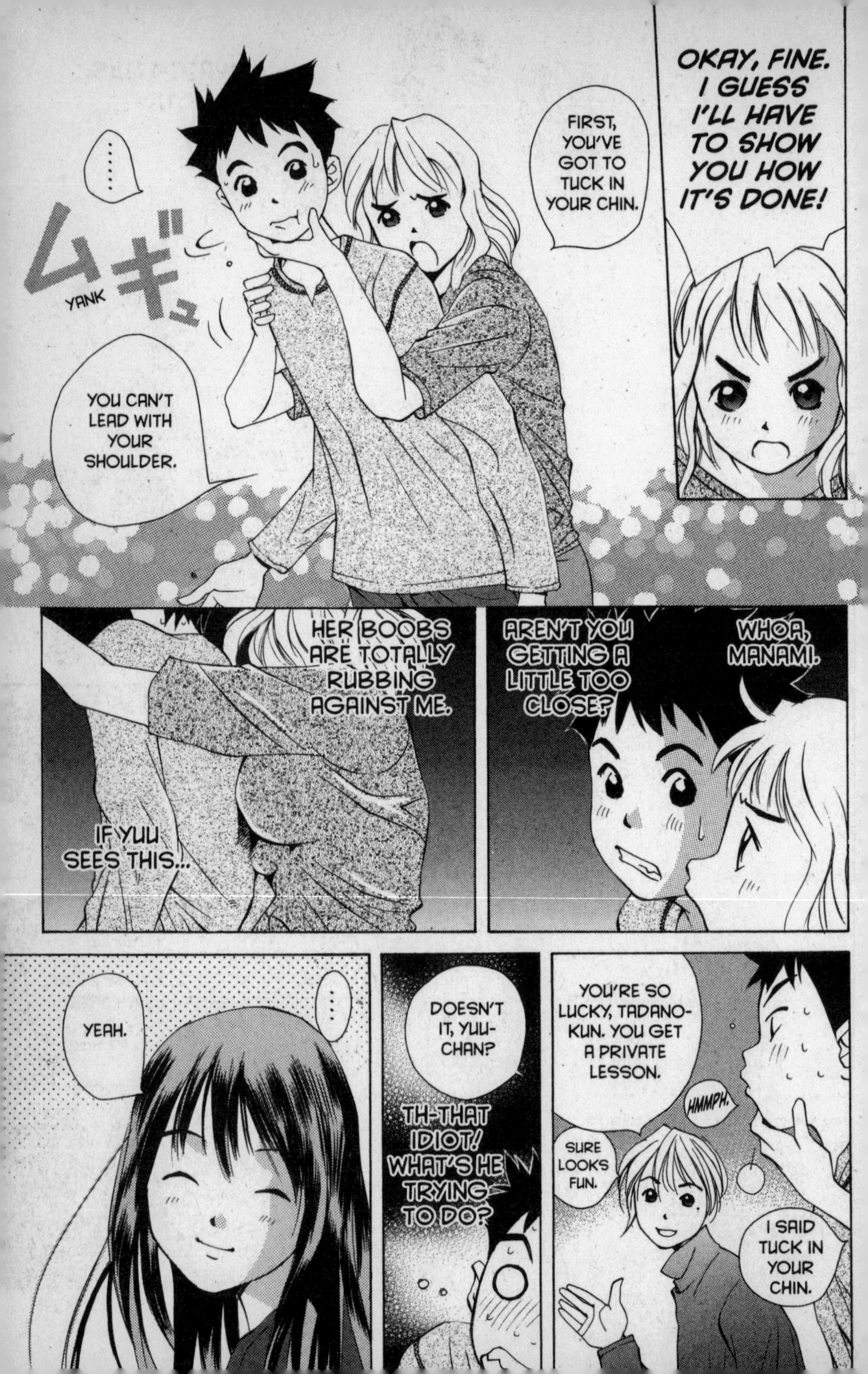
OKAY, FINE. I GUESS I'LL HAVE TO SHOW YOU HOW IT'S DONE!
FIRST, YOU'VE GOT TO TUCK IN YOUR CHIN.
......
ムギュ
YANK
YOU CAN'T LEAD WITH YOUR SHOULDER.
WHOA, MANAMI.
AREN'T YOU GETTING A LITTLE TOO CLOSE?
HER BOOBS ARE TOTALLY RUBBING AGAINST ME.
IF YUU SEES THIS...
YOU'RE SO LUCKY, TADANO-KUN. YOU GET A PRIVATE LESSON.
HMMPH.
SURE LOOKS FUN.
I SAID TUCK IN YOUR CHIN.
DOESN'T IT, YUU-CHAN?
TH-THAT IDIOT! WHAT'S HE TRYING TO DO?
......
YEAH.

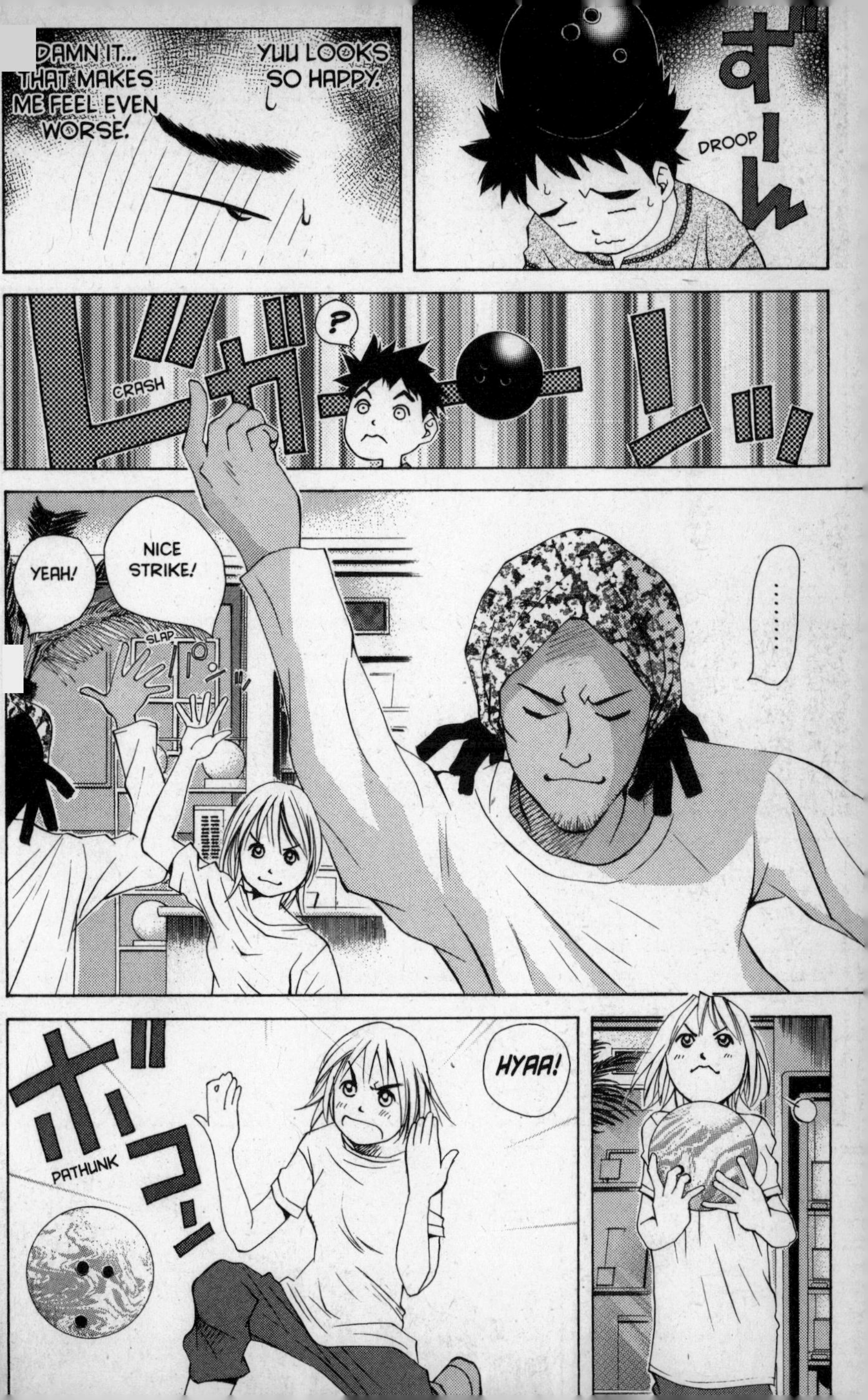
DROOP
YUU LOOKS SO HAPPY.
DAMN IT... THAT MAKES ME FEEL EVEN WORSE!
CRASH
?
......
NICE STRIKE!
YEAH!
SLAP
HYAA!
PATHUNK

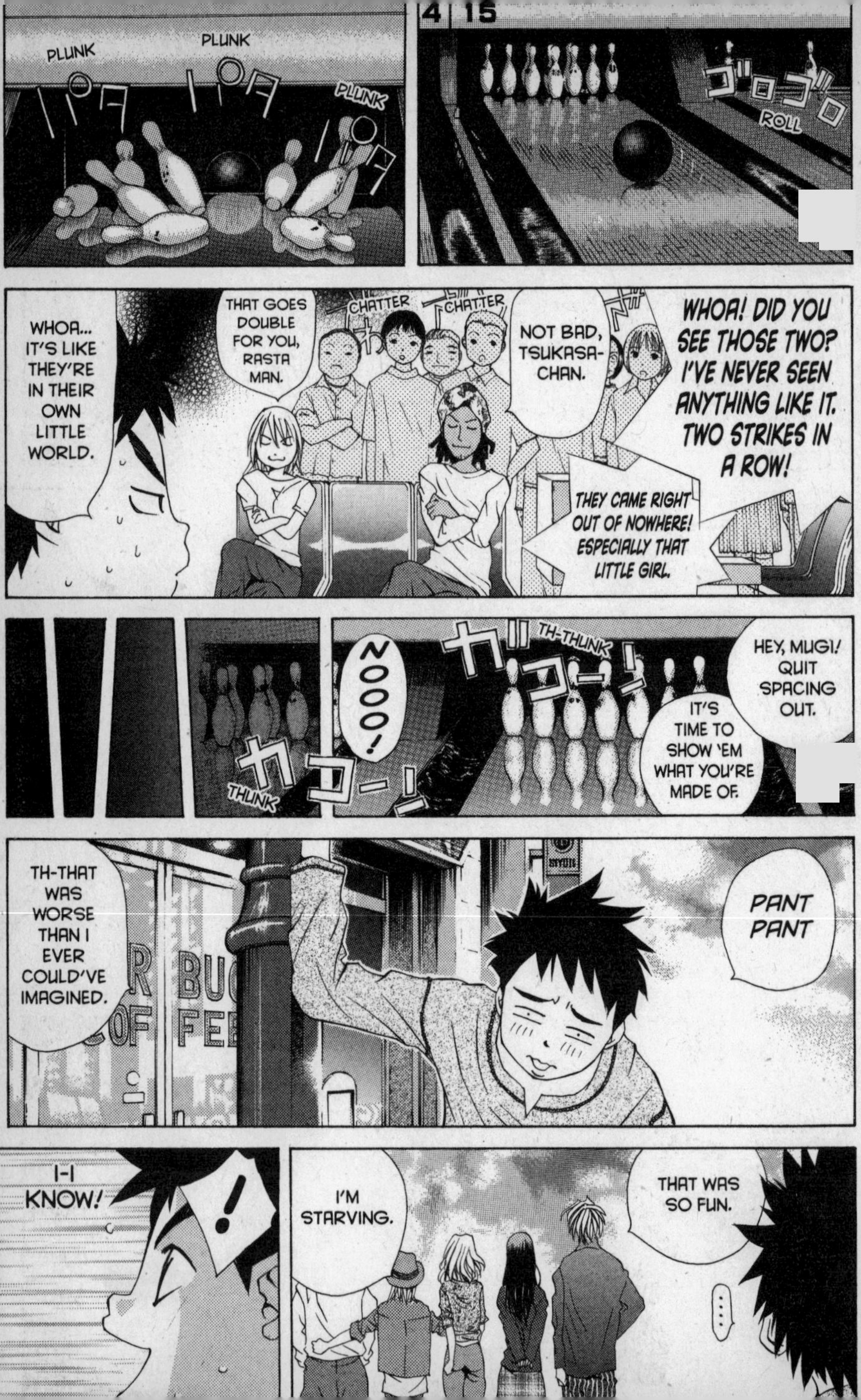
4 15
ROLL
PLUNK
PLUNK
PLUNK
WHOA! DID YOU SEE THOSE TWO? I'VE NEVER SEEN ANYTHING LIKE IT. TWO STRIKES IN A ROW!
THEY CAME RIGHT OUT OF NOWHERE! ESPECIALLY THAT LITTLE GIRL.
NOT BAD, TSUKASA-CHAN.
CHATTER
CHATTER
THAT GOES DOUBLE FOR YOU, RASTA MAN.
WHOA... IT'S LIKE THEY'RE IN THEIR OWN LITTLE WORLD.
HEY, MUGI! QUIT SPACING OUT.
IT'S TIME TO SHOW 'EM WHAT YOU'RE MADE OF.
TH-THUNK
NOOO!
THUNK
PANT PANT
TH-THAT WAS WORSE THAN I EVER COULD'VE IMAGINED.
THAT WAS SO FUN.
....
I'M STARVING.
I-I KNOW!

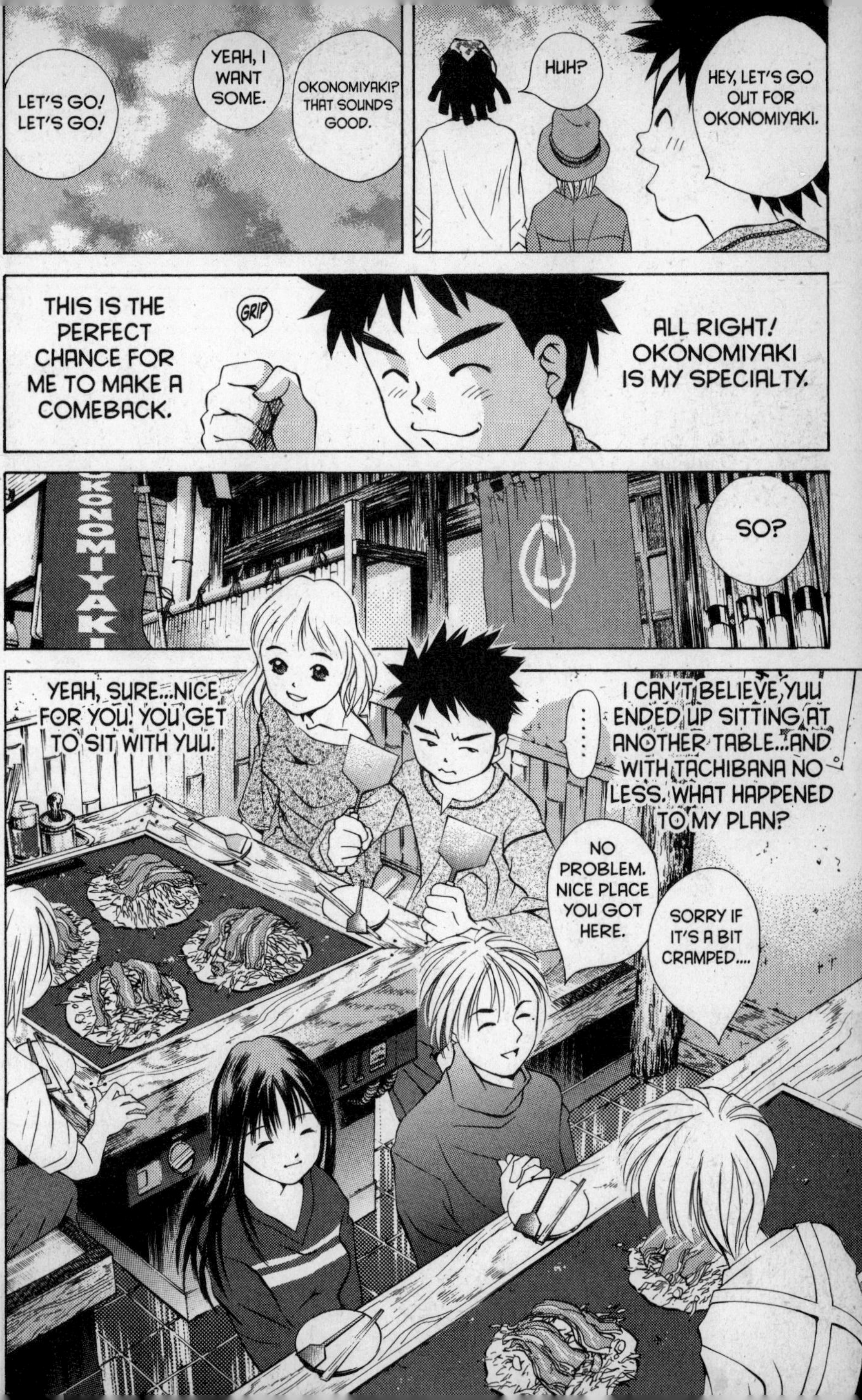
HEY, LET'S GO OUT FOR OKONOMIYAKI.
HUH?
OKONOMIYAKI? THAT SOUNDS GOOD.
YEAH, I WANT SOME.
LET'S GO! LET'S GO!
ALL RIGHT! OKONOMIYAKI IS MY SPECIALTY.
GRIP
THIS IS THE PERFECT CHANCE FOR ME TO MAKE A COMEBACK.
SO?
OKONOMIYAKI
I CAN'T BELIEVE YUU ENDED UP SITTING AT ANOTHER TABLE...AND WITH TACHIBANA NO LESS. WHAT HAPPENED TO MY PLAN?
......
YEAH, SURE...NICE FOR YOU. YOU GET TO SIT WITH YUU.
SORRY IF IT'S A BIT CRAMPED....
NO PROBLEM. NICE PLACE YOU GOT HERE.

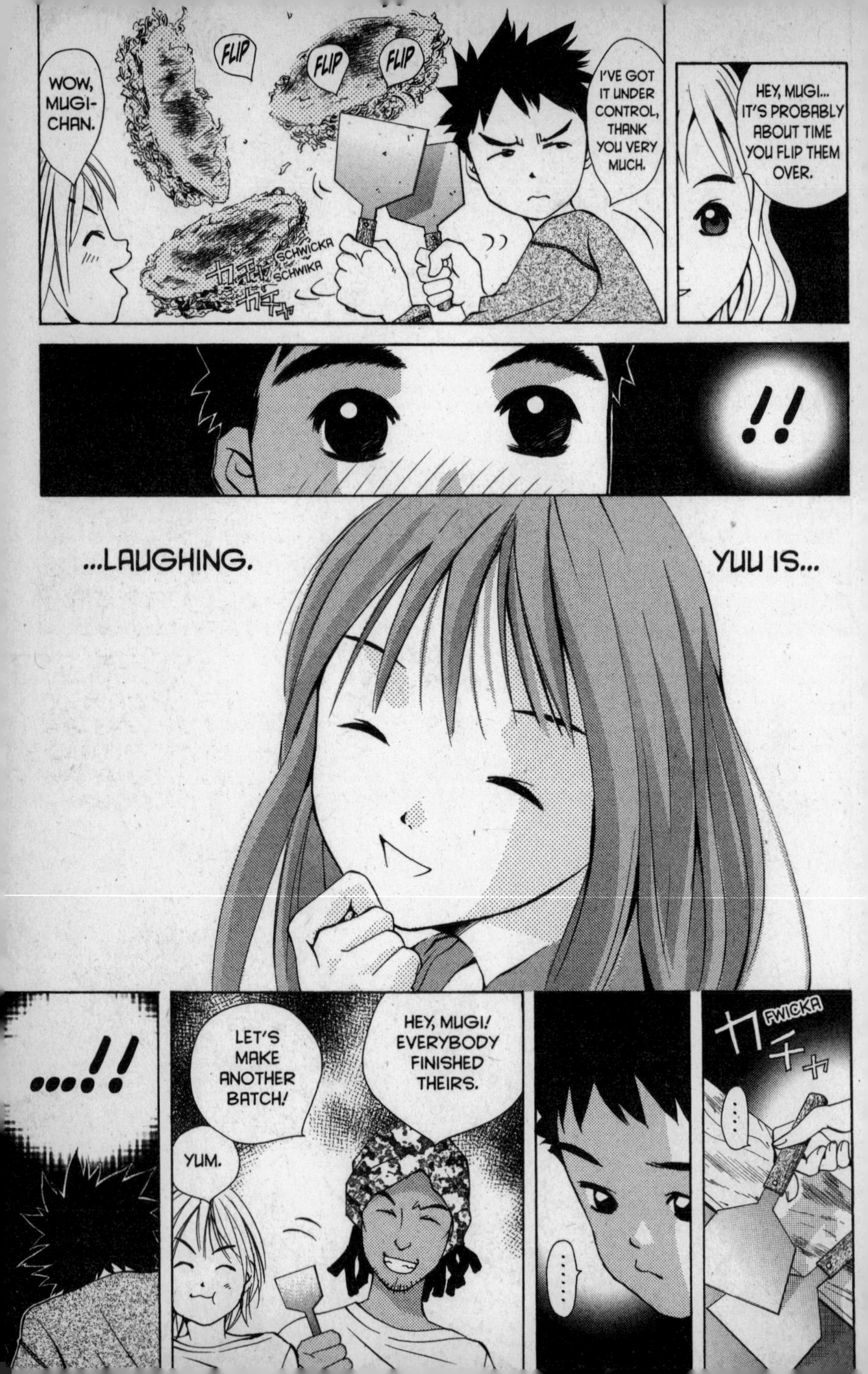
HEY, MUGI... IT'S PROBABLY ABOUT TIME YOU FLIP THEM OVER.
I'VE GOT IT UNDER CONTROL, THANK YOU VERY MUCH.
FLIP
FLIP
FLIP
WOW, MUGI-CHAN.
SCHWICKA SCHWIKA
!!
YUU IS...
...LAUGHING.
FWICKA
......
......
HEY, MUGI! EVERYBODY FINISHED THEIRS.
LET'S MAKE ANOTHER BATCH!
YUM.
....!!

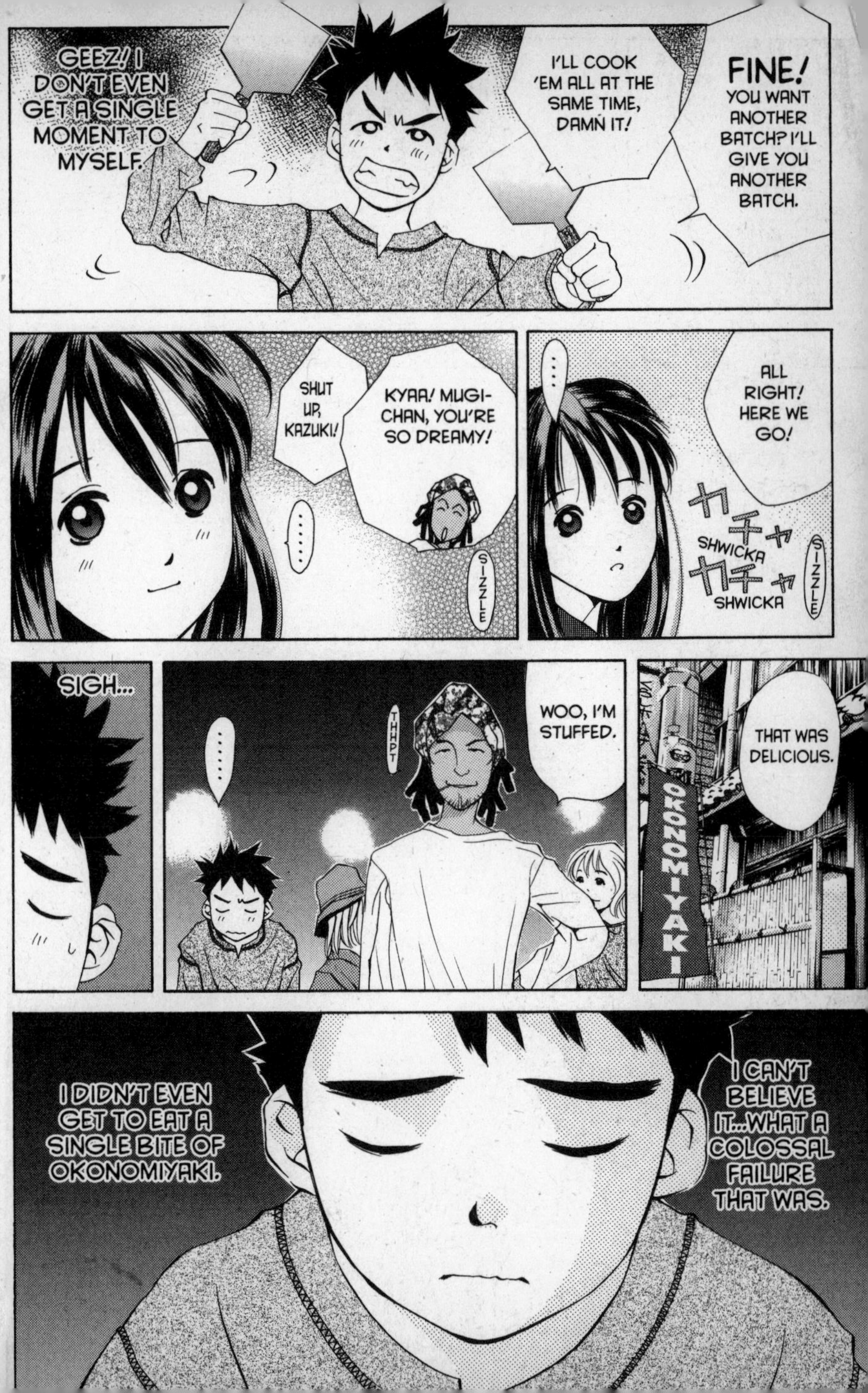
FINE! YOU WANT ANOTHER BATCH? I'LL GIVE YOU ANOTHER BATCH.
I'LL COOK 'EM ALL AT THE SAME TIME, DAMN IT!
GEEZ! I DON'T EVEN GET A SINGLE MOMENT TO MYSELF.
...
ALL RIGHT! HERE WE GO!
SHWICKA
SHWICKA
SIZZLE
KYAA! MUGI-CHAN, YOU'RE SO DREAMY!
SHUT UP, KAZUKI!
......
SIZZLE
OKONOMIYAKI
THAT WAS DELICIOUS.
WOO, I'M STUFFED.
THHPT
......
SIGH...
I CAN'T BELIEVE IT...WHAT A COLOSSAL FAILURE THAT WAS.
I DIDN'T EVEN GET TO EAT A SINGLE BITE OF OKONOMIYAKI.

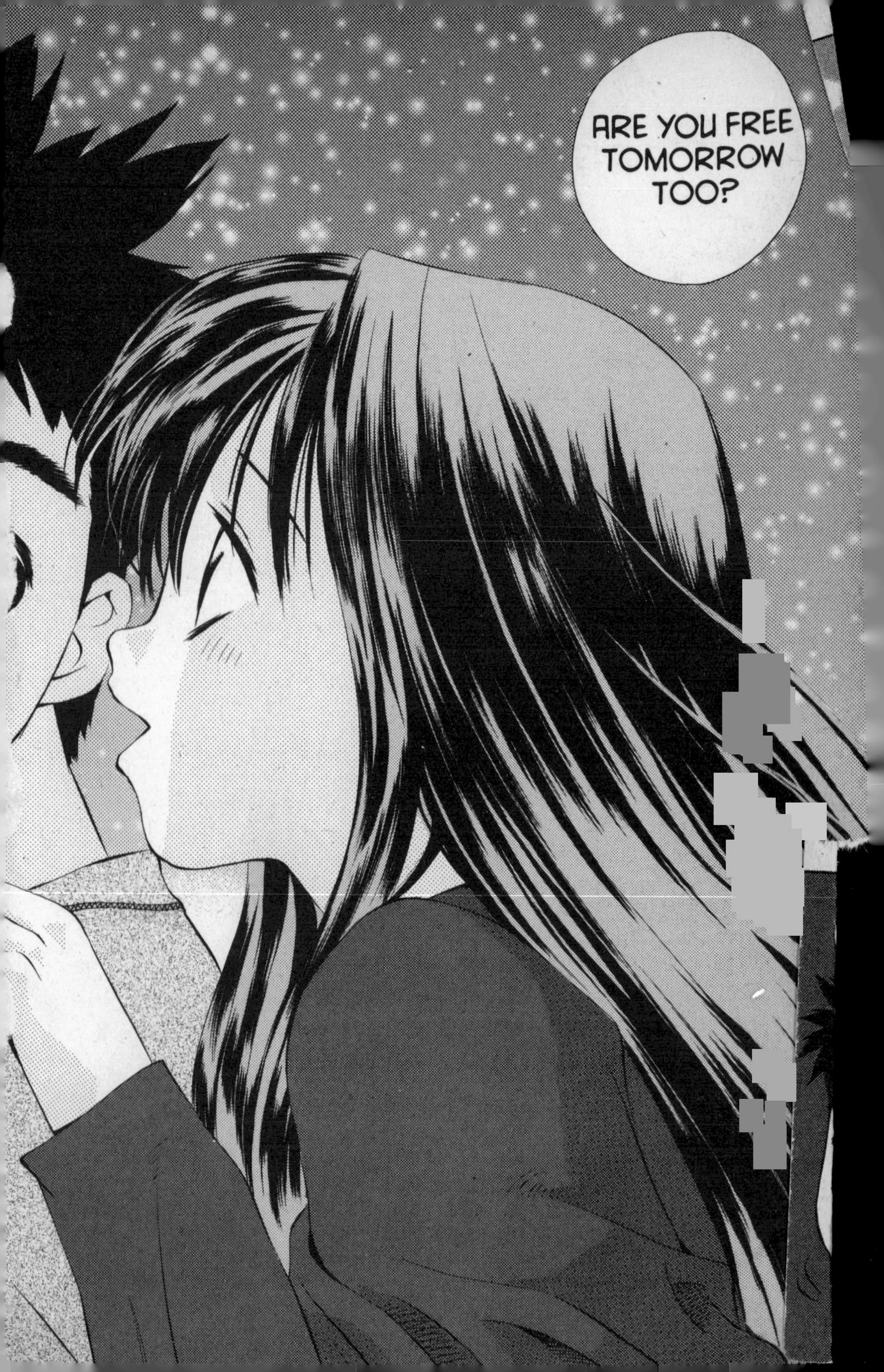
ARE YOU FREE TOMORROW TOO?

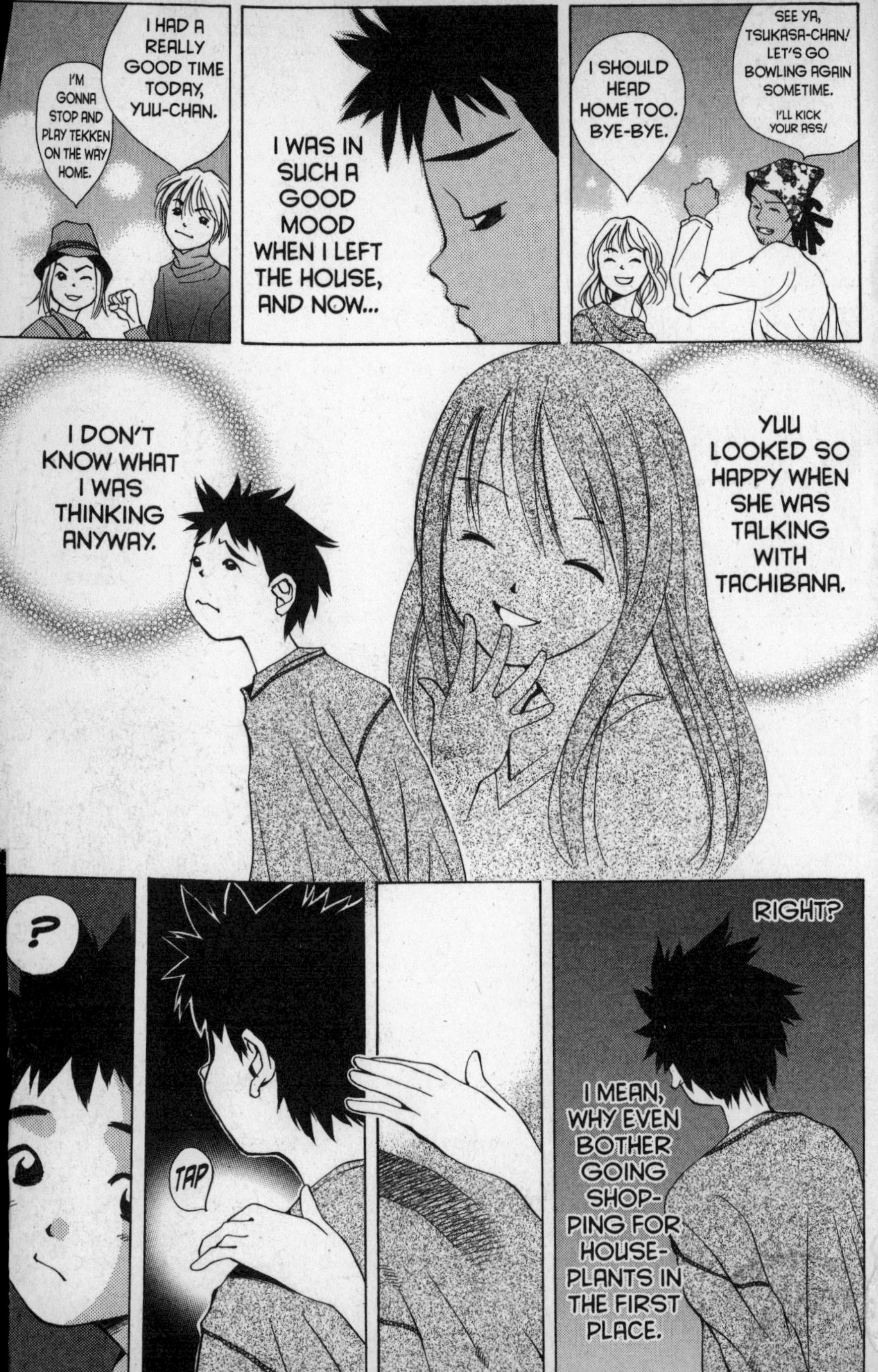
SEE YA, TSUKASA-CHAN! LET'S GO BOWLING AGAIN SOMETIME.
I'LL KICK YOUR ASS!
I SHOULD HEAD HOME TOO. BYE-BYE.
I WAS IN SUCH A GOOD MOOD WHEN I LEFT THE HOUSE, AND NOW...
I HAD A REALLY GOOD TIME TODAY, YUU-CHAN.
I'M GONNA STOP AND PLAY TEKKEN ON THE WAY HOME.
YUU LOOKED SO HAPPY WHEN SHE WAS TALKING WITH TACHIBANA.
I DON'T KNOW WHAT I WAS THINKING ANYWAY.
RIGHT?
I MEAN, WHY EVEN BOTHER GOING SHOP-PING FOR HOUSE-PLANTS IN THE FIRST PLACE.
TAP
?

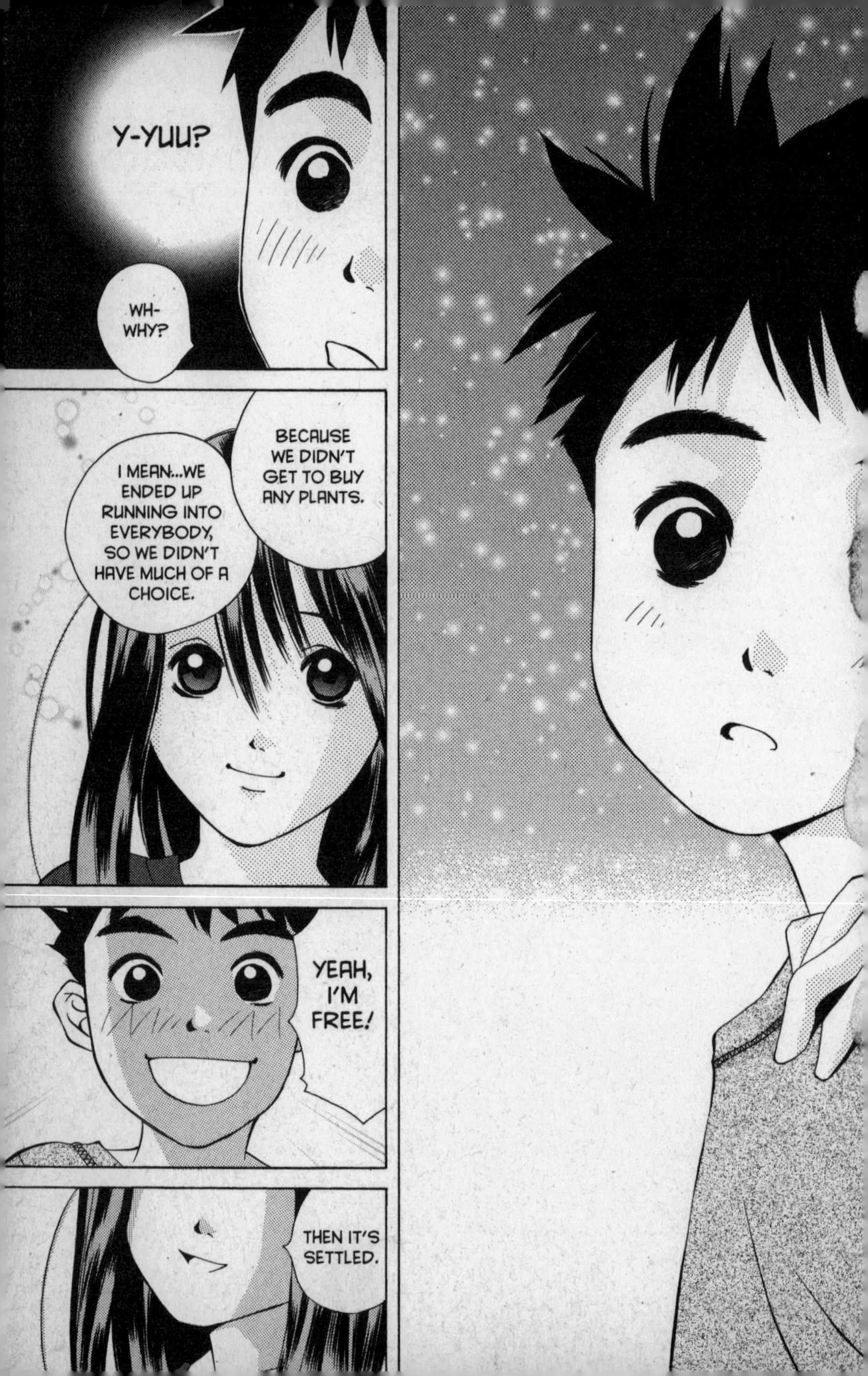
Y-YUU?
WH- WHY?
BECAUSE WE DIDN'T GET TO BUY ANY PLANTS.
I MEAN...WE ENDED UP RUNNING INTO EVERYBODY, SO WE DIDN'T HAVE MUCH OF A CHOICE.
YEAH, I'M FREE!
THEN IT'S SETTLED.

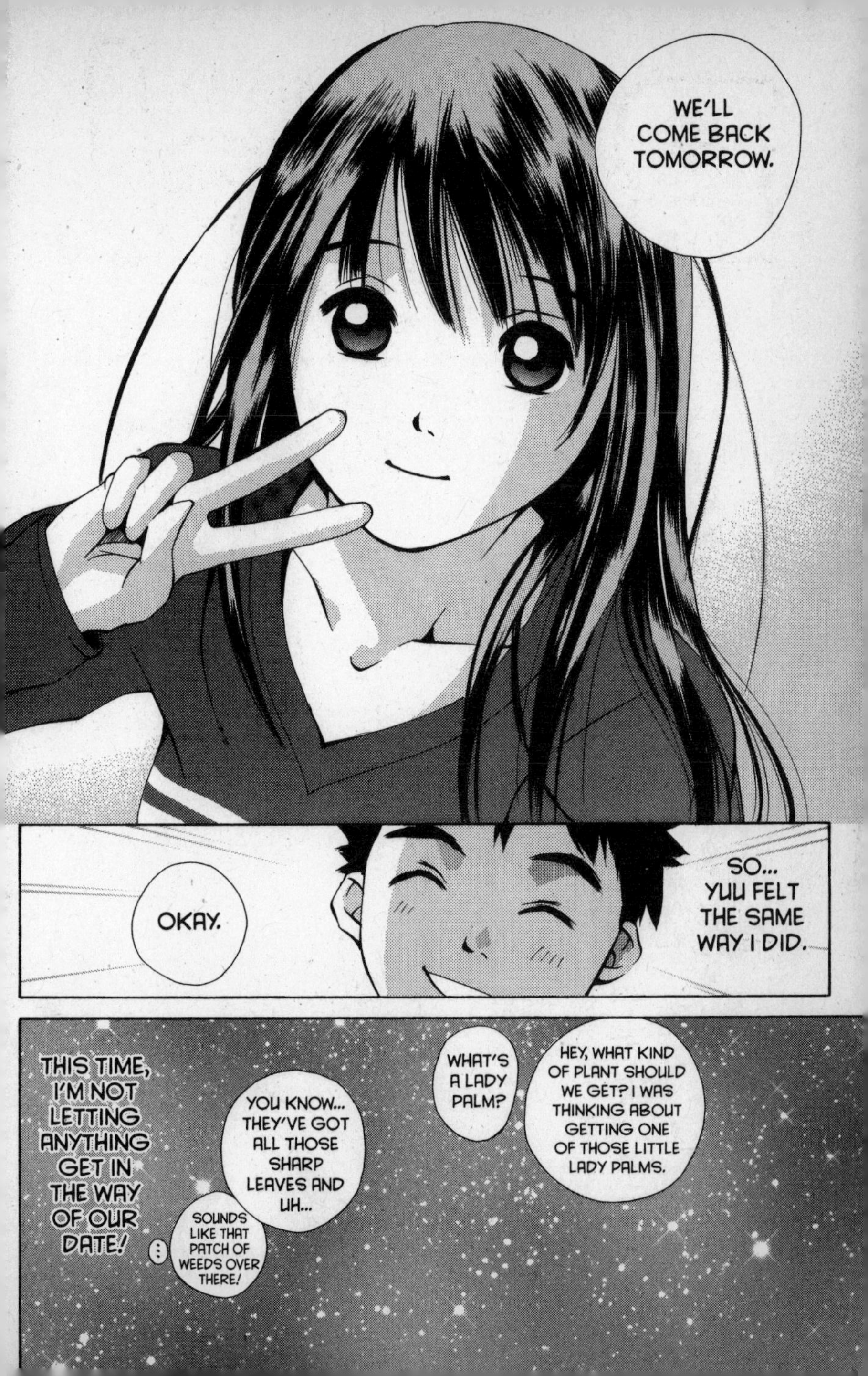
WE'LL COME BACK TOMORROW.
SO... YUU FELT THE SAME WAY I DID.
OKAY.
HEY, WHAT KIND OF PLANT SHOULD WE GET? I WAS THINKING ABOUT GETTING ONE OF THOSE LITTLE LADY PALMS.
WHAT'S A LADY PALM?
YOU KNOW... THEY'VE GOT ALL THOSE SHARP LEAVES AND UH...
SOUNDS LIKE THAT PATCH OF WEEDS OVER THERE!
...
THIS TIME, I'M NOT LETTING ANYTHING GET IN THE WAY OF OUR DATE!

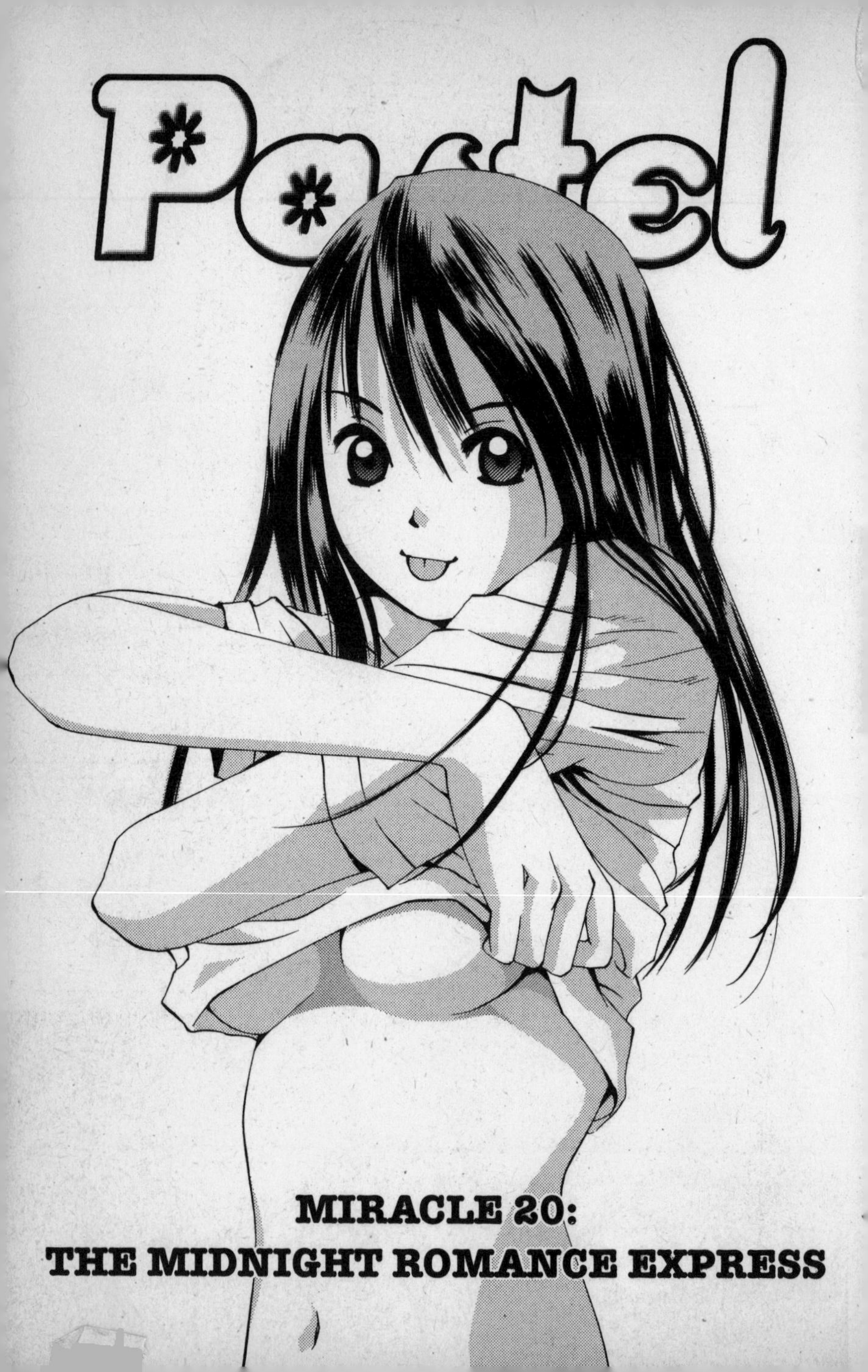
Pastel

MIRACLE 20:
THE MIDNIGHT ROMANCE EXPRESS

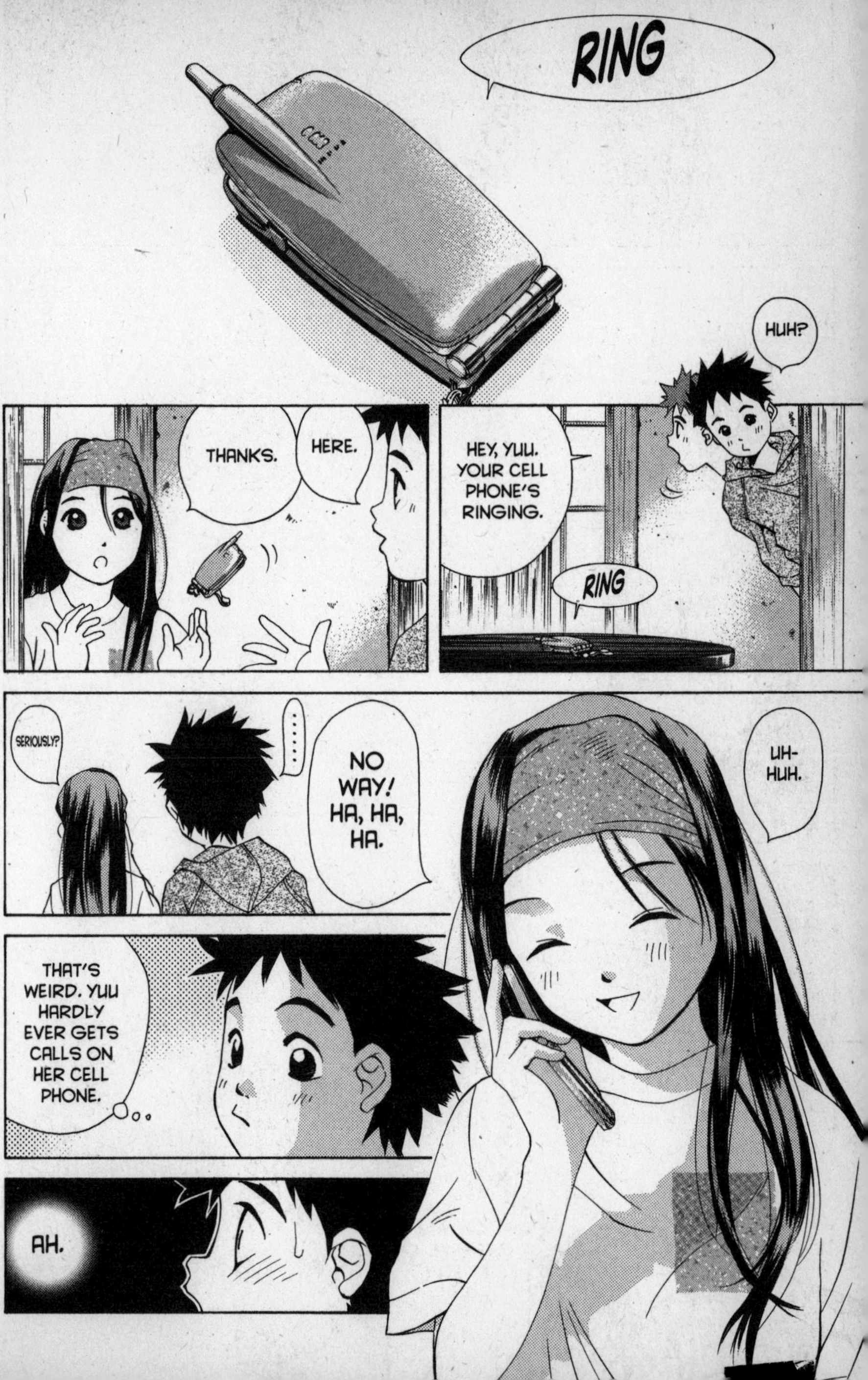
RING
HUH?
HEY, YUU. YOUR CELL PHONE'S RINGING.
RING
HERE.
THANKS.
UH-HUH.
NO WAY! HA, HA, HA.
......
SERIOUSLY?
THAT'S WEIRD. YUU HARDLY EVER GETS CALLS ON HER CELL PHONE.
AH.

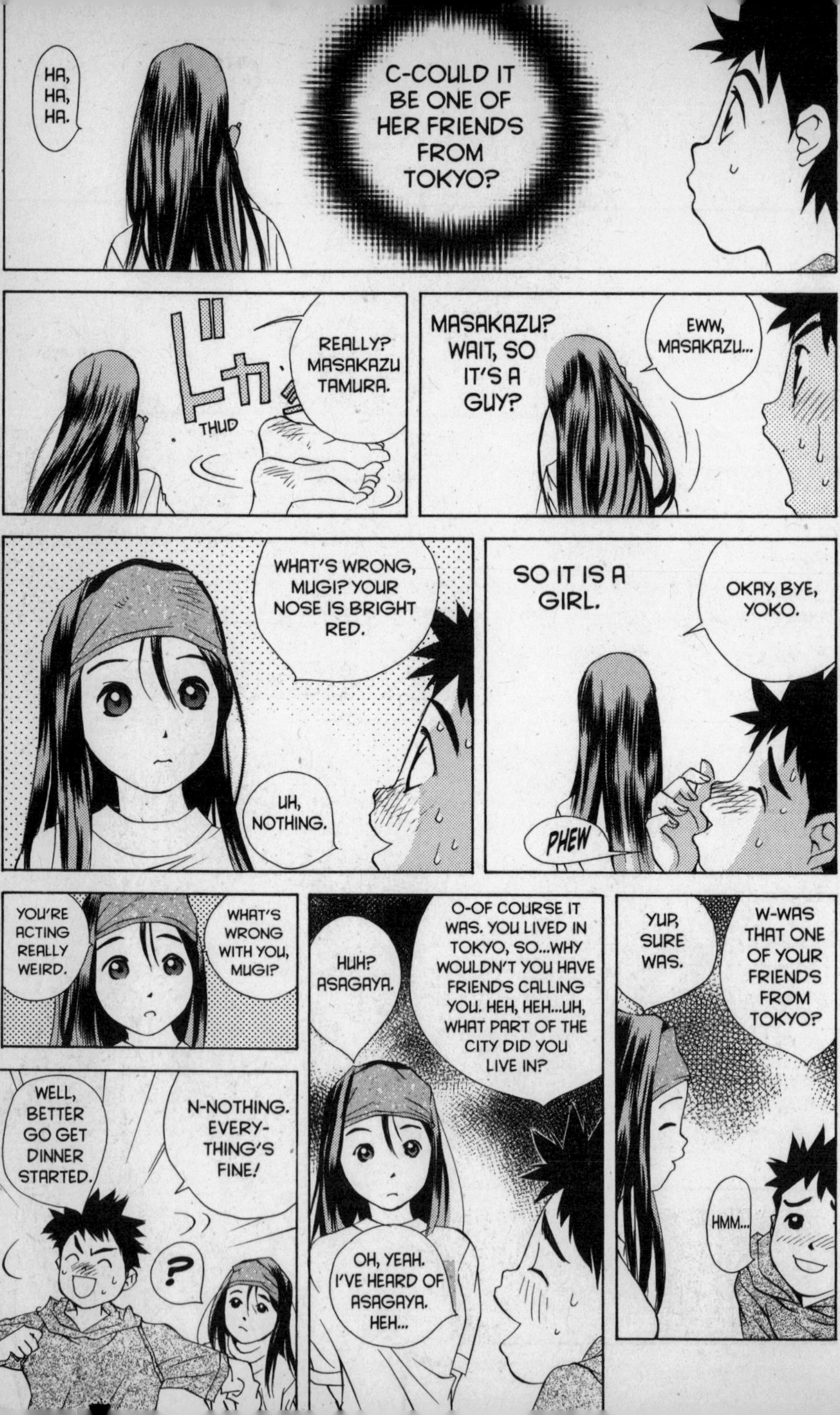
C-COULD IT BE ONE OF HER FRIENDS FROM TOKYO?
HA, HA, HA.
EWW, MASAKAZU...
MASAKAZU? WAIT, SO IT'S A GUY?
REALLY? MASAKAZU TAMURA.
ドカ
THUD
OKAY, BYE, YOKO.
SO IT IS A GIRL.
PHEW
WHAT'S WRONG, MUGI? YOUR NOSE IS BRIGHT RED.
UH, NOTHING.
W-WAS THAT ONE OF YOUR FRIENDS FROM TOKYO?
YUP, SURE WAS.
HMM...
O-OF COURSE IT WAS. YOU LIVED IN TOKYO, SO...WHY WOULDN'T YOU HAVE FRIENDS CALLING YOU. HEH, HEH...UH, WHAT PART OF THE CITY DID YOU LIVE IN?
HUH? ASAGAYA.
OH, YEAH. I'VE HEARD OF ASAGAYA. HEH...
WHAT'S WRONG WITH YOU, MUGI?
YOU'RE ACTING REALLY WEIRD.
N-NOTHING. EVERY-THING'S FINE!
WELL, BETTER GO GET DINNER STARTED.
?

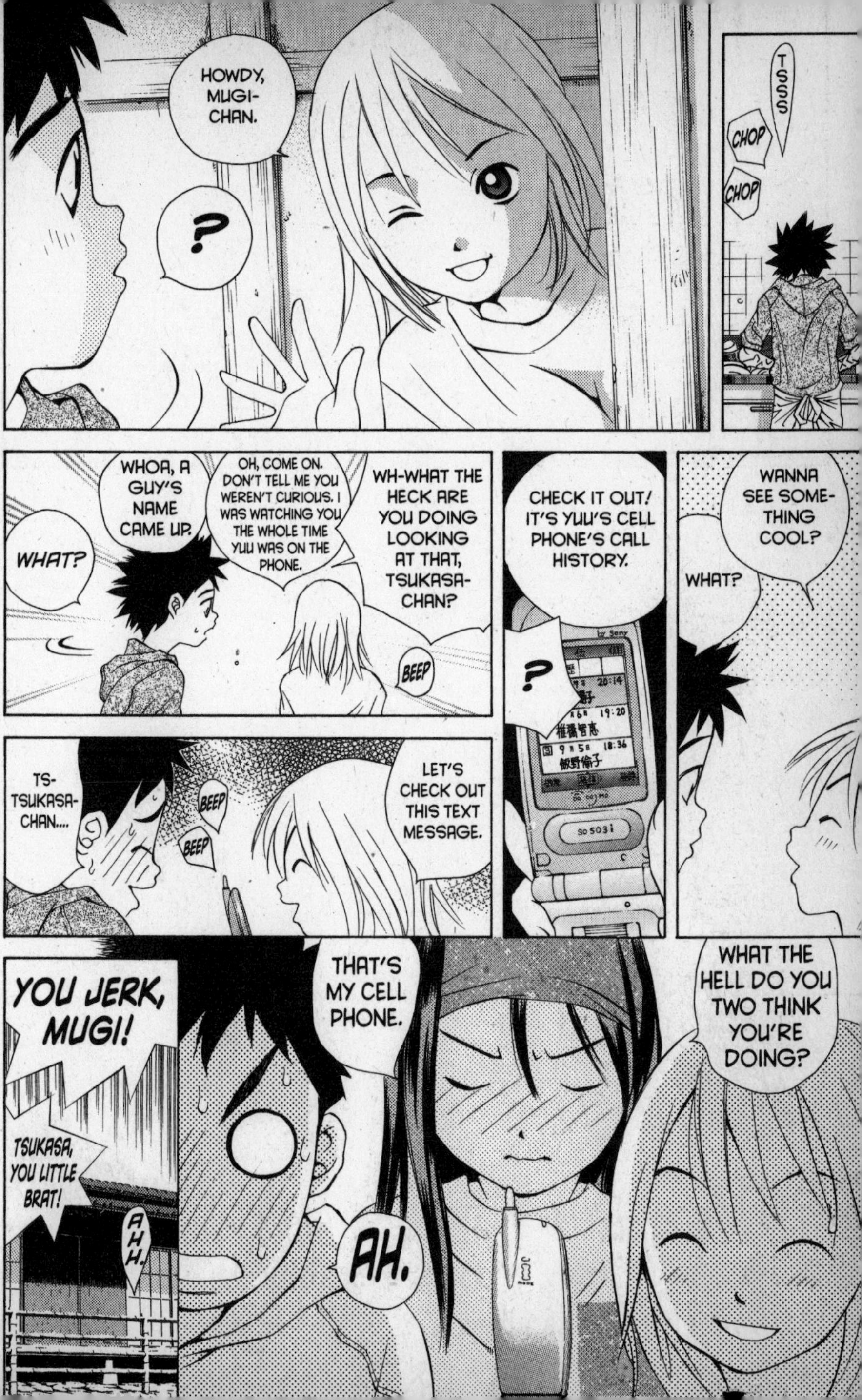
TSSS
CHOP
CHOP
HOWDY, MUGI-CHAN.
?
WANNA SEE SOME-THING COOL?
WHAT?
CHECK IT OUT! IT'S YUU'S CELL PHONE'S CALL HISTORY.
?
WH-WHAT THE HECK ARE YOU DOING LOOKING AT THAT, TSUKASA-CHAN?
OH, COME ON. DON'T TELL ME YOU WEREN'T CURIOUS. I WAS WATCHING YOU THE WHOLE TIME YUU WAS ON THE PHONE.
WHOA, A GUY'S NAME CAME UP.
WHAT?
BEEP
LET'S CHECK OUT THIS TEXT MESSAGE.
BEEP
BEEP
TS-TSUKASA-CHAN....
WHAT THE HELL DO YOU TWO THINK YOU'RE DOING?
THAT'S MY CELL PHONE.
AH.
YOU JERK, MUGI!
TSUKASA, YOU LITTLE BRAT!
AHH.

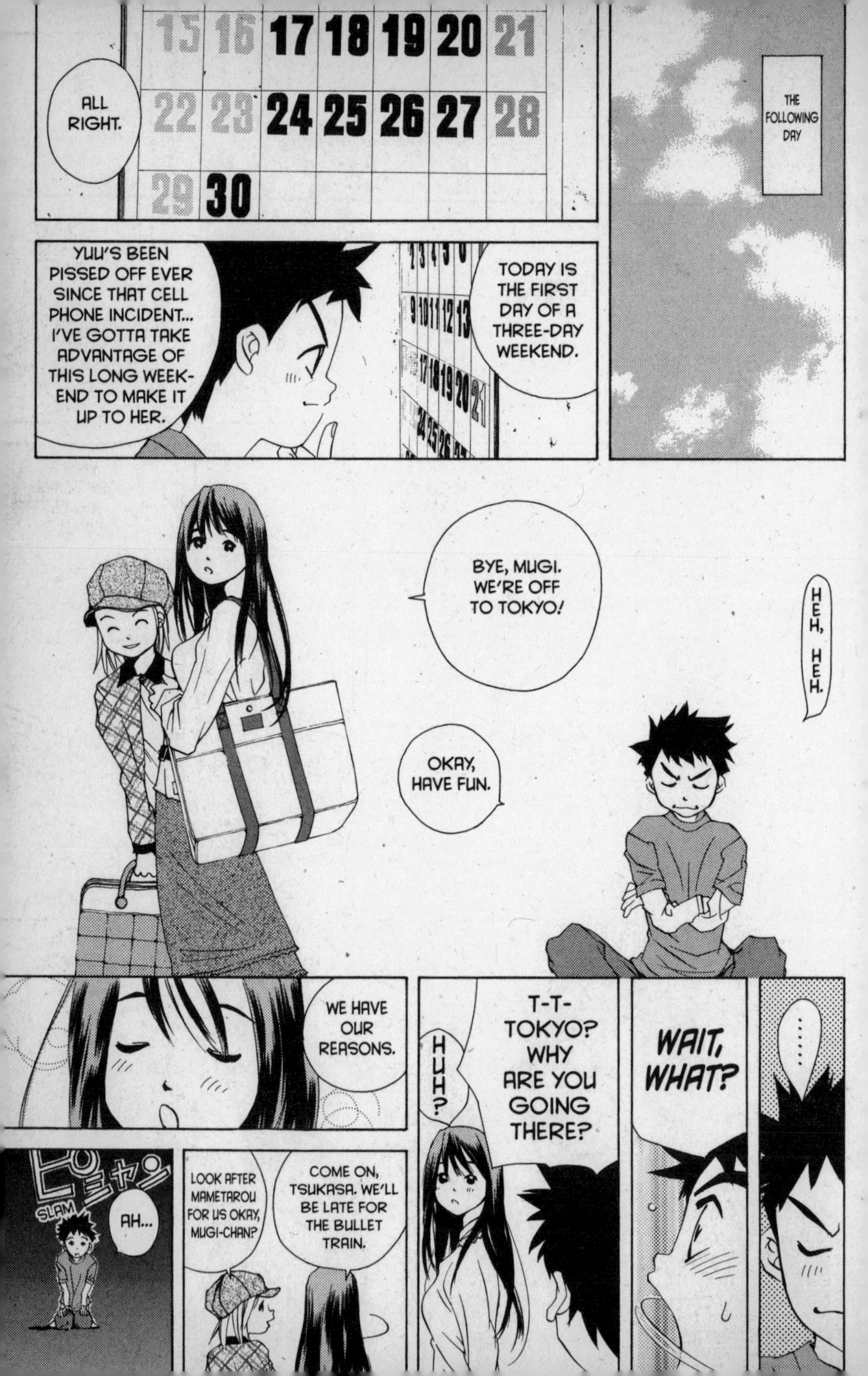
THE FOLLOWING DAY
ALL RIGHT.
TODAY IS THE FIRST DAY OF A THREE-DAY WEEKEND.
YUU'S BEEN PISSED OFF EVER SINCE THAT CELL PHONE INCIDENT... I'VE GOTTA TAKE ADVANTAGE OF THIS LONG WEEK-END TO MAKE IT UP TO HER.
HEH, HEH.
BYE, MUGI. WE'RE OFF TO TOKYO!
OKAY, HAVE FUN.
......
WAIT, WHAT?
T-T-TOKYO? WHY ARE YOU GOING THERE?
HUH?
WE HAVE OUR REASONS.
COME ON, TSUKASA. WE'LL BE LATE FOR THE BULLET TRAIN.
LOOK AFTER MAMETAROU FOR US OKAY, MUGI-CHAN?
AH...
SLAM

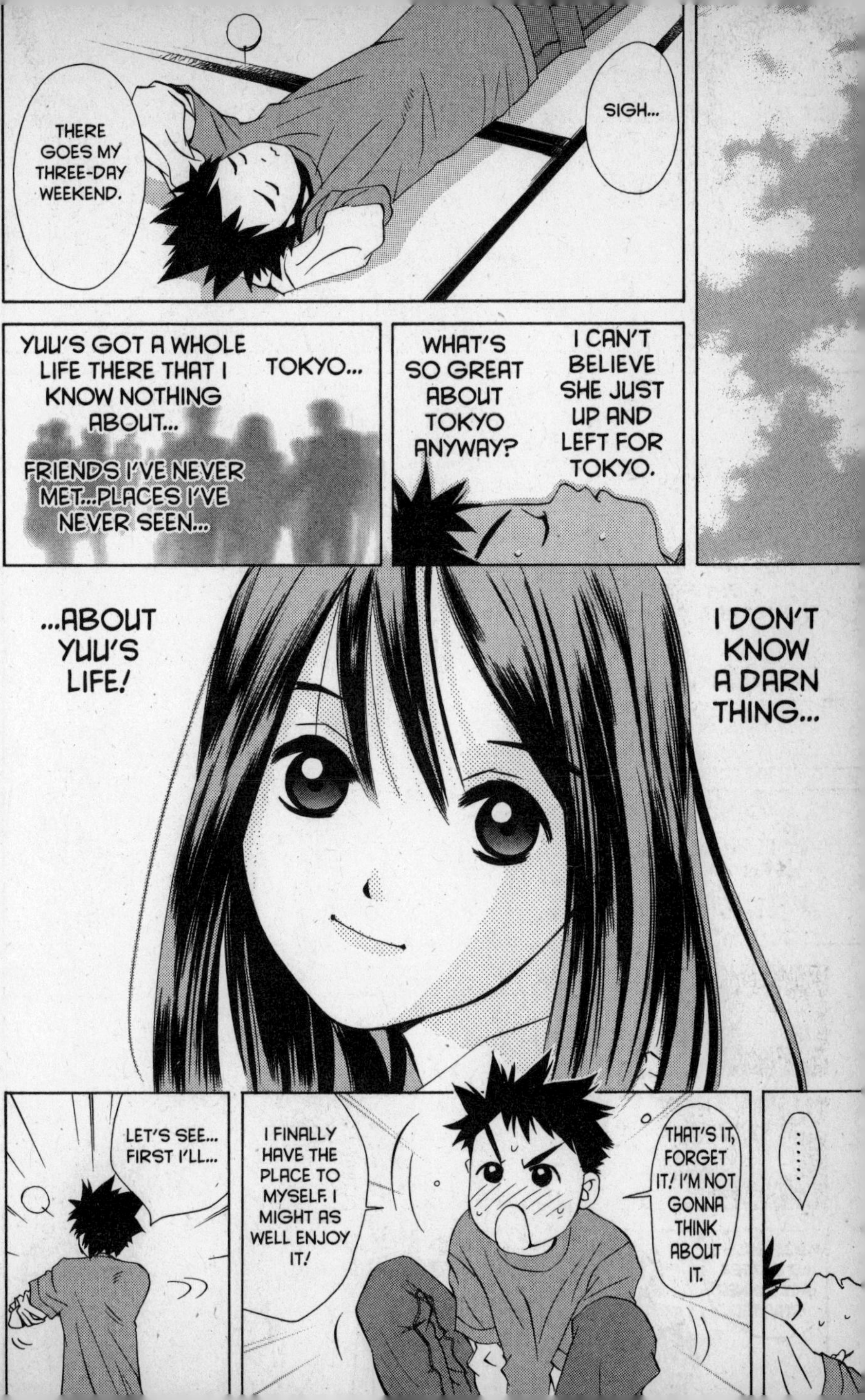
SIGH...
THERE GOES MY THREE-DAY WEEKEND.
I CAN'T BELIEVE SHE JUST UP AND LEFT FOR TOKYO.
WHAT'S SO GREAT ABOUT TOKYO ANYWAY?
TOKYO...
YUU'S GOT A WHOLE LIFE THERE THAT I KNOW NOTHING ABOUT...
FRIENDS I'VE NEVER MET...PLACES I'VE NEVER SEEN...
I DON'T KNOW A DARN THING...
...ABOUT YUU'S LIFE!
......
THAT'S IT, FORGET IT! I'M NOT GONNA THINK ABOUT IT.
I FINALLY HAVE THE PLACE TO MYSELF. I MIGHT AS WELL ENJOY IT!
LET'S SEE... FIRST I'LL...

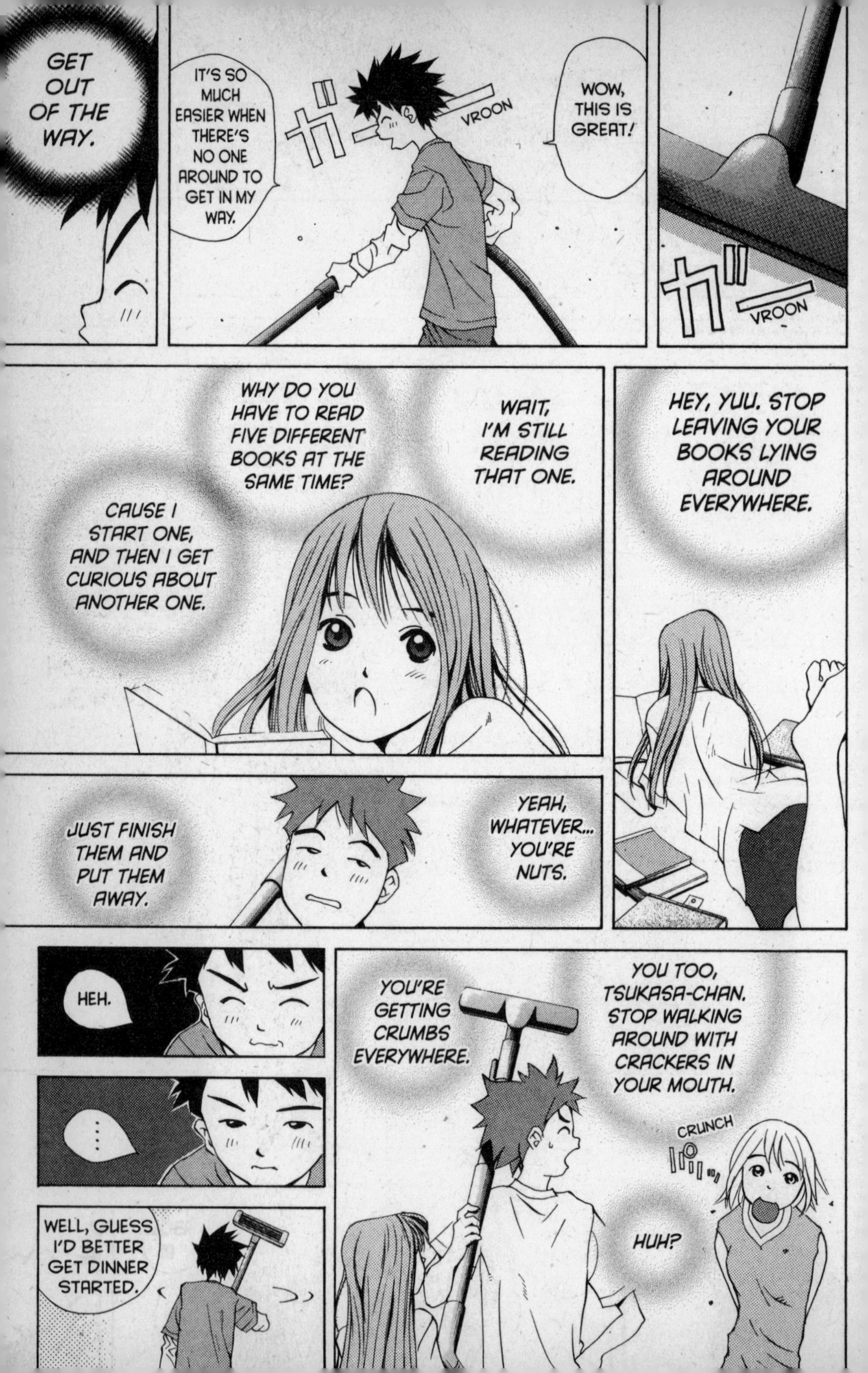
ガー
VROON
WOW, THIS IS GREAT!
ガー
VROON
IT'S SO MUCH EASIER WHEN THERE'S NO ONE AROUND TO GET IN MY WAY.
GET OUT OF THE WAY.
HEY, YUU. STOP LEAVING YOUR BOOKS LYING AROUND EVERYWHERE.
WAIT, I'M STILL READING THAT ONE.
WHY DO YOU HAVE TO READ FIVE DIFFERENT BOOKS AT THE SAME TIME?
CAUSE I START ONE, AND THEN I GET CURIOUS ABOUT ANOTHER ONE.
YEAH, WHATEVER... YOU'RE NUTS.
JUST FINISH THEM AND PUT THEM AWAY.
YOU TOO, TSUKASA-CHAN. STOP WALKING AROUND WITH CRACKERS IN YOUR MOUTH.
YOU'RE GETTING CRUMBS EVERYWHERE.
CRUNCH
HUH?
HEH.
....
WELL, GUESS I'D BETTER GET DINNER STARTED.

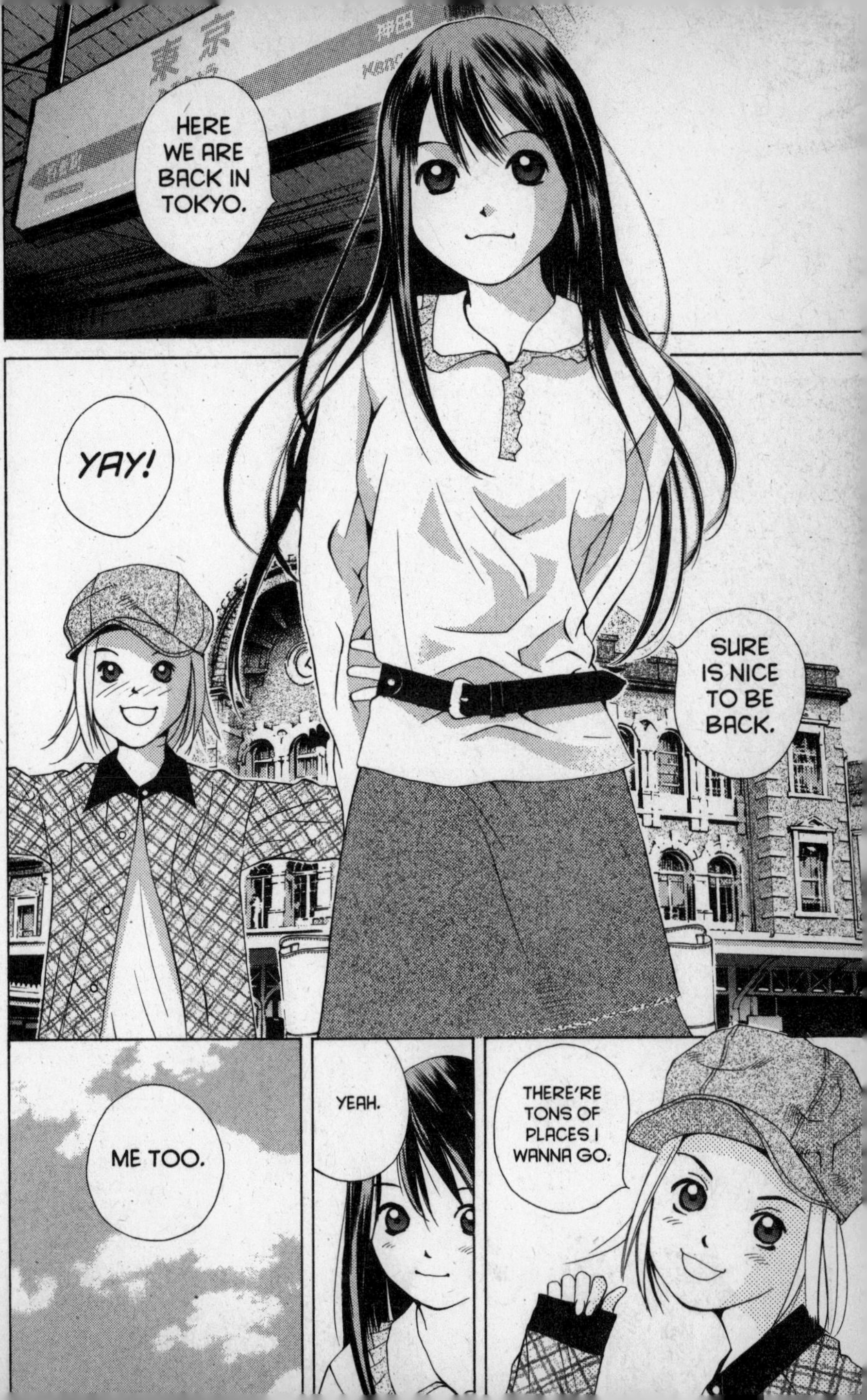
HERE WE ARE BACK IN TOKYO.
東京
SURE IS NICE TO BE BACK.
YAY!
THERE'RE TONS OF PLACES I WANNA GO.
YEAH.
ME TOO.

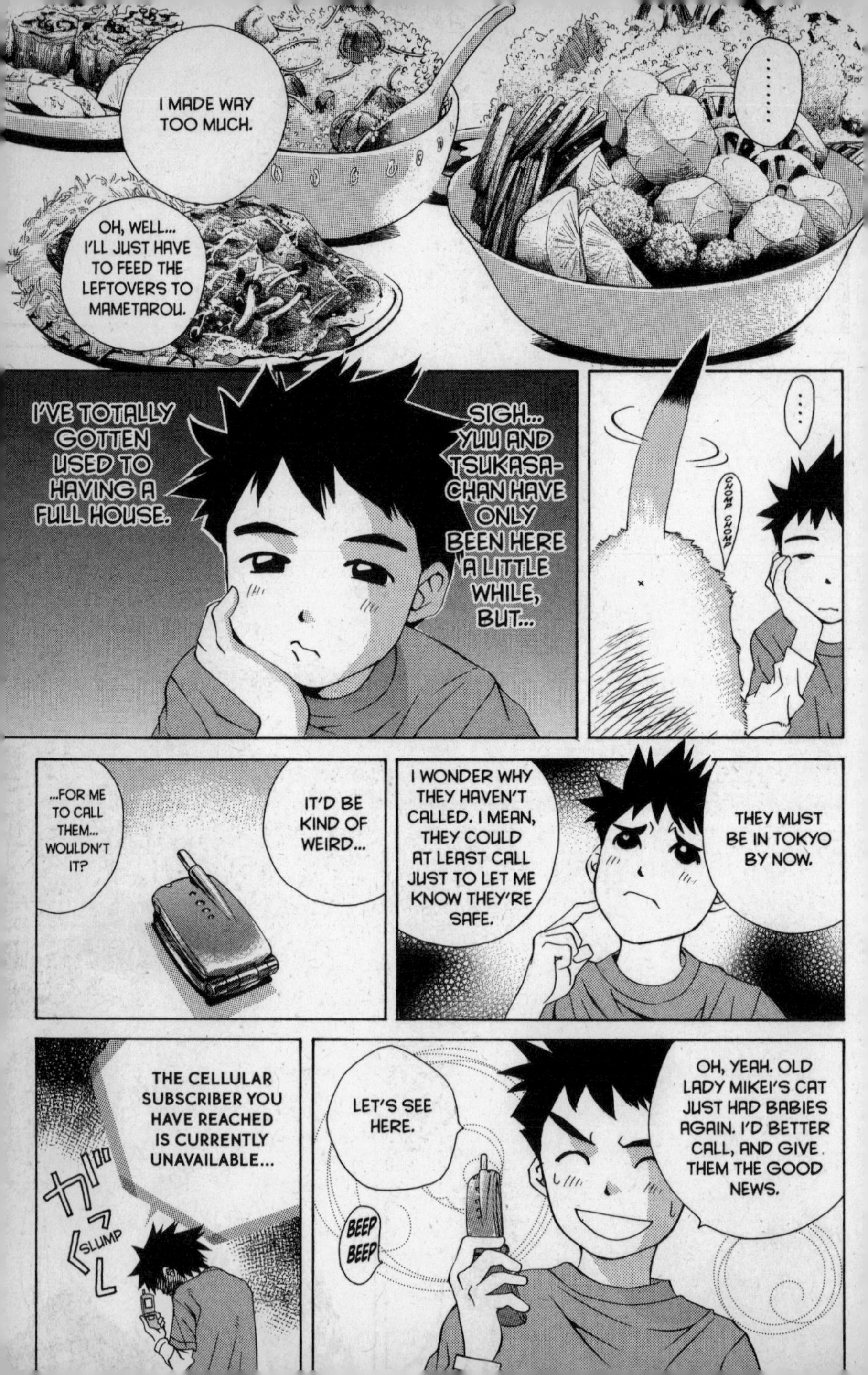
......
I MADE WAY TOO MUCH.
OH, WELL... I'LL JUST HAVE TO FEED THE LEFTOVERS TO MAMETAROU.
.....
CHOMP CHOMP
SIGH... YUU AND TSUKASA-CHAN HAVE ONLY BEEN HERE A LITTLE WHILE, BUT...
I'VE TOTALLY GOTTEN USED TO HAVING A FULL HOUSE.
THEY MUST BE IN TOKYO BY NOW.
I WONDER WHY THEY HAVEN'T CALLED. I MEAN, THEY COULD AT LEAST CALL JUST TO LET ME KNOW THEY'RE SAFE.
IT'D BE KIND OF WEIRD...
...FOR ME TO CALL THEM... WOULDN'T IT?
OH, YEAH. OLD LADY MIKEI'S CAT JUST HAD BABIES AGAIN. I'D BETTER CALL, AND GIVE THEM THE GOOD NEWS.
LET'S SEE HERE.
BEEP BEEP
THE CELLULAR SUBSCRIBER YOU HAVE REACHED IS CURRENTLY UNAVAILABLE...
SLUMP

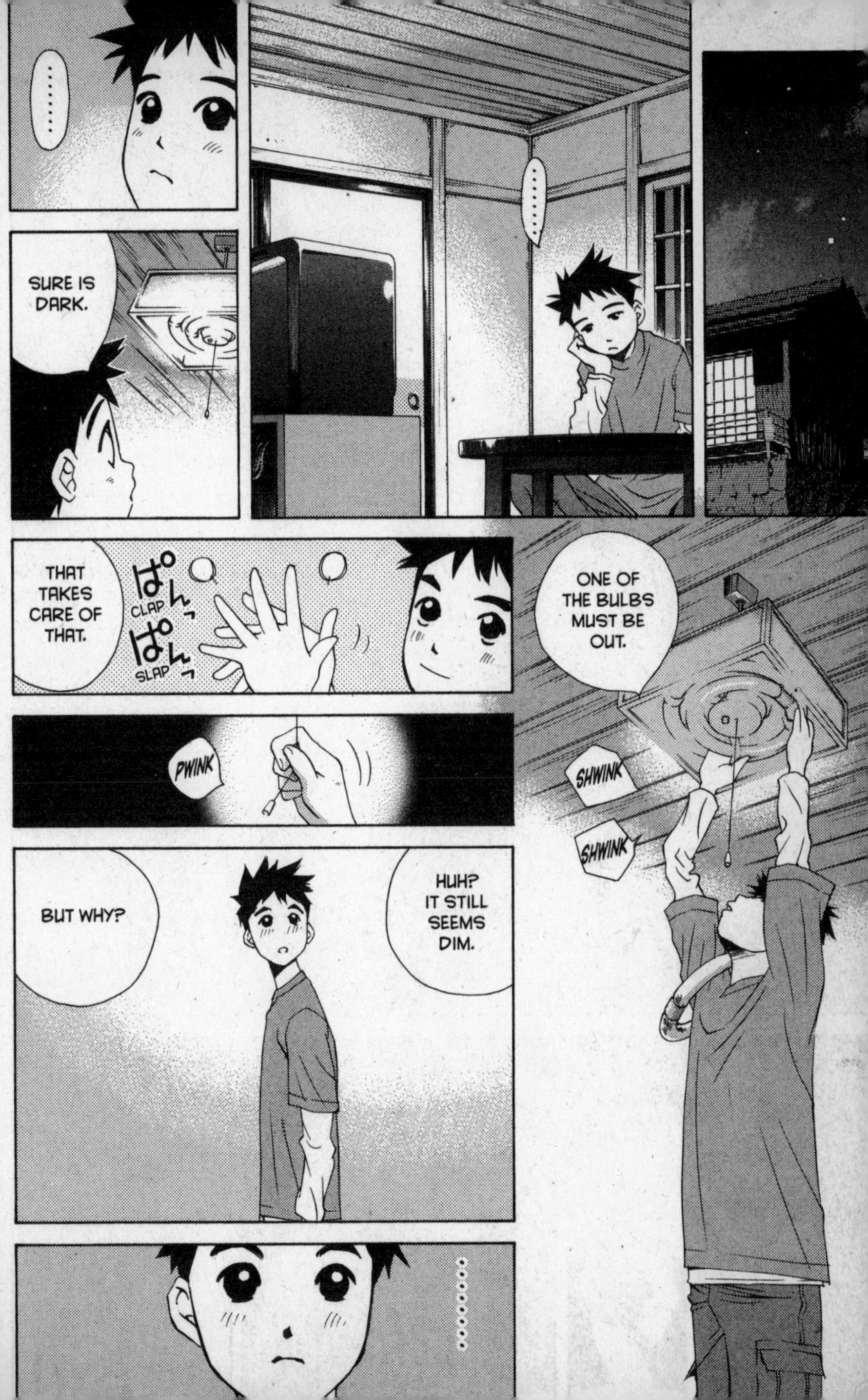

......
......
SURE IS DARK.
ONE OF THE BULBS MUST BE OUT.
SHWINK
SHWINK
ぱん CLAP
ぱん SLAP
THAT TAKES CARE OF THAT.
PWINK
HUH? IT STILL SEEMS DIM.
BUT WHY?
......

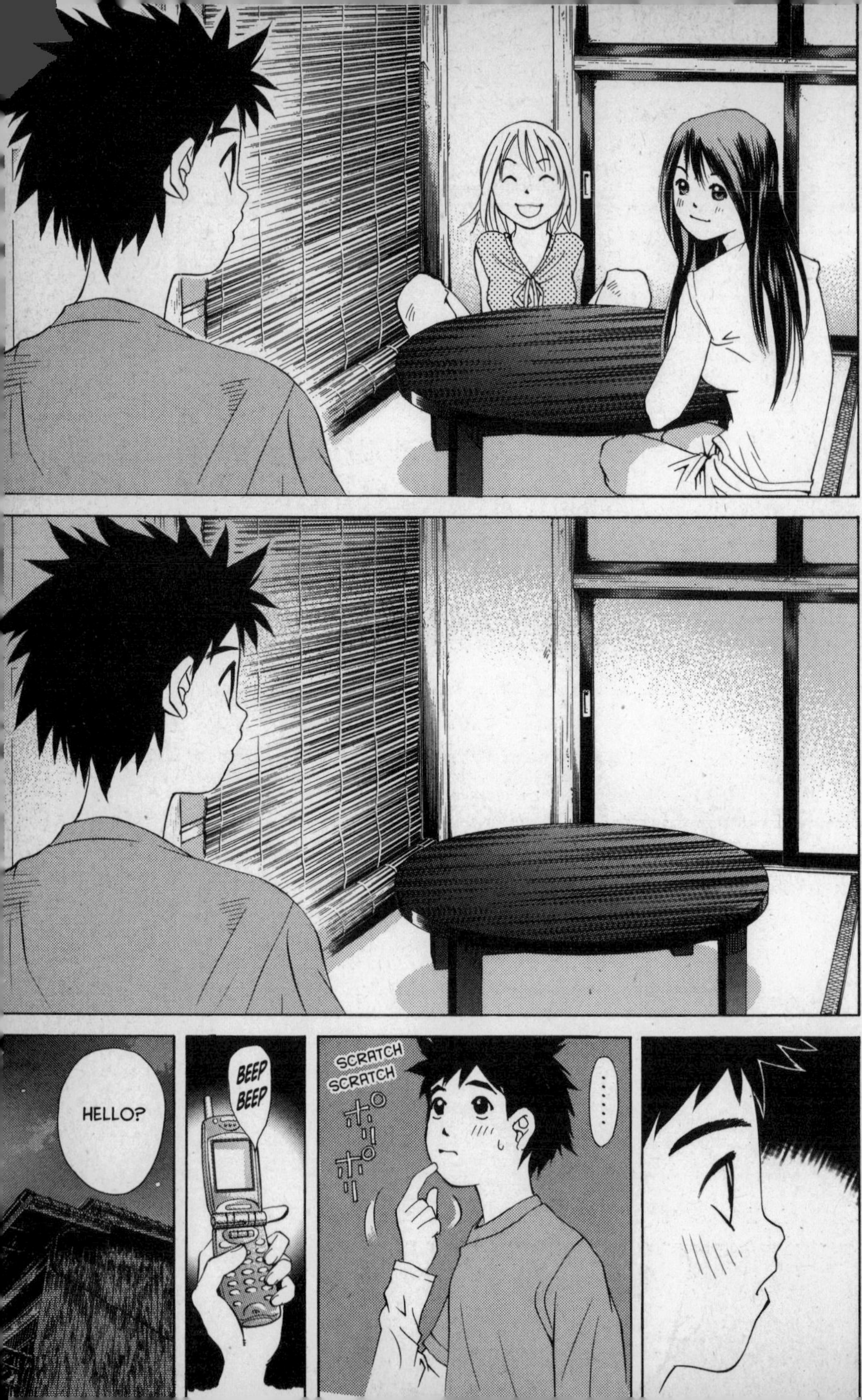
......
SCRATCH SCRATCH
ポリポリ
BEEP BEEP
HELLO?

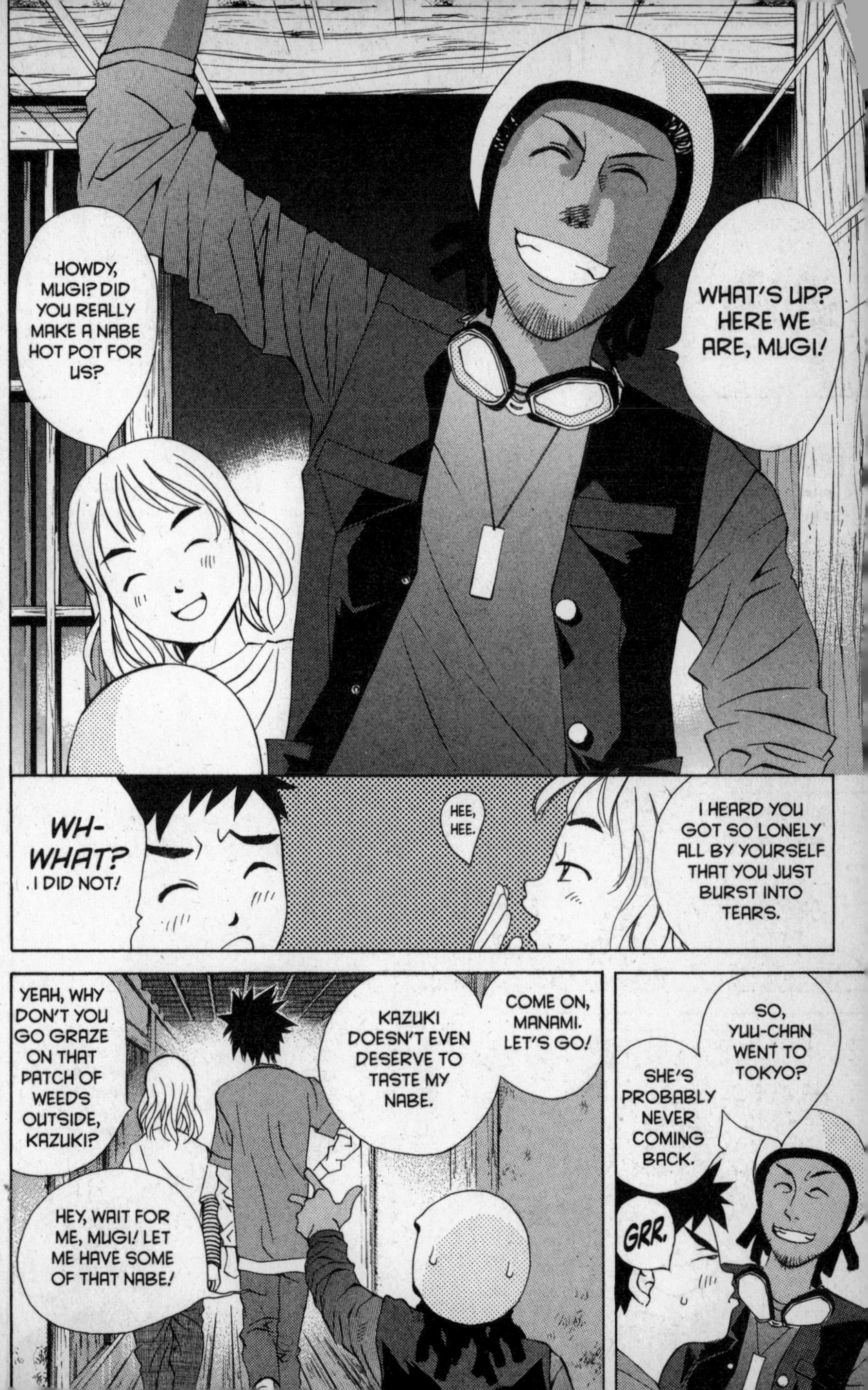
WHAT'S UP? HERE WE ARE, MUGI!
HOWDY, MUGI? DID YOU REALLY MAKE A NABE HOT POT FOR US?
I HEARD YOU GOT SO LONELY ALL BY YOURSELF THAT YOU JUST BURST INTO TEARS.
HEE, HEE.
WH- WHAT? I DID NOT!
SO, YUU-CHAN WENT TO TOKYO?
SHE'S PROBABLY NEVER COMING BACK.
GRR.
COME ON, MANAMI. LET'S GO!
KAZUKI DOESN'T EVEN DESERVE TO TASTE MY NABE.
YEAH, WHY DON'T YOU GO GRAZE ON THAT PATCH OF WEEDS OUTSIDE, KAZUKI?
HEY, WAIT FOR ME, MUGI! LET ME HAVE SOME OF THAT NABE!

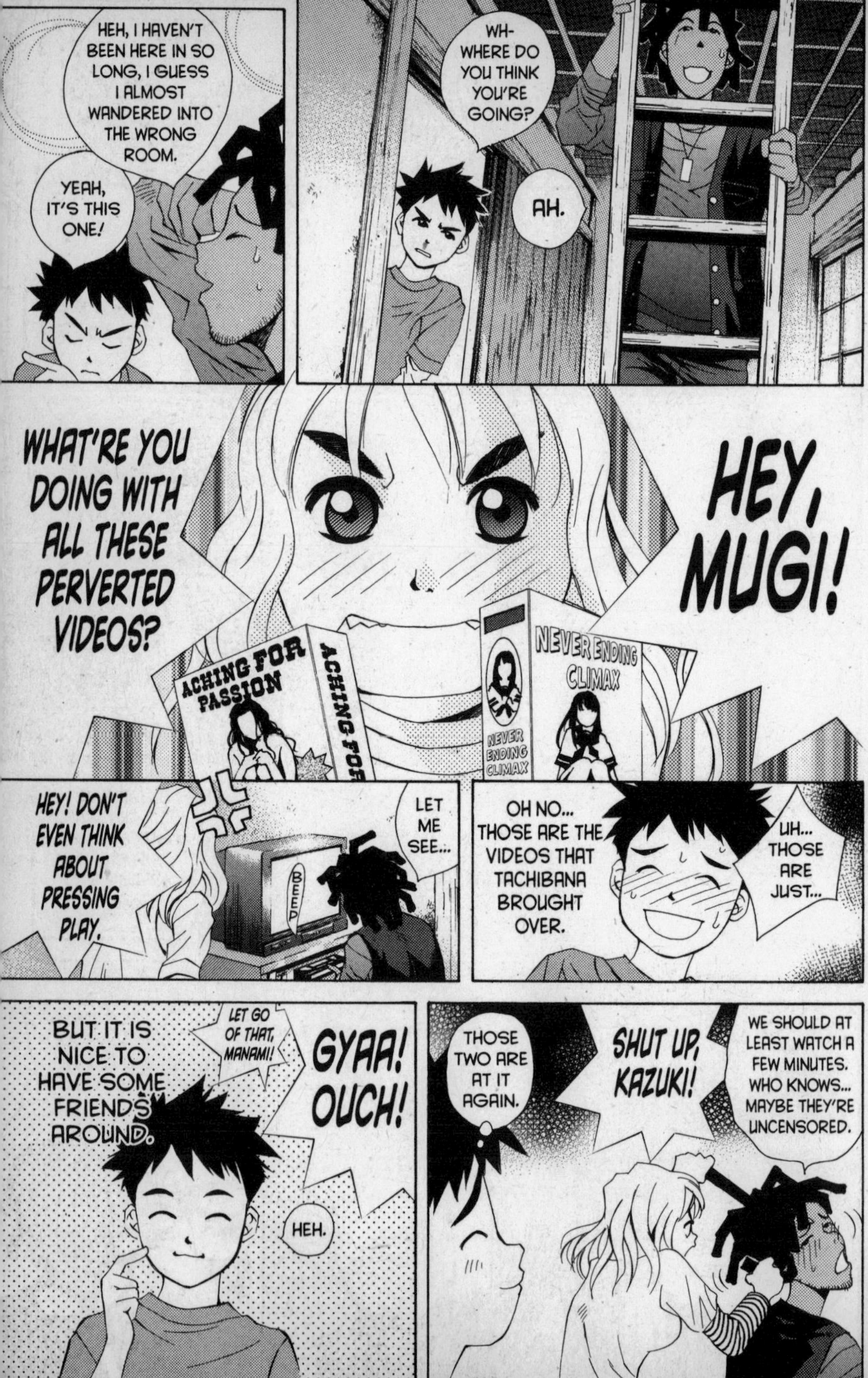
WH- WHERE DO YOU THINK YOU'RE GOING?
AH.
HEH, I HAVEN'T BEEN HERE IN SO LONG, I GUESS I ALMOST WANDERED INTO THE WRONG ROOM.
YEAH, IT'S THIS ONE!
HEY, MUGI!
WHAT'RE YOU DOING WITH ALL THESE PERVERTED VIDEOS?
NEVER ENDING CLIMAX
NEVER ENDING CLIMAX
ACHING FOR PASSION
ACHING FOR
UH... THOSE ARE JUST...
OH NO... THOSE ARE THE VIDEOS THAT TACHIBANA BROUGHT OVER.
LET ME SEE...
BEEP
HEY! DON'T EVEN THINK ABOUT PRESSING PLAY.
WE SHOULD AT LEAST WATCH A FEW MINUTES. WHO KNOWS... MAYBE THEY'RE UNCENSORED.
SHUT UP, KAZUKI!
THOSE TWO ARE AT IT AGAIN.
GYAA! OUCH!
LET GO OF THAT, MANAMI!
BUT IT IS NICE TO HAVE SOME FRIENDS AROUND.
HEH.

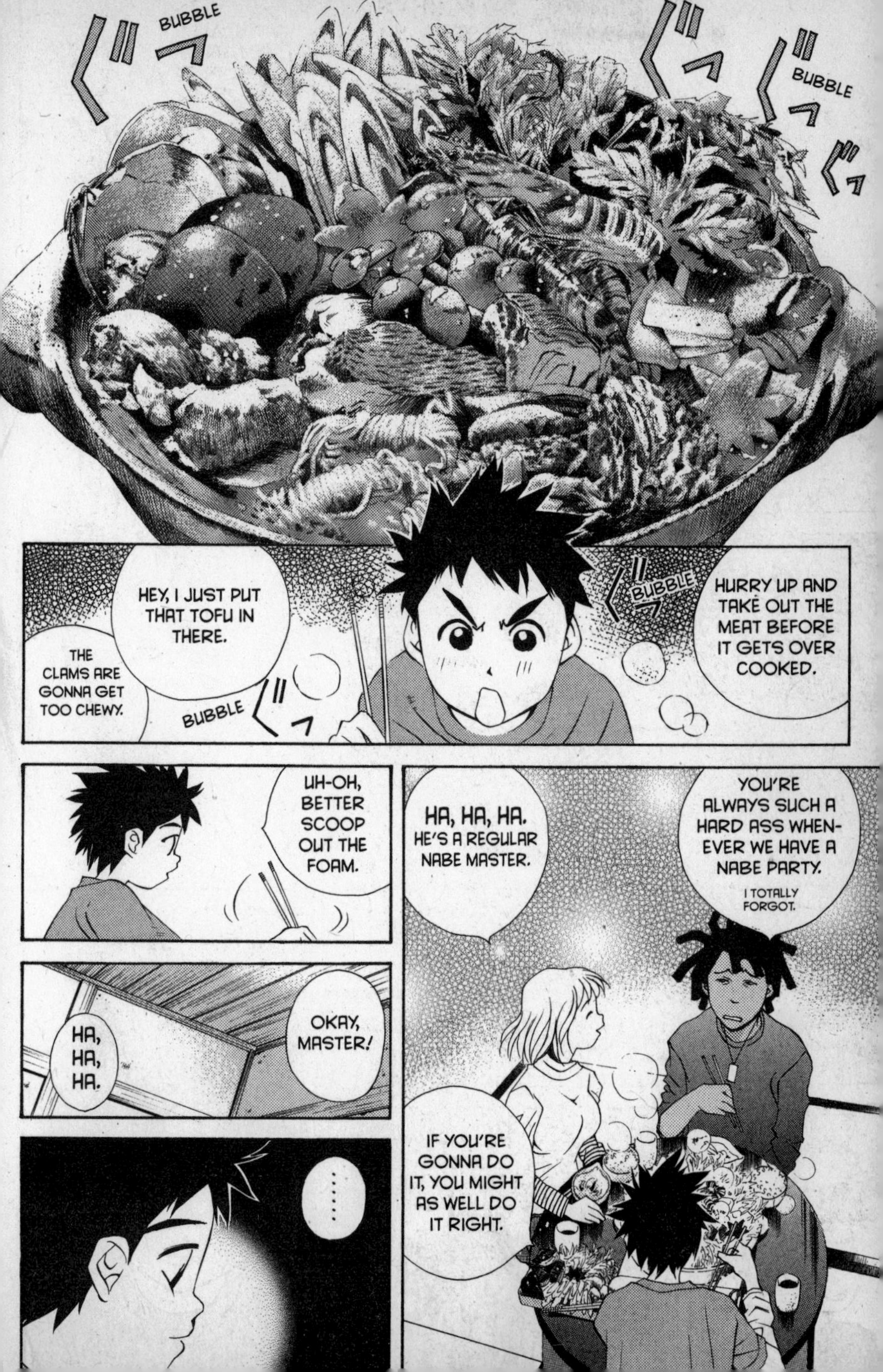
BUBBLE
BUBBLE
HURRY UP AND TAKE OUT THE MEAT BEFORE IT GETS OVER COOKED.
BUBBLE
HEY, I JUST PUT THAT TOFU IN THERE.
THE CLAMS ARE GONNA GET TOO CHEWY.
BUBBLE
YOU'RE ALWAYS SUCH A HARD ASS WHEN-EVER WE HAVE A NABE PARTY.
I TOTALLY FORGOT.
HA, HA, HA. HE'S A REGULAR NABE MASTER.
IF YOU'RE GONNA DO IT, YOU MIGHT AS WELL DO IT RIGHT.
UH-OH, BETTER SCOOP OUT THE FOAM.
OKAY, MASTER!
HA, HA, HA.
......

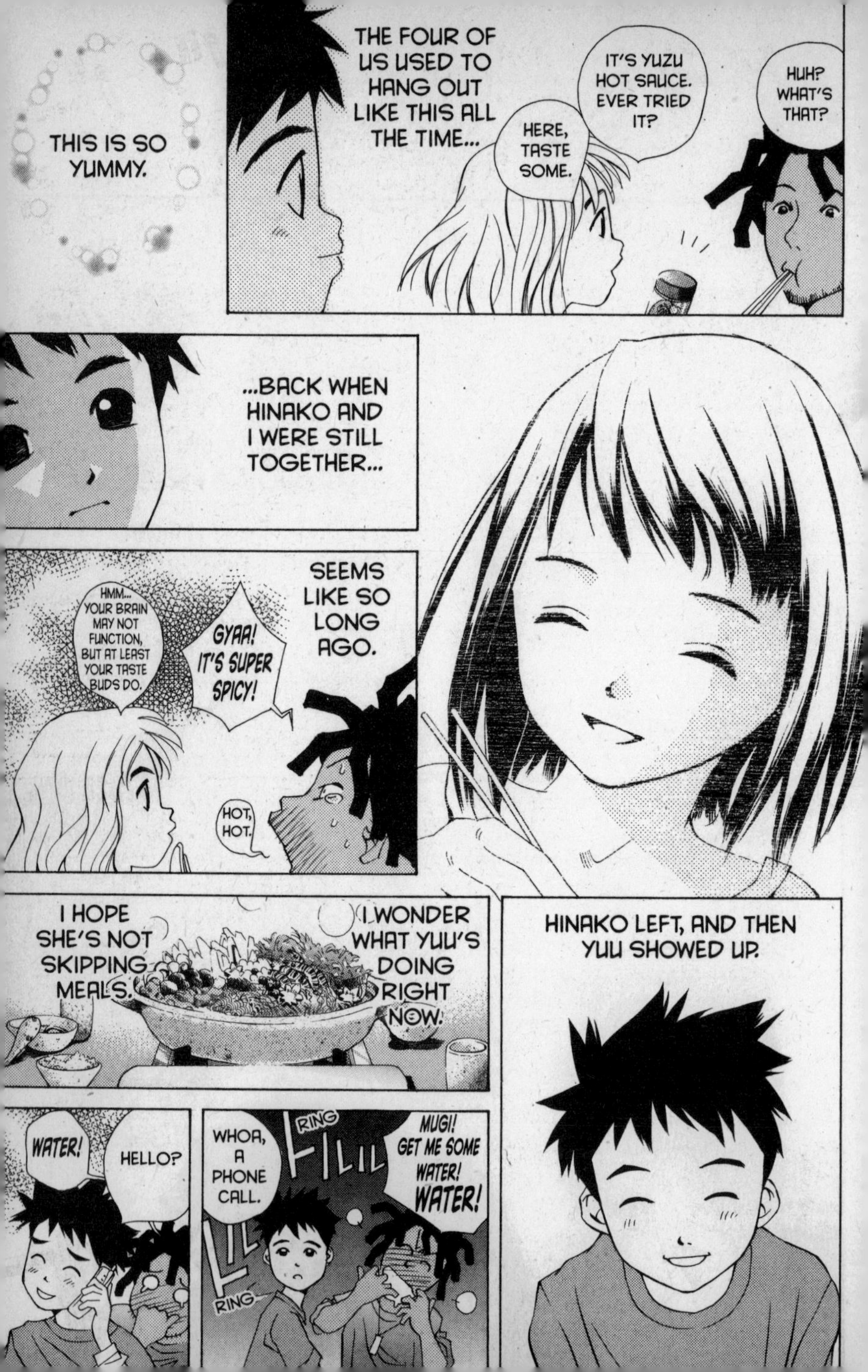
HUH? WHAT'S THAT?
IT'S YUZU HOT SAUCE. EVER TRIED IT?
HERE, TASTE SOME.
THE FOUR OF US USED TO HANG OUT LIKE THIS ALL THE TIME...
THIS IS SO YUMMY.
...BACK WHEN HINAKO AND I WERE STILL TOGETHER...
SEEMS LIKE SO LONG AGO.
GYAA! IT'S SUPER SPICY!
HMM... YOUR BRAIN MAY NOT FUNCTION, BUT AT LEAST YOUR TASTE BUDS DO.
HOT, HOT.
HINAKO LEFT, AND THEN YUU SHOWED UP.
I WONDER WHAT YUU'S DOING RIGHT NOW.
I HOPE SHE'S NOT SKIPPING MEALS.
MUGI! GET ME SOME WATER! WATER!
RING
WHOA, A PHONE CALL.
RING
HELLO?
WATER!

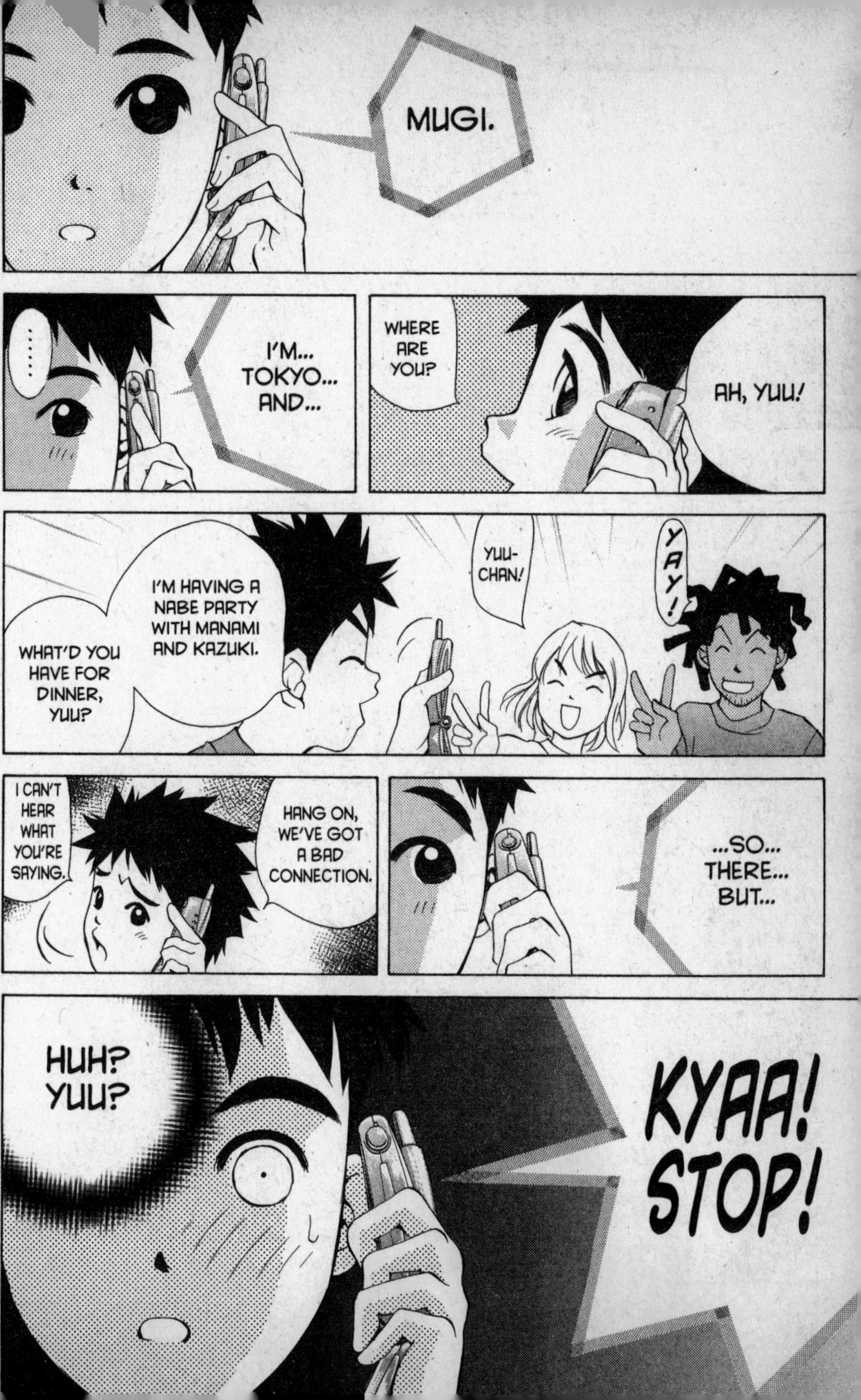
MUGI.
AH, YUU!
WHERE ARE YOU?
I'M... TOKYO... AND...
......
YAY!
YUU-CHAN!
I'M HAVING A NABE PARTY WITH MANAMI AND KAZUKI.
WHAT'D YOU HAVE FOR DINNER, YUU?
...SO... THERE... BUT...
HANG ON, WE'VE GOT A BAD CONNECTION.
I CAN'T HEAR WHAT YOU'RE SAYING.
KYAA! STOP!
HUH? YUU?

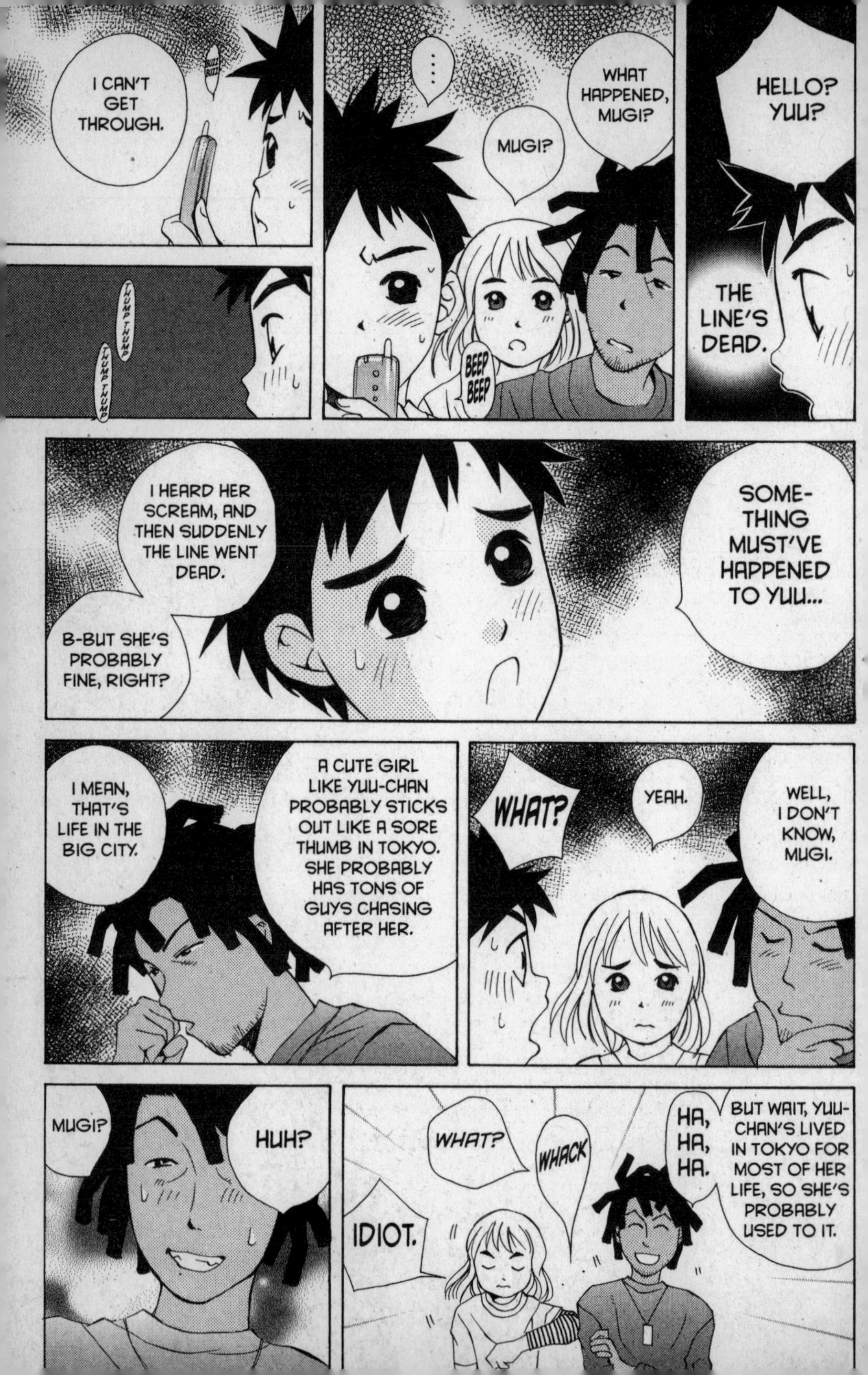
HELLO? YUU?
THE LINE'S DEAD.
WHAT HAPPENED, MUGI?
MUGI?
.....
BEEP BEEP
I CAN'T GET THROUGH.
BUZZ BUZZ
THUMP THUMP
THUMP THUMP
SOME-THING MUST'VE HAPPENED TO YUU...
I HEARD HER SCREAM, AND THEN SUDDENLY THE LINE WENT DEAD.
B-BUT SHE'S PROBABLY FINE, RIGHT?
WELL, I DON'T KNOW, MUGI.
YEAH.
WHAT?
A CUTE GIRL LIKE YUU-CHAN PROBABLY STICKS OUT LIKE A SORE THUMB IN TOKYO. SHE PROBABLY HAS TONS OF GUYS CHASING AFTER HER.
I MEAN, THAT'S LIFE IN THE BIG CITY.
BUT WAIT, YUU-CHAN'S LIVED IN TOKYO FOR MOST OF HER LIFE, SO SHE'S PROBABLY USED TO IT.
HA, HA, HA.
WHACK
WHAT?
IDIOT.
HUH?
MUGI?

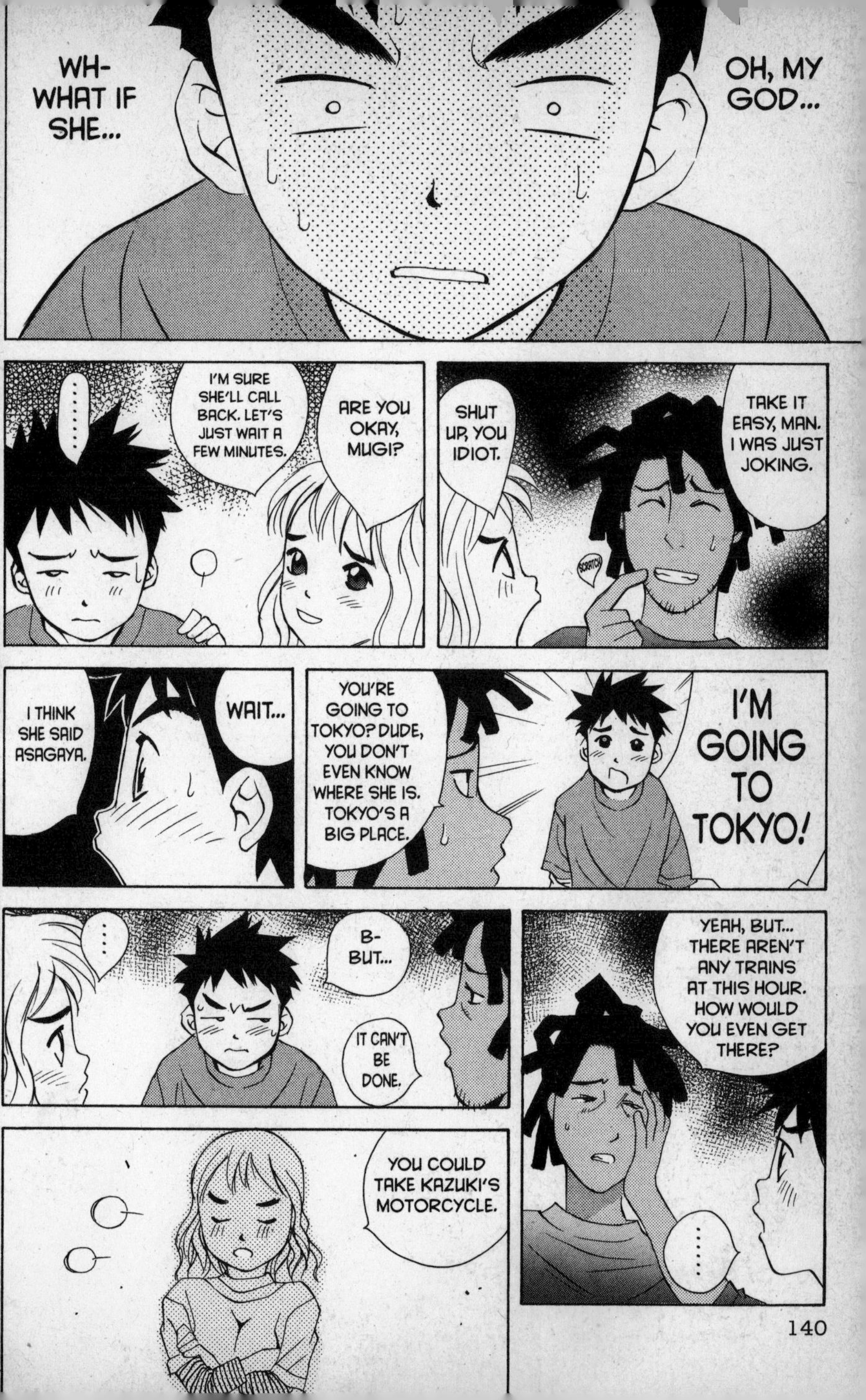
OH, MY GOD...
WH- WHAT IF SHE...
TAKE IT EASY, MAN. I WAS JUST JOKING.
SCRATCH
SHUT UP, YOU IDIOT.
ARE YOU OKAY, MUGI?
I'M SURE SHE'LL CALL BACK. LET'S JUST WAIT A FEW MINUTES.
......
I'M GOING TO TOKYO!
YOU'RE GOING TO TOKYO? DUDE, YOU DON'T EVEN KNOW WHERE SHE IS. TOKYO'S A BIG PLACE.
WAIT...
I THINK SHE SAID ASAGAYA.
YEAH, BUT... THERE AREN'T ANY TRAINS AT THIS HOUR. HOW WOULD YOU EVEN GET THERE?
......
B- BUT...
IT CAN'T BE DONE.
....
YOU COULD TAKE KAZUKI'S MOTORCYCLE.

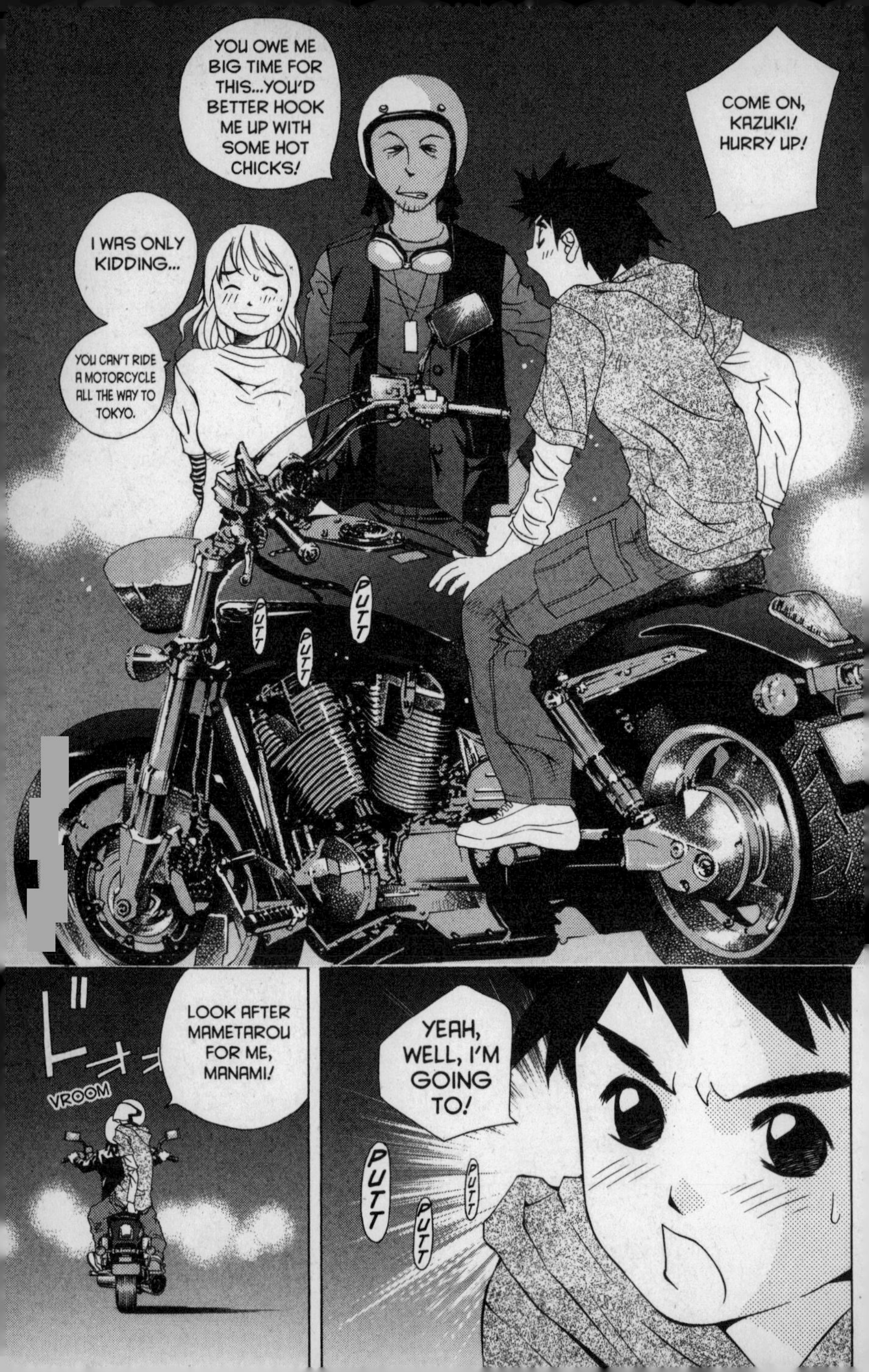
COME ON, KAZUKI! HURRY UP!
YOU OWE ME BIG TIME FOR THIS...YOU'D BETTER HOOK ME UP WITH SOME HOT CHICKS!
I WAS ONLY KIDDING...
YOU CAN'T RIDE A MOTORCYCLE ALL THE WAY TO TOKYO.
PUTT
PUTT
PUTT
YEAH, WELL, I'M GOING TO!
PUTT
PUTT
PUTT
LOOK AFTER MAMETAROU FOR ME, MANAMI!
ドォォ
VROOM

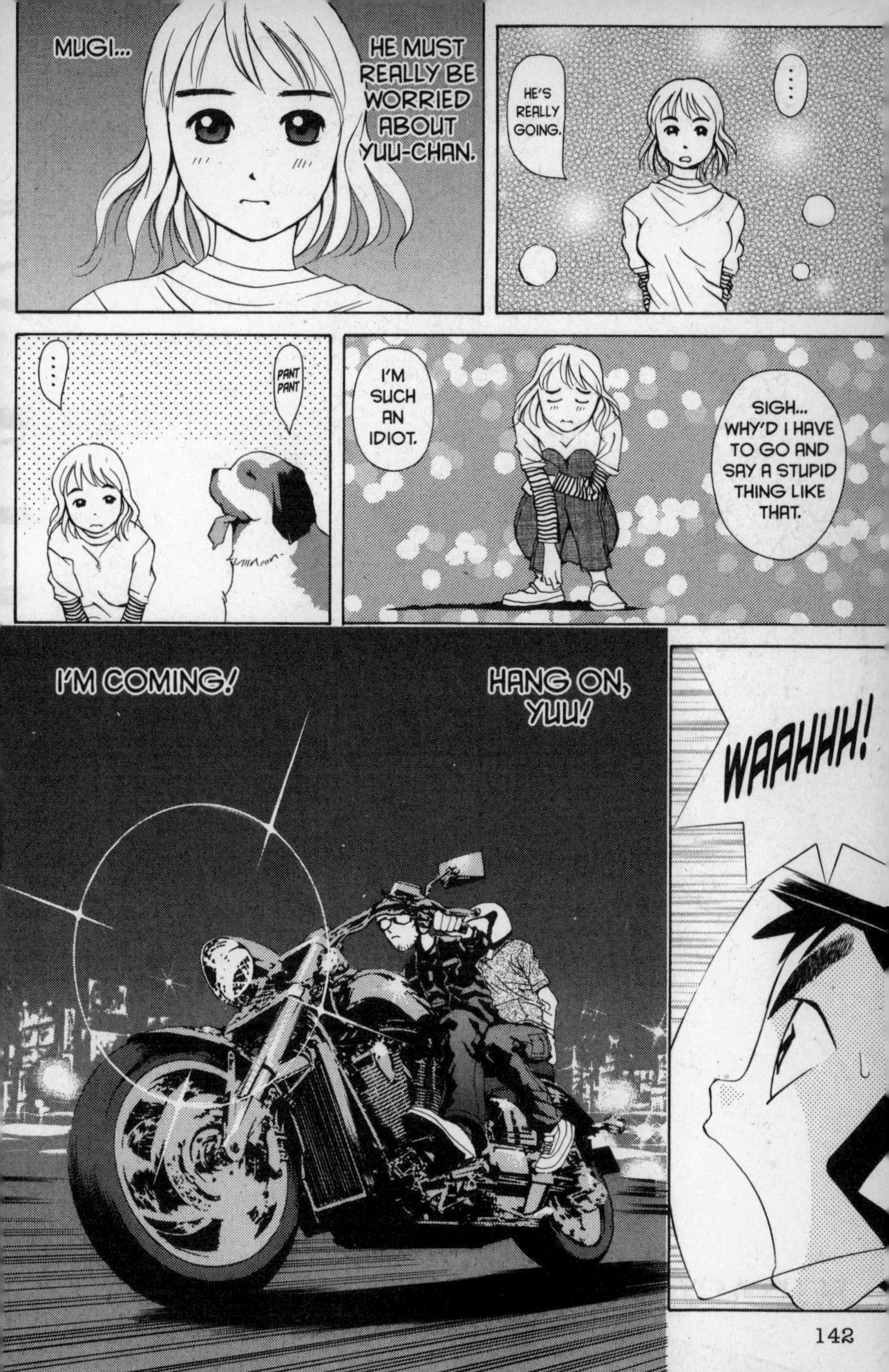

. . . .
HE'S REALLY GOING.
HE MUST REALLY BE WORRIED ABOUT YUU-CHAN.
MUGI...
SIGH... WHY'D I HAVE TO GO AND SAY A STUPID THING LIKE THAT.
I'M SUCH AN IDIOT.
PANT PANT
. . . .
WAAHHH!
HANG ON, YUU!
I'M COMING!

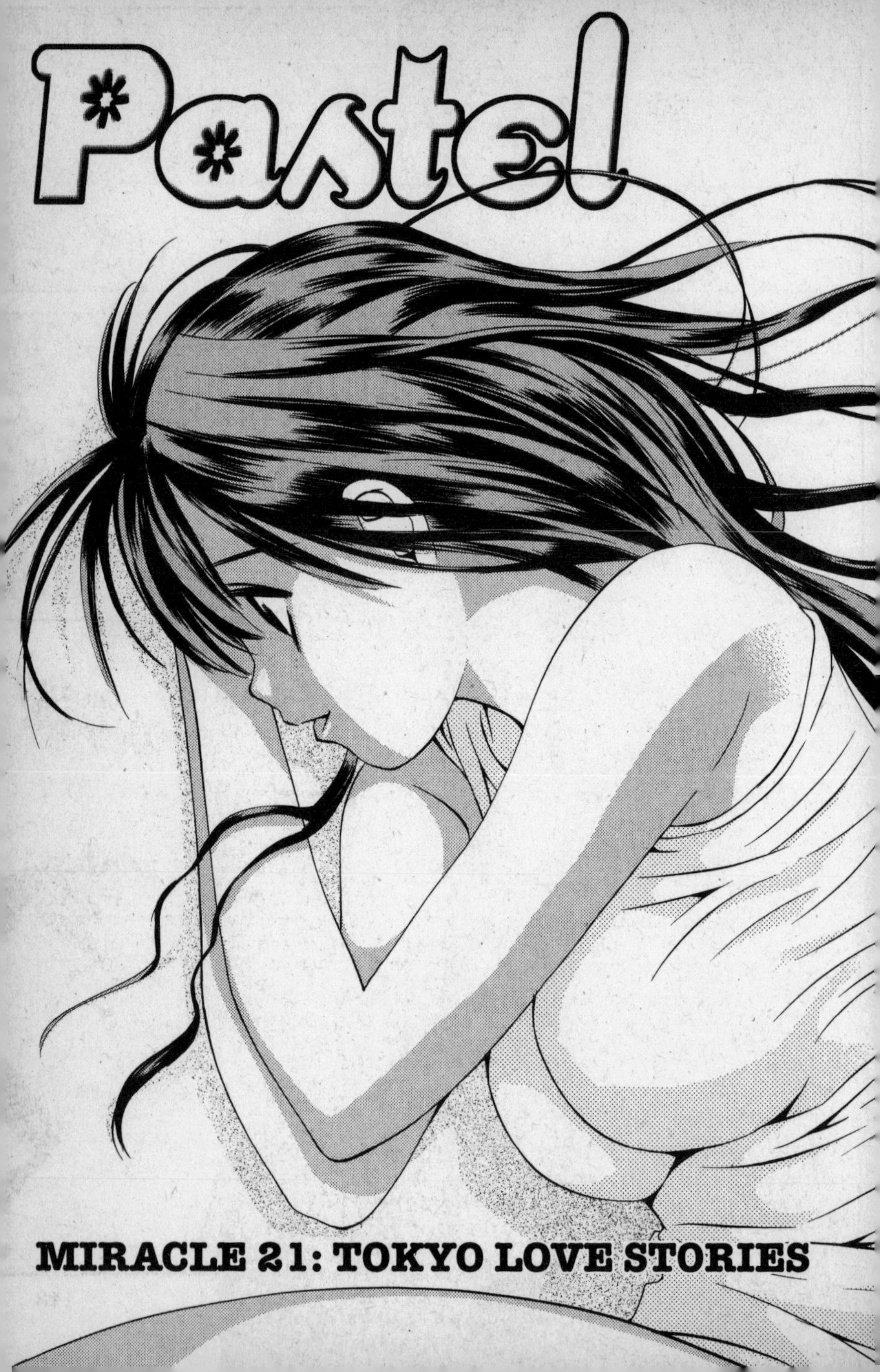
Pastel
MIRACLE 21: TOKYO LOVE STORIES

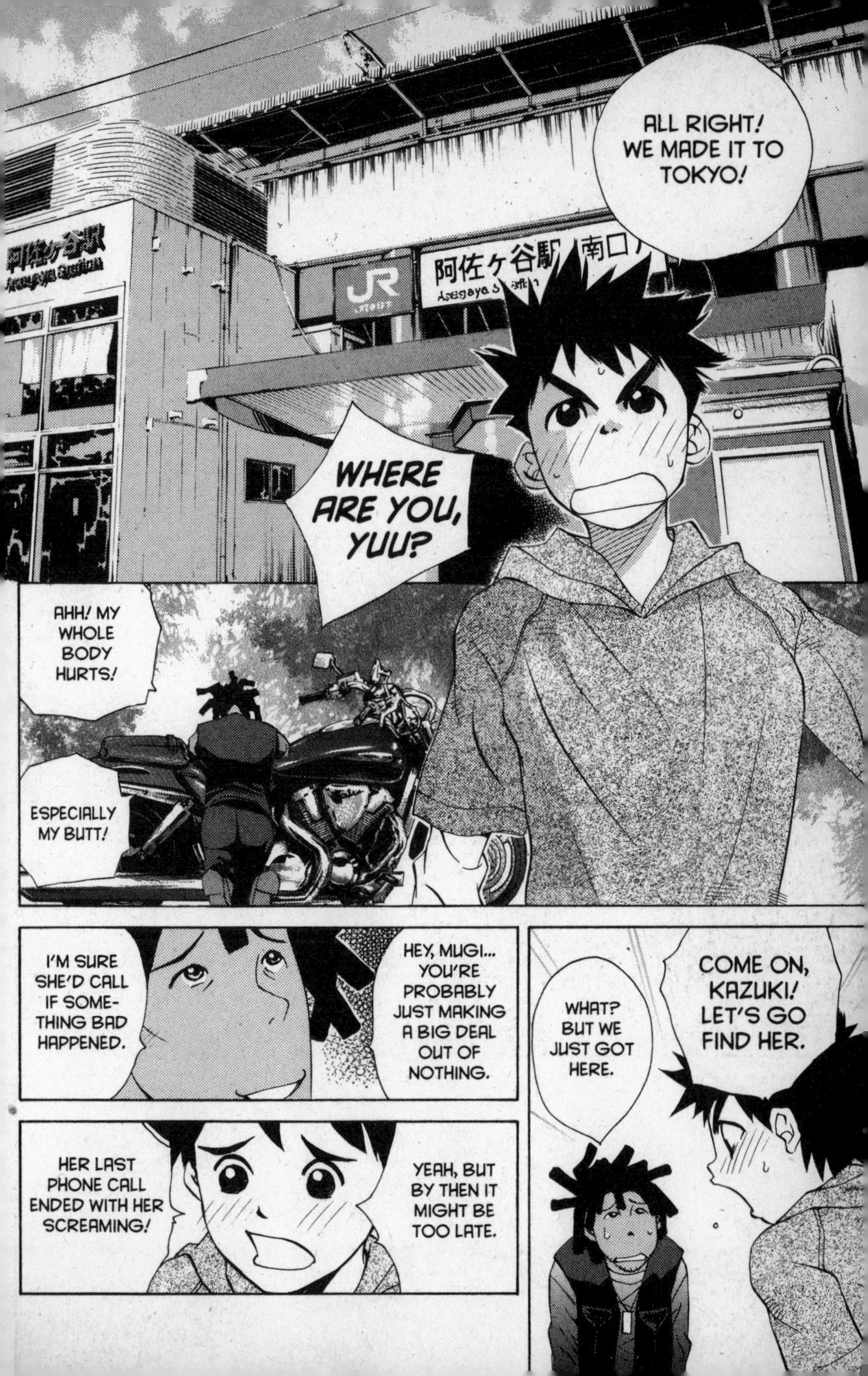
阿佐ヶ谷駅 南口
ALL RIGHT! WE MADE IT TO TOKYO!
WHERE ARE YOU, YUU?
AHH! MY WHOLE BODY HURTS!
ESPECIALLY MY BUTT!
COME ON, KAZUKI! LET'S GO FIND HER.
WHAT? BUT WE JUST GOT HERE.
HEY, MUGI... YOU'RE PROBABLY JUST MAKING A BIG DEAL OUT OF NOTHING.
I'M SURE SHE'D CALL IF SOME-THING BAD HAPPENED.
YEAH, BUT BY THEN IT MIGHT BE TOO LATE.
HER LAST PHONE CALL ENDED WITH HER SCREAMING!

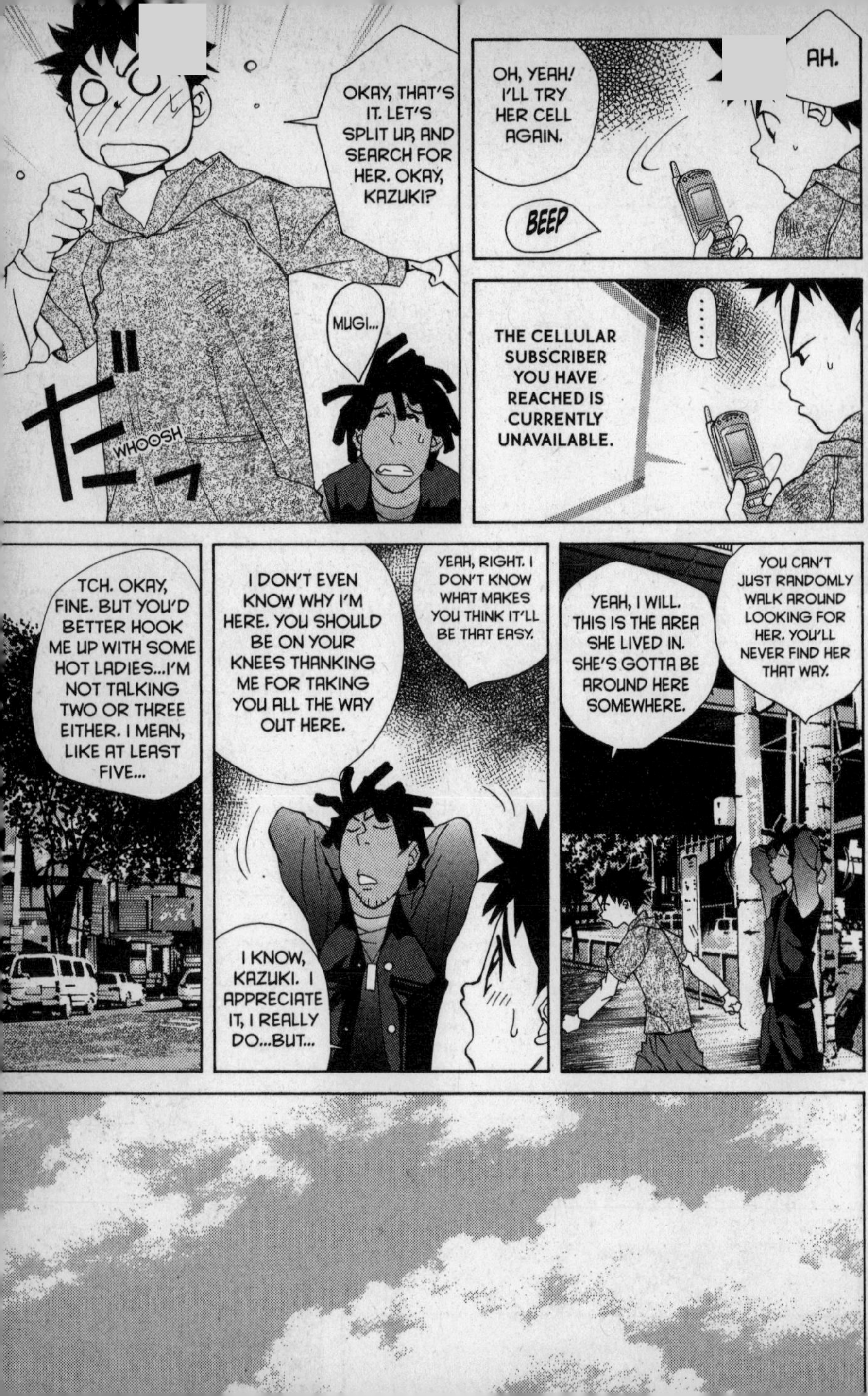
AH.
OH, YEAH! I'LL TRY HER CELL AGAIN.
BEEP
......
THE CELLULAR SUBSCRIBER YOU HAVE REACHED IS CURRENTLY UNAVAILABLE.
OKAY, THAT'S IT. LET'S SPLIT UP, AND SEARCH FOR HER. OKAY, KAZUKI?
MUGI...
WHOOSH
YOU CAN'T JUST RANDOMLY WALK AROUND LOOKING FOR HER. YOU'LL NEVER FIND HER THAT WAY.
YEAH, I WILL. THIS IS THE AREA SHE LIVED IN. SHE'S GOTTA BE AROUND HERE SOMEWHERE.
YEAH, RIGHT. I DON'T KNOW WHAT MAKES YOU THINK IT'LL BE THAT EASY.
I DON'T EVEN KNOW WHY I'M HERE. YOU SHOULD BE ON YOUR KNEES THANKING ME FOR TAKING YOU ALL THE WAY OUT HERE.
I KNOW, KAZUKI. I APPRECIATE IT, I REALLY DO...BUT...
TCH. OKAY, FINE. BUT YOU'D BETTER HOOK ME UP WITH SOME HOT LADIES...I'M NOT TALKING TWO OR THREE EITHER. I MEAN, LIKE AT LEAST FIVE...

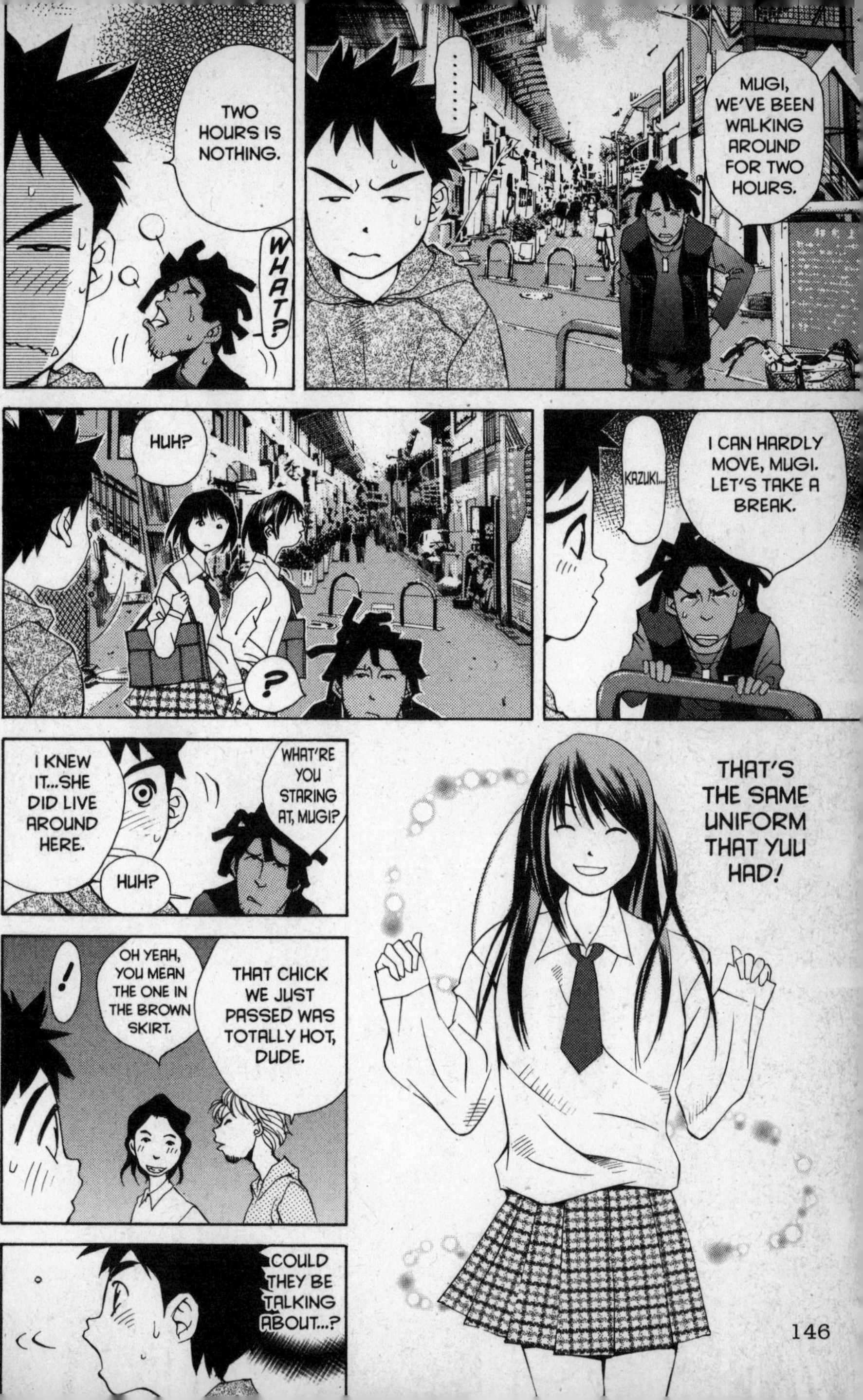
MUGI, WE'VE BEEN WALKING AROUND FOR TWO HOURS.
......
TWO HOURS IS NOTHING.
WHAT?
I CAN HARDLY MOVE, MUGI. LET'S TAKE A BREAK.
KAZUKI...
HUH?
?
THAT'S THE SAME UNIFORM THAT YUU HAD!
WHAT'RE YOU STARING AT, MUGI?
I KNEW IT...SHE DID LIVE AROUND HERE.
HUH?
THAT CHICK WE JUST PASSED WAS TOTALLY HOT, DUDE.
OH YEAH, YOU MEAN THE ONE IN THE BROWN SKIRT.
!
COULD THEY BE TALKING ABOUT...?

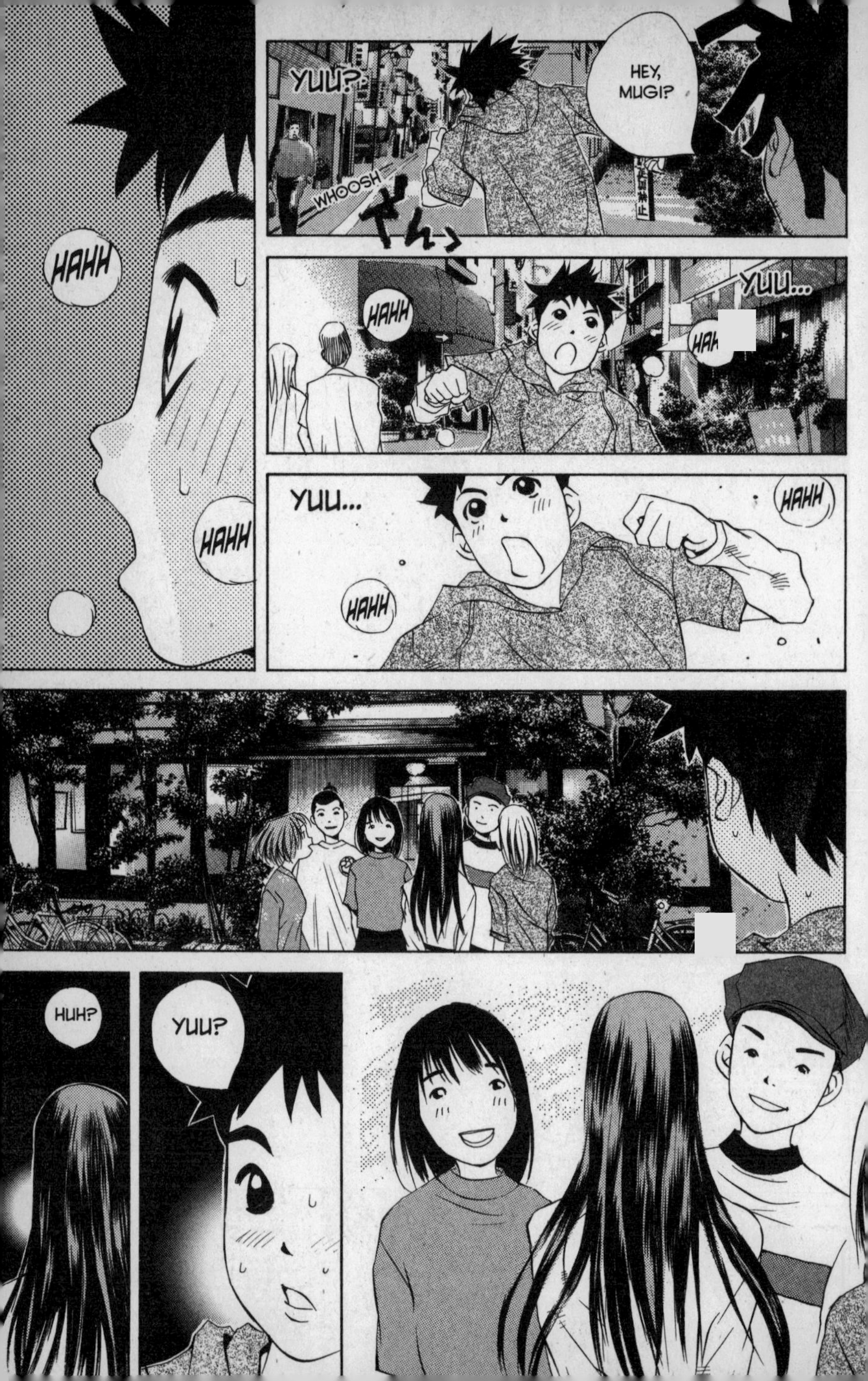
HEY, MUGI?
YUU?
WHOOSH
YUU...
HAHH
HAHH
HAHH
YUU...
HAHH
HAHH
HAHH
YUU?
HUH?

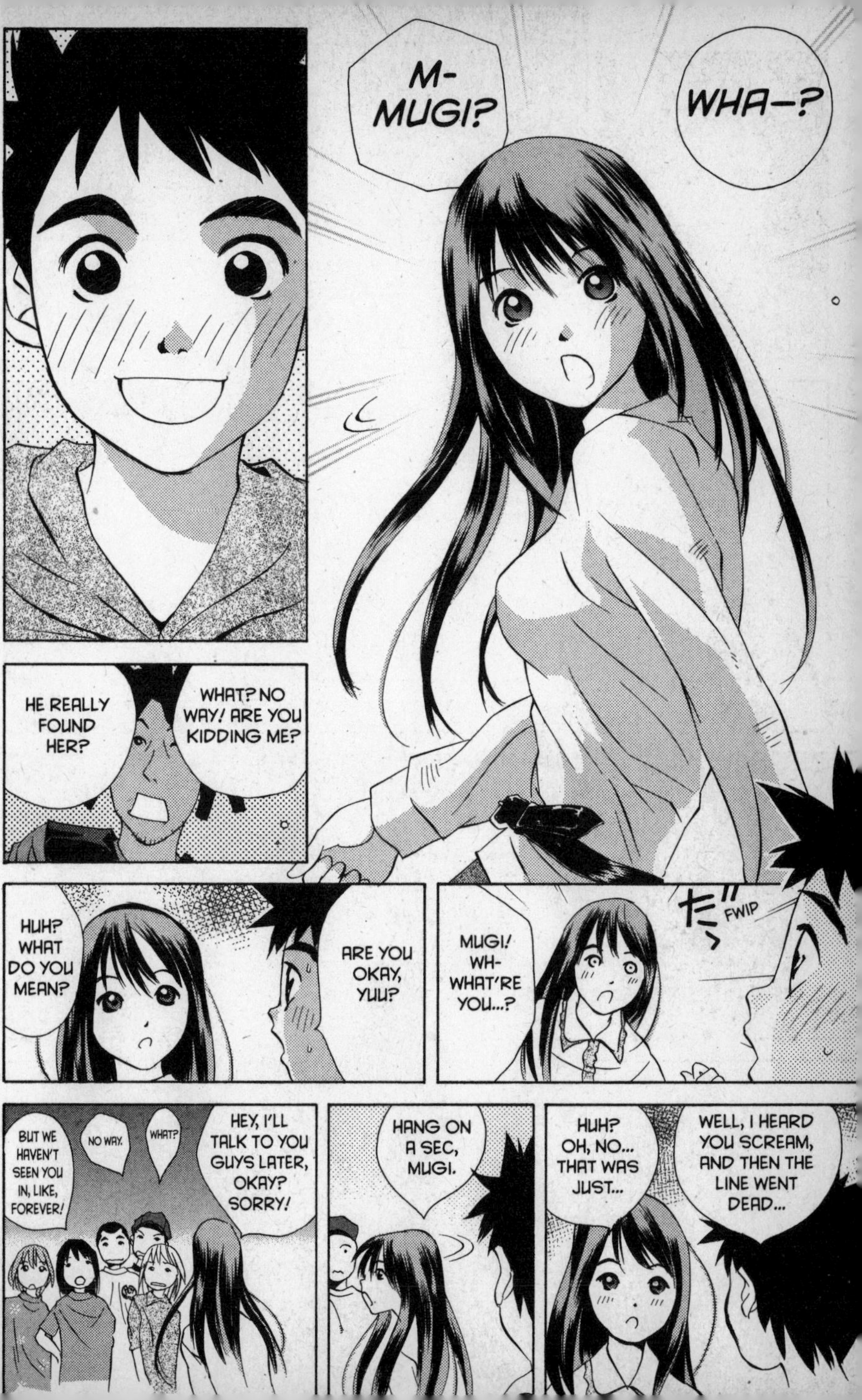
WHA–?
M-MUGI?
WHAT? NO WAY! ARE YOU KIDDING ME?
HE REALLY FOUND HER?
FWIP
MUGI! WH-WHAT'RE YOU...?
ARE YOU OKAY, YUU?
HUH? WHAT DO YOU MEAN?
WELL, I HEARD YOU SCREAM, AND THEN THE LINE WENT DEAD...
HUH? OH, NO... THAT WAS JUST...
HANG ON A SEC, MUGI.
HEY, I'LL TALK TO YOU GUYS LATER, OKAY? SORRY!
WHAT?
NO WAY.
BUT WE HAVEN'T SEEN YOU IN, LIKE, FOREVER!

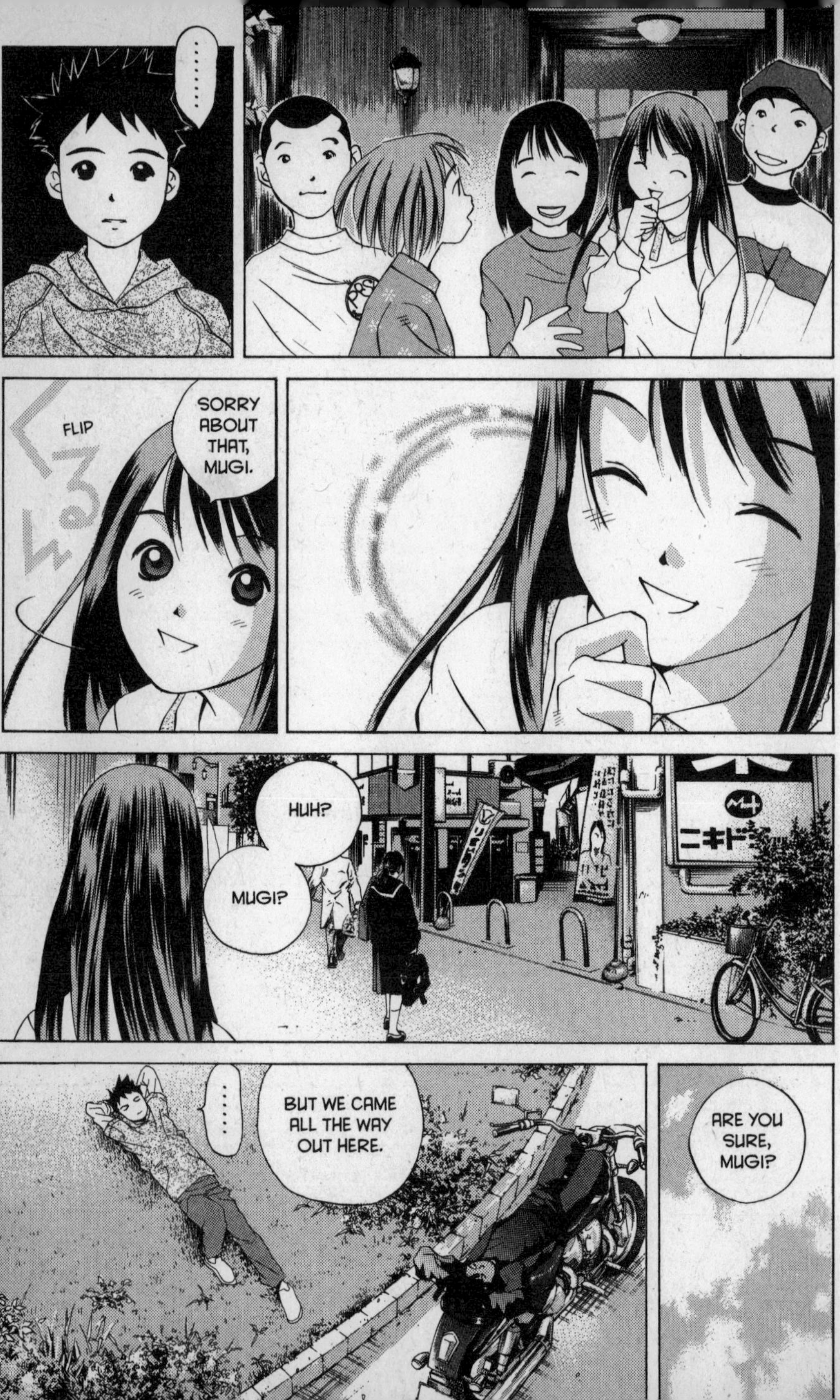
......
SORRY ABOUT THAT, MUGI.
FLIP
HUH?
MUGI?
ARE YOU SURE, MUGI?
BUT WE CAME ALL THE WAY OUT HERE.
......

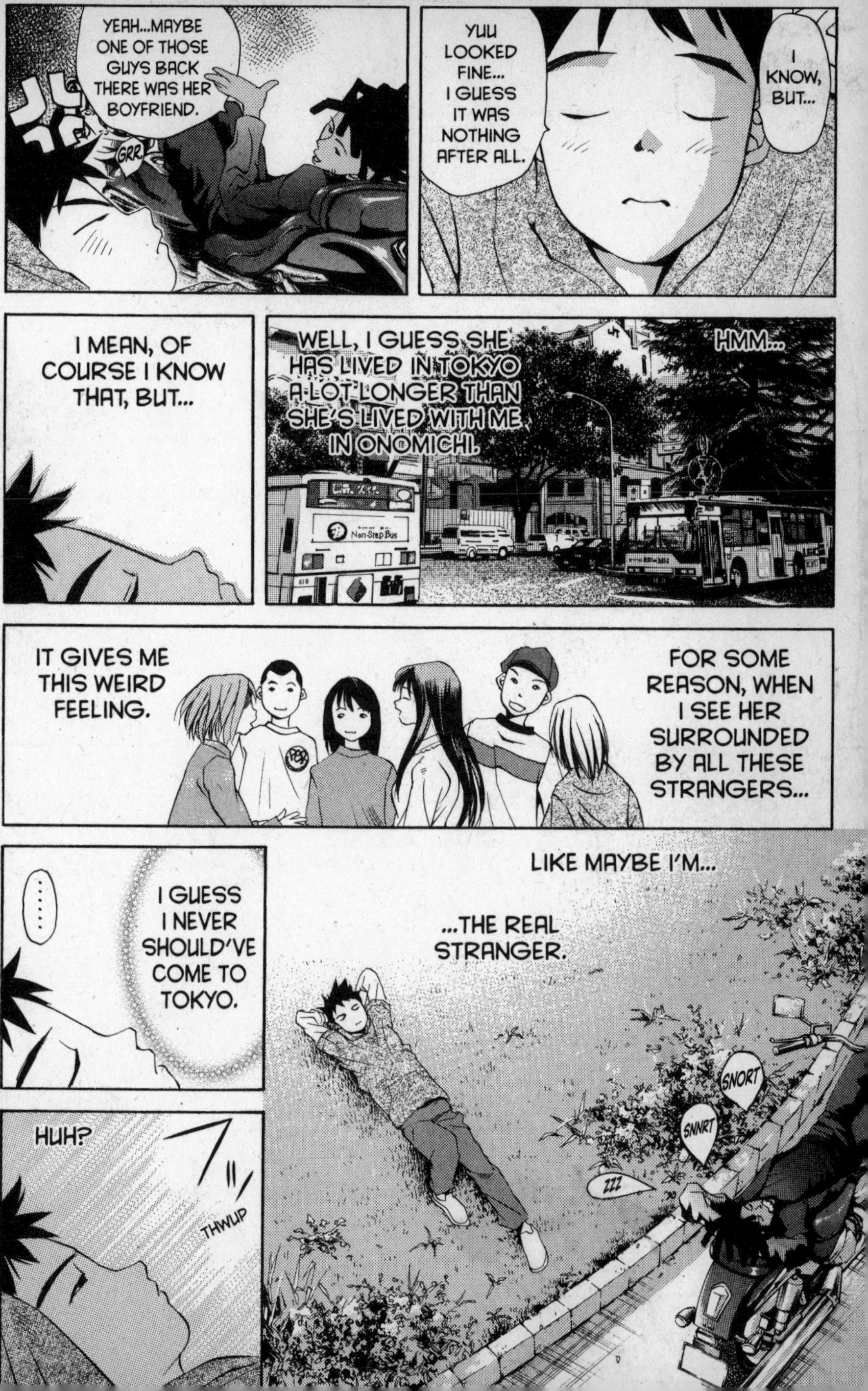
I KNOW, BUT...
YUU LOOKED FINE... I GUESS IT WAS NOTHING AFTER ALL.
YEAH...MAYBE ONE OF THOSE GUYS BACK THERE WAS HER BOYFRIEND.
GRR.
HMM...
WELL, I GUESS SHE HAS LIVED IN TOKYO A LOT LONGER THAN SHE'S LIVED WITH ME IN ONOMICHI.
Non-Step Bus
I MEAN, OF COURSE I KNOW THAT, BUT...
FOR SOME REASON, WHEN I SEE HER SURROUNDED BY ALL THESE STRANGERS...
IT GIVES ME THIS WEIRD FEELING.
LIKE MAYBE I'M...
...THE REAL STRANGER.
SNORT
SNNRT
ZZZ
......
I GUESS I NEVER SHOULD'VE COME TO TOKYO.
HUH?
THWUP

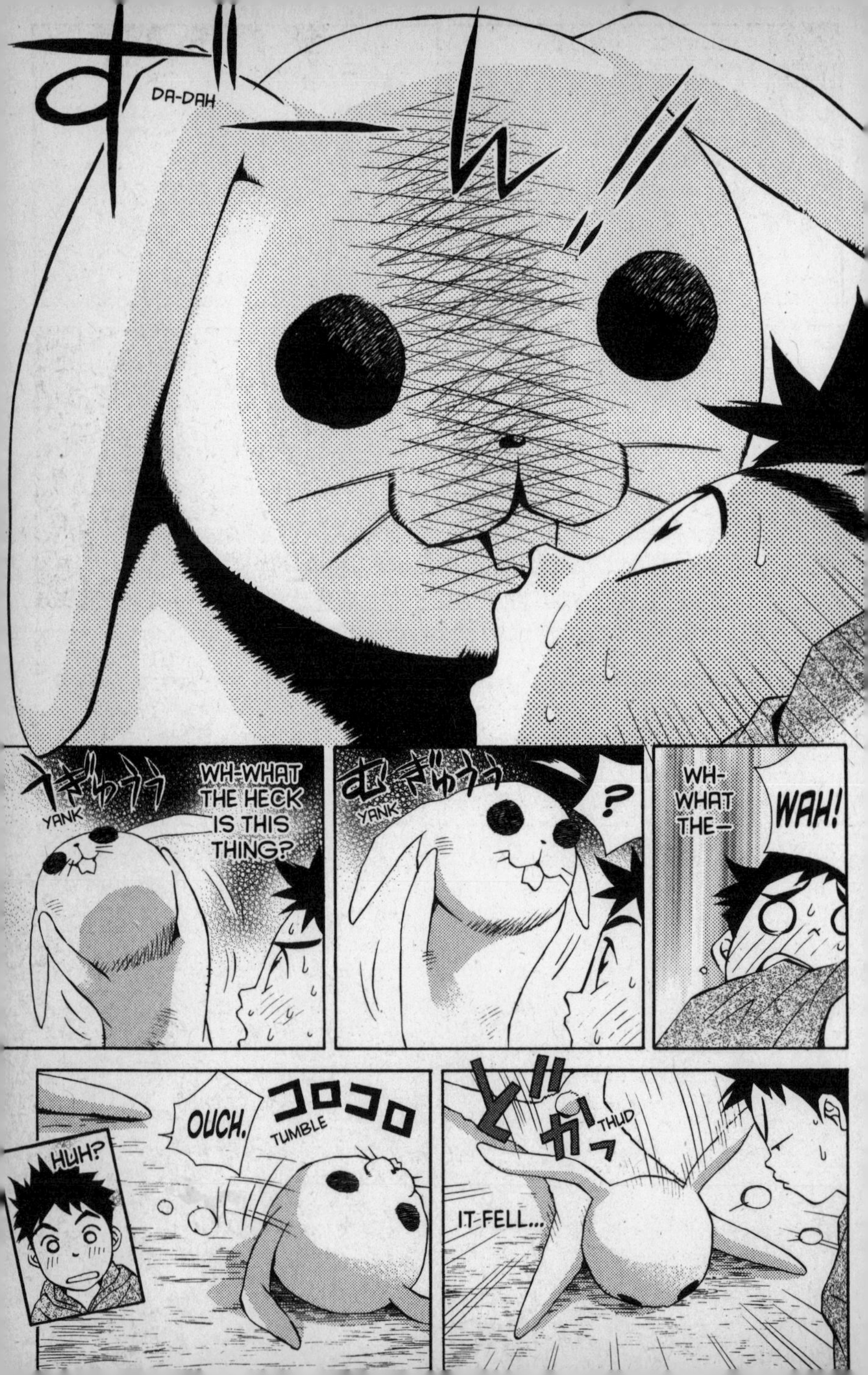

すーん!!
DA-DAH
WAH!
WH-WHAT THE—
?
むぎゅうっ
YANK
ぎゅううう
YANK
WH-WHAT THE HECK IS THIS THING?
どがっ
THUD
IT FELL...
OUCH.
コロコロ
TUMBLE
HUH?

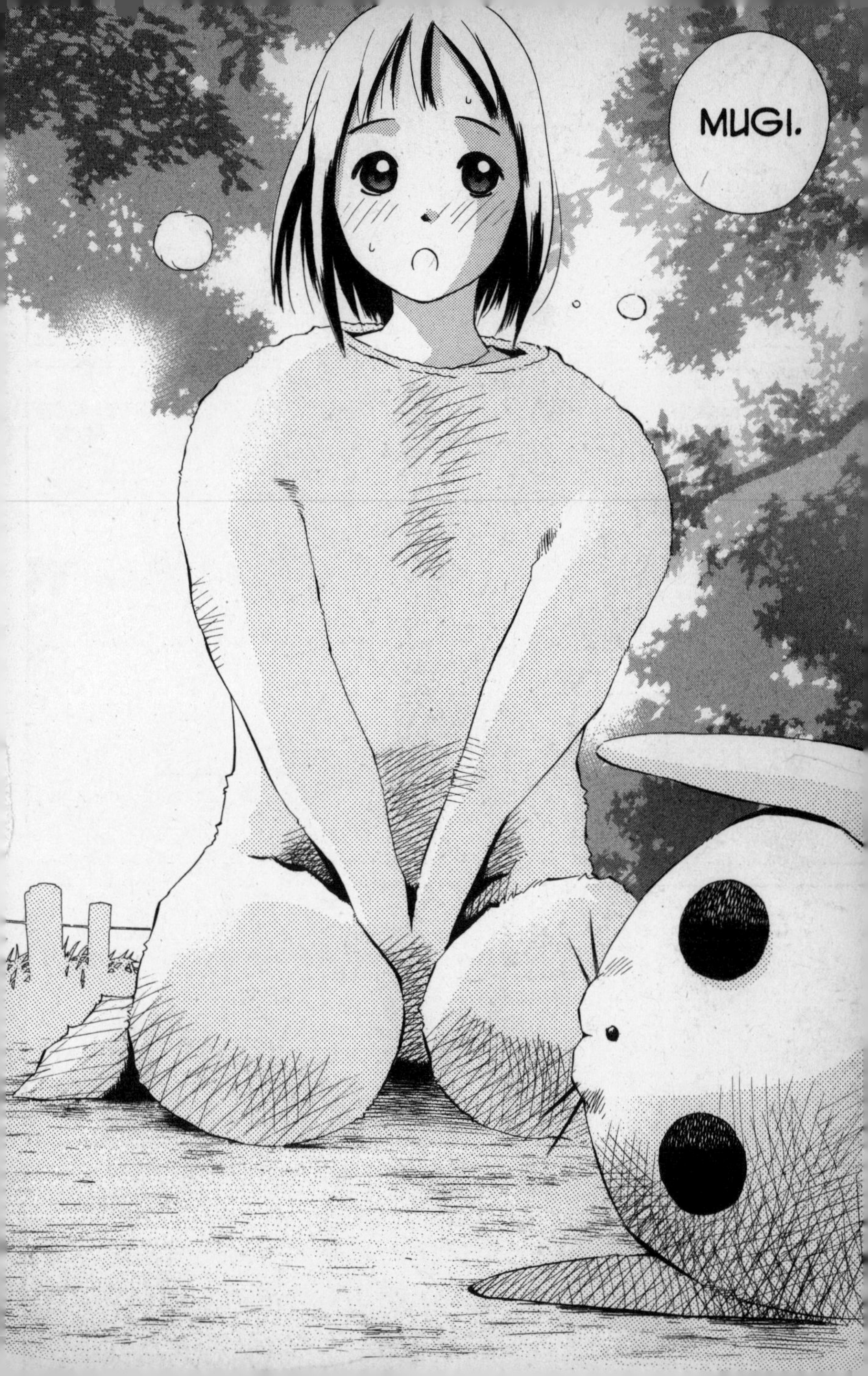
MUGI.

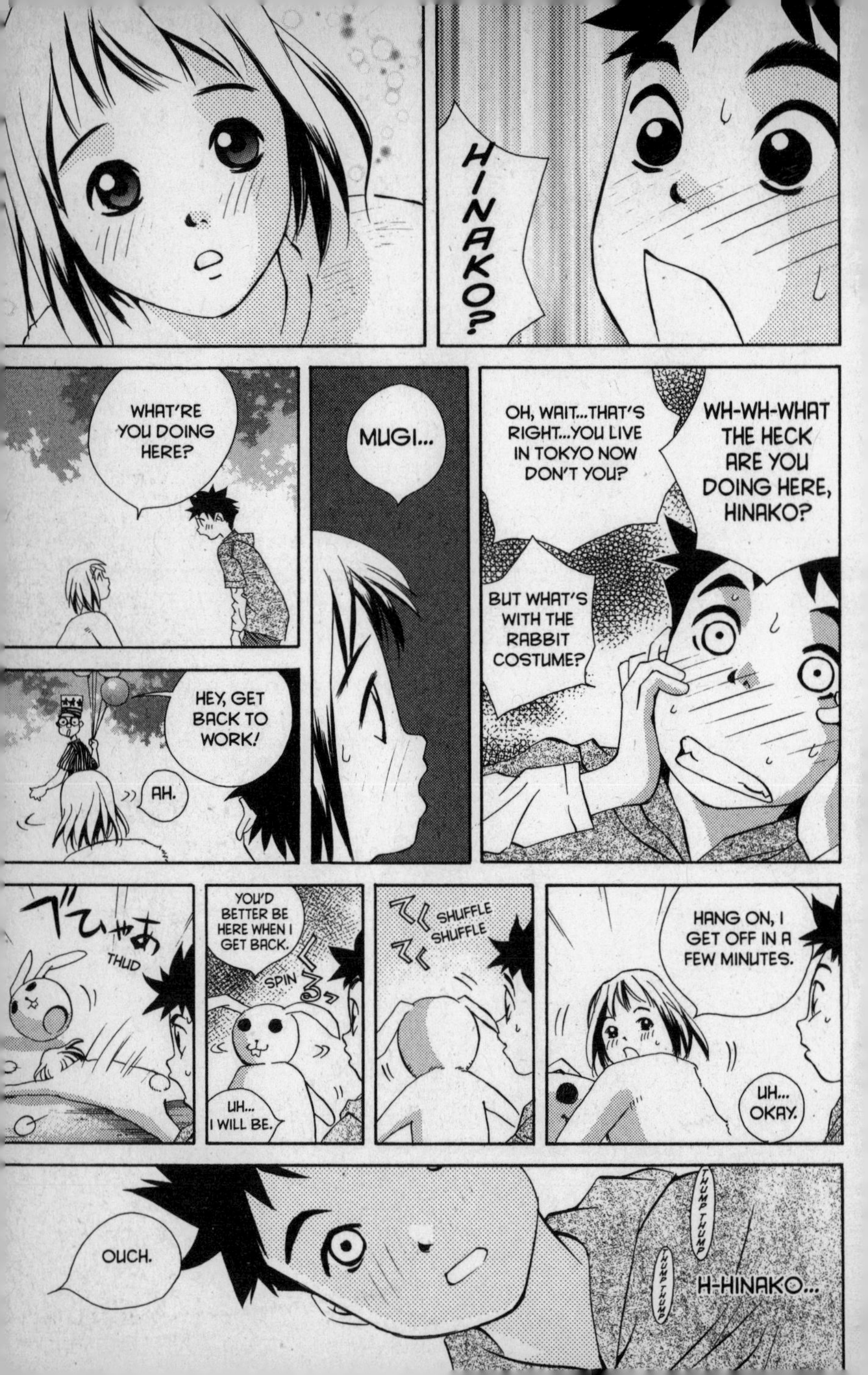
HINAKO?
WH-WH-WHAT THE HECK ARE YOU DOING HERE, HINAKO?
OH, WAIT...THAT'S RIGHT...YOU LIVE IN TOKYO NOW DON'T YOU?
BUT WHAT'S WITH THE RABBIT COSTUME?
MUGI...
WHAT'RE YOU DOING HERE?
HEY, GET BACK TO WORK!
AH.
HANG ON, I GET OFF IN A FEW MINUTES.
UH... OKAY.
SHUFFLE SHUFFLE
YOU'D BETTER BE HERE WHEN I GET BACK.
SPIN
UH... I WILL BE.
THUD
THUMP THUMP
THUMP THUMP
H-HINAKO...
OUCH.

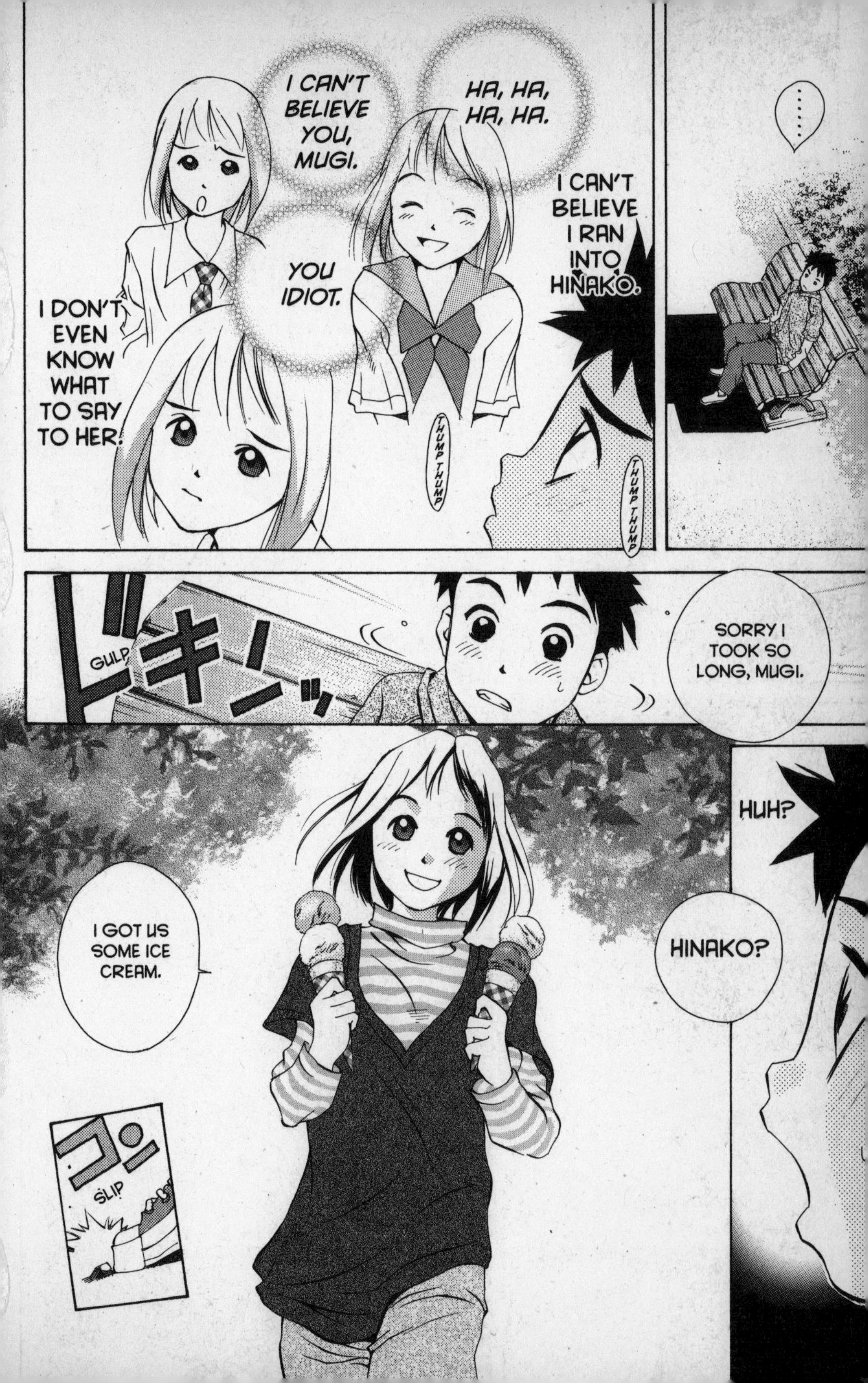
……
HA, HA, HA, HA.
I CAN'T BELIEVE YOU, MUGI.
I CAN'T BELIEVE I RAN INTO HIÑAKO.
YOU IDIOT.
THUMP THUMP
THUMP THUMP
I DON'T EVEN KNOW WHAT TO SAY TO HER.
SORRY I TOOK SO LONG, MUGI.
GULP
HUH?
HINAKO?
I GOT US SOME ICE CREAM.
SLIP

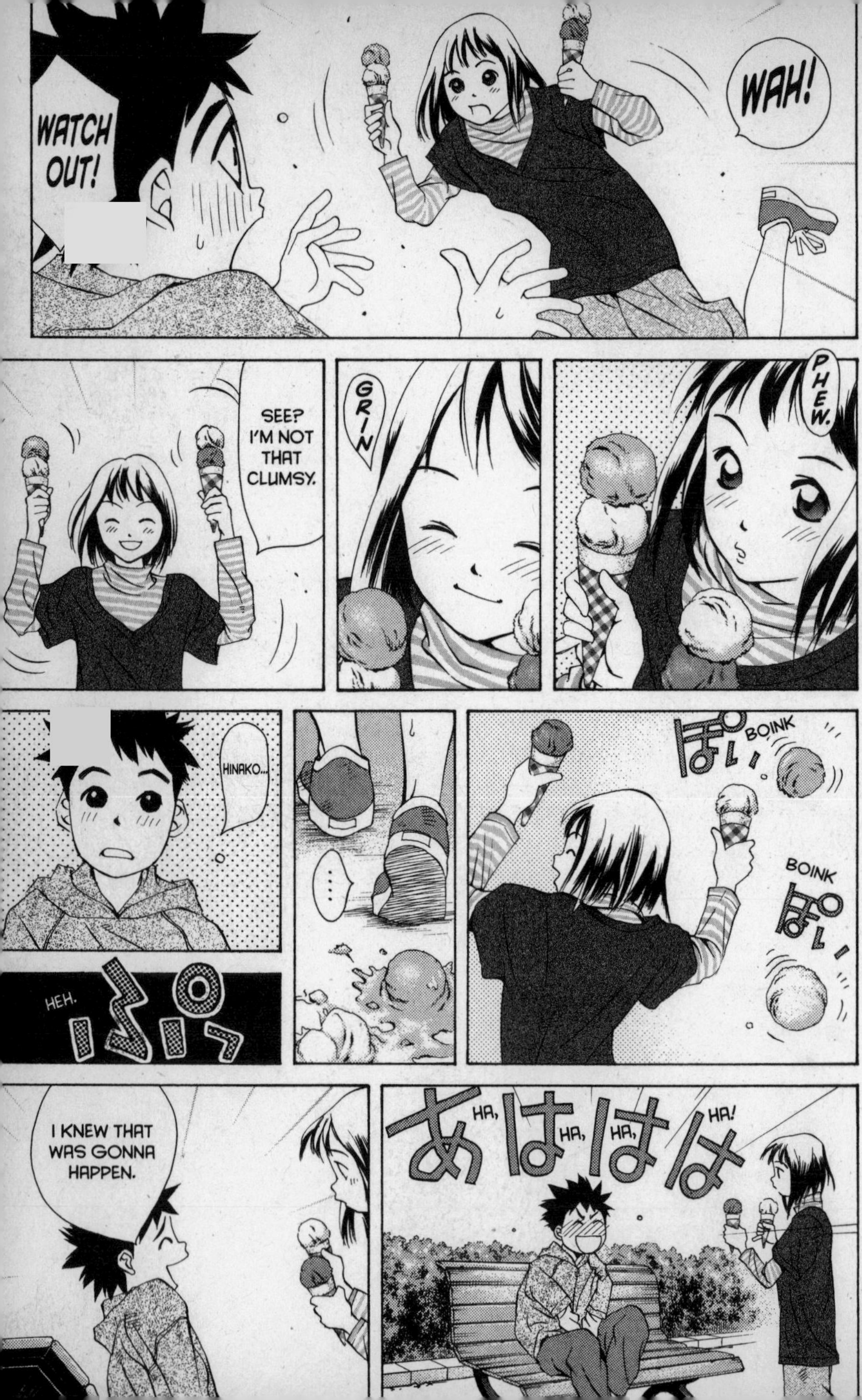
WAH!
WATCH OUT!
PHEW.
GRIN
SEE? I'M NOT THAT CLUMSY.
ぽい BOINK
BOINK ぽい
...
HINAKO...
ぷっ HEH.
あははは HA, HA, HA, HA!
I KNEW THAT WAS GONNA HAPPEN.

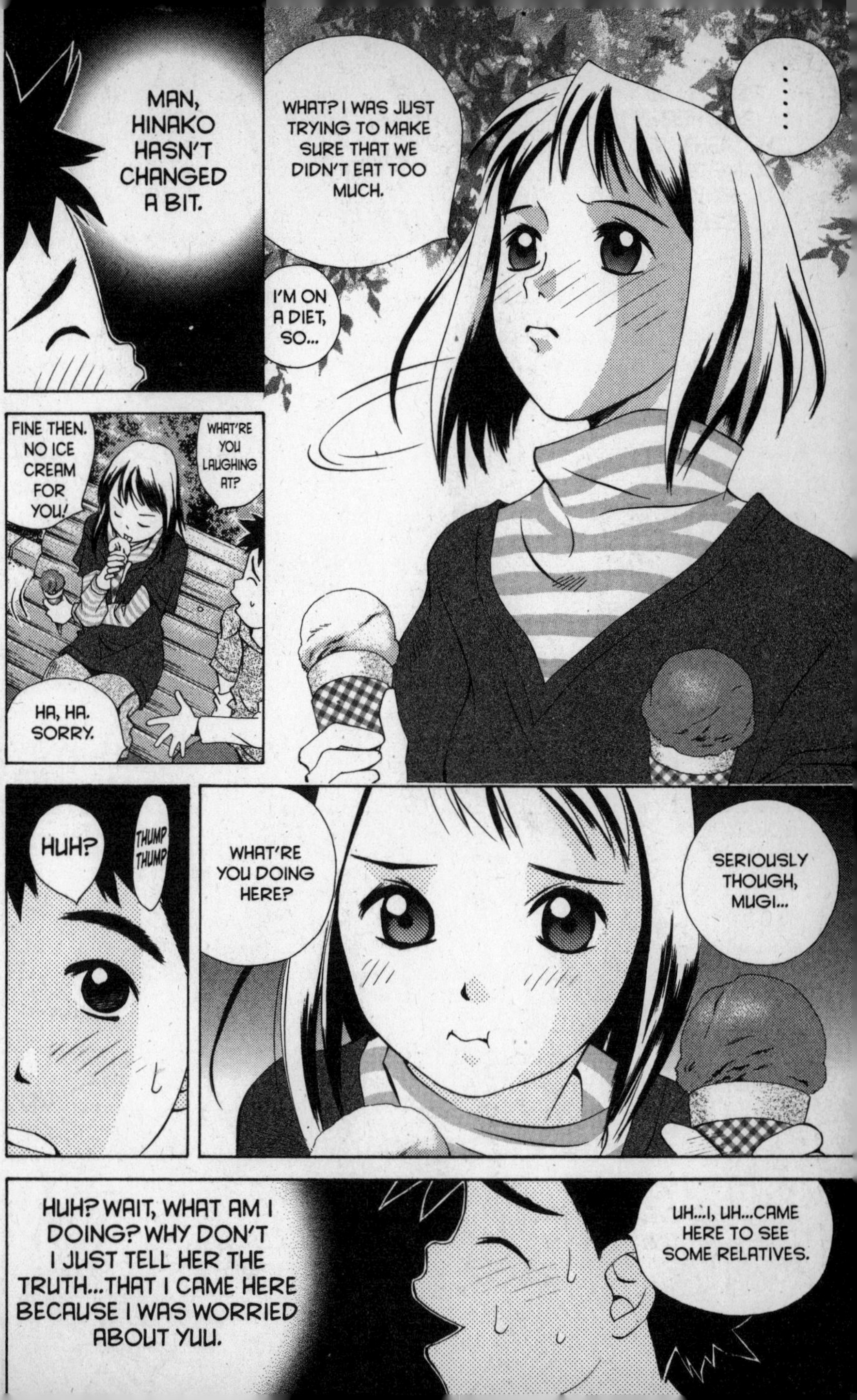
......
WHAT? I WAS JUST TRYING TO MAKE SURE THAT WE DIDN'T EAT TOO MUCH.
I'M ON A DIET, SO...
MAN, HINAKO HASN'T CHANGED A BIT.
WHAT'RE YOU LAUGHING AT?
FINE THEN. NO ICE CREAM FOR YOU!
HA, HA. SORRY.
SERIOUSLY THOUGH, MUGI...
WHAT'RE YOU DOING HERE?
THUMP THUMP
HUH?
UH...I, UH...CAME HERE TO SEE SOME RELATIVES.
HUH? WAIT, WHAT AM I DOING? WHY DON'T I JUST TELL HER THE TRUTH...THAT I CAME HERE BECAUSE I WAS WORRIED ABOUT YUU.

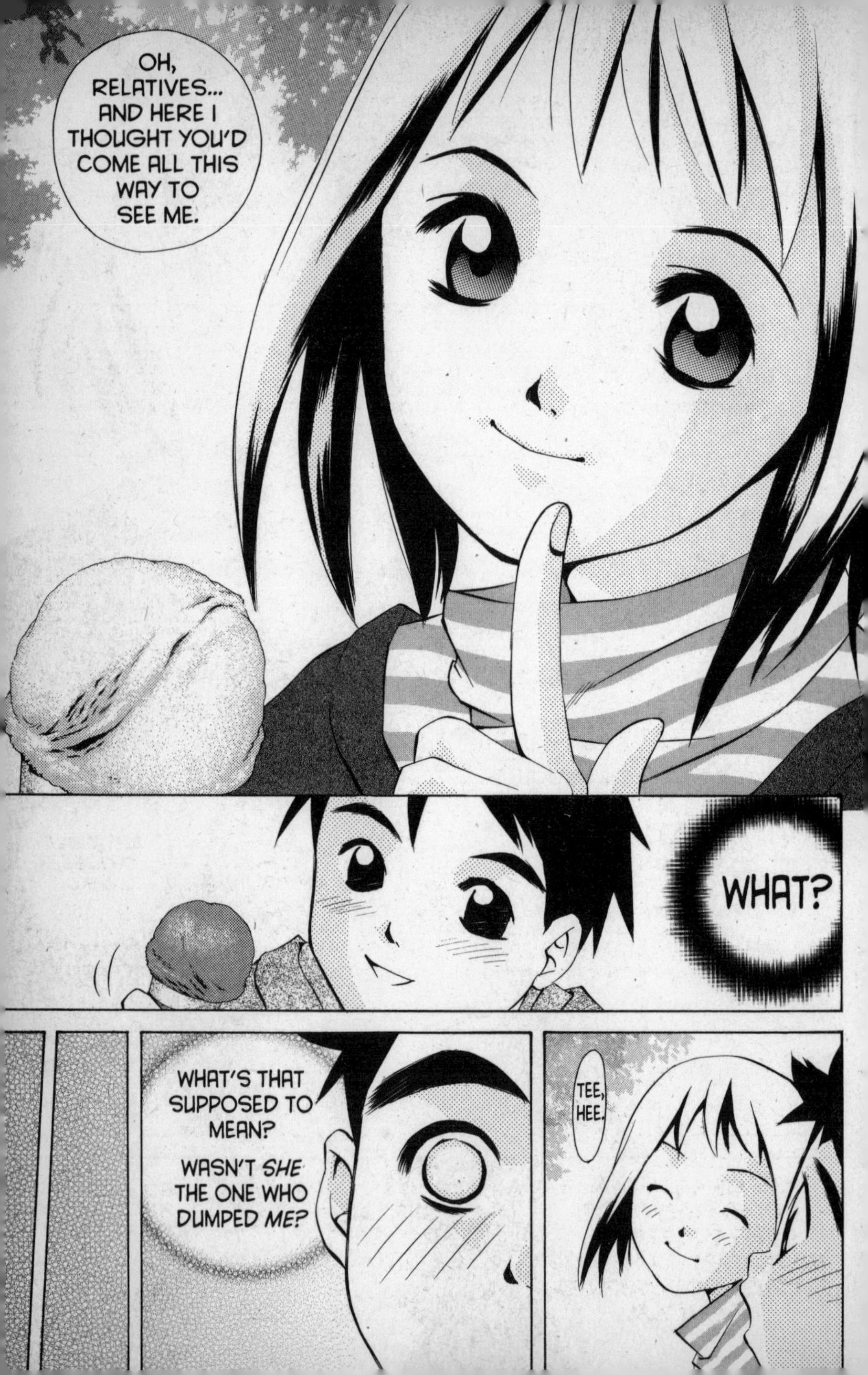
OH, RELATIVES... AND HERE I THOUGHT YOU'D COME ALL THIS WAY TO SEE ME.
WHAT?
TEE, HEE.
WHAT'S THAT SUPPOSED TO MEAN?
WASN'T *SHE* THE ONE WHO DUMPED *ME*?

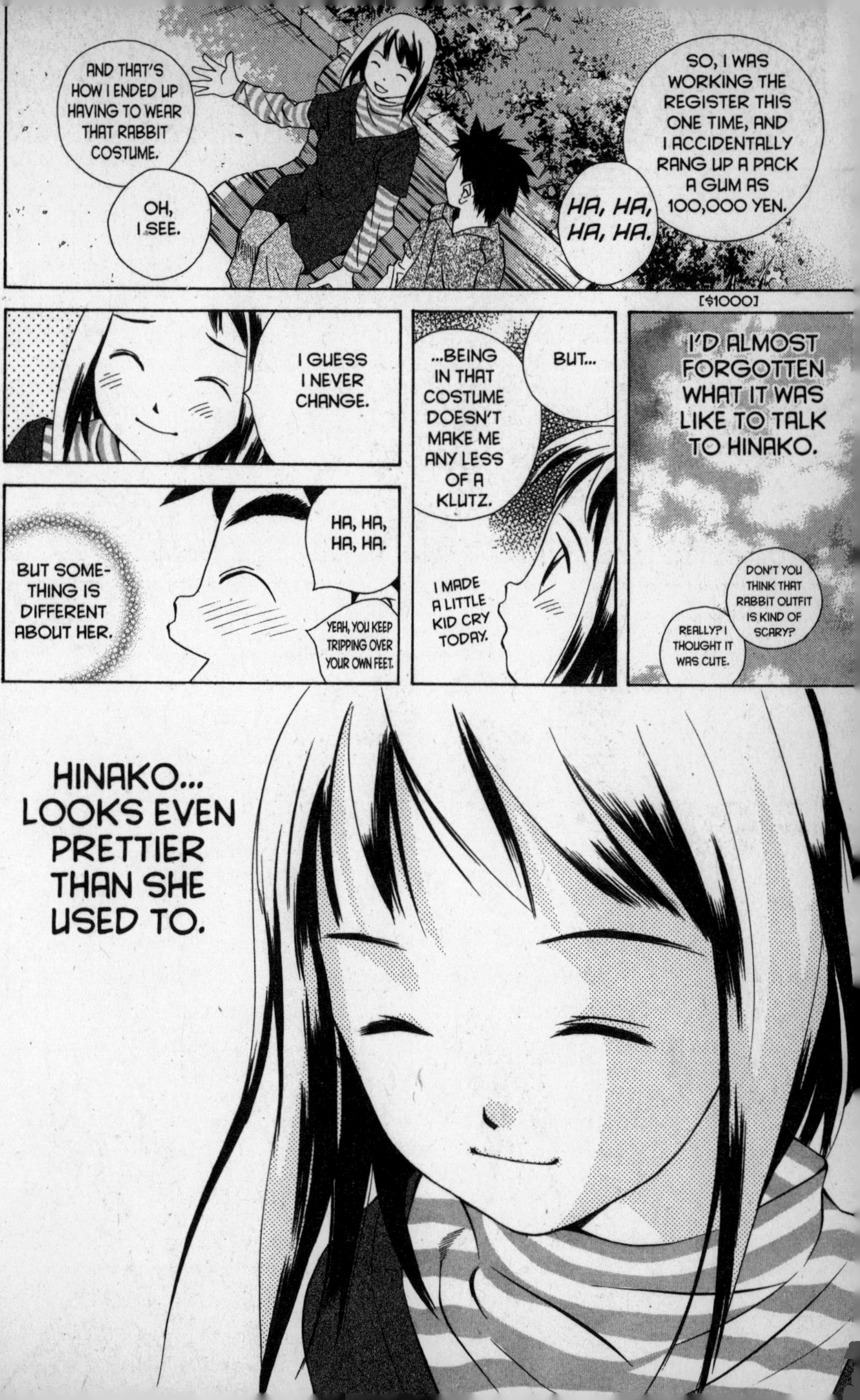
SO, I WAS WORKING THE REGISTER THIS ONE TIME, AND I ACCIDENTALLY RANG UP A PACK A GUM AS 100,000 YEN.
[$1000]
HA, HA, HA, HA.
AND THAT'S HOW I ENDED UP HAVING TO WEAR THAT RABBIT COSTUME.
OH, I SEE.
I'D ALMOST FORGOTTEN WHAT IT WAS LIKE TO TALK TO HINAKO.
DON'T YOU THINK THAT RABBIT OUTFIT IS KIND OF SCARY?
REALLY? I THOUGHT IT WAS CUTE.
BUT...
...BEING IN THAT COSTUME DOESN'T MAKE ME ANY LESS OF A KLUTZ.
I MADE A LITTLE KID CRY TODAY.
I GUESS I NEVER CHANGE.
HA, HA, HA, HA.
YEAH, YOU KEEP TRIPPING OVER YOUR OWN FEET.
BUT SOMETHING IS DIFFERENT ABOUT HER.
HINAKO... LOOKS EVEN PRETTIER THAN SHE USED TO.

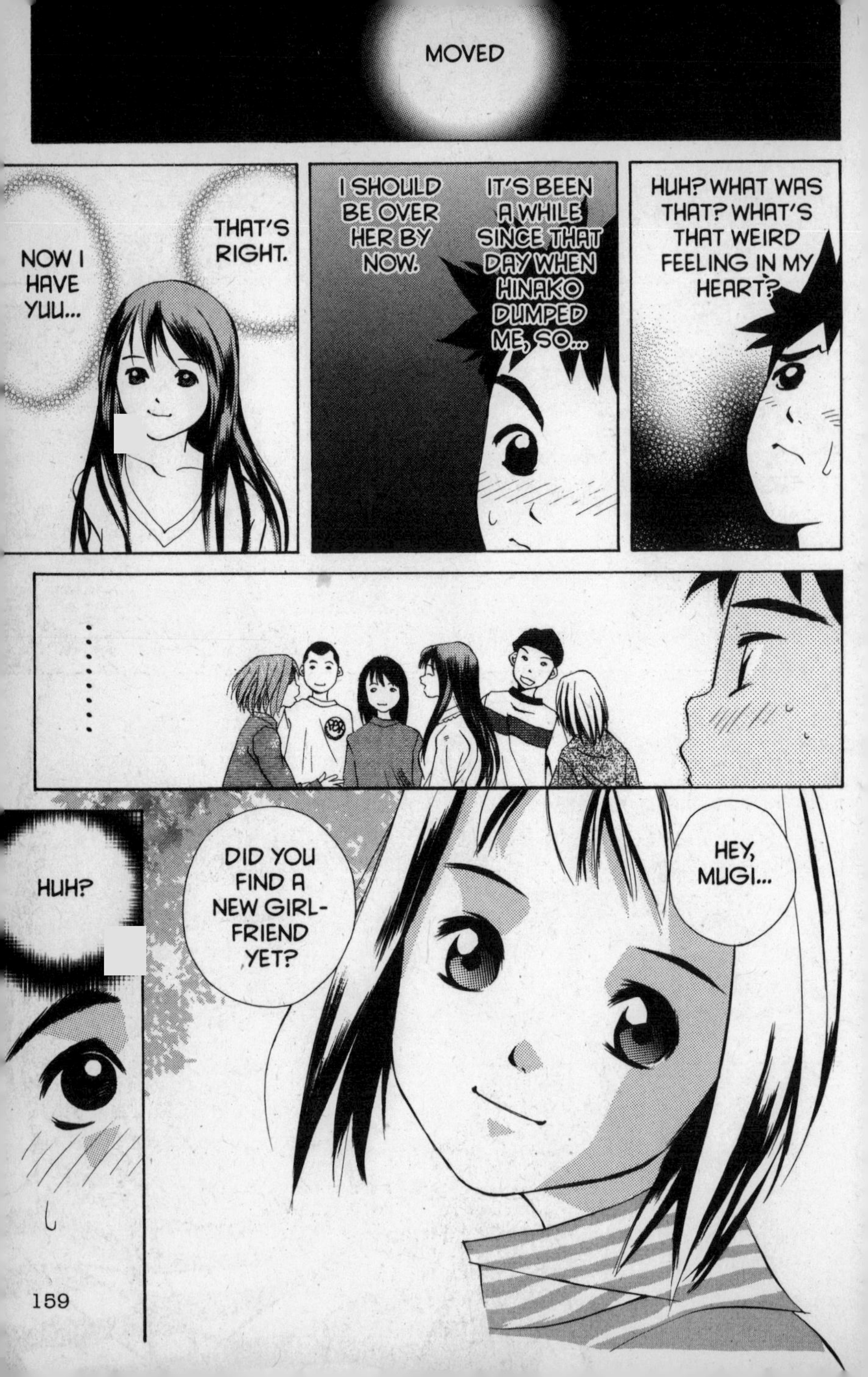
MOVED
HUH? WHAT WAS THAT? WHAT'S THAT WEIRD FEELING IN MY HEART?
IT'S BEEN A WHILE SINCE THAT DAY WHEN HINAKO DUMPED ME, SO...
I SHOULD BE OVER HER BY NOW.
THAT'S RIGHT.
NOW I HAVE YUU...
....
HEY, MUGI...
DID YOU FIND A NEW GIRL-FRIEND YET?
HUH?

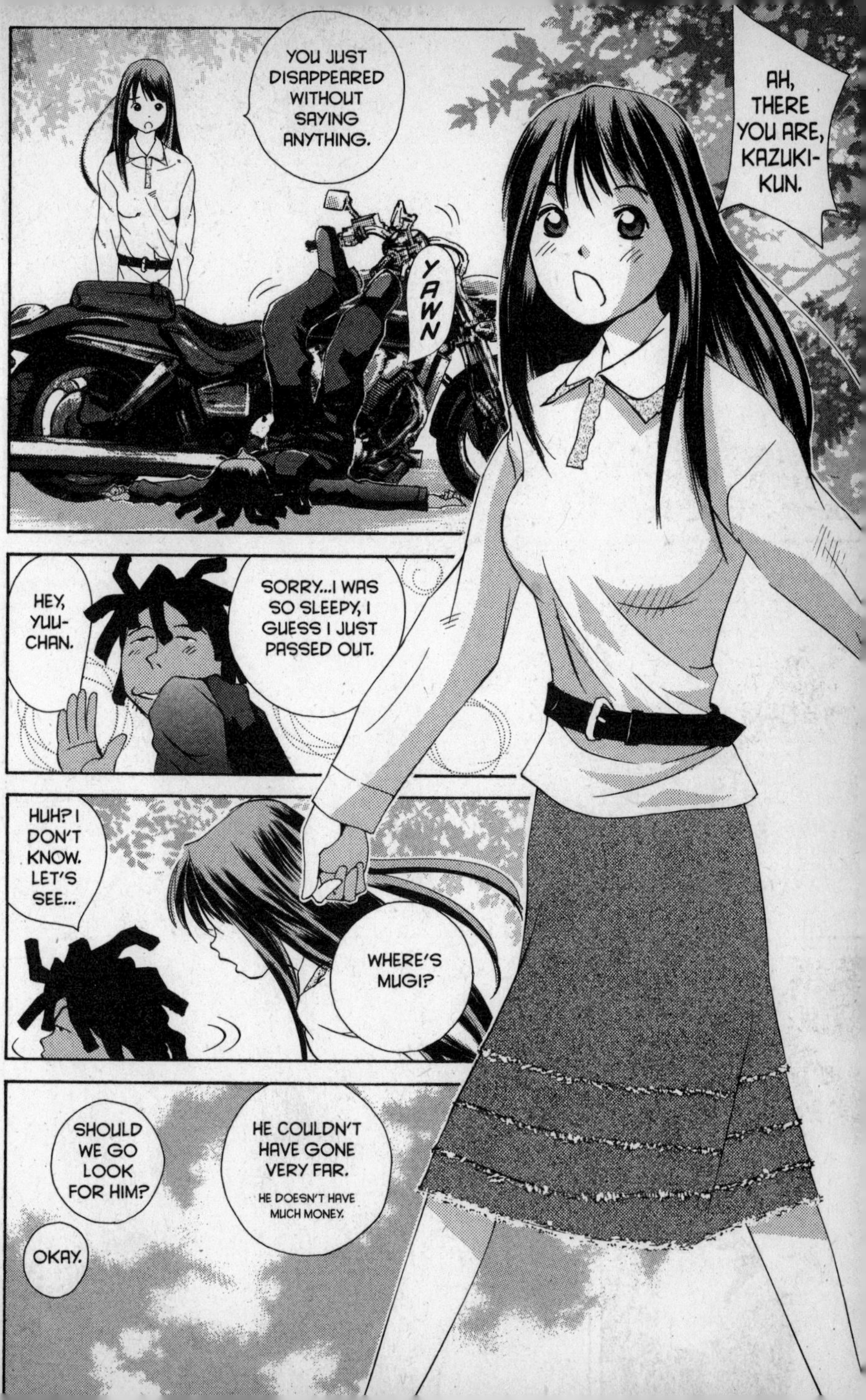
AH, THERE YOU ARE, KAZUKI-KUN.
YOU JUST DISAPPEARED WITHOUT SAYING ANYTHING.
YAWN
SORRY...I WAS SO SLEEPY, I GUESS I JUST PASSED OUT.
HEY, YUU-CHAN.
WHERE'S MUGI?
HUH? I DON'T KNOW. LET'S SEE...
HE COULDN'T HAVE GONE VERY FAR.
HE DOESN'T HAVE MUCH MONEY.
SHOULD WE GO LOOK FOR HIM?
OKAY.

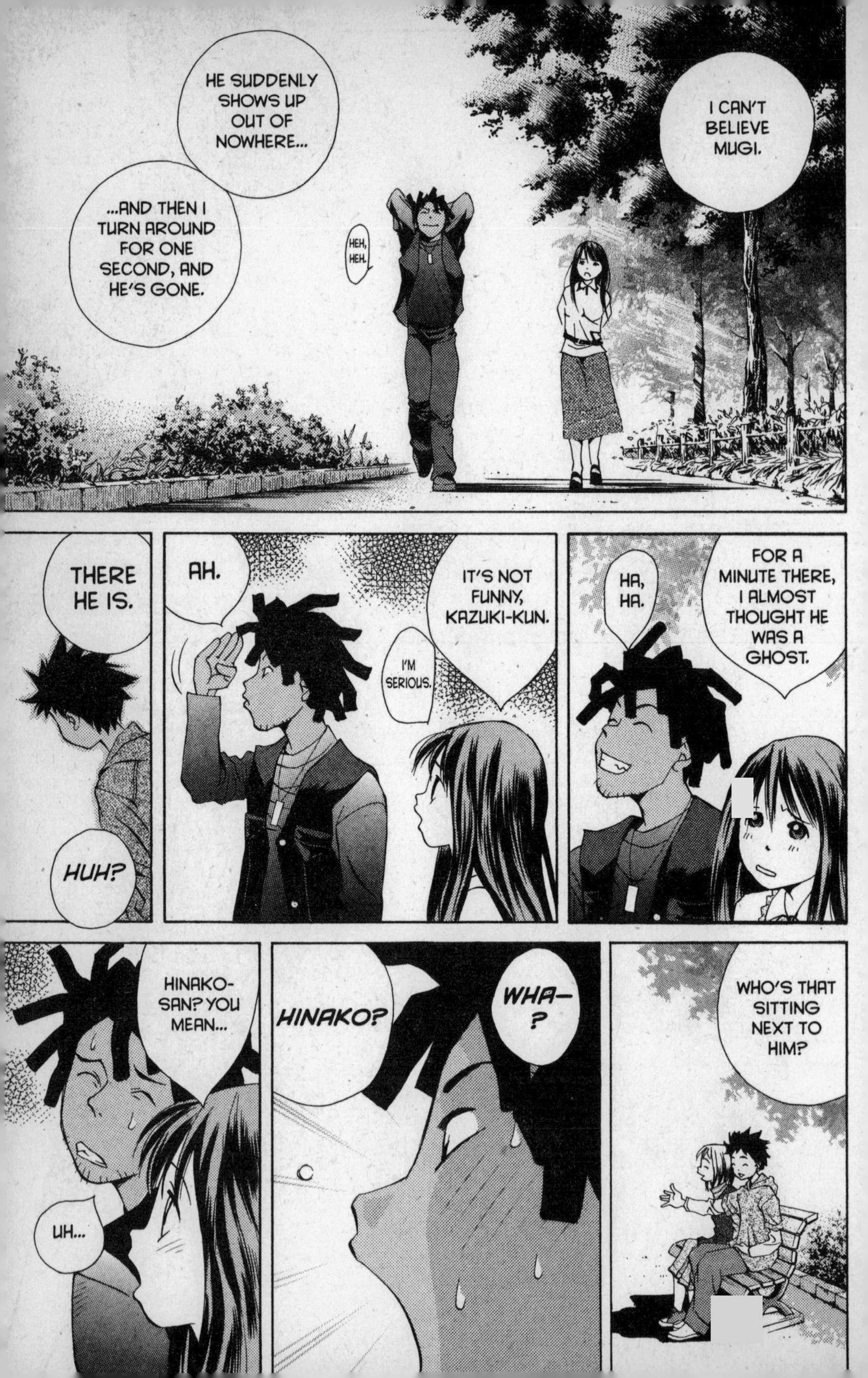
I CAN'T BELIEVE MUGI.
HE SUDDENLY SHOWS UP OUT OF NOWHERE...
...AND THEN I TURN AROUND FOR ONE SECOND, AND HE'S GONE.
HEH, HEH.
FOR A MINUTE THERE, I ALMOST THOUGHT HE WAS A GHOST.
HA, HA.
IT'S NOT FUNNY, KAZUKI-KUN.
I'M SERIOUS.
AH.
THERE HE IS.
HUH?
WHO'S THAT SITTING NEXT TO HIM?
WHA—?
HINAKO?
HINAKO-SAN? YOU MEAN...
UH...

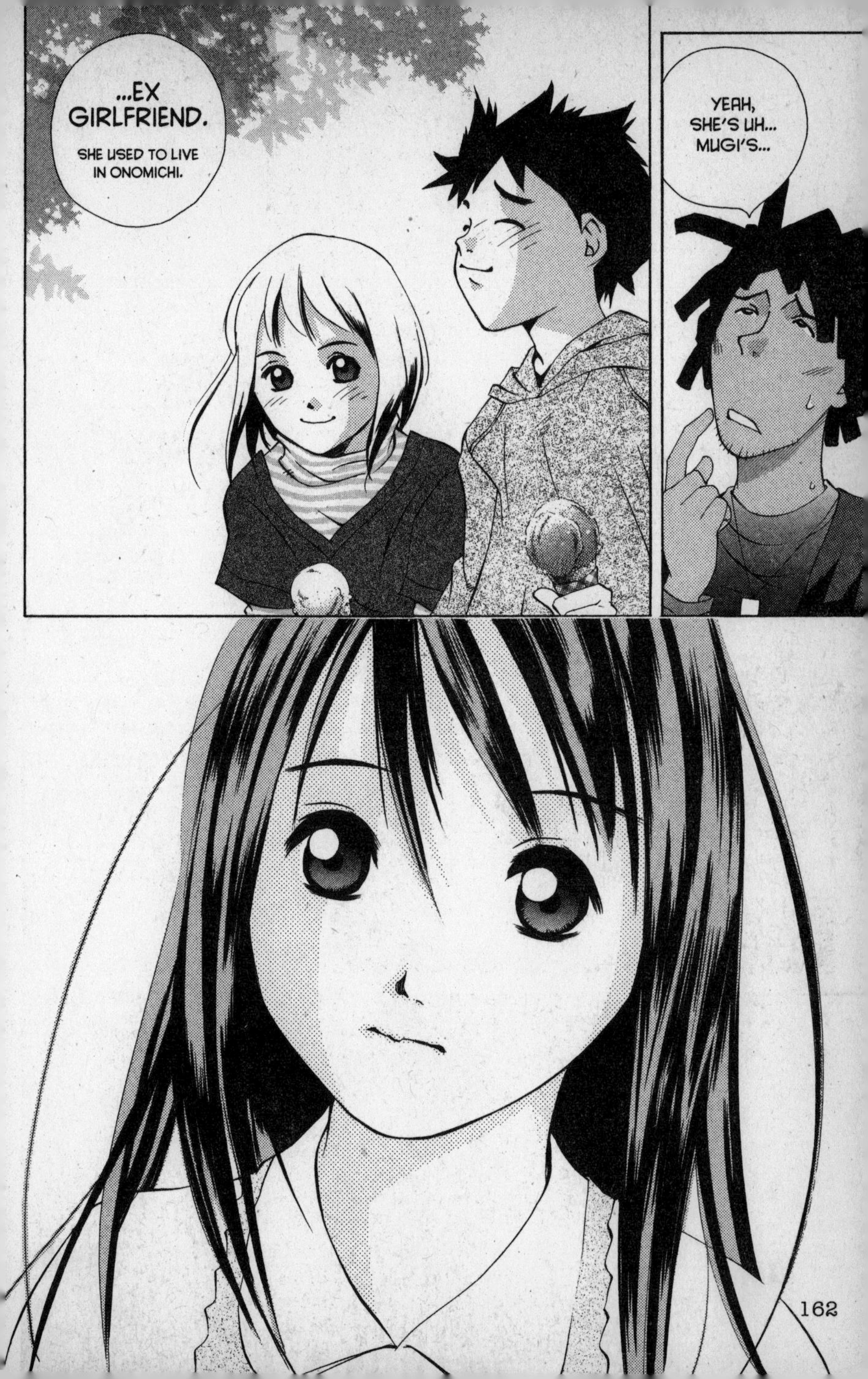
YEAH, SHE'S UH... MUGI'S...
...EX GIRLFRIEND.
SHE USED TO LIVE IN ONOMICHI.

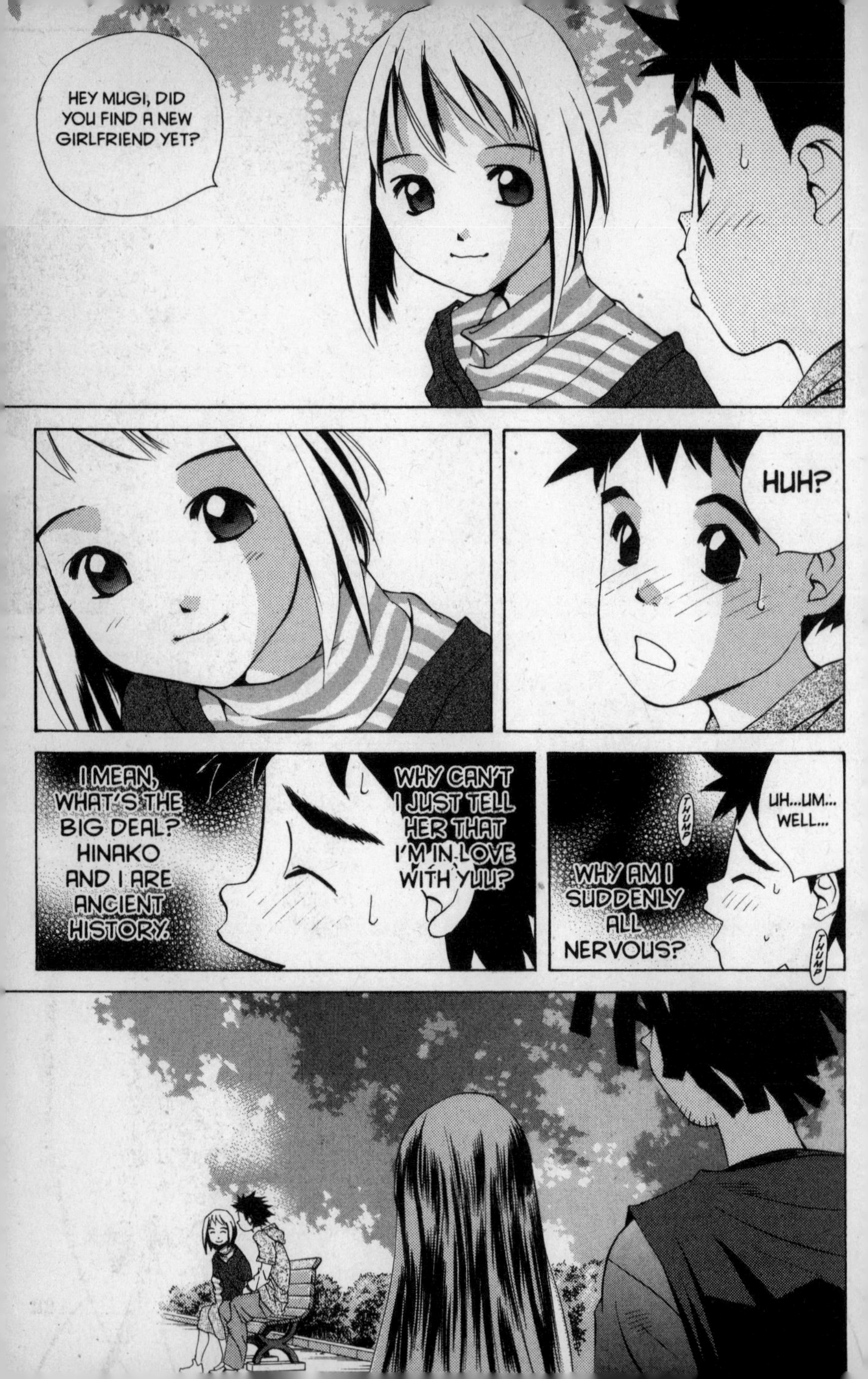
HEY MUGI, DID YOU FIND A NEW GIRLFRIEND YET?
HUH?
UH...UM... WELL...
THUMP
WHY AM I SUDDENLY ALL NERVOUS?
THUMP
WHY CAN'T I JUST TELL HER THAT I'M IN LOVE WITH YUU?
I MEAN, WHAT'S THE BIG DEAL? HINAKO AND I ARE ANCIENT HISTORY.

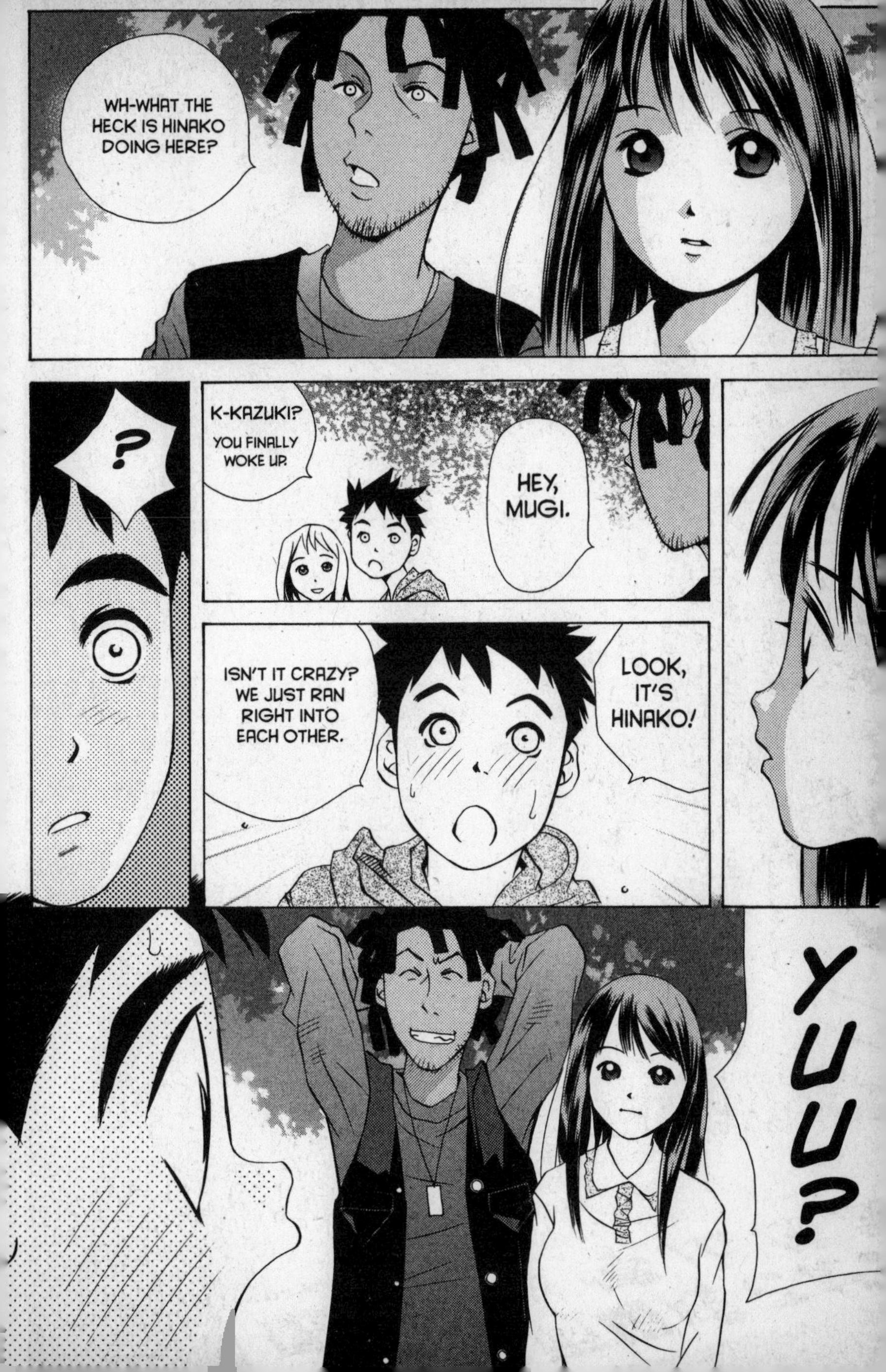
WH-WHAT THE HECK IS HINAKO DOING HERE?
HEY, MUGI.
K-KAZUKI? YOU FINALLY WOKE UP.
LOOK, IT'S HINAKO!
ISN'T IT CRAZY? WE JUST RAN RIGHT INTO EACH OTHER.
?
YUUU?

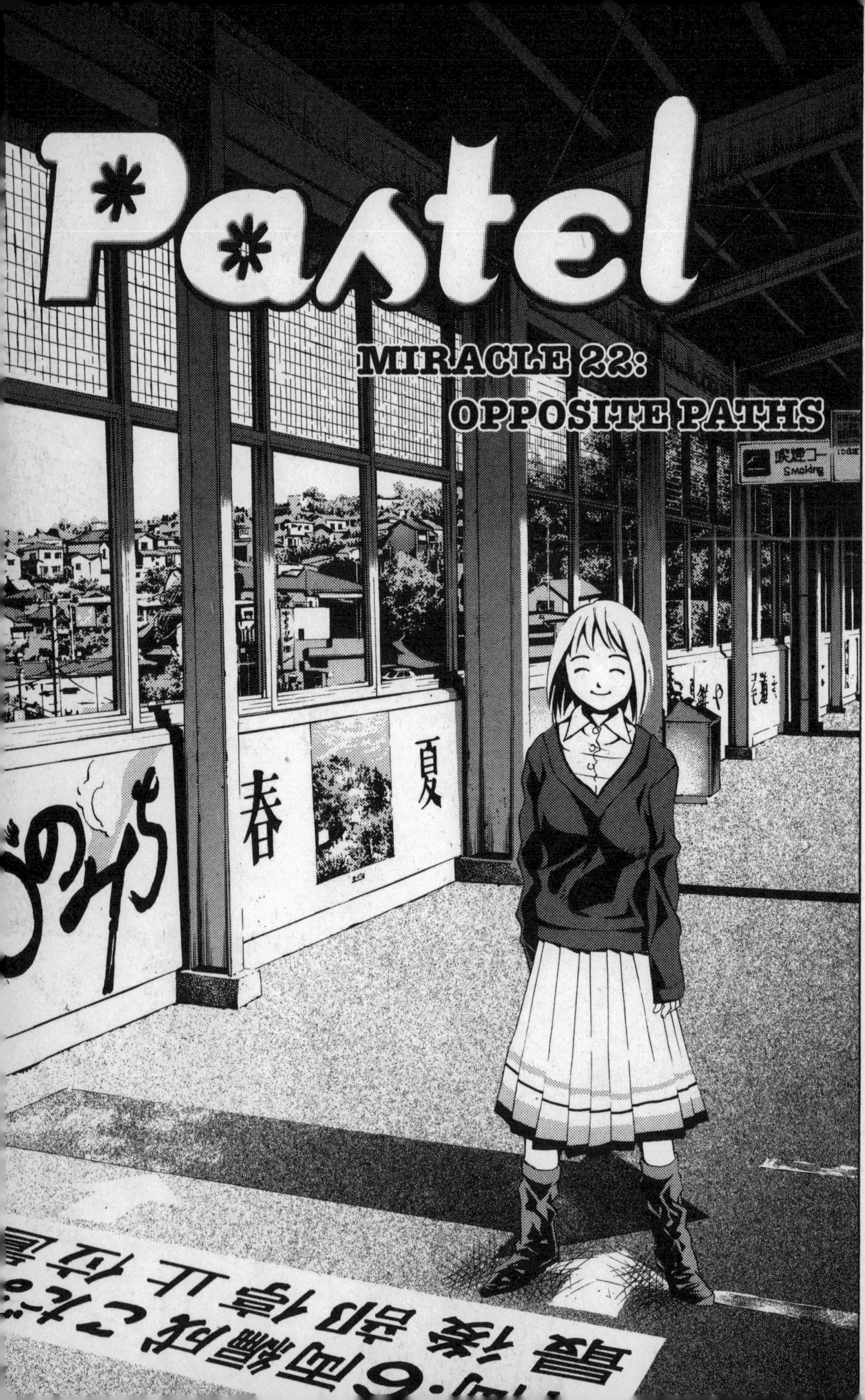
Pastel
MIRACLE 22:
OPPOSITE PATHS
春
夏

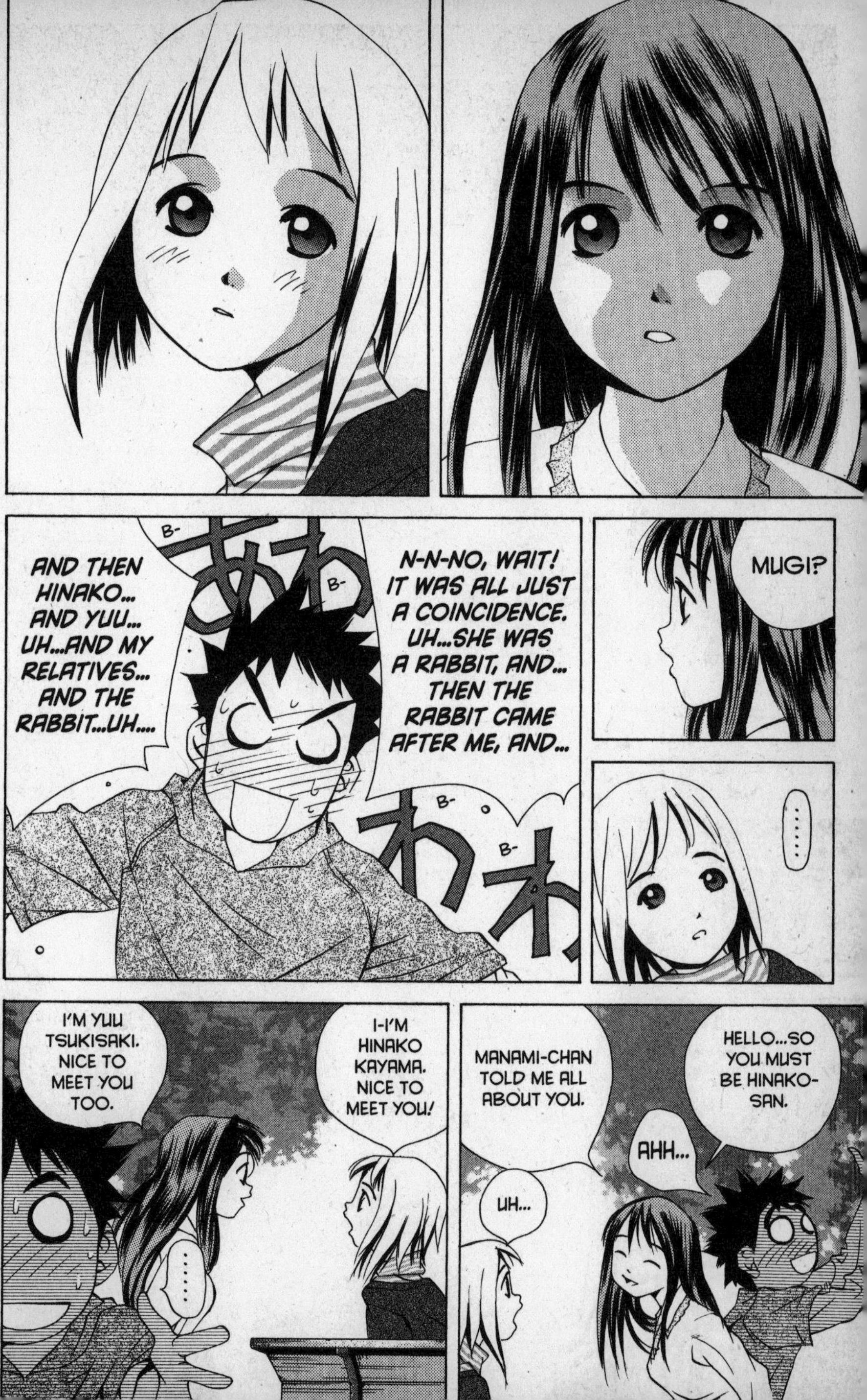
MUGI?
......
N-N-NO, WAIT! IT WAS ALL JUST A COINCIDENCE. UH...SHE WAS A RABBIT, AND... THEN THE RABBIT CAME AFTER ME, AND...
B-
B-
AND THEN HINAKO... AND YUU... UH...AND MY RELATIVES... AND THE RABBIT...UH....
B-
B-
HELLO...SO YOU MUST BE HINAKO-SAN.
MANAMI-CHAN TOLD ME ALL ABOUT YOU.
AHH...
UH...
I-I'M HINAKO KAYAMA. NICE TO MEET YOU!
I'M YUU TSUKISAKI. NICE TO MEET YOU TOO.
......

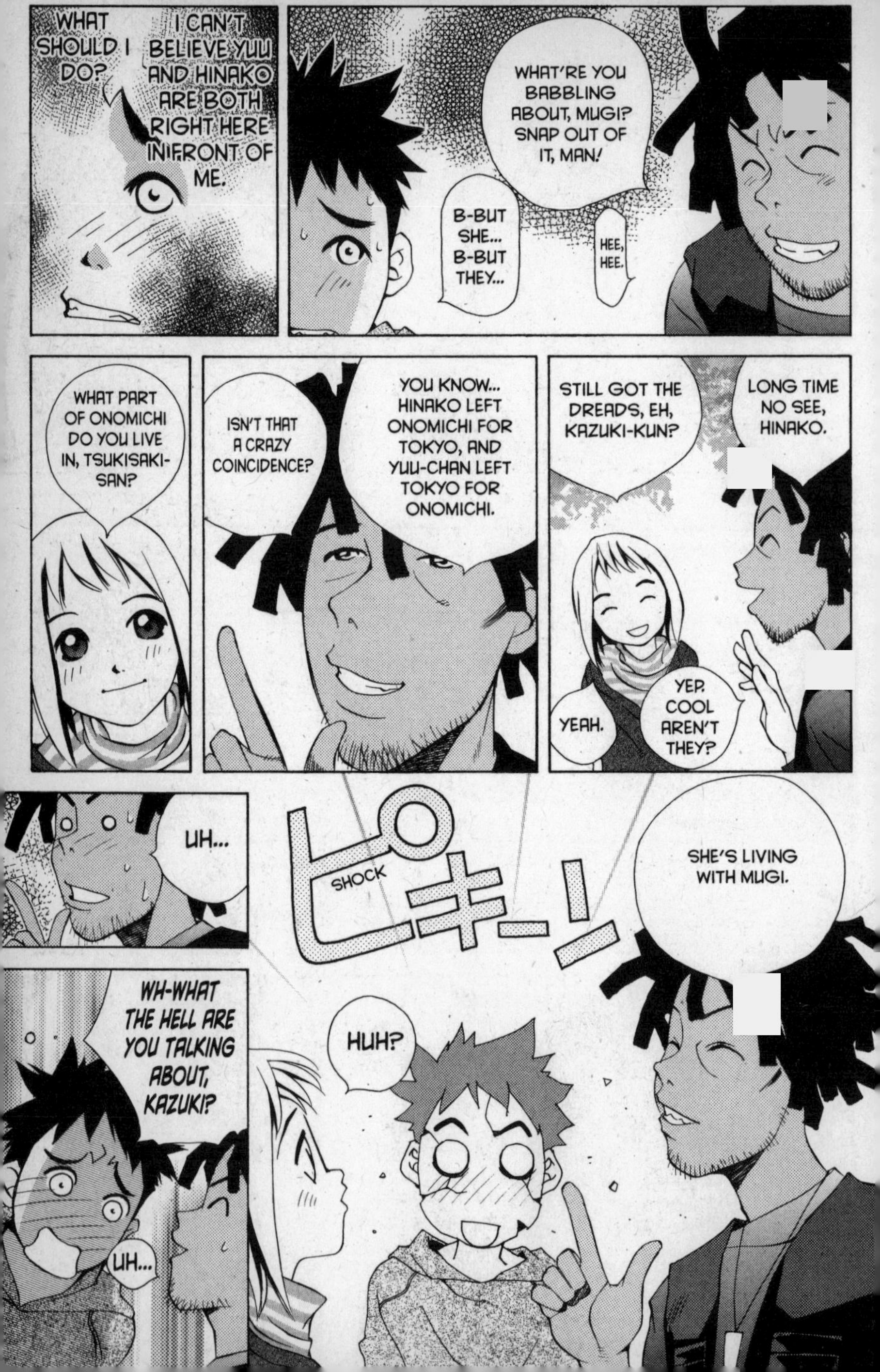
WHAT'RE YOU BABBLING ABOUT, MUGI? SNAP OUT OF IT, MAN!
HEE, HEE.
B-BUT SHE... B-BUT THEY...
I CAN'T BELIEVE YUU AND HINAKO ARE BOTH RIGHT HERE IN FRONT OF ME.
WHAT SHOULD I DO?
LONG TIME NO SEE, HINAKO.
STILL GOT THE DREADS, EH, KAZUKI-KUN?
YEP. COOL AREN'T THEY?
YEAH.
YOU KNOW... HINAKO LEFT ONOMICHI FOR TOKYO, AND YUU-CHAN LEFT TOKYO FOR ONOMICHI.
ISN'T THAT A CRAZY COINCIDENCE?
WHAT PART OF ONOMICHI DO YOU LIVE IN, TSUKISAKI-SAN?
SHE'S LIVING WITH MUGI.
ピキーン
SHOCK
HUH?
UH...
WH-WHAT THE HELL ARE YOU TALKING ABOUT, KAZUKI?
UH...

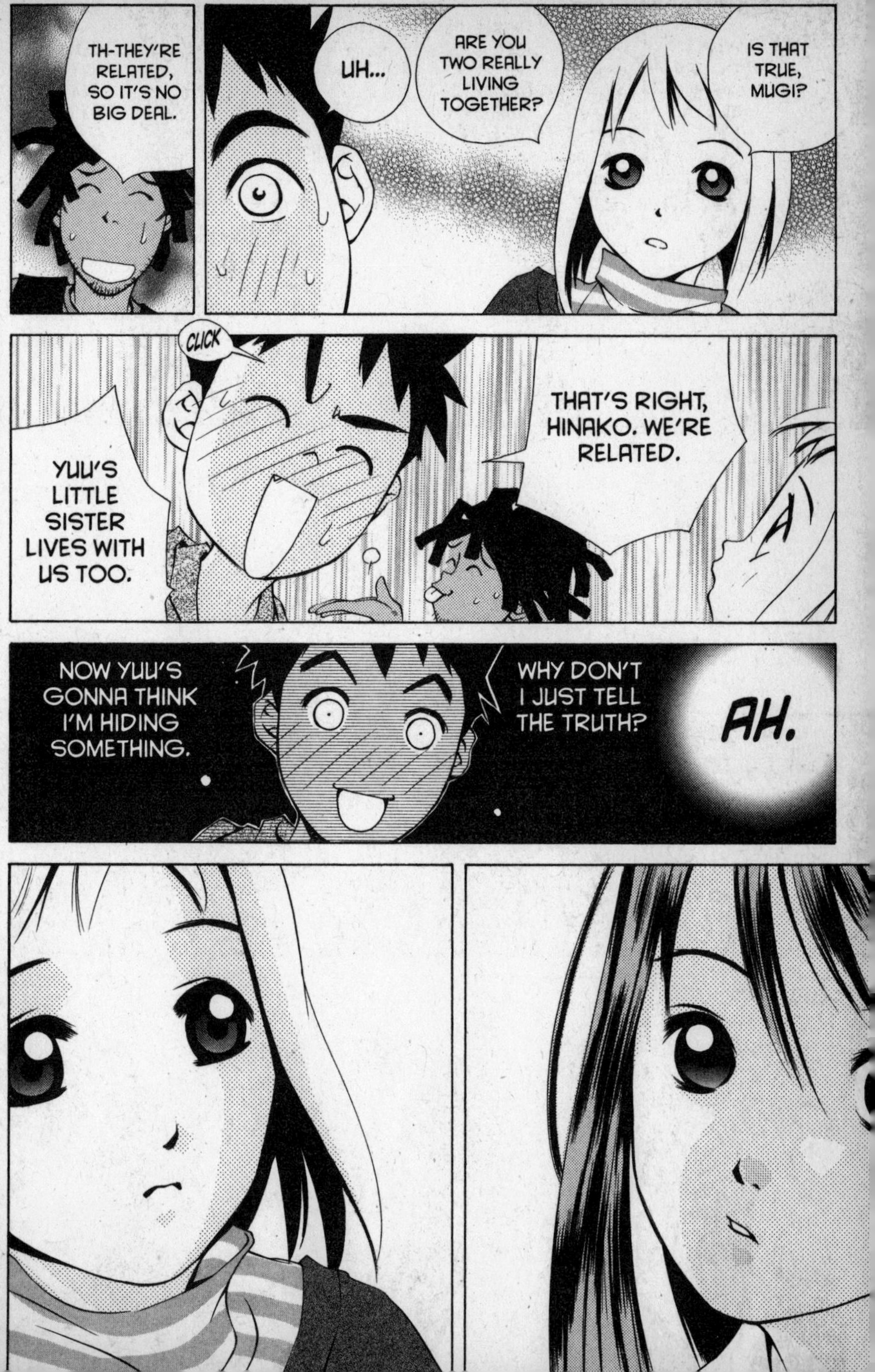
IS THAT TRUE, MUGI?
ARE YOU TWO REALLY LIVING TOGETHER?
UH...
TH-THEY'RE RELATED, SO IT'S NO BIG DEAL.
THAT'S RIGHT, HINAKO. WE'RE RELATED.
CLICK
YUU'S LITTLE SISTER LIVES WITH US TOO.
AH.
WHY DON'T I JUST TELL THE TRUTH?
NOW YUU'S GONNA THINK I'M HIDING SOMETHING.

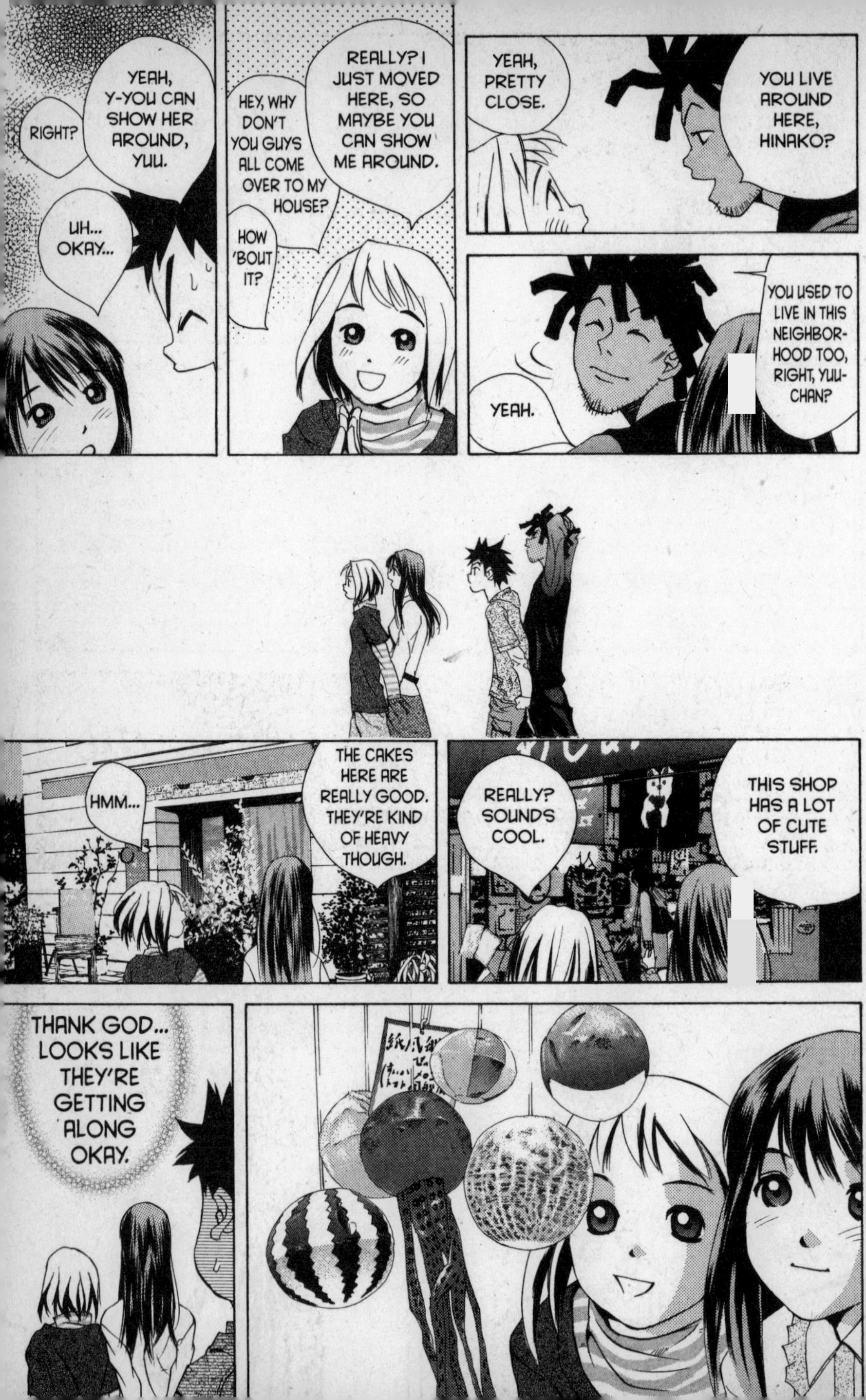
YOU LIVE AROUND HERE, HINAKO?
YEAH, PRETTY CLOSE.
YOU USED TO LIVE IN THIS NEIGHBOR-HOOD TOO, RIGHT, YUU-CHAN?
YEAH.
REALLY? I JUST MOVED HERE, SO MAYBE YOU CAN SHOW ME AROUND.
HEY, WHY DON'T YOU GUYS ALL COME OVER TO MY HOUSE?
HOW 'BOUT IT?
YEAH, Y-YOU CAN SHOW HER AROUND, YUU.
RIGHT?
UH... OKAY...
THIS SHOP HAS A LOT OF CUTE STUFF.
REALLY? SOUNDS COOL.
THE CAKES HERE ARE REALLY GOOD. THEY'RE KIND OF HEAVY THOUGH.
HMM...
THANK GOD... LOOKS LIKE THEY'RE GETTING ALONG OKAY.

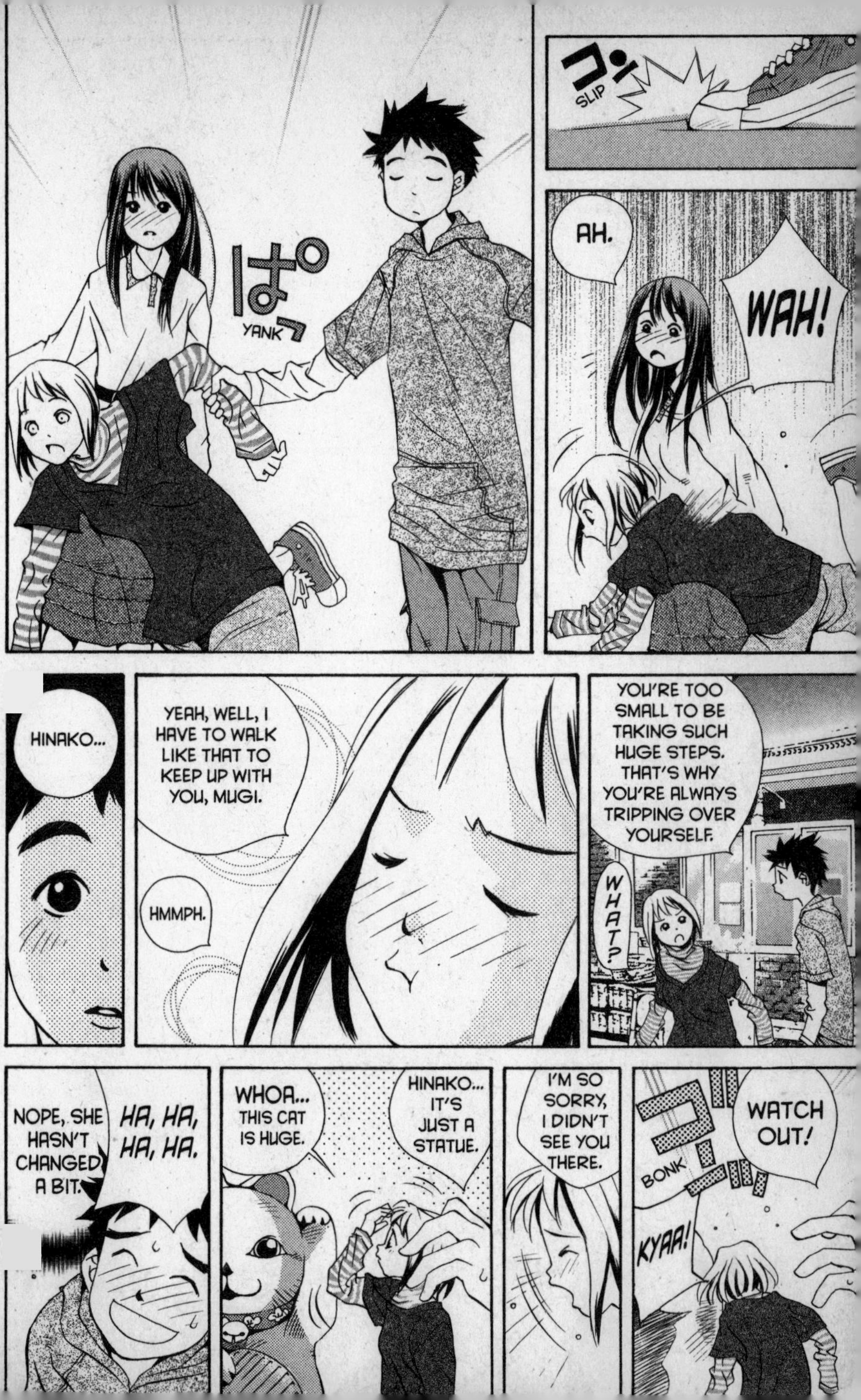
SLIP
AH.
WAH!
YANK
YOU'RE TOO SMALL TO BE TAKING SUCH HUGE STEPS. THAT'S WHY YOU'RE ALWAYS TRIPPING OVER YOURSELF.
WHAT?
YEAH, WELL, I HAVE TO WALK LIKE THAT TO KEEP UP WITH YOU, MUGI.
HMMPH.
HINAKO...
WATCH OUT!
BONK
KYAA!
I'M SO SORRY, I DIDN'T SEE YOU THERE.
HINAKO... IT'S JUST A STATUE.
WHOA... THIS CAT IS HUGE.
HA, HA, HA, HA.
NOPE, SHE HASN'T CHANGED A BIT.

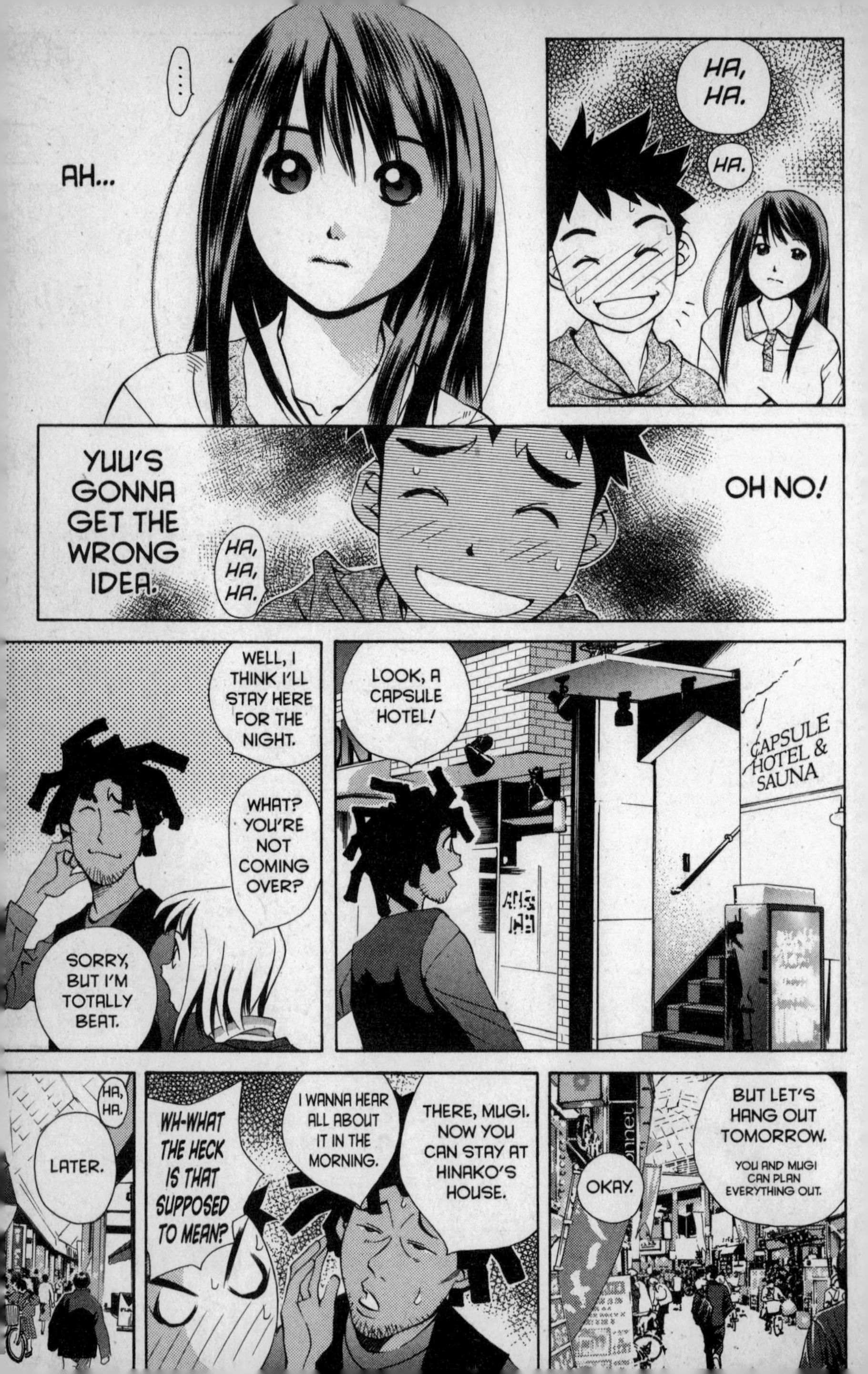
HA, HA.
HA.
...
AH...
OH NO!
YUU'S GONNA GET THE WRONG IDEA.
HA, HA, HA.
LOOK, A CAPSULE HOTEL!
CAPSULE HOTEL & SAUNA
WELL, I THINK I'LL STAY HERE FOR THE NIGHT.
WHAT? YOU'RE NOT COMING OVER?
SORRY, BUT I'M TOTALLY BEAT.
BUT LET'S HANG OUT TOMORROW.
YOU AND MUGI CAN PLAN EVERYTHING OUT.
OKAY.
THERE, MUGI. NOW YOU CAN STAY AT HINAKO'S HOUSE.
I WANNA HEAR ALL ABOUT IT IN THE MORNING.
WH-WHAT THE HECK IS THAT SUPPOSED TO MEAN?
HA, HA.
LATER.

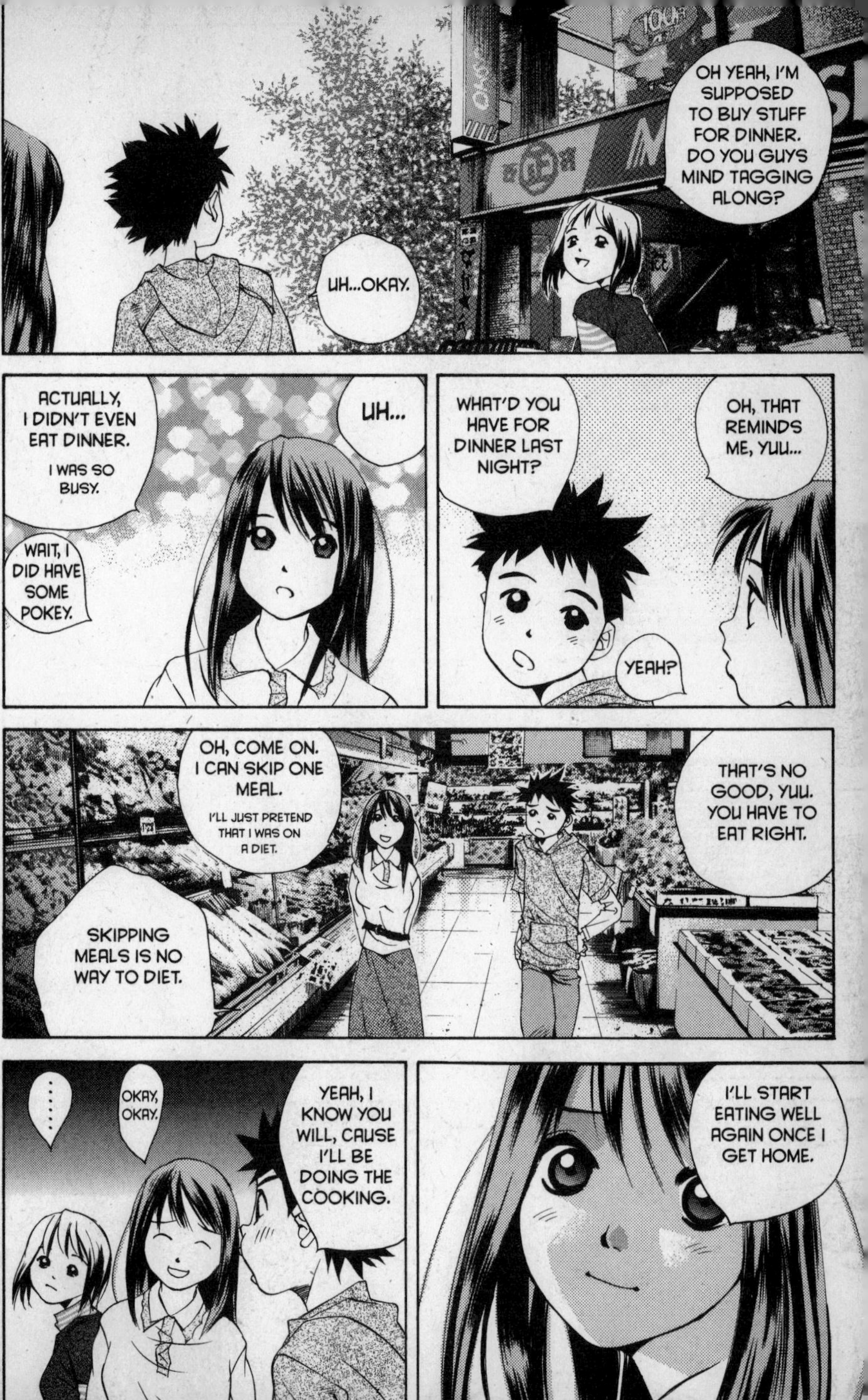
OH YEAH, I'M SUPPOSED TO BUY STUFF FOR DINNER. DO YOU GUYS MIND TAGGING ALONG?
UH...OKAY.
OH, THAT REMINDS ME, YUU...
WHAT'D YOU HAVE FOR DINNER LAST NIGHT?
YEAH?
UH...
ACTUALLY, I DIDN'T EVEN EAT DINNER.
I WAS SO BUSY.
WAIT, I DID HAVE SOME POKEY.
THAT'S NO GOOD, YUU. YOU HAVE TO EAT RIGHT.
OH, COME ON. I CAN SKIP ONE MEAL.
I'LL JUST PRETEND THAT I WAS ON A DIET.
SKIPPING MEALS IS NO WAY TO DIET.
I'LL START EATING WELL AGAIN ONCE I GET HOME.
YEAH, I KNOW YOU WILL, CAUSE I'LL BE DOING THE COOKING.
OKAY, OKAY.
......

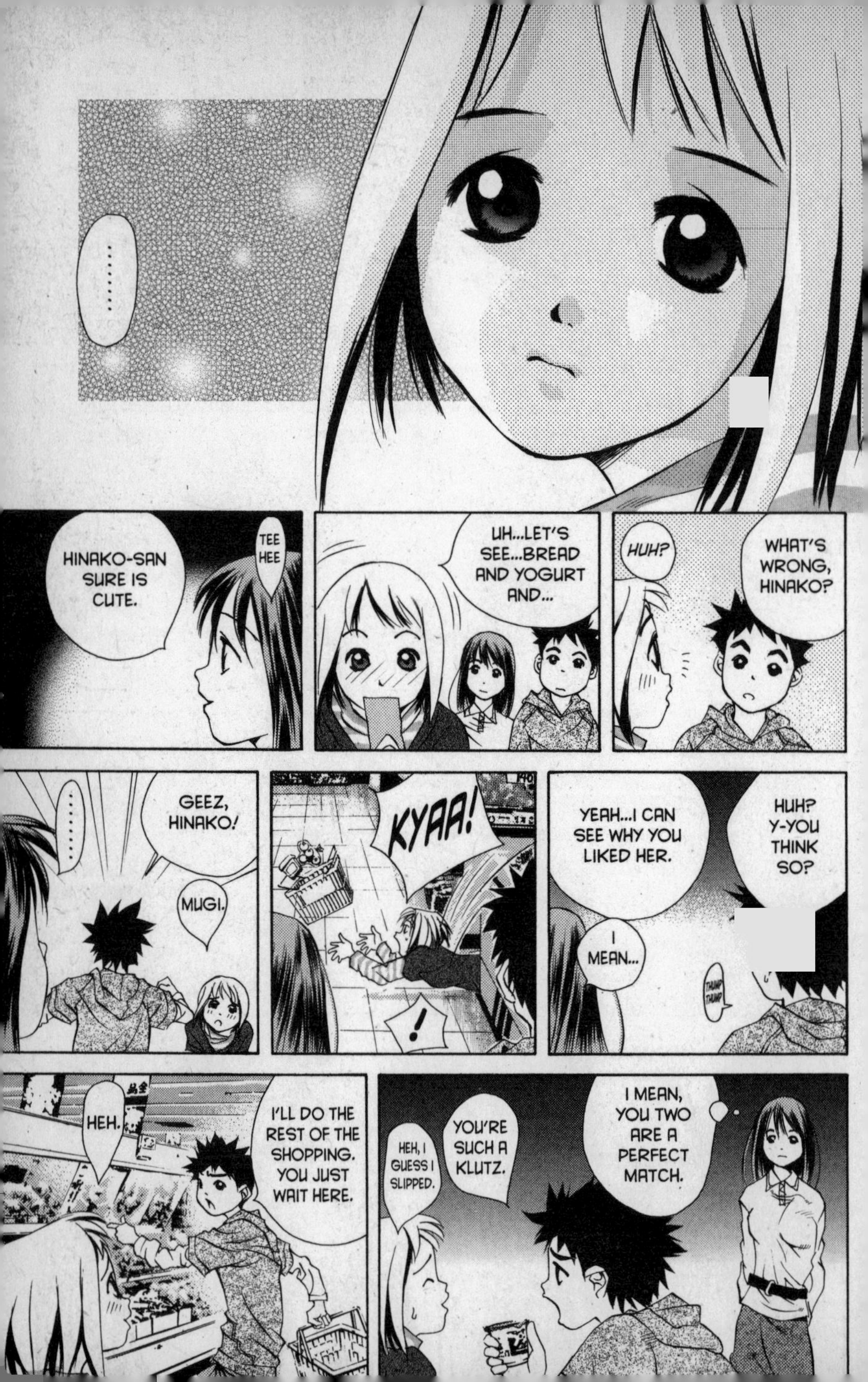
......
WHAT'S WRONG, HINAKO?
HUH?
UH...LET'S SEE...BREAD AND YOGURT AND...
TEE HEE
HINAKO-SAN SURE IS CUTE.
HUH? Y-YOU THINK SO?
YEAH...I CAN SEE WHY YOU LIKED HER.
I MEAN...
THUMP THUMP
KYAA!
!
GEEZ, HINAKO!
......
MUGI.
I MEAN, YOU TWO ARE A PERFECT MATCH.
YOU'RE SUCH A KLUTZ.
HEH, I GUESS I SLIPPED.
I'LL DO THE REST OF THE SHOPPING. YOU JUST WAIT HERE.
HEH.

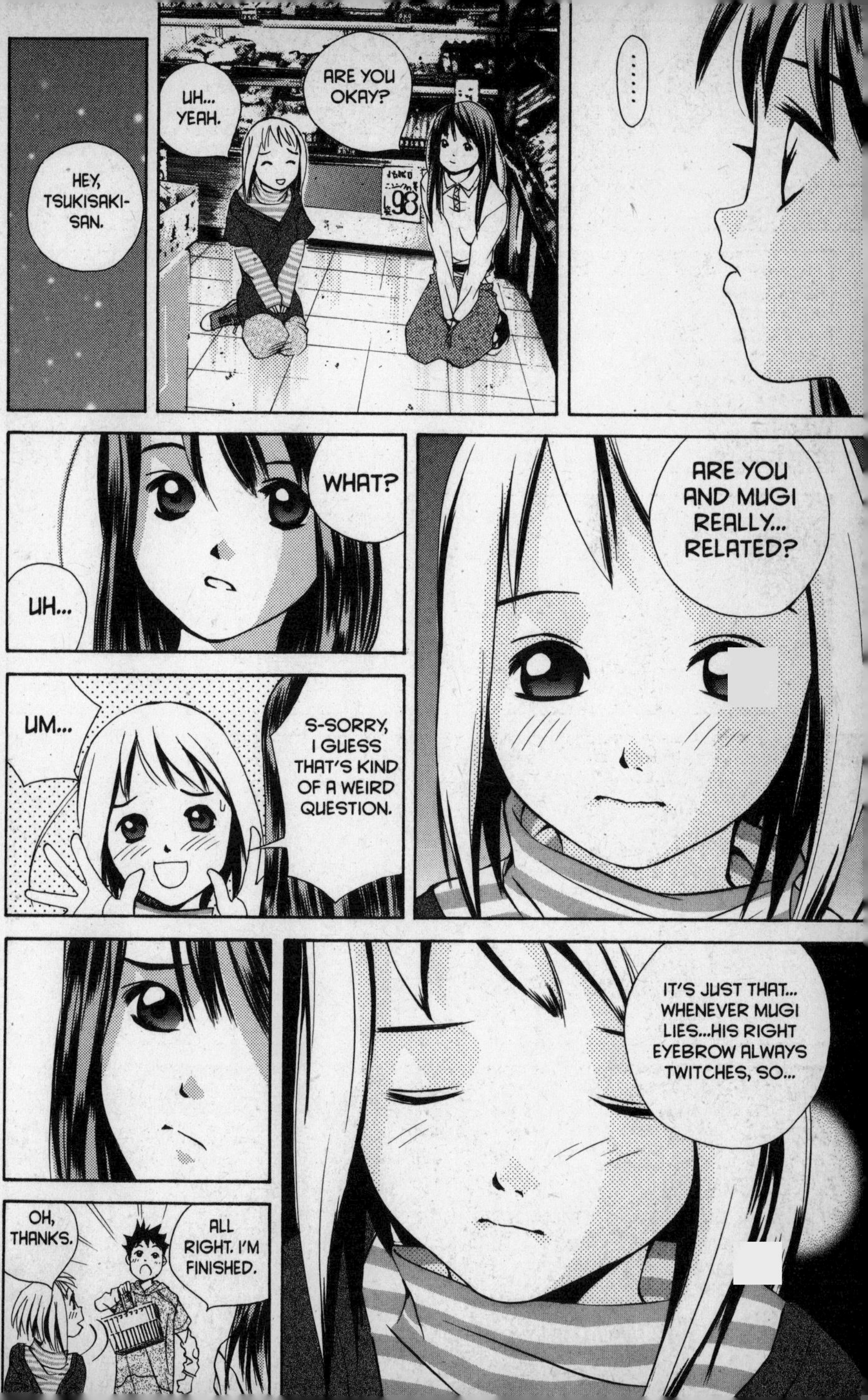
......
ARE YOU OKAY?
UH... YEAH.
HEY, TSUKISAKI-SAN.
ARE YOU AND MUGI REALLY... RELATED?
WHAT?
UH...
S-SORRY, I GUESS THAT'S KIND OF A WEIRD QUESTION.
UM...
IT'S JUST THAT... WHENEVER MUGI LIES...HIS RIGHT EYEBROW ALWAYS TWITCHES, SO...
ALL RIGHT. I'M FINISHED.
OH, THANKS.

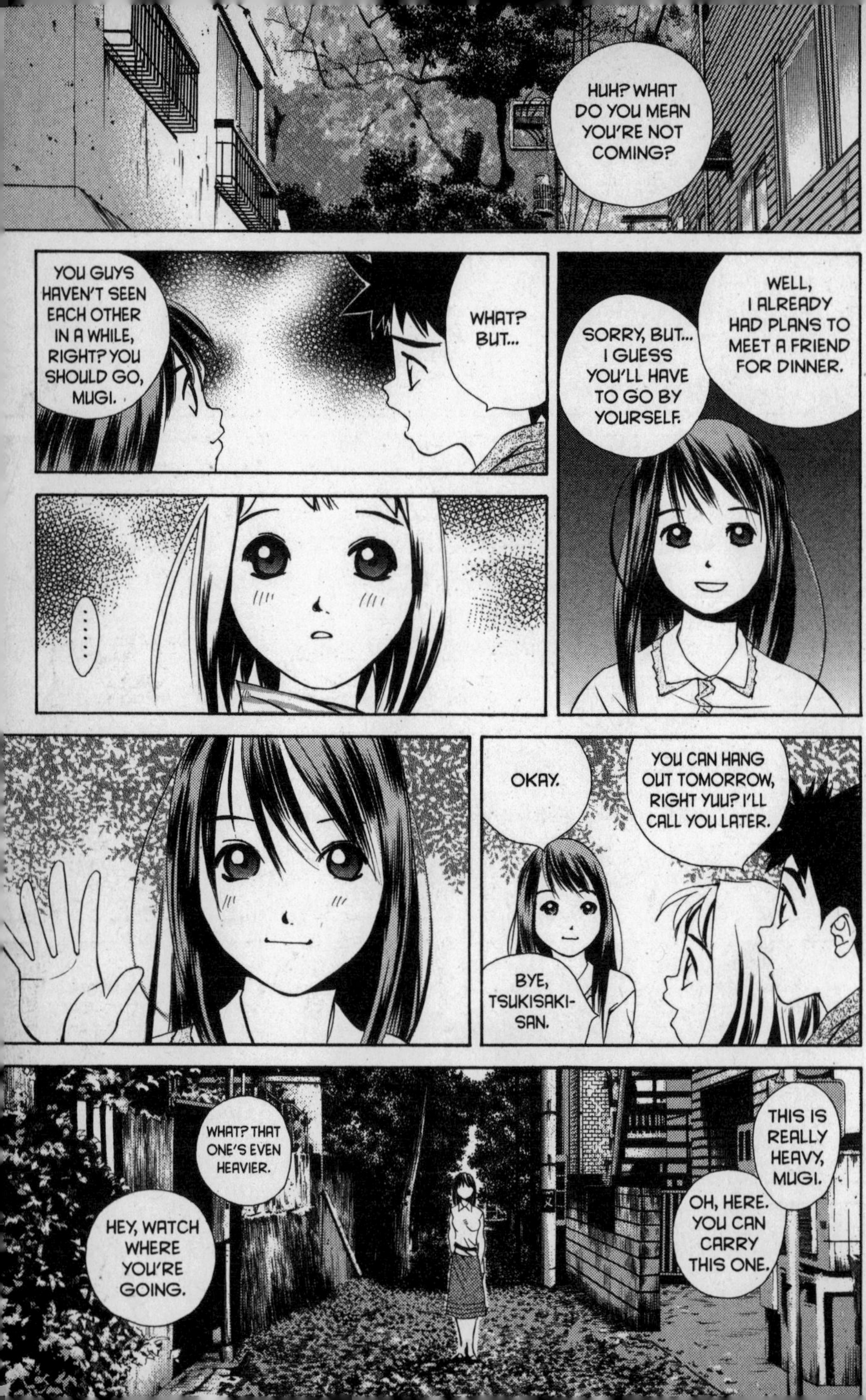
HUH? WHAT DO YOU MEAN YOU'RE NOT COMING?
WELL, I ALREADY HAD PLANS TO MEET A FRIEND FOR DINNER.
SORRY, BUT... I GUESS YOU'LL HAVE TO GO BY YOURSELF.
WHAT? BUT...
YOU GUYS HAVEN'T SEEN EACH OTHER IN A WHILE, RIGHT? YOU SHOULD GO, MUGI.
......
YOU CAN HANG OUT TOMORROW, RIGHT YUU? I'LL CALL YOU LATER.
OKAY.
BYE, TSUKISAKI-SAN.
THIS IS REALLY HEAVY, MUGI.
OH, HERE. YOU CAN CARRY THIS ONE.
WHAT? THAT ONE'S EVEN HEAVIER.
HEY, WATCH WHERE YOU'RE GOING.

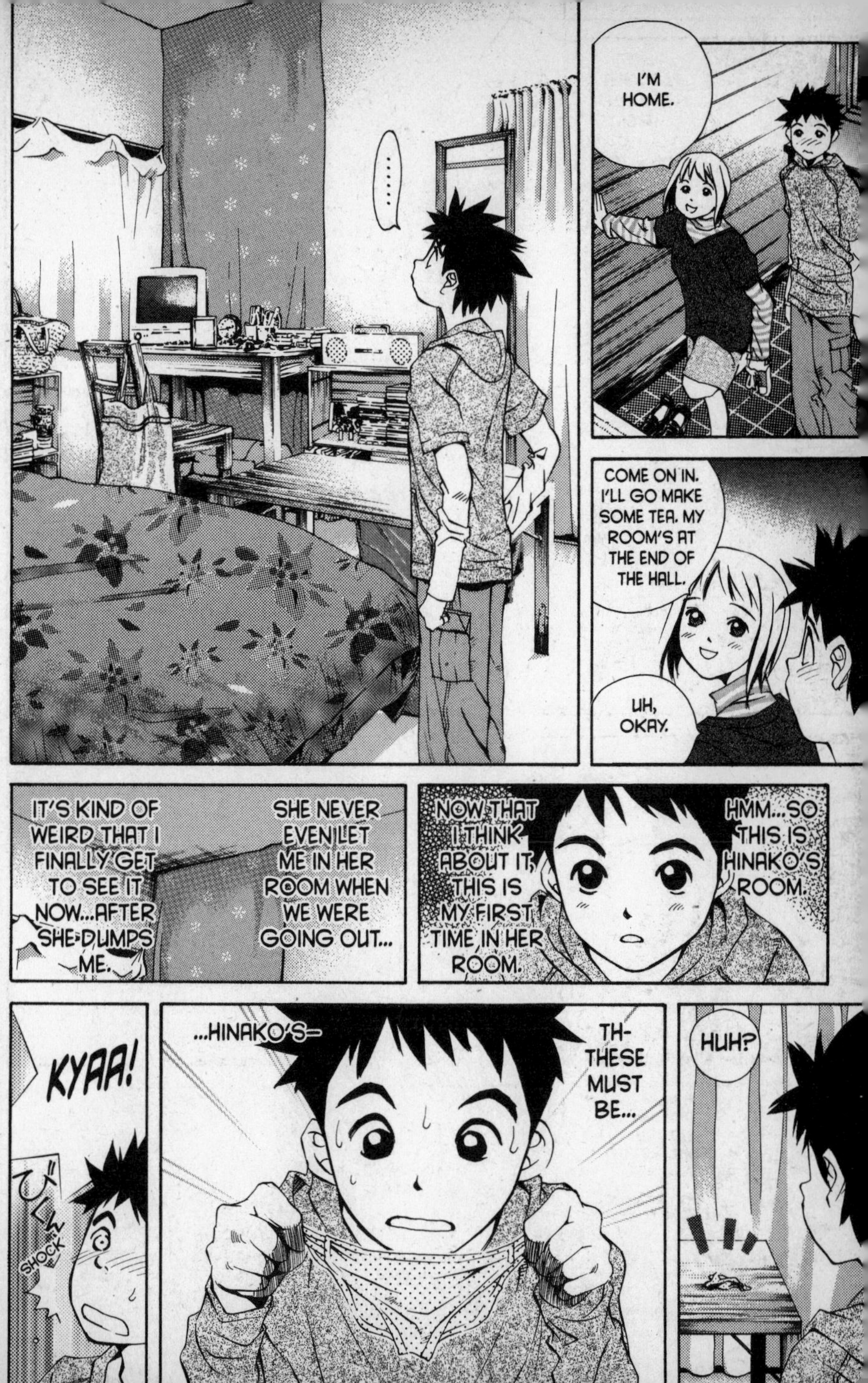
I'M HOME.
COME ON IN. I'LL GO MAKE SOME TEA. MY ROOM'S AT THE END OF THE HALL.
UH, OKAY.
......
HMM...SO THIS IS HINAKO'S ROOM.
NOW THAT I THINK ABOUT IT, THIS IS MY FIRST TIME IN HER ROOM.
SHE NEVER EVEN LET ME IN HER ROOM WHEN WE WERE GOING OUT...
IT'S KIND OF WEIRD THAT I FINALLY GET TO SEE IT NOW...AFTER SHE DUMPS ME.
HUH?
TH- THESE MUST BE...
...HINAKO'S—
KYAA!
びくん
SHOCK

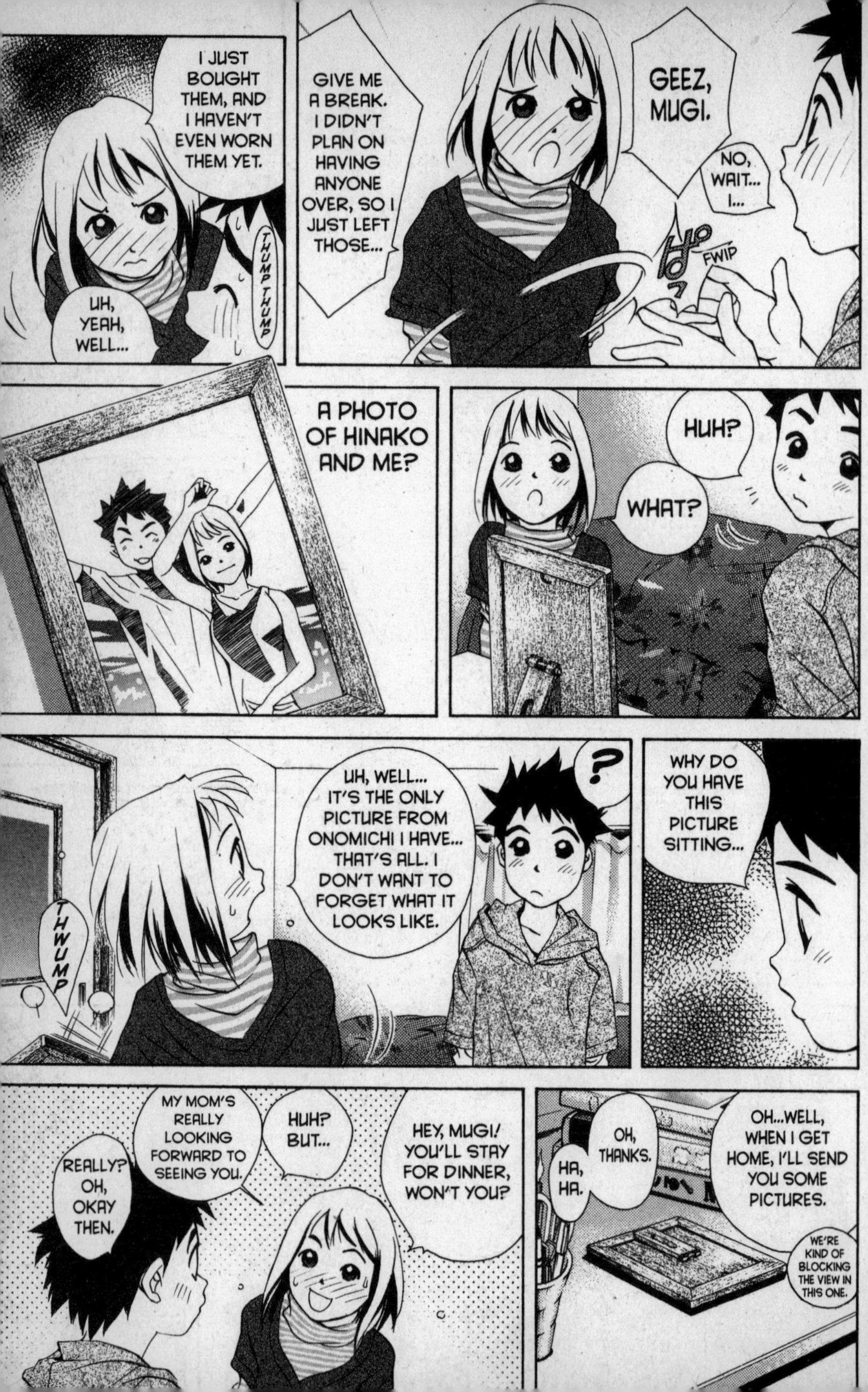
GEEZ, MUGI.
GIVE ME A BREAK. I DIDN'T PLAN ON HAVING ANYONE OVER, SO I JUST LEFT THOSE...
NO, WAIT... I...
FWIP
I JUST BOUGHT THEM, AND I HAVEN'T EVEN WORN THEM YET.
THUMP THUMP
UH, YEAH, WELL...
HUH?
WHAT?
A PHOTO OF HINAKO AND ME?
WHY DO YOU HAVE THIS PICTURE SITTING...
?
UH, WELL... IT'S THE ONLY PICTURE FROM ONOMICHI I HAVE... THAT'S ALL. I DON'T WANT TO FORGET WHAT IT LOOKS LIKE.
THWUMP
OH...WELL, WHEN I GET HOME, I'LL SEND YOU SOME PICTURES.
OH, THANKS.
HA, HA.
WE'RE KIND OF BLOCKING THE VIEW IN THIS ONE.
HEY, MUGI! YOU'LL STAY FOR DINNER, WON'T YOU?
HUH? BUT...
MY MOM'S REALLY LOOKING FORWARD TO SEEING YOU.
REALLY? OH, OKAY THEN.

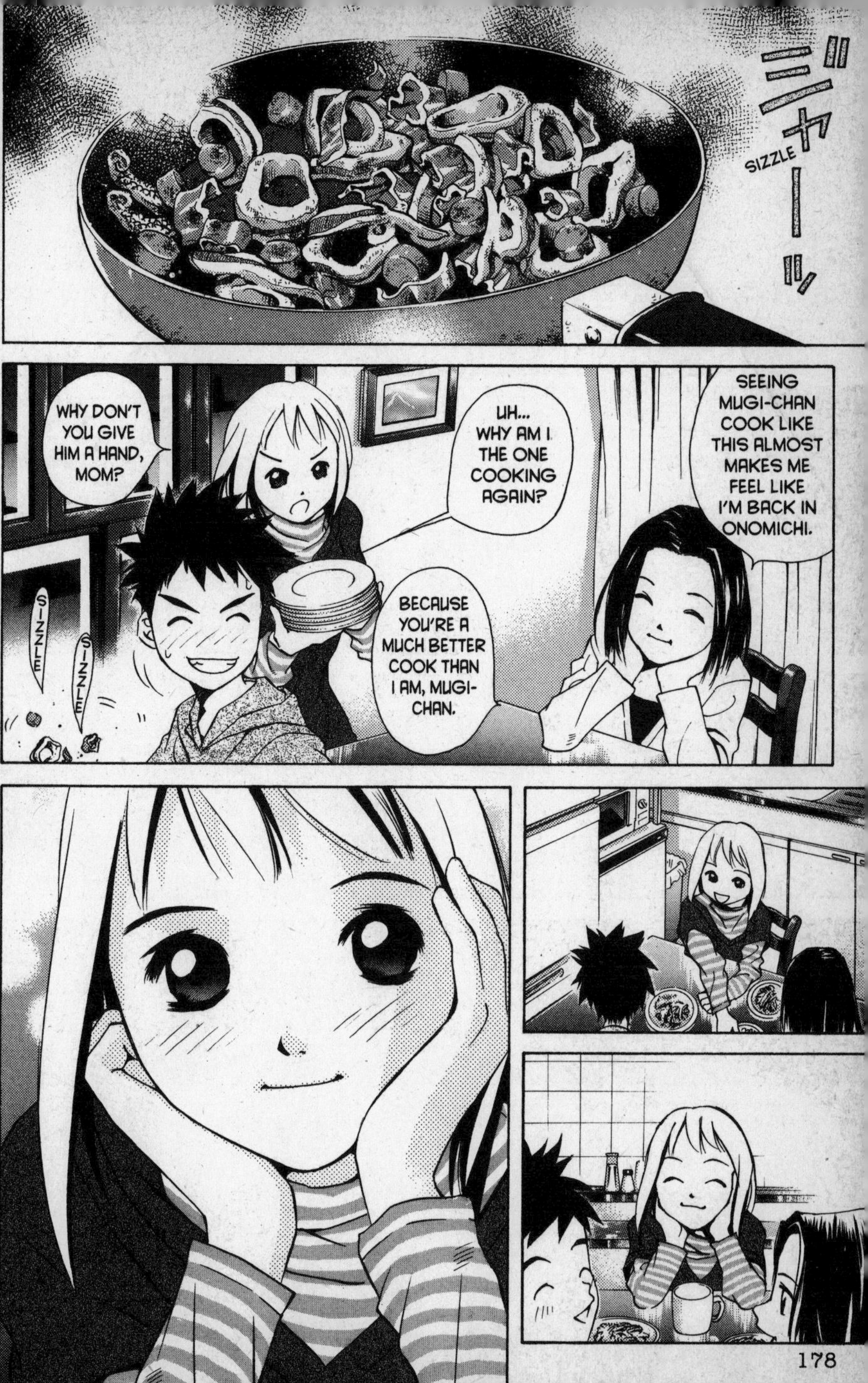
SIZZLE
SEEING MUGI-CHAN COOK LIKE THIS ALMOST MAKES ME FEEL LIKE I'M BACK IN ONOMICHI.
UH... WHY AM I THE ONE COOKING AGAIN?
WHY DON'T YOU GIVE HIM A HAND, MOM?
BECAUSE YOU'RE A MUCH BETTER COOK THAN I AM, MUGI-CHAN.
SIZZLE
SIZZLE

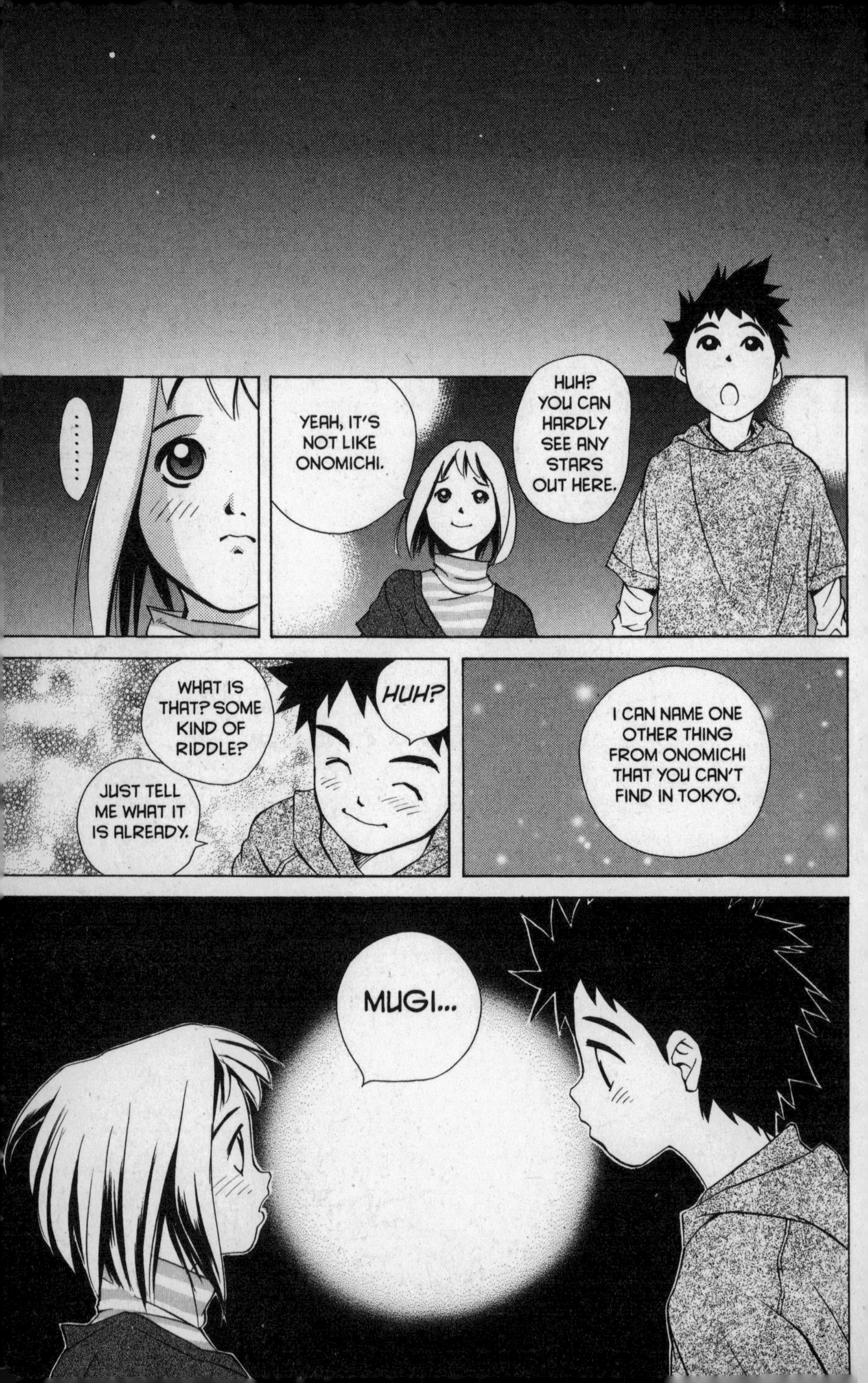
HUH? YOU CAN HARDLY SEE ANY STARS OUT HERE.
YEAH, IT'S NOT LIKE ONOMICHI.
......
I CAN NAME ONE OTHER THING FROM ONOMICHI THAT YOU CAN'T FIND IN TOKYO.
HUH?
WHAT IS THAT? SOME KIND OF RIDDLE?
JUST TELL ME WHAT IT IS ALREADY.
MUGI...

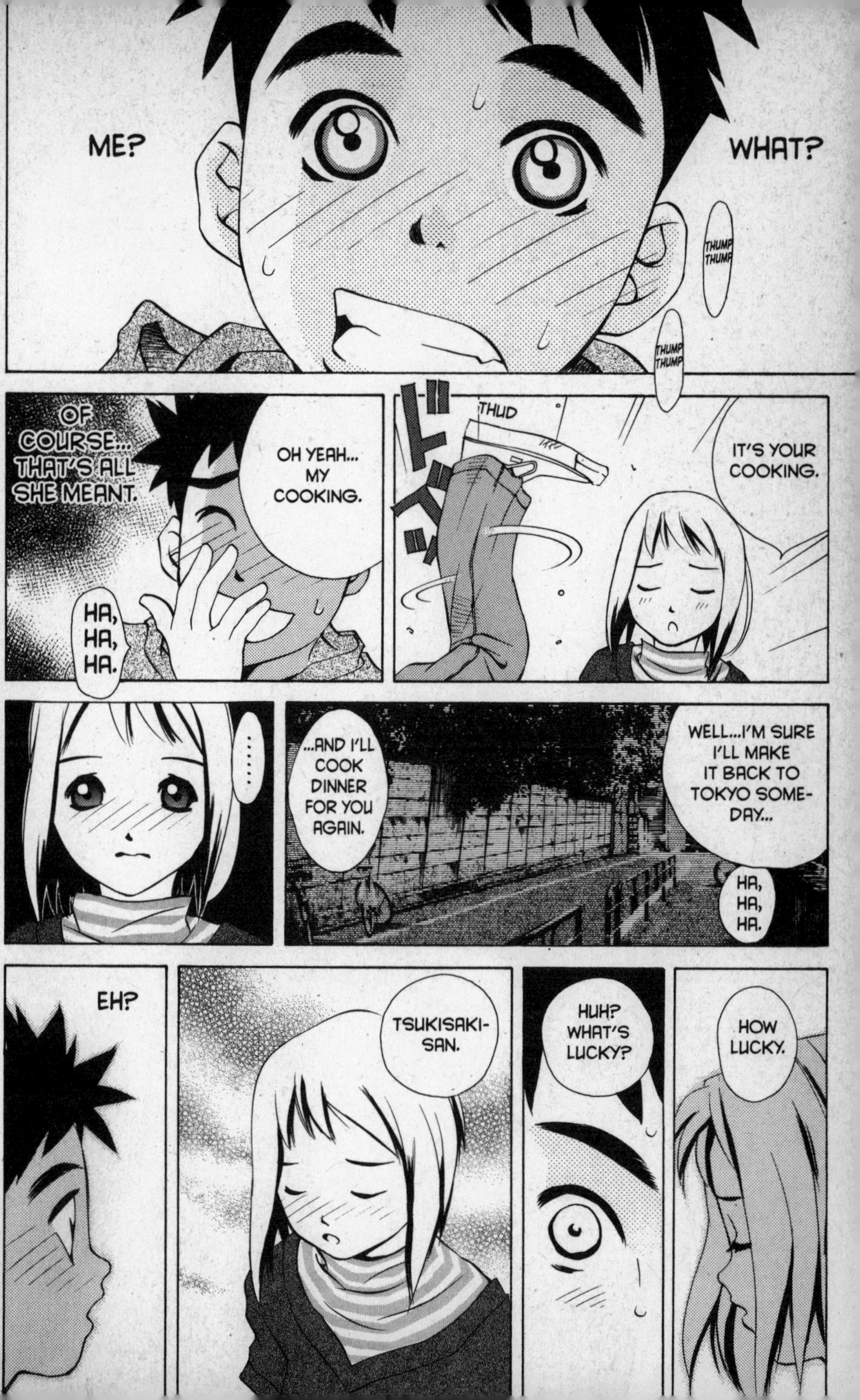
WHAT?
ME?
THUMP THUMP
THUMP THUMP
IT'S YOUR COOKING.
THUD
OH YEAH... MY COOKING.
OF COURSE... THAT'S ALL SHE MEANT.
HA, HA, HA.
WELL...I'M SURE I'LL MAKE IT BACK TO TOKYO SOME-DAY...
HA, HA, HA.
...AND I'LL COOK DINNER FOR YOU AGAIN.
......
HOW LUCKY.
HUH? WHAT'S LUCKY?
TSUKISAKI-SAN.
EH?

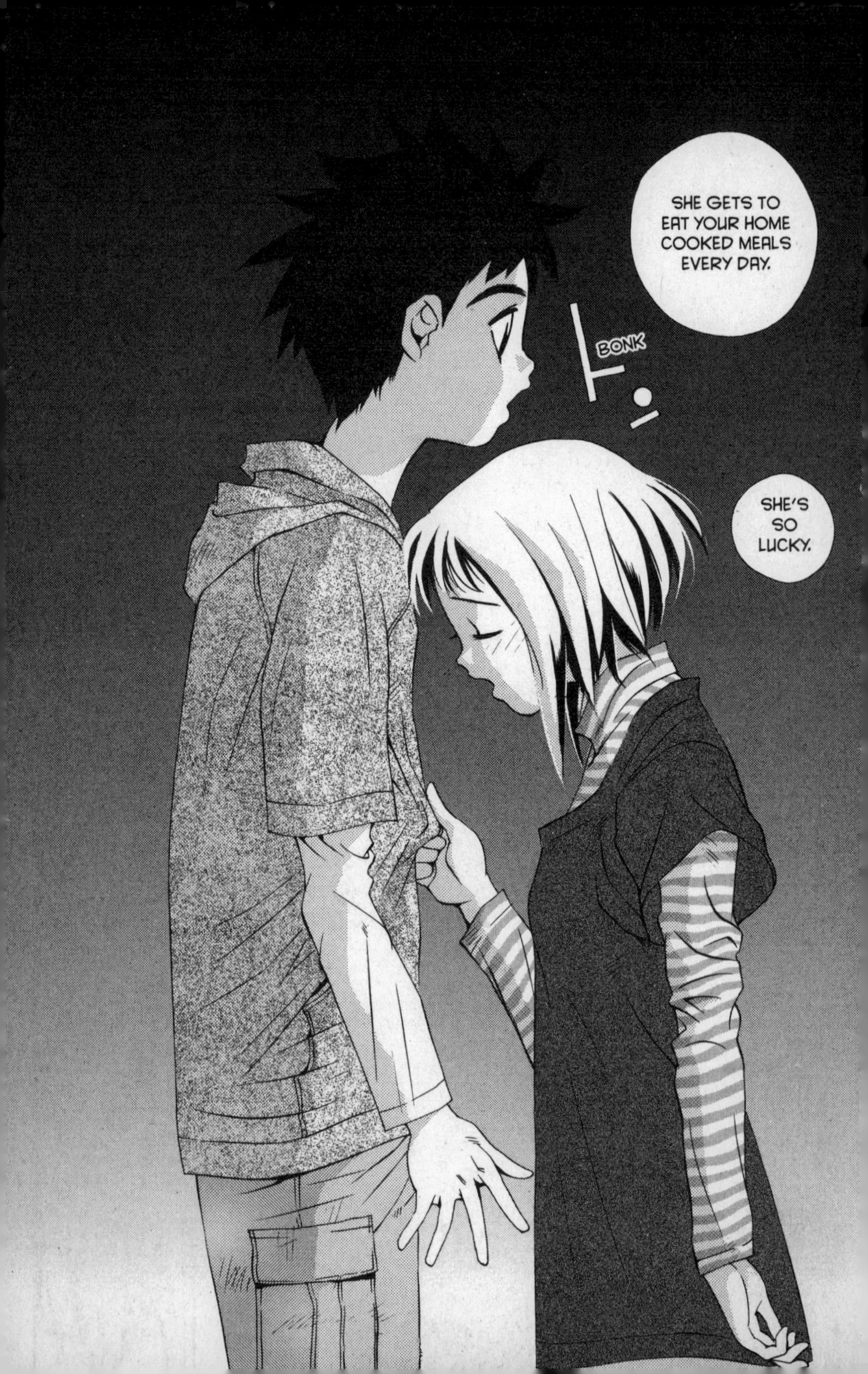
SHE GETS TO EAT YOUR HOME COOKED MEALS EVERY DAY.
BONK
SHE'S SO LUCKY.

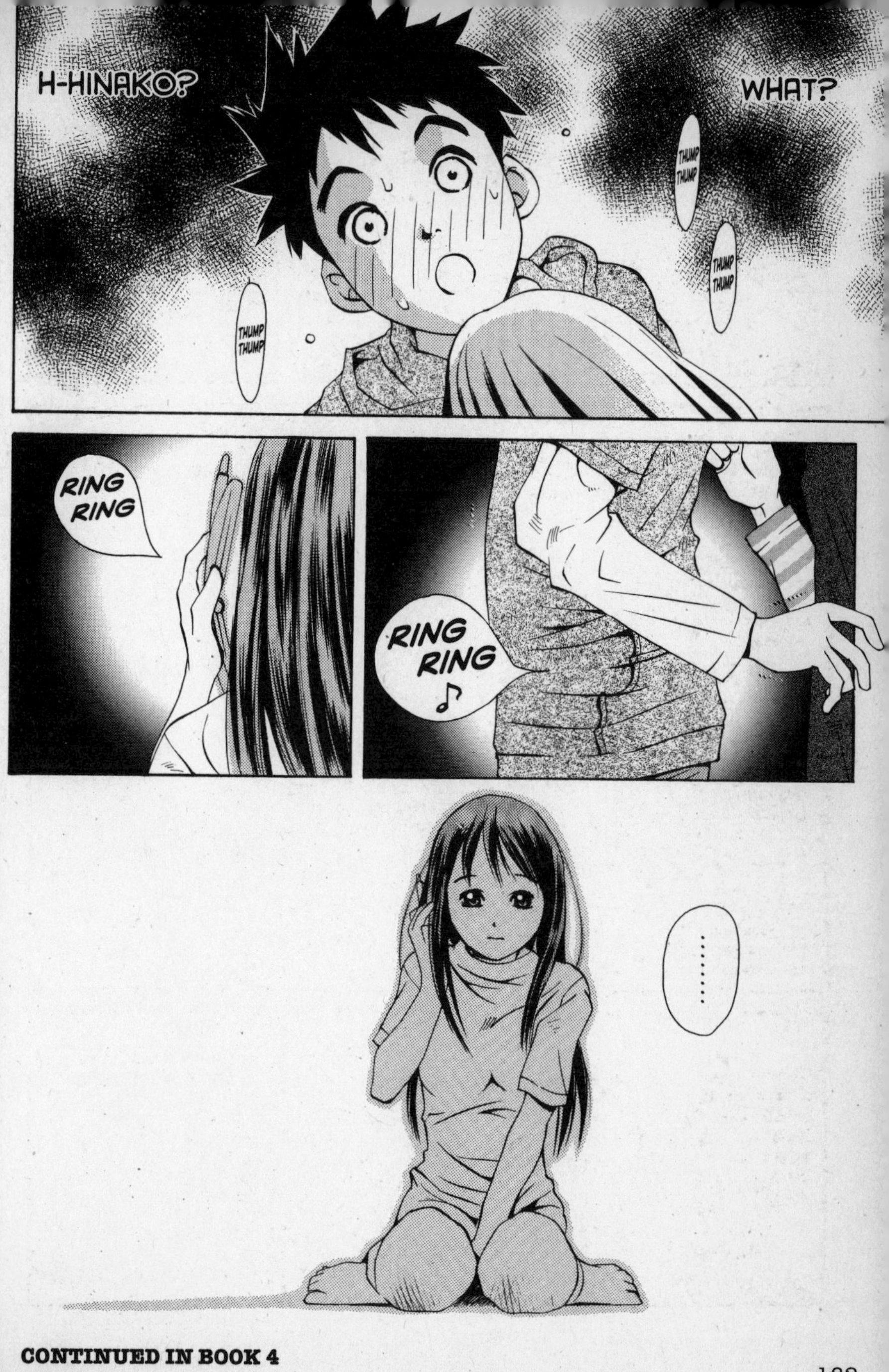
WHAT?
THUMP THUMP
THUMP THUMP
H-HINAKO?
THUMP THUMP
RING RING ♪
RING RING
......

CONTINUED IN BOOK 4

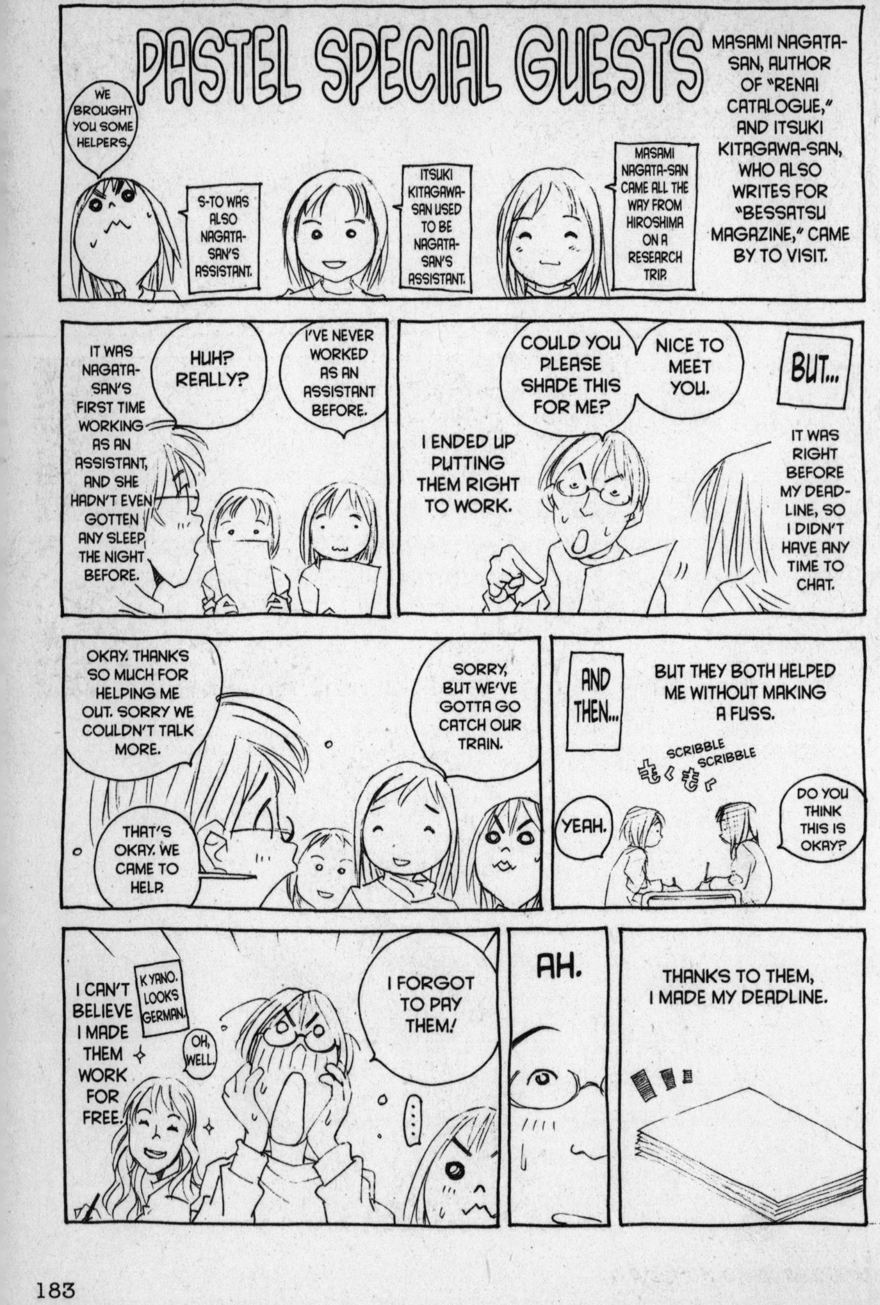
PASTEL SPECIAL GUESTS
MASAMI NAGATA-SAN, AUTHOR OF "RENAI CATALOGUE," AND ITSUKI KITAGAWA-SAN, WHO ALSO WRITES FOR "BESSATSU MAGAZINE," CAME BY TO VISIT.
MASAMI NAGATA-SAN CAME ALL THE WAY FROM HIROSHIMA ON A RESEARCH TRIP.
ITSUKI KITAGAWA-SAN USED TO BE NAGATA-SAN'S ASSISTANT.
S-TO WAS ALSO NAGATA-SAN'S ASSISTANT.
WE BROUGHT YOU SOME HELPERS.
BUT...
IT WAS RIGHT BEFORE MY DEADLINE, SO I DIDN'T HAVE ANY TIME TO CHAT.
NICE TO MEET YOU.
COULD YOU PLEASE SHADE THIS FOR ME?
I ENDED UP PUTTING THEM RIGHT TO WORK.
I'VE NEVER WORKED AS AN ASSISTANT BEFORE.
HUH? REALLY?
IT WAS NAGATA-SAN'S FIRST TIME WORKING AS AN ASSISTANT, AND SHE HADN'T EVEN GOTTEN ANY SLEEP THE NIGHT BEFORE.
AND THEN...
BUT THEY BOTH HELPED ME WITHOUT MAKING A FUSS.
SCRIBBLE SCRIBBLE
DO YOU THINK THIS IS OKAY?
YEAH.
SORRY, BUT WE'VE GOTTA GO CATCH OUR TRAIN.
OKAY. THANKS SO MUCH FOR HELPING ME OUT. SORRY WE COULDN'T TALK MORE.
THAT'S OKAY. WE CAME TO HELP.
THANKS TO THEM, I MADE MY DEADLINE.
AH.
I FORGOT TO PAY THEM!
OH, WELL.
K YANO. LOOKS GERMAN.
I CAN'T BELIEVE I MADE THEM WORK FOR FREE.

TOSHIHIKO KOBAYASHI

Born in Mihara city in Hiroshima. Birthday is February 25.
In 1995, "Half Coat" was serialized in "Magazine Special" from No.1 to
No.11. After the serial publication of "Parallel" in "Magazine Special"
from No.8 in 2000 to No.1 in 2002, "Pastel" was serialized in "Weekly
Shonen Magazine" from the 32nd issue in 2002 to the 33rd issue in
2003. And now "Pastel" has been running as a serial ever since
"Magazine Special" No.10 in 2003.

Favorites
Fruits
Sleeping
Hot green tea

Dislikes
Being scolded
Excessive expectations
Cigarette smoke

Translation Notes

Japanese is a tricky language for most Westerners, and translation is often more art than science. For your edification and reading pleasure, here are notes on some of the places where we could have gone in a different direction in our translation of the work, or where a Japanese cultural reference is used.

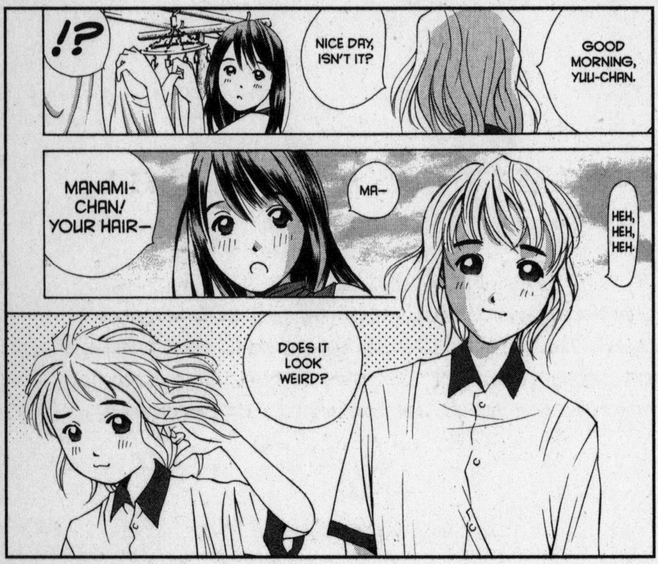
GOOD MORNING, YUU-CHAN.
NICE DAY, ISN'T IT?
!?
HEH, HEH, HEH.
MA—
MANAMI-CHAN! YOUR HAIR—
DOES IT LOOK WEIRD?

Cutting Hair, page 19

In Japanese Manga and television dramas, brokenhearted female characters often cut off their hair.

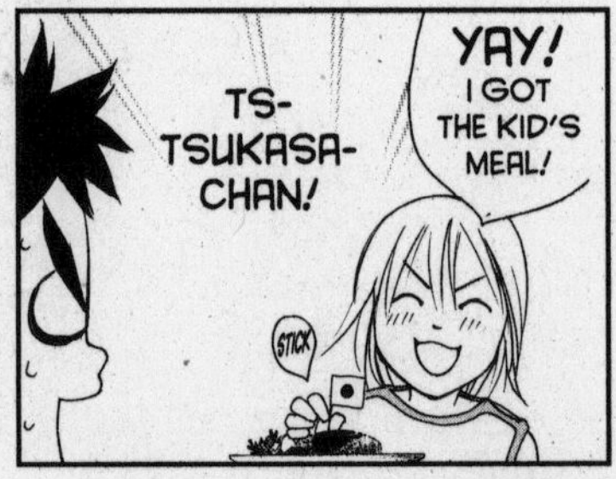
YAY! I GOT THE KID'S MEAL!
TS- TSUKASA-CHAN!
STICK

Kid's meals, page 38

At Japanese restaurants, kid's meals usually come with a little flag attached to part of the plate.

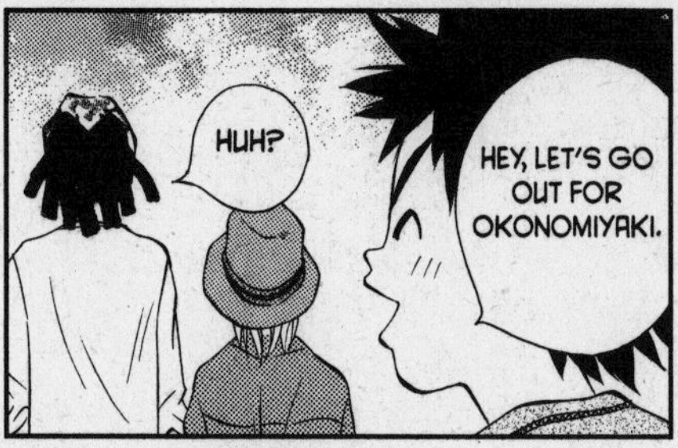
HEY, LET'S GO OUT FOR OKONOMIYAKI.
HUH?

Okonomiyaki, page 116

Okonomiyaki is commonly referred to as a Japanese style pancake. It's a concoction made up of batter and a mixture of meat, vegetables, egg, and sometimes noodles. At *okonomiyaki* restaurants, guests usually get to grill their *okonomiyaki* right at the table.

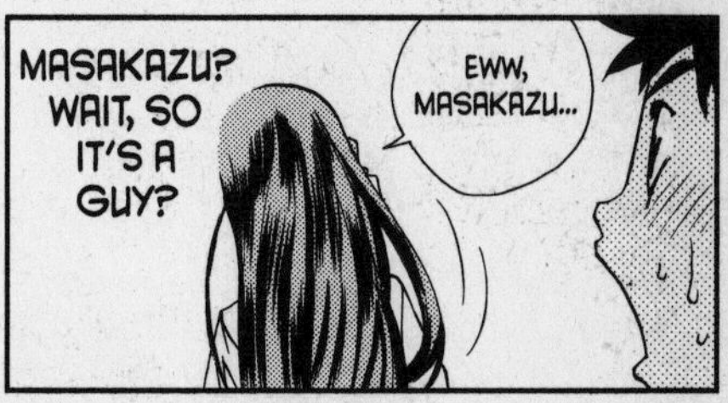
EWW, MASAKAZU...
MASAKAZU? WAIT, SO IT'S A GUY?

Masakazu Tamura, page 125

Masakazu Tamura is a famous actor. When Mugi hears Yuu say, "Eww, Masakazu," he thinks she's talking to a guy named Masakazu.

Nabe, page 134

A *nabe* is literally a large pot, but the term is used generically to describe any kind of soup, stew or boiled dish made in a hot pot. Generally, the hot pot sits in the middle of the table, and each diner serves herself.

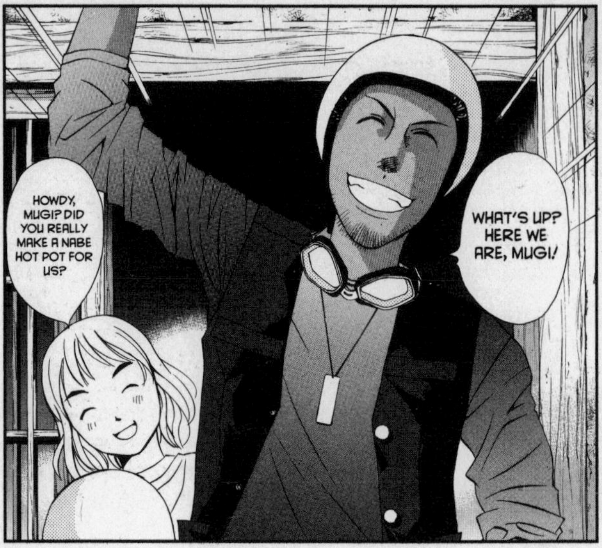
WHAT'S UP? HERE WE ARE, MUGI!
HOWDY, MUGI? DID YOU REALLY MAKE A NABE HOT POT FOR US?

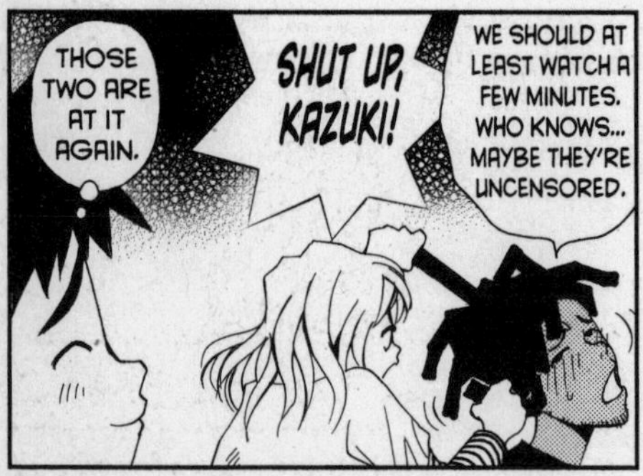
WE SHOULD AT LEAST WATCH A FEW MINUTES. WHO KNOWS... MAYBE THEY'RE UNCENSORED.
SHUT UP, KAZUKI!
THOSE TWO ARE AT IT AGAIN.

Censoring, page 135

In Japan, it's illegal to show genitalia in any kind of media. The genital areas in pornographic films and magazines must be blurred in order to skirt the pornography laws.

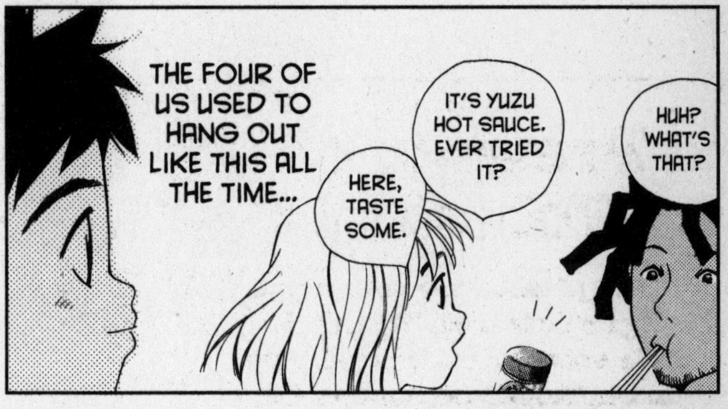
HUH? WHAT'S THAT?
IT'S YUZU HOT SAUCE. EVER TRIED IT?
HERE, TASTE SOME.
THE FOUR OF US USED TO HANG OUT LIKE THIS ALL THE TIME...

Yuzu, page 137

Yuzu is a tiny, fragrant citrus fruit that is sort of like a cross between an orange and a lime.

Preview of Volume 4

We're pleased to present you a preview from Volume 4. This volume will be available in English on September 26, 2006, but for now you'll have to make do with Japanese!

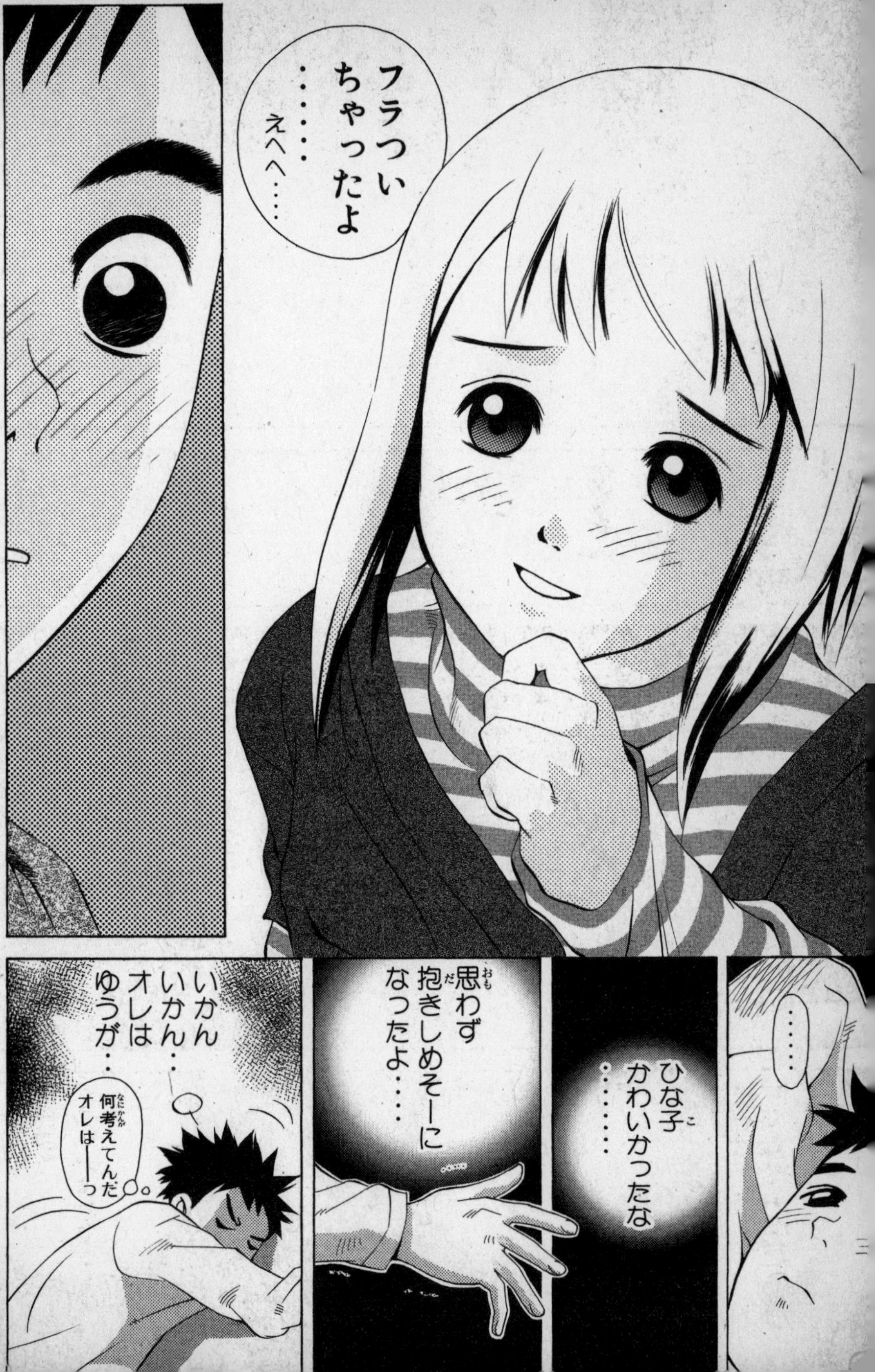
フラつい
ちゃったよ
……えへへ……
……
ひな子
かわいかったな
……
思わず
抱きしめそーに
なったよ……
いかん
いかん…
オレは
ゆうが…
何考えてんだ
オレは——っ

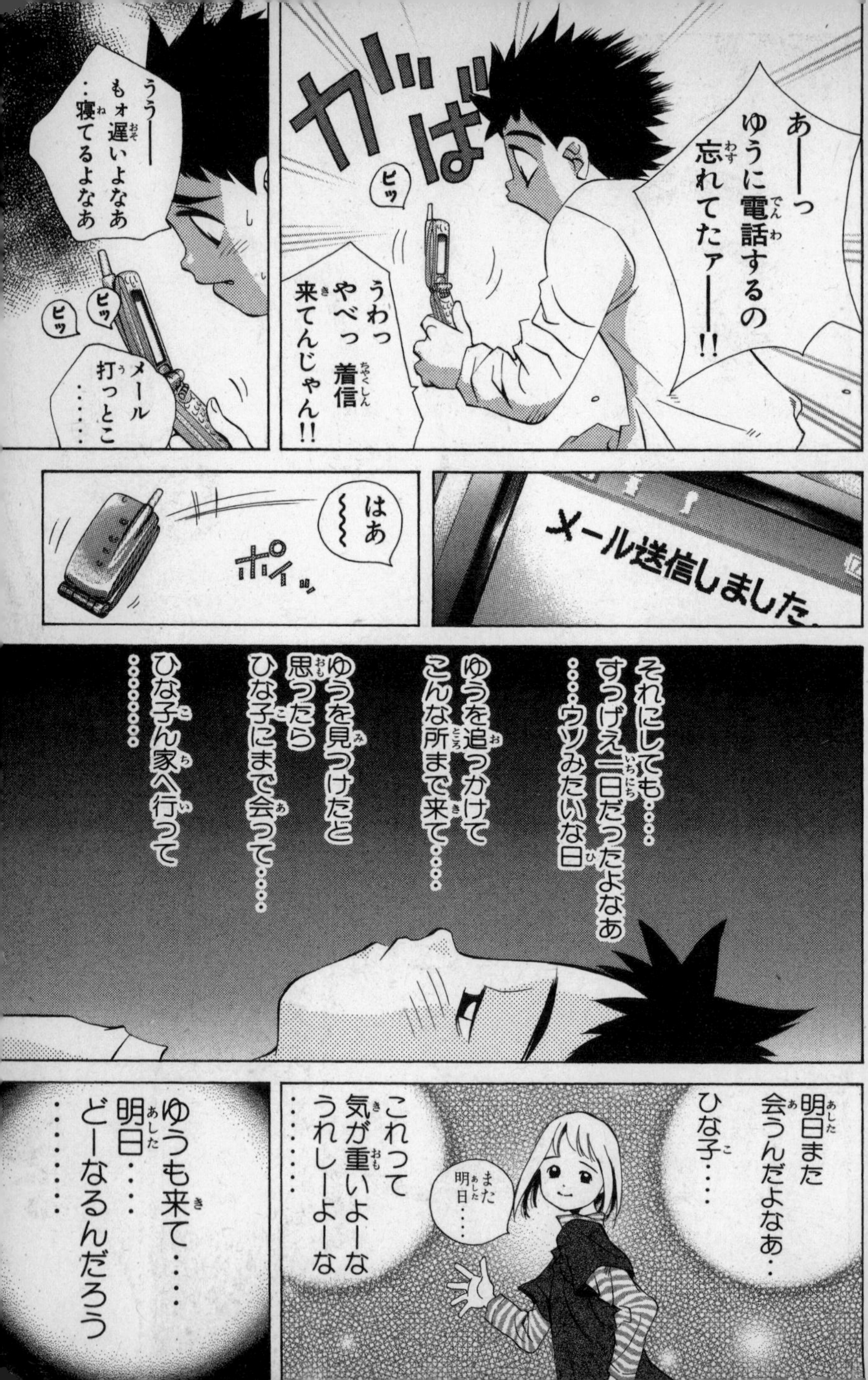
あーっ ゆうに電話するの忘れてたァーー!!
がばっ
ピッ
うわっ やべっ 着信来てんじゃん!!
うう―― もォ遅いよなあ ‥寝てるよなあ
ピッ
ピッ
メール打っとこ……
メール送信しました。
はあ～
ポイッ
それにしても‥‥ すっげえ一日だったよなあ ‥‥ウソみたいな日
ゆうを追っかけてこんな所まで来て‥‥
ゆうを見つけたと思ったら ひな子にまで会って‥‥
ひな子ん家へ行って ‥‥‥‥‥
明日また会うんだよなあ‥ ひな子‥‥
また明日‥‥
これって気が重いよーな うれしーよーな ‥‥‥
ゆうも来て‥‥ 明日‥‥ どーなるんだろう ‥‥‥

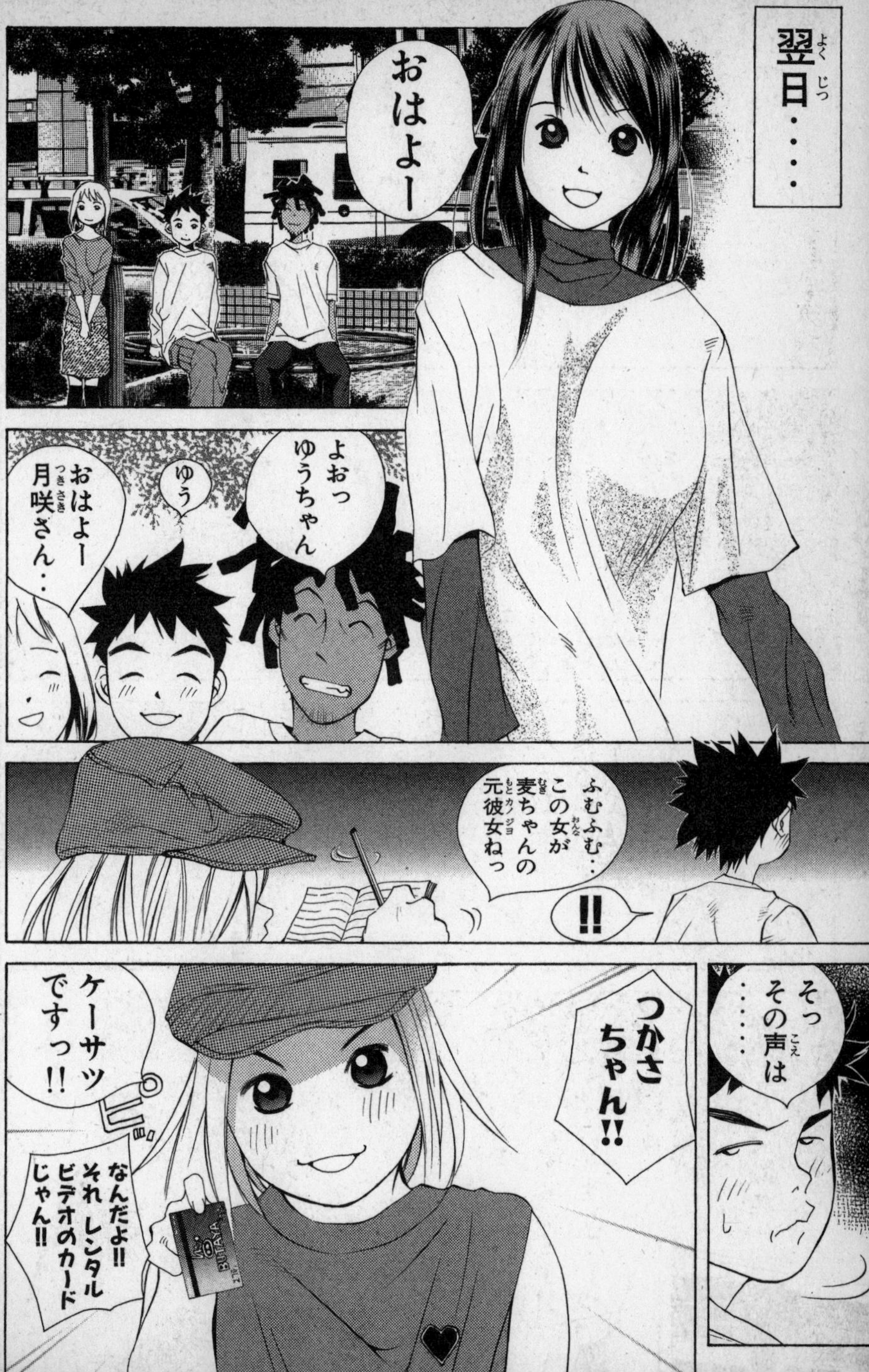
翌日・・・・
おはよー
よおっ ゆうちゃん
ゆう
おはよー 月咲さん・・
ふむふむ・・ この女が 麦ちゃんの 元彼女ねっ
!!
そっ その声は ・・・・・
つかさ ちゃん!!
ケーサツ ですっ!!
なんだよ!! それ レンタル ビデオのカード じゃん!!

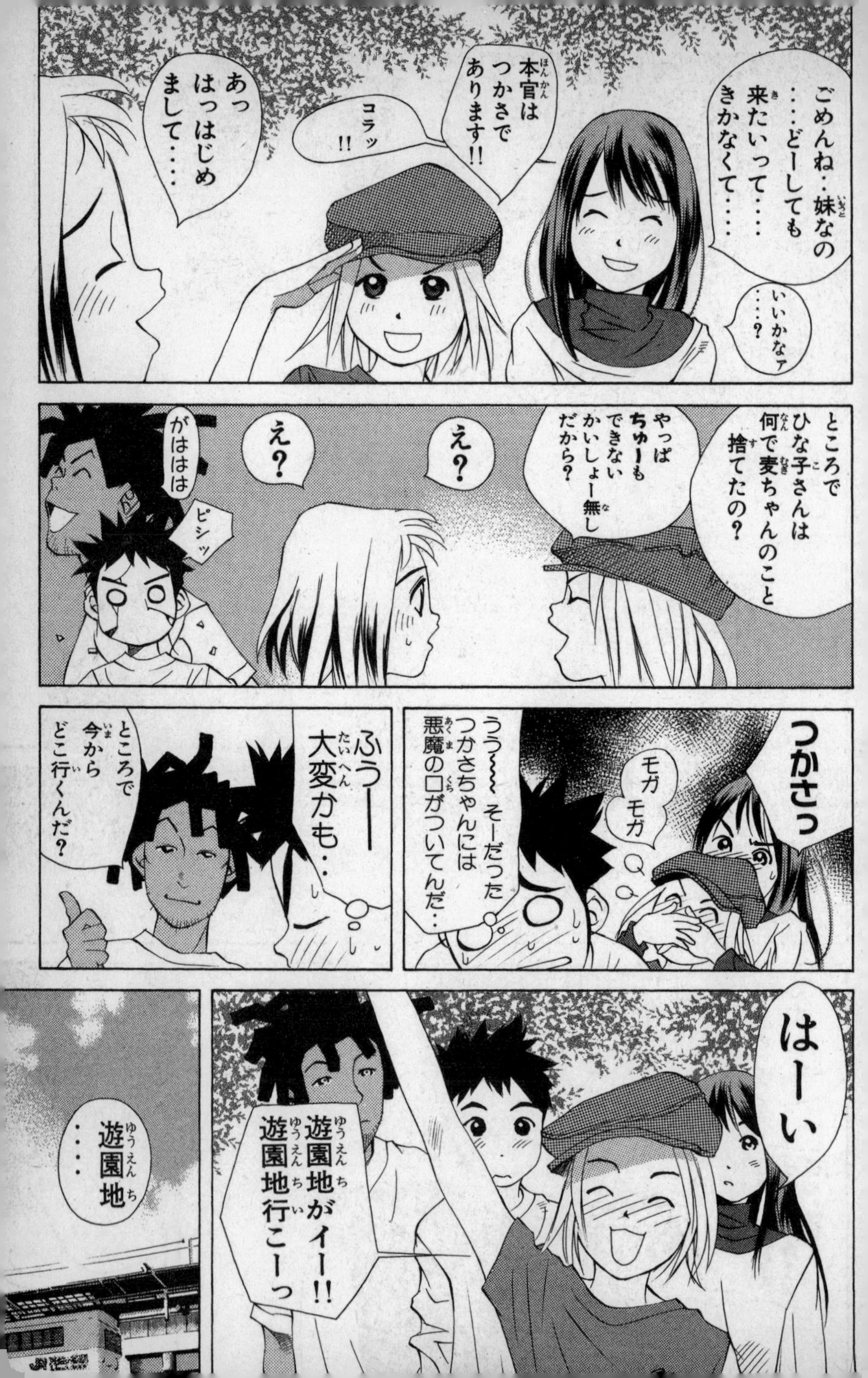
ごめんね‥妹なの‥‥どーしても来たいって‥‥きかなくて‥‥
いいかなァ‥‥？
本官はつかさであります!!
コラッ!!
あっはっはじめまして‥‥
ところでひな子さんは何で麦ちゃんのこと捨てたの？
やっぱちゅーもできないかいしょー無しだから？
え？
え？
がははは
ピシッ
つかさっ
モガモガ
うう〰 そーだったつかさちゃんには悪魔の口がついてんだ‥
ふうーー大変かも‥
ところで今からどこ行くんだ？
はーい
遊園地がイーー!!遊園地行こーっ
遊園地‥‥

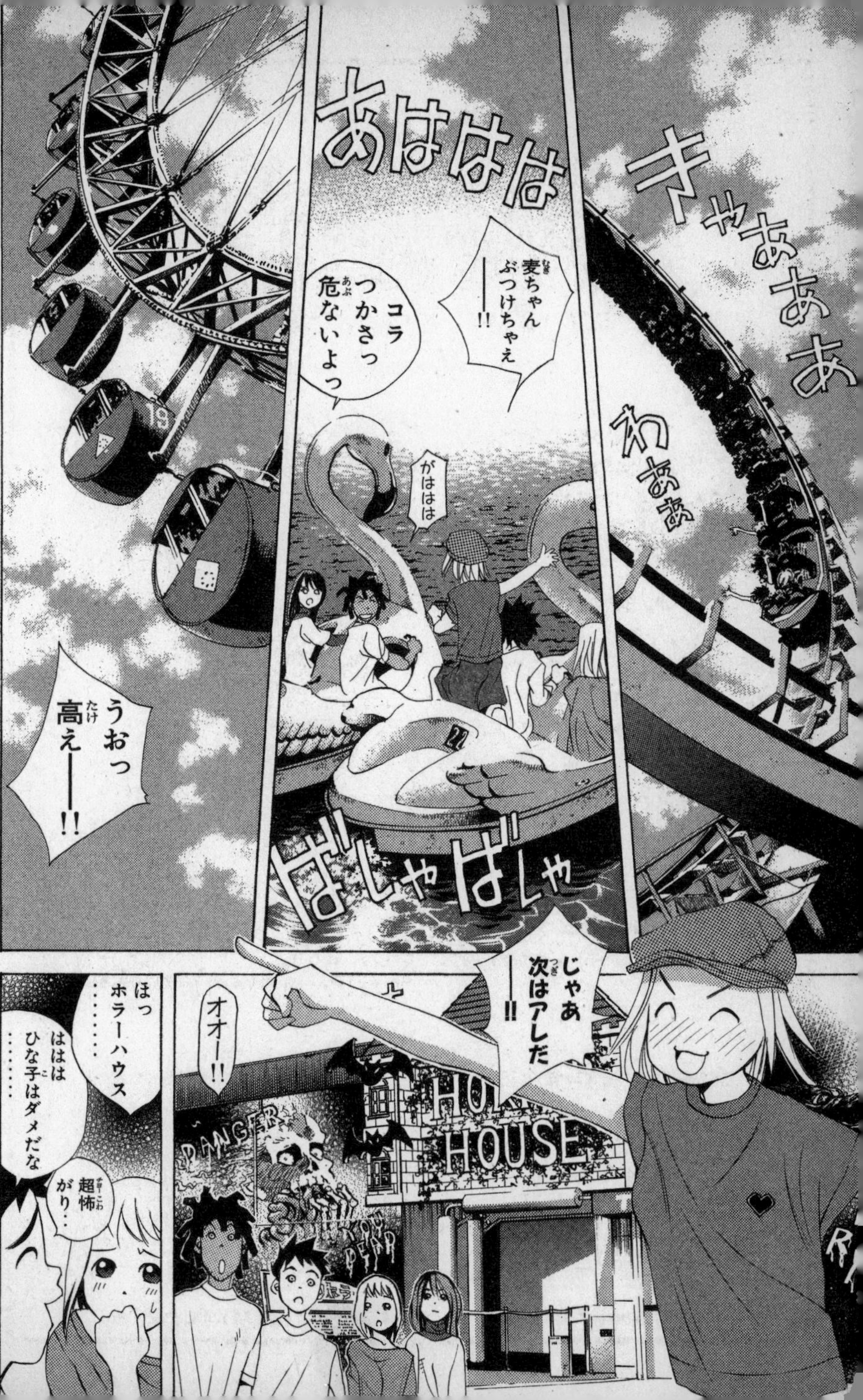
きゃああああ
わああ
あははは
麦ちゃんぶつけちゃえ——!!
コラつかさっ危ないよっ
がははは
ばしゃばしゃ
うおっ高え——!!
じゃあ次はアレだ——!!
オオー!!
HOUSE
DANGER
ほっホラーハウス……
はははひな子はダメだな……
超怖がり…

School Rumble

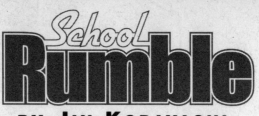

BY JIN KOBAYASHI

SUBTLETY IS FOR WIMPS!

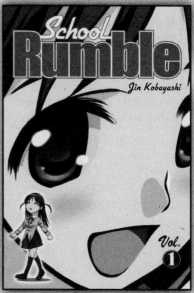

She . . . is a second-year high school student with a single all-consuming question: Will the boy she likes ever really notice her?

He . . . is the school's most notorious juvenile delinquent, and he's suddenly come to a shocking realization: He's got a huge crush, and now he must tell her how he feels.

Life-changing obsessions, colossal foul-ups, grand schemes, deep-seated anxieties, and raging hormones—School Rumble portrays high school as it really is: over-the-top comedy!

School Rumble
Jin Kobayashi
Vol. 1

Ages: 16+

Special extras in each volume! Read them all!

DEL REY

VISIT WWW.DELREYMANGA.COM TO:
- **Read sample pages**
- **View release date calendars for upcoming volumes**
- **Sign up for Del Rey's free manga e-newsletter**
- **Find out the latest about new Del Rey Manga series**

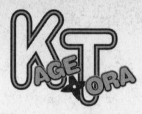

KAGETORA

BY AKIRA SEGAMI

MISSION IMPOSSIBLE

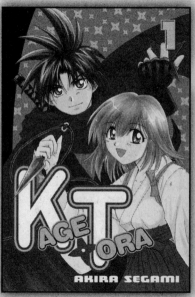

The young ninja Kagetora has been given a great honor—to serve a renowned family of skilled martial artists. But on arrival, he's handed a challenging assignment: teach the heir to the dynasty, the charming but clumsy Yuki, the deft moves of self-defense and combat.

Yuki's inability to master the martial arts is not what makes this job so difficult for Kagetora. No, it is Yuki herself. Someday she will lead her family dojo, and for a ninja like Kagetora to fall in love with his master is a betrayal of his duty, the ultimate dishonor, and strictly forbidden. Can Kagetora help Yuki overcome her ungainly nature . . . or will he be overcome by his growing feelings?

Ages: 13 +

Special extras in each volume! Read them all!

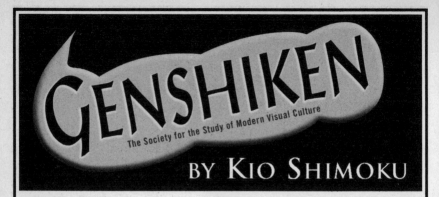

GENSHIKEN
The Society for the Study of Modern Visual Culture

BY KIO SHIMOKU

ARE YOU OTAKU?

It's the spring of freshman year, and Kanji Sasahara is in a quandary. Should he fulfill his long-cherished dream of joining an otaku club? Saki Kasukabe also faces a dilemma. Can she ever turn her boyfriend, anime fanboy Kousaka, into a normal guy? Kanji triumphs where Saki fails, when both Kanji and Kousaka sign up for Genshiken: The Society for the Study of Modern Visual Culture.

Undeterred, Saki chases Kousaka through various activities of the club, from cosplay and comic conventions to video gaming and collecting anime figures—all the while discovering more than she ever wanted to know about the humorous world of the Japanese otaku!

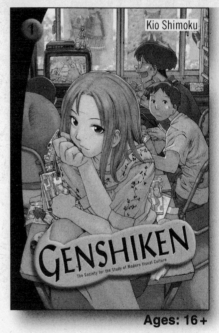

Ages: 16 +

Special extras in each volume! Read them all!

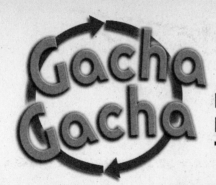

Gacha Gacha

By Hiroyuki Tamakoshi

Gacha Gacha
1
HIROYUKI TAMAKOSHI

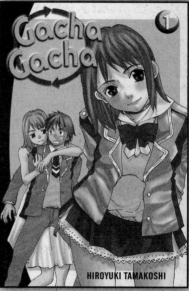

Kouhei is your typical Japanese high school student—he's usually late, he loves beef bowls, he pals around with his buddies, and he's got his first-ever crush on his childhood friend Kurara. Before he can express his feelings, however, Kurara heads off to Hawaii with her mother for summer vacation. When she returns, she seems like a totally different person . . . and that's because she is! While she was away, Kurara somehow developed an alternate personality: Arisa! And where Kurara has no time for boys, Arisa isn't interested in much else. Now Kouhei must help protect his friend's secret, and make sure that Arisa doesn't do anything Kurara would regret!

Ages: 16+

Special extras in each volume! Read them all!

DEL REY

VISIT WWW.DELREYMANGA.COM TO:
- View release date calendars for upcoming volumes
- Sign up for Del Rey's free manga e-newsletter
- Find out the latest about new Del Rey Manga series

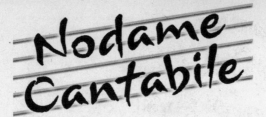

Nodame Cantabile

BY TOMOKO NINOMIYA

WINNER OF THE 2003 MANGA OF THE YEAR AWARD FROM KODANSHA

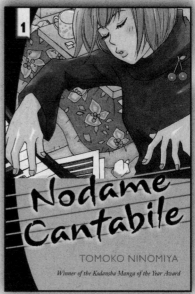

The son of a famous pianist, music student Shinichi Chiaki has always wanted to study abroad and become a conductor like his mentor. However, his fear of planes and water make it impossible for him to follow his dream. As he watches other young students achieve what he has always wanted, Shinichi ponders whether to quit music altogether.

Then one day he meets a fellow music student named Megumi Noda, also known as Nodame. This oddball girl cannot cook, clean, or even read her own score, but she can play the piano in incomparable Cantabile style. And she teaches Shinichi something that he has forgotten: to enjoy his music no matter where he is.

1
Nodame Cantabile
TOMOKO NINOMIYA
Winner of the Kodansha Manga of the Year Award

Ages: 16 +

Special extras in each volume! Read them all!

VISIT WWW.DELREYMANGA.COM TO:

- Read sample pages
- View release date calendars for upcoming volumes
- Sign up for Del Rey's free manga e-newsletter
- Find out the latest about new Del Rey Manga series

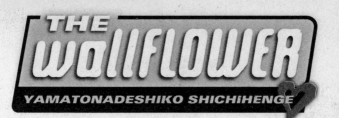
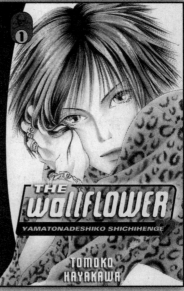

TOMARE!

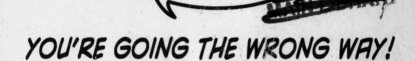

STOP!

YOU'RE GOING THE WRONG WAY!

MANGA IS A COMPLETELY DIFFERENT TYPE
OF READING EXPERIENCE.

TO START AT THE BEGINNING, GO TO THE END!

THAT'S RIGHT!

AUTHENTIC MANGA IS READ THE TRADITIONAL
JAPANESE WAY—FROM RIGHT TO LEFT. EXACTLY THE OPPOSITE
OF HOW AMERICAN BOOKS ARE READ. IT'S EASY TO FOLLOW:
JUST GO TO THE OTHER END OF THE BOOK, AND READ EACH PAGE
—AND EACH PANEL—FROM RIGHT SIDE TO LEFT SIDE,
STARTING AT THE TOP RIGHT. NOW YOU'RE EXPERIENCING
MANGA AS IT WAS MEANT TO BE.